Routledge Revivals

Industrial Organization in India

First published in 1935, *Industrial Organization in India* examines the structure and efficiency of industrial organization in India. It explores the origins, evolution, and unique features of the managing agency system, comparing the organizational practices and methods of Indian and British managing agency firms.

The book analyzes the system's influence on the industrial structure, focusing on how British firms achieved administrative integration under this model. It discusses the future of the managing agency system, concluding that Indian industry would benefit more from addressing its flaws than from abolishing it entirely.

The text also studies the factors shaping the localization of industry and the scale of industrial units in India. It provides a detailed account of the methods used to finance industry, followed by an examination of industrial finance challenges and potential solutions based on foreign experience. The book concludes with an assessment of industrial worker efficiency, emphasizing the relationship between wages and living standards. It will be of interest to students and researchers of industrial economics and business and economic history.

Industrial Organization in India

P.S. Lokanathan

Routledge
Taylor & Francis Group

First published in 1935
by George Allen & Unwin Ltd

This edition first published in 2026 by Routledge
4 Park Square, Milton Park, Abingdon, Oxon, OX14 4RN

and by Routledge
605 Third Avenue, New York, NY 10158

Routledge is an imprint of the Taylor & Francis Group, an informa business

A Library of Congress record exists under LCCN: 35017030

ISBN: 978-1-041-26829-1 (hbk)
ISBN: 978-1-003-75176-2 (ebk)
ISBN: 978-1-041-26859-8 (pbk)

Book DOI 10.4324/9781003751762

INDUSTRIAL ORGANIZATION IN INDIA

by

P. S. LOKANATHAN
M.A., D.Sc. (Econ.), London
Reader in Economics in the
University of Madras

LONDON
GEORGE ALLEN & UNWIN LTD
MUSEUM STREET

FIRST PUBLISHED IN 1935

Thesis for Degree of Doctor of Science

PRINTED IN GREAT BRITAIN BY
UNWIN BROTHERS LTD., WOKING

TO THE MEMORY OF MY FATHER

PREFACE

THIS work is the result of investigation and study pursued for nearly five years, during which the writer visited important industrial centres in India, England, Austria, and Germany.

It attempts to examine the structure and efficiency of industrial organization in India. It traces the origin, evolution, and features of the managing agency system which is peculiar to India, and explains the differences in methods and organization between Indian and British managing agency firms. It examines the influence of the managing agency system on the structure of industry, and shows how administrative integration is secured under the system, particularly by British firms. The future of the system is then discussed and the conclusion reached, that Indian industry, which owes already so much to the system, has more to gain by curing it of its admitted defects than by abolishing it altogether.

The various factors which have influenced the localization of industry and the size of industrial units in India are studied in detail. An account of the prevalent methods of financing industry is followed by an inquiry into the problems of industrial finance and the lines on which they may be solved in the light of foreign experience. The book concludes with an examination of the efficiency of the industrial worker in relation to wages and standard of living.

Since this work was completed, the Report of the Indian Tariff Board on the cotton industry has been published. In Chapter IV of the Report the Board examines some of the features of the managing agency system as it has been in operation in Bombay and Ahmedabad, and its conclusions agree in the main with those reached here.

In the preparation of this work the writer has received help from various persons. To Sir Campbell Rhodes, C.B.E., Head of Messrs. Hoare, Miller & Co., London, who so generously placed his wide experience and vast knowledge of the managing agency system at the disposal of the present writer and who found time to go through Chapter I and offer helpful criticisms, he is indebted to an especial degree. He is also under obligation to Sir Thomas Catto, Bart., Head of Messrs. Morgan, Grenfell & Co., London, who both in interview and correspondence elucidated doubtful points and checked some of the conclusions. He desires to express his gratitude to his advisers, Dr. Gilbert Slater, who has for many years taken a friendly interest in his work, and to Professor Coatman, who read through parts of the MS. and offered valuable suggestions. The writer cannot adequately express his thanks to Dr. Vera Anstey for the willing and generous help she gave throughout the preparation of this work. Thanks are also due to the Librarians at the London School of Economics, the High Commissioner's Office, and the India Office, London, for their unfailing courtesy.

The publication of this work has been aided by a grant from the Publication Fund of the University of London, and the writer desires to acknowledge gratefully this aid. Special thanks are due to Mr. B. M. Headicar, Librarian, London School of Economics, for help in arranging for the publication of the book.

P. S. L.

CONTENTS

NOTE

In India units of 100,000 are called lakhs. 100 lakhs or 10 millions are equal to 1 crore.

The unit of account is the rupee which is linked to the pound sterling and is equal to 1s. 6d. at the par of exchange. A lakh of rupees is thus equal to £7,500, and a crore of rupees, £750,000.

The rupee is divided into 16 annas, and an anna into 12 pies.

INDUSTRIAL ORGANIZATION IN INDIA

CHAPTER I

PIONEERING OF INDUSTRY IN INDIA

ALTHOUGH the history of the development of Indian industry has been the subject of many recent books, the actual methods by which the individual units in each of the important industries are organized and floated have so far received little attention. Yet the pioneering and promoting of industry in India reveal some distinct and almost unique features which differ from those of company promotion in other countries and are almost without parallel in any part of the world. The neglect by Indian economists of this aspect of organization may be explained partly by the general tendency, until recently, to ignore the role of the promoter, as his function was not sufficiently differentiated from that of the entrepreneur. Although with the growth of joint-stock forms of organization the promoter-entrepreneur has been largely replaced by a Board of Directors in most countries, it was thought that the methods of setting up a business and floating it were not sufficiently distinctive to invite special study. In countries, however, in which there arose a separate class of "promoters" whose main function was that of starting or organizing a business, and who very often were not interested in its further career and development, some attention has been given and judgment formed as to their soundness and economy. In India, although here and there a few men of the professional promoter type have floated industrial concerns—and their activities were pronounced during the boom period 1919–21—it cannot be said that the promoting function has become sufficiently specialized to have brought into the field a new and separate class of promoters.

Another reason for neglect was that Indian economists did not fully realize the exceptional and distinctive features of a system which evolved in the special circumstances of the country and which was accepted as perfectly normal by them. It is only in recent years that they have realized that the differences between the system in India and elsewhere are much greater than the similarities, and that it is necessary not merely to explain the Indian system but to examine its features from the point of view of past conditions and future requirements.

There is no doubt that one of the factors on which the success of an industrial unit depends is the careful planning of the scheme and its launching under favourable conditions. This requires great constructive ability on the part of the organizer, and a country rich in such talents will be able to achieve industrial success sooner than one which, however well endowed with natural resources, is lacking in the supply of initiative and enterprise. Modern industry in India owed its development primarily to two classes of people: British merchants who had come out to represent British trading firms, and the cotton merchants of Bombay and, latterly, of Ahmedabad and other centres. These, directly or indirectly, were responsible for much of the development that has occurred. India was fortunate in having in the country British merchants with wide experience and considerable financial resources who were able to pioneer and establish new industrial concerns. But the peculiarity of the system lay in the fact that enterprises were promoted and controlled by persons who belonged to what are known as Managing Agency firms or, as more popularly known, managing agents. Even when, as in western India, Indian merchants pioneered the cotton industry, the same system was developed, although there were differences in the circumstances that gave rise to it.

The significant role played by managing agents in the development and organization of industry will be marked in almost every chapter of this book, but we are now concerned with their role as promoters or undertakers of business.

I

BRITISH MANAGING AGENTS

It is not possible to trace the origin of the managing agency system, as it was the result of gradual evolution. The history of some of the managing agents like Martin & Co., Andrew Yule & Co., Killick, Nixon & Co., or W. H. Brady & Co., shows how much the system owes to the enterprise and ability of the individual men who came out to India as representatives of some trading companies. They were men who were first engaged in the general trading business, but soon turned their attention to other lines of activity. They found a country with vast undeveloped resources; but unlike Canada or Australia, India had a large consuming population and a plentiful labour supply. They found that the country was lacking in industrial leaders, in fact, in any industries in the modern acceptation of the term, and that they had the whole field clear to themselves. The experience they had gained in their general merchandise business was such as was capable of being utilized in the organization and advancement of industrial concerns, and they were fully prepared to engage experts for technical purposes. Thus industrial advancement in India was in the hands of men who were keen business men and not technical experts. Being pioneers, they realized such profits in each line of business that they could afford to make mistakes without burning their fingers. From one industry they turned to another, not only because the experience gained in the one was equally valuable in the other, so that all that they needed was to get experts versed in the technique of each industry, but also because each line of business opened the way for another, and the market for the products of one line of business was found in another. Thus managing agents of jute mills started colliery concerns, and found that the jute mills were good customers for their coal. Then again, when some of them floated boating and inland steamer companies, these latter were able to get their own jute mills and colliery companies and tea estates to send their goods by their line of steamers. It was thus a great thing for them to know that they had a market which was controlled by themselves, and thus one line of activity naturally led to another. That is why in India managing agency firms have neither specialized in one or two industries nor developed a vertical form of organization. They have used their knowledge in developing quite a miscellaneous range of enterprises, including jute mills, tea gardens, flour mills, coal companies, shipping companies, insurance agencies, etc. Some idea of the range of their activities can be had by a reference to the statement annexed to the chapter. But though managing agents usually concerned themselves with a variety of enterprises there are a few firms specializing in one branch of industry, and these may be regarded as specialist managing firms. The main reason for such growth was that the field open to them was large and had to be shared out only among a limited number of firms.

ORGANIZATION OF MANAGING AGENTS

For the purpose of promoting the different concerns in which they were interested, these pioneers formed themselves into partnerships. In many cases they merely comprised a few members of the family with one or two outsiders. More recently, the tendency has been to form limited liability companies with shares privately held. Thus about six firms in Bengal are limited companies. English managing agency firms are generally servants of the corresponding firms in England, or, in these days of income-tax difficulty and differentiation of the legal systems in the two countries, are technically separate, though actually the firms in England are able to exercise general control by means of their capital invested therein.[1] The evolution of family agency concerns into private limited liability companies is rather interesting. It

[1] Thus the managing agents of the Bengal Paper Mill Co., Ltd., are Balmer, Lawrie & Co., Ltd. Their London correspondents are Alexander Lawrie & Co., Ltd. The partners of this latter firm are partners of the Calcutta firm, and thus control the Bengal Paper Mill Co.

Indian Tariff Board : Paper and Paper Pulp Industries, Evidence, 1932, Vol. 1, p. 462.

often happens that the sons of some of the family concerns are not willing to spend their time in India and are therefore eager to avail themselves of the services of able assistants.[1] The assistants are engaged in London, often University men, through the University Appointments Board, or technical men gathered from British industrial firms. The "sons" get pushed on, but often prefer to spend their inherited money in England, and the assistant gets his chance, stimulated by the fact that he has to make his own way in the world. The men among the staff who have made good are brought into the concerns as partners, and in this way not merely is the firm energized and vitalized, but the knowledge that such opportunities are more easily available in India than elsewhere has led to some of the abler youths of England taking up junior posts with prospects of rising to the position of partners. Retirement at a comparatively early age also holds out prospects of early promotion for the younger men. The opportunities which Indian industry has thus afforded to the young brains of England are quite exceptional, and India has served as a good training-ground for business talents. There are again instances of some managing agency firms making a definite rule against having as partners or employees, more than a limited number of persons belonging to one family. Thus in a firm of managing agents in Calcutta, the founder of the firm which has 15 partners, of whom 6 were serving in India, and 9 in England in 1926, made a definite rule prohibiting the taking in of relatives.[2] On the whole it may be said that although family influences predominate and the partnership is carried on among the same families from generation to generation, there has always been plenty of scope for the more enterprising and ambitious of the junior assistants to look forward to becoming ultimately partners and in many instances heads of firms;[3] succeeding frequently after retirement to the headship

[1] Sir C. Rhodes's letter to the writer dated September 19, 1933.

[2] *Indian Tariff Board: Cotton Industry*, Evidence, 1927, Vol. 3, p. 324.

[3] The names of Sir Percy Newson, Sir Campbell Rhodes, and Sir Alexander Murray, who, however, was only the head of the Indian branch, may be cited as examples.

of the associated London firm. Thus the infusion of "outside" blood in British firms in India has been stimulating and fruitful. The responsibilities abroad are great, and even a desire to see a son in a prominent position does not always outweigh the father's desire not to have his business ruined. In a few instances managing agency concerns have even been turned into joint-stock public limited companies, although the shares are held by only a limited number of persons.[1] There is no uniform practice in regard to the number of partners in each concern. The number depends upon the extent and sphere of influence of each agency firm and the number of enterprises it has to manage. From 3 to 15 is quite common, though it sometimes goes up to the maximum of 20. Some of them work in India, while others work in England, and, as the Industrial Commission stated, the system arose out of the "difficulty in the case of companies under European control of finding among the relatively small class of leading men of business available in India directors, especially managing directors, who will remain in the country long enough to guarantee the continuous supervision requisite for the successful conduct of such businesses. An agency firm as a rule comprises several partners, some of whom are taking their turn of duty in India, while the others attend to the firm's affairs in London or elsewhere."[2] But this view of the constant interchange of partners between India and England is not borne out by actual facts. The practice seems to be for some partners to serve in India throughout the period of their service and then to retire from India, either permanently or with a view to working in England. Similarly, those who serve in England pay occasional visits to India.

From the point of view of starting a new concern, what is more important to note is that in India at the time when the system was evolving itself there was hardly any investing class as such. Capital could not be attracted from the people of India, and the

[1] Burn & Co., Ltd., is a public limited company which has been amalgamated with Martin & Co., and which manages the Indian Iron & Steel Co., Indian Standard Wagon Co., etc.

[2] *Report of the Indian Industrial Commission*, 1916–18, p. 13.

managing agents were prepared to put in a large capital. After the concerns were established and shown to be working profitably, it was possible to attract investors to them, and thus build up in India an investing public. They thus nursed a large number of enterprises in their early years of struggle and till they could come out into the open market for capital. In some cases a long interval has occurred between the starting of a concern and its conversion into a joint-stock public company, during the whole of which the managing agents have nursed the enterprise. As a writer put it in the *Capital, Trade Supplement*, December 1932, "the managing agents nourished the growth of new enterprises and carefully nursed the young and immature." When the time was opportune for the conversion into public companies, the managing agents got the bulk of their capital out by selling a large portion of their interests, and having unloosened their capital were ready to enter into fresh enterprises. But in each case in parting with their interests they were careful to retain their power and control either by securing a long fixed tenure of management or by including in the articles of agreement terms ensuring their permanence and rendering it extremely difficult for anyone to turn them out.[1] In theory, 51 per cent of

[1] The following extracts from the Articles of Association relating to two mills managed by Messrs. Andrew Yule & Co. will show how the agents secure a permanent right of management:

(*a*) *Budge-Budge Mills.*—"The firm of Messrs. Andrew Yule & Co. and their successors in business under that or any other name or style and their assignees shall be and continue to be the managing agents of the Company and shall as such managing agents be remunerated by a commission of 5 per cent on the net profits of the Company and Rs. 500 per month for a suitable office and establishment in Calcutta to be provided by the agents, but in case such net profits and the said sum of Rs. 500 per month shall not amount to Rs. 42,000 per annum the remuneration shall be made up to Rs. 42,000."

(*b*) *Central Jute Mills.*—"The firm of Messrs. Andrew Yule & Co. and their successors in business under that or any other name or style, already irrevocably declared by the Memorandum of Association to be the managing agent of the Company shall as such managing agent be remunerated by a Commission of 2 per cent on the gross proceeds of sales of goods made by the Company, but in case the said 2 per cent on

the shares is needed to secure absolute control of a concern, and there are some concerns where the agency firms do have as much as that.[1] But as is more usually the case, their holdings are far less, but even with a 25 or 30 per cent of the holdings in one hand they are able to control the destinies of the concerns as effectually as if they were absolute masters. The Indian Company Law of 1882, favoured the growth of the system of managing agents by the very elastic nature of its provisions. Up till 1913 the law did not compel the constitution of an elected Board of Directors; still less did it require the creation of a managing director. It was, therefore, possible to evolve a system by which the persons interested in the enterprise constituted themselves managing agents. When, later on, the law required the constitution of a Board of Directors, the managing agents had no difficulty in getting together a few friends as directors from among their business associates, who were perfectly aware that their continuance on the Board depended on their loyalty to the managing agents who had the power to choose their own friends. Thus although outwardly many of the concerns were joint-stock companies with Boards of Directors, in effect they were more akin to partnerships with control in the hands of the managing agents. At its best the system was eminently suited to the needs of the country and the limitations under which British capitalists had to work. On the one hand there was the fact that owing to climatic and other conditions it would have been difficult for British capitalists to work continuously in India and to find for every concern competent men who could serve as directors and as managing directors. The system of managing agents made it possible to administer and manage industrial ventures with a few able leaders, and thus it was possible to effect great economy

the sales shall not amount to Rs. 30,000, then the remuneration shall be made up to Rs. 30,000 in any year."

Quoted from the *Capital*, Calcutta, by the *Indian Textile Journal*, March 1904, p. 188.

[1] See Appendix I at the end of the chapter, where the holdings of some of the managing agents in those companies which they manage are given.

in the labour of higher grade administrative staff. On the other hand the flow of British capital to Indian industry was greatly facilitated by a system which enabled control to be vested in British hands, though there was a leavening of Indian element in some of the concerns. The English managing agents in Bengal, Assam, and other provinces constituted a sort of bottle-neck through which British capital flowed to India and got distributed among the varied enterprises promoted by the British managing agents. But for the managing agency system the pace of industrial development in India would have been slower, and the opportunities for British capital and British enterprise to function in India would have been limited. Thus England and India both gained. The lack of indigenous capital and Indian industrial leadership gave the British merchants their opportunity. The available British capital seeking investment found among these British merchants just the right sort of men who could safely be entrusted with it. Once the system came into existence its very success led to its growth and development.

II

INDIAN MANAGING AGENTS

If, therefore, the managing agency system grew up, particularly in Bengal and Upper India, out of the special economic conditions in which British merchants and officers representing British trading firms in India found themselves, for reasons slightly different but essentially the same, there evolved a similar system on the western side of India. There, too, the merchants who were engaged in general trade, and more particularly in the cotton trade, began to take interest in the development of industry, and were helped considerably by the resident English representatives of British machine-manufacturing firms. They were also faced by the same set of facts. Capital was extremely limited and, such as it was, remained entirely with a few wealthy merchants like themselves engaged in commerce. The wealth acquired during the American Civil War formed, indeed, the basis for the promotion of cotton companies in Bombay city.[1] There was no large investing class in the country, and industrial leadership was lacking. As in Lancashire, where the wealth acquired in commerce became the basis for the starting of the textile industry, so in Bombay the merchants who amassed fortunes in trade and commerce pioneered the new industry. There have been instances where men who had once been "Bardan carriers"[2] and became rich by trading in cotton and cotton yarn, used their wealth in the development of the industry.[3] Thus it was inevitable that the pioneering and promoting of industry in western India was undertaken by a few wealthy merchant communities such as the Parsis and the Bhatias.[4] The first successful cotton company in India, the Oriental Mill, was promoted by a wealthy Parsi merchant and converted into a joint-stock company in 1858, and was managed by Messrs. Framji & Co., who were appointed as Secretaries and agents. Thus began the system of management by managing agents in the cotton-mill industry in India.[5] Later, wealthy merchants belonging to other communities followed. The money required for the cotton mills was subscribed by the promoters and their friends, and those who had large financial interests in the concerns constituted themselves as managing agents. While in Bengal the difficulty of finding among the few British residents a sufficient number of able men to serve as directors and managing directors was partly responsible for the growth of the managing agency system, in the Bombay Presidency the scarcity of industrial leaders in the country led to similar results. The whole task of pioneering, promoting, financing, and managing the mills fell on the shoulders of a few merchants, and although

[1] "The merchants reaped a rich harvest of profits. These came mostly in the shape of nuggets of gold and silver authentically recorded at 51 crores of rupees." D. E. Wacha, *Life of Tata*, 1918, p. 17.

[2] "Bardan carriers" are persons who carry cotton bales.

[3] *Indian Textile Journal*, October 1893.

[4] See Appendix II, where an account is given of the life of some of the chief promoters of cotton mills in Bombay and Ahmedabad which would give an idea of the evolution of cotton merchants into cotton manufacturers.

[5] S. M. Rutnagur, *The Cotton Mills*, 1927, p. 9.

with a view to getting a certain amount of additional capital they were prepared to take in some from outside, they always took care that control remained in their own hands. Thus a form of organization was evolved which, while formally joint stock, was in reality largely proprietary in character, and the managing agency system tended to combine the virtues of the unity of management of a proprietary or partnership concern with the ampler resources of a joint-stock company. To a foreign student of Indian industry it might appear paradoxical that the most important of its organized industries, like cotton, jute, coal mining, flour, and tea companies, should have been organized on a joint-stock basis when everyone knows that there had been a dearth of managerial and directing ability, and that capital seeking investment was limited and confined to only a few wealthy groups. But the explanation for this apparent paradox lies in the evolution of the managing agency system. The managing agents retained a considerable share in the interests of the firms they promoted, and took in a few rich capitalists as shareholders with a view to getting an increase of capital. As will be noticed when studying the system as it works in Ahmedabad, many of the so-called public joint-stock companies are essentially private in character, the bulk of the shares being held by only half a dozen persons. How far this type of organization was efficient in the past, and developed on proper lines, and how far it should prove beneficial in the future we shall consider later; but that in the early stages of its evolution it fitted the country admirably, and that, indeed, there was no alternative to it, cannot be doubted. Everything began to adjust itself to the system. Investors who had any money to invest in industries were willing to put their money in any enterprise promoted or backed by a reputable firm of managing agents. The imprimatur of a managing agent was found essential for the successful flotation of any public company in India. Even at a time of depression, as in 1931–2, when capital was justifiably shy, many new sugar companies were successfully floated by managing agents because of the confidence of the public in the promoters. The banking organization of the country came to be adapted to the development of the managing agency system to such an extent that credit was often refused to an industrial concern unless guaranteed by the managing agents. This was most general in Bombay, though in Bengal the managing agents did not have to give their personal guarantee in the case of bank loans and overdrafts.[1] Thus industrial finance was entirely provided either directly by the agents or indirectly through their guaranteeing the banks. In short, managing agents became the pivot of the whole industrial system.

III

STEPS IN THE FORMATION OF MANAGING AGENCY FIRMS

It is now necessary to consider in greater detail the actual steps in the formation of managing agency firms and the nature of the agreements entered into between them and the concerns they manage. As was already pointed out, managing agents started either as family concerns like Messrs. Tata, Sons & Co., Nowrosji Wadia & Sons, and Currimbhai Ebrahim & Sons, Ltd., which later were converted into partnerships, or more often directly as partnerships comprising 3 to 15, or even up to the maximum of 20 persons.[2] When such a limited liability company is formed, the major portion of the shares is held by the persons who have promoted it, and the outside public are allowed to come in for a limited number of shares, generally up to 25 per cent. It is necessary broadly to distinguish between three types of managing agency firms, each type predominating in certain parts of India. Thus the British managing agency firms in India, the Indian agency firms in Bombay, and those in Ahmedabad show some differences in organization. In all three one finds proprietary firms, partnerships with unlimited liability, limited companies with

[1] *Indian Central Banking Enquiry Committee*, Report, 1931, Vol. 1, p. 276.

[2] *Indian Tariff Board: Cotton Industry*, 1927, Vol. 3, Evidence of the Ahmedabad Mill Owners' Association, p. 441. The company law prohibited the formation of limited or unlimited partnerships of more than twenty persons.

shares privately held, and in a very few cases also public joint-stock limited liability companies.[1] In Bombay, where partnership

[1] *Indian Central Banking Enquiry Committee*, Report, p. 643. Out of thirty-six firms whose names appear in the Calcutta Stock Exchange list, only seven are limited companies and the rest are private firms.

Family Concerns

Most of the Ahmedabad mill agency companies are more or less family concerns. In Bombay, Morarji Gokuldass & Co. is a private partnership with only one person from outside (Sir D. E. Wacha). Messrs. Thackersey, Mooljee & Co., Mathradass Gokuldass & Co., D. M. Petit, Sons & Co., Nowrosjee Wadia & Sons, C. N. Wadia & Co., and Narottam Morarjee & Co. are all more or less family concerns, though legally they are private partnerships.

Public Limited Companies :—

(*a*) Messrs. W. H. Brady & Co., Ltd., was registered as a joint-stock company (Bombay) in June 1913. No shares were offered to the public, and the conversion into a public limited company involved no change either in the management or policy. The business which was established in 1893 had since grown very much, thus necessitating the change of organization (*Indian Textile Journal*, June 1913, p. 299).

(*b*) Binny & Co., Ltd., became a public limited company with 1,350 lakhs of capital (Madras).

(*c*) Burn & Co., Ltd., public limited company (Calcutta).

(*d*) Steel Bros. Co., Ltd., public limited company (Calcutta).

(*e*) Stanes Co., Ltd., public limited company (Madras).

Private Limited Companies:—

(1) Messrs. Tata, Sons & Co., Ltd., registered in 1917 with a capital of Rs. 117 lakhs, Bombay.

(2) Messrs. E. D. Sassoon & Co., Ltd., registered in 1920 with a capital of Rs. 100 lakhs, Bombay.

(3) Messrs. Cowasji Jehangir & Co., Ltd., registered in 1920 with a capital of Rs. 100 lakhs, Bombay.

(4) Messrs. Currimbhai Ebrahim & Sons, Ltd., registered in 1916 with a capital of Rs. 93 lakhs, Bombay.

(5) Messrs. Andrew Yule & Co., registered in 1919, paid up capital Rs. 180 lakhs, Calcutta.

(6) Messrs. Birla Bros. Co., registered in 1918, paid up capital Rs. 50 lakhs, Calcutta.

(7) Messrs. Begg, Dunlop & Co., registered in 1922, paid up capital Rs. 51 lakhs, Calcutta.

(8) Messrs. Balmer, Lawrie & Co., registered in 1924, authorized capital Rs. 60 lakhs, Calcutta.

[*Continued on p. 26*

agency firms predominate, the partners agree to take over a certain minimum number of shares, and usually about 25 per cent of the mill companies' shares are owned by the partners taken together.[1] The usual method of organizing a managing agency firm with a view to floating a cotton-mill company in Ahmedabad is for a limited liability company to be formed with a nominal capital of Rs. 1,000, there being 1,000 shares of R. 1 each. To buy this one-rupee share, a person has to lay down Rs. 5,000, partly in the shares of the mill company, and partly in cash deposits with the mill. "Anyone who comes forward with Rs. 5,000, i.e. Rs. 3,000 in the shape of ordinary share capital and Rs. 2,000 in the shape of deposits for a fixed period of seven years, is given one share of the managing agency or one-thousandth part of the agency commission."[2] This one-rupee share has considerably more value than its nominal value, and in some cases it is said to fetch a premium of Rs. 700 or 800. Formerly the managing agents used to take into their agency firms any person or persons who supplied a certain amount of capital as something like sleeping partners, but now most of the agencies have been made into limited liability concerns and shares are issued, a portion of which the holders may sell at their discretion. In the past it was also the practice when loans were taken from private firms of Shroffs, to grant them a share in the managing agency commission in addition to the usual interest on the loan. When a cotton mill

(9) Messrs. Villiers & Co., Ltd., registered in 1919, authorized capital Rs. 20 lakhs, Calcutta.

(10) Messrs. Low & Co., registered in 1919, authorized capital Rs. 30 lakhs, Calcutta.

The above information relating to public and private limited companies was extracted from *The Investor's India Year Book*, 1930–1, and from Pat Lovett, *The Mirror of Investment*, 1927.

[1] "I began business in 1883 with a share in the agency of the Bombay Cotton Manufacturing Co., and *thereby* incurred a liability to take up shares of the value of Rs. 30,000." Letter left behind by a mill agent who committed suicide, quoted in the *Indian Textile Journal*, September 1909.

[2] *Indian Central Banking Enquiry Committee*, Report, 1931, Vol. 1, p. 277.

is floated as a joint-stock company, the several partners of the managing agency firm subscribe to the shares of the company and take them up fully in some agreed proportion. Although the shares are nominally open to the public, it is the partners that are responsible for a certain percentage of the shares, and it is open to any partner to distribute the shares later among his friends or the outside public. These latter do not come in directly in the beginning, but only when a partner unloads the shares.[1] But even when he does, he gets his usual commission based on the total holding, while the owners of the shares get only the declared dividend. The partnership agreement is non-terminable for at least eighty years.[2] In cases where a partner desires to transfer his rights, the other partners must be given the first choice to buy him out.

It will thus be evident that in each type mentioned above, the relation between the managing agents and the concerns floated by them is very intimate. When an agreement is entered into between a mill company and a managing agent, it is in effect an agreement between themselves in their dual capacity. The managing agents are the leading shareholders of the concern, and so the agreement is between themselves as (*a*) managers and (*b*) shareholders. Of course, in so far as shares are gradually taken up by outsiders, and as managing agents unload their capital on the market, the agreement becomes more real and has consequences of great economic and social importance. The draft of the agreement is settled by the Board of Directors, who again are the individuals comprising the managing agency firm or their friends. The agreements contain various features which differ greatly in detail one from another. In many cases the agreement provides for a long fixed tenure of management extending to twenty or thirty years. In Ahmedabad the agency cannot be terminated at all, and the only circumstance in which it can change hands is

[1] *Indian Central Banking Enquiry Committee*, Evidence of the Ahmedabad Mill Owners' Association, Vol. 2, p. 480.

[2] See Appendix III for some specimen clauses of managing agency agreements.

when a concern does not work well, and is unable to find the requisite finance, in which case the agency is voluntarily surrendered to a new firm of partners. But even in terminable agreements care is taken to ensure that managing agents are not turned out easily. Some of the provisions state the conditions under which the managing agency agreement may be terminated, and it will be noticed that except in cases of gross mismanagement or incompetence they cannot be turned out, and even so a two-thirds majority is often required. Since managing agents retain a certain percentage of shares, it is not easy to get such a large majority against them. Again, the agreement sometimes requires a minimum share amount to be held by the managing agents, and this in turn ensures their continuance.

IV

PROMOTION OF CONCERNS IN THE COTTON INDUSTRY

The early cotton mills in India were first established in Bombay city and owed their existence, as already stated, to the enterprise and energy of a few wealthy Parsi merchants and bankers who were assisted by the agents of British machine-making firms. Soon after the Hindu community of Bhatias entered the field as promoters and started mills with the aid of their own resources and those of their friends. Although they were ignorant of the technical conditions of the industry they were men who had an intimate knowledge of the cotton trade and gave personal attention to the details of the working of the mill companies. Their want of technical experience was made up by the importing of skilled technical labour, and but for the Lancashire men who came out as managers to supervise Lancashire machinery, the cotton industry could not have developed so rapidly in India. The mills started in the earlier period were all adequately financed and equipped. The profits that were earned by them were such as to invite more and more mill promotions. But the later entrants were of the type well known in all countries. They were the speculative class of company promoters who had little experience and less resources of their own. They held out much promise of high profits to investors, and their interest was only to win substantial gains by floating the companies. The system of remuneration based on output increased the number of concerns floated. A mill agent assured of a minimum commission on production (quarter anna per lb. of yarn) had every inducement to promote a mill because, whatever be the ultimate success or failure of the concern, the commission would enable him to recover the capital he had put in. By holding out promises of buying stores, supplies, machinery, etc., and by offering to utilize their services for building and construction, various persons were persuaded to take up shares in the mill agents' concern. Thus apart from the mill agents themselves, the chief shareholders were the friends and relations of the agents, the machinery and store suppliers, the coal dealer, the cotton merchant, the broker, the maccadam, the building contractor—all who were in a greater or lesser degree obliged to the agents and drawing benefit directly from the new enterprise.[1] In many cases, even before the engines emitted steam, the companies had to wind up.[2] Instances were not unknown when a few people sought to start a company with only the vaguest notion of how to work a cotton mill, and governed only by the motive of making enormous profit by selling out their interest in the concern. As one lawyer remarked, speaking of the prospectus of a mill company shown to him, "this company is being formed to purchase the land of B at a fabulous price, to build a cotton mill thereon for the benefit of B and to appoint him and his nominees as agents for life and secure employment for their friends and relations."[3] Companies projected on these lines often did not reach the stage of registration or the issue of a prospectus, while those which could gather a little capital from unwary investors soon came to grief. But these cannot be regarded as the normal feature. On the other hand, in many cases the methods of promotion were characterized by careful investigation and prudent planning. The industry owed much to the pioneering work of men

[1] *Indian Textile Journal*, December 1904, p. 73.

[2] S. M. Rutnagur, *The Cotton Mills*, 1927, p. 47.

[3] Ibid.

like J. N. Tata, who went over to England to study the working of the mills in Lancashire, and to obtain machinery suitable for spinning and weaving in the different climatic conditions of India. The influence of Greaves, Cotton & Co., Ltd., who became managing agents of several cotton mills, and of Bradbury, Brady & Co., who were machinery agents, and who advised the mills in regard to equipment, was also important in the development of the cotton industry. But when cotton mills came to be floated by smaller capitalists and less well-known managing agents, whose only motive was to get the agency commission, certain serious evils came to be associated with the system of flotation which led to fluctuations in the progress of the industry. By holding out promises of buying materials from cotton merchants, coal dealers, store suppliers, etc., sufficient funds were secured for the company from such persons, but the mills suffered greatly owing to the poor quality of the goods delivered and the obligation to buy from those who had subscribed to the shares of the company on such assurances.[1] The contract for the cartage of the company's cotton, machinery, and other goods was given to those who took a large number of shares, while the building contractor had to accept a substantial sum in script for his work in lieu of cash. Again, part of the subscription to mill shares came from the local agents of machinery firms,[2] and machinery was purchased only

[1] In Lancashire, too, the mills sometimes had credit from merchants and became "tied" to them with the same adverse consequences. *Committee on Industry and Trade, Survey of Textile Industries*, 1928, p. 27.

[2] S. M. Rutnagur, *The Cotton Mills*, p. 47.

In Ahmedabad, too, the system by which local agents of British machinery firms were asked to subscribe to the shares of the concern was by no means exceptional.

Indian Textile Journal, July 1904, p. 324: "By an agreement made on 19th April, 1895, by the Ahmedabad Advance Spinning and Weaving Co., Ltd., with one Mr. T. Ralph Douse, in consideration of a sum of £33,000 he was to supply to the company 15,000 spindles and 300 looms with all preparatory machinery, engines and boilers, and it was arranged that the sum of £33,000 should be paid *half* in cash and *half in fully paid up* shares in the Company."

Out of a total of 799 shares of Rs. 1,000 each in the Queen Mills, Mr. Abdul Husen Abdul Karim became the owner of 592 shares, and

from those who were prepared not only to supply it on credit but also willing to make a contribution to the share capital. The machinery agents could afford to subscribe initially to the shares of a company and gradually unload their capital because with machinery costing about Rs. 7 to 8 lakhs for a moderately sized mill, the commission amounted to Rs. 50,000, part of which they could easily invest in the mill. But such a system of mill flotation meant the import of unsuitable machinery, and mills started sometimes with a load of debt to the machine-makers, which they could not repay. Some of them therefore became "the museum of all kinds of obsolete machinery"[1] and had to close down or to be reorganized. There was enormous waste in such a system of promotion, but luckily it became rarer with the passage of time. The public came to look with suspicion upon such methods, and soon it was made impossible for any but influential mill agents of ability and prestige to float cotton mills with success. But this is not to say that even to-day wasteful and unsound methods of flotation do not exist. In the boom period of 1919 to 1921 many a concern was started in India which had not the least title to public support.[2] Professional promoters sprang up all over the country, holding out absurd promises of huge profits, with the result that an enormous amount of capital was wasted. Mills were transferred from one agency to another and capitalized at enormously inflated values. But on the whole the agency system of mill flotation has ensured to India a certain economy, and the flotation of wild-cat enterprises has been rendered less easy.

The methods of promoting cotton mills in Ahmedabad and elsewhere have differed from those prevalent in Bombay. In Ahmedabad, as has already been pointed out in a general way, and as will be considered in greater detail in Chapters III and VI, the mills have been started, controlled, and financed by the managing agents who, together with some of their friends, practi-

these were shares given to him in lieu of cash for supplying machinery (*Indian Textile Journal*, September 1909, p. 434).

[1] Arno Pearse, *The Cotton Industry of India*, 1930, p. 8.

[2] *Report of the Bombay Stock Exchange Enquiry Committee*, 1924.

cally owned the mills. Unlike the cotton merchants of Bombay, the mill agents of Ahmedabad were financiers and capitalists who, with the profits of money-lending and banking, became the pioneers of the mill industry. The public were invited to come into the industry only after a lapse of time, and on the whole their confidence in the mill industry had been such that they were not only willing to take shares but to make heavy deposits with the mill companies. Of all this more later.

JUTE MILLS

As with the cotton industry where Lancashire men came out to run the cotton mills and train Indian workers to tend the machinery, so in the jute industry Dundee mill overseers came out to look after the machinery in the mills in Bengal. The first jute mill was started by one Acland with the help of an Indian financial agent,[1] and these two partners managed the mill. Even when the first limited liability company in the jute industry was started, it is significant that it was managed by a firm of managing agents (Messrs. Borradaile, Schiller & Co.) although there was also a managing director in the concern. The history of the flotation of jute mills in Bengal shows the part played by individual merchants who later founded the managing agency firms in their own names or in those of local agents of British firms. Although the first jute mill had a chequered career and was restarted in 1868 as a new company, and the managing agency transferred to a new firm, the industry was so prosperous that many new mills were floated between 1872 and 1873. Indeed, in that period it was only necessary to issue a prospectus for the shares to be fully subscribed forthwith. Naturally some of the new companies were conceived rather hastily and started with insufficient resources and equipment. They became moribund and had to be reorganized and restarted under new names and new management.[2] The pioneers of the jute mills belonged to two or three distinct classes of people. Some of them were men

[1] D. R. Wallace, *The Romance of Jute*, second edition, 1928, p. 11.
[2] Ibid., p. 31.

who had come out as representatives of British firms and started jute mills with the help of a few partners and founded managing agency firms in their own name. There were instances of the servants and officers of the managing agency firms persuading their head office to float new concerns, and in this way some mills were floated. The Borneo Jute Company was started in 1859 at the instance of the local agents of the Borneo Company. On the other hand the Gouripore mill was started by a Doctor Barrie representing Messrs. Scott, Thomson & Co. in conjunction with one Smith representing a sugar refining company. Thus either the old agency firms went on promoting new mills, or new agency partnership firms were organized by persons representing British trading firms with a view specially to floating new concerns.

IRON AND STEEL INDUSTRY

Perhaps in no other industry has the extent or importance of the pioneering and experimenting work been revealed to a greater extent and the part played by managing agents seen in truer perspective than in the promotion of the Tata Iron and Steel Co.[1] From 1900 to 1907, when the company was actually floated, the time and money spent by J. N. Tata and his friends in the investigation of the suitable conditions for the manufacture of pig-iron and steel were enormous. After getting a prospecting licence in 1900 and arranging for the prospecting work to be done by some agents, he went over to Germany and America and realized that if his scheme was to mature it was necessary to spend a large amount in preliminary investigation and in a thorough and scientific survey of local conditions, raw materials, markets, etc. But nothing daunted him. An expert engineer was got out, and for the next two years an enormous amount of wandering, combined with great privation, marked the adventurous prospecting operations. The preliminary cost had reached the sum of £30,000, which would have been sheer loss if the enterprise had never

[1] For the pioneering work of J. N. Tata the reader is referred to the admirable works: D. E. Wacha, *Life of J. N. Tata*, 1918, and F. R. Harris, *Life of J. N. Tata*, 1925.

reached the stage of successful flotation, and indeed the project on which Tata and the expert were engaged in prospecting was not destined to be started in his lifetime. It was the discovery of the rich ores in the lofty Gurumaishini Hill and the great assistance rendered by Mr. P. N. Bose, a retired official of the Geological Survey Department, that finally led to the maturing of the project; and in 1907, after experiencing a great check in the attempt to float a company with British capital, the Tata Iron and Steel Co. was finally started with Indian capital. The industry owed its rise and development entirely to the initiative and ability of J. N. Tata, the head of the managing agency firm founded by him. But for the expenditure which he was prepared to risk in the enterprise, the steel company would never have been founded.

V

PROMOTERS' REMUNERATION

Has the cost of promotion in India been excessive? It is difficult to answer this question with any exactness, as in the large majority of cases the remuneration to promoters takes the form of managing agency commissions and profits, and is not directly in the form of promoters' shares, thus identifying their interests not only with the promotion but also with the continuing prosperity of the concern. In return for organizing a business unit, the promoter enters into an agreement by which he becomes the managing agent of that concern for a definite period of time and cannot ordinarily be turned out. In a word, the return to the promoter is the right of managing the concern with all the privileges and rights pertaining to management, and, as we shall see later, these extend to the right of taking commissions on all kinds of activities pursued on behalf of the business. It is therefore difficult to separate the share belonging to him in his capacity of promoter from that accruing to him in his capacity as manager.

There have been cases where the promoters have sought to make money by the sale of their own properties to the business which they floated. But the Indian company law has ensured a certain amount of publicity by insisting that the names of all vendors from whom any property is acquired must be published, and by providing that full particulars of the nature and extent of the interests of every director in the promotion of the company and in the property proposed to be acquired by the company must be published in the prospectus. This has given a fair security against fraud and exploitation of the investors by the promoters.

A typical case of promoters' rights and privileges and the remuneration granted to them is that furnished by the agreement between Messrs. Tata, Sons & Co. and the Tata Iron and Steel Co., when the latter was started. "All the ore fields, railway, and freight concessions, together with all the other privileges conceded by the Government of India, were handed over to the company by Messrs. Tata, Sons & Co. in consideration of the allotment to them of 15 lakhs of rupees in ordinary shares, issued as fully paid up, and $5\frac{1}{4}$ lakhs of rupees in cash to reimburse them for their preliminary out-of-pocket outlay upon the scheme. This latter amount, with an addition of $4\frac{3}{4}$ lakhs of rupees of their own (making a total of 10 lakhs), the firm undertook to invest in the shares of the company and not to sell any of those shares for five years. The firm was also to receive a royalty of 4 annas per ton sold as ore in India or exported. The firm was also to act as agents for the company for a period of eighteen years, their remuneration being a commission of 5 per cent on annual net profits, after deducting interest on debentures and amount set aside for depreciation, with a minimum commission of Rs. 50,000 per year."[1]

Since it is impossible to assess separately the amount of promoter's profits as it is absorbed in his profits of management, the question whether the promotion of industry is done economically is one intimately connected with the efficiency and economy of management, a question to be examined fully later. The managing agent gets profits in a dual capacity. As holder of a considerable amount of shares it is to his interest that the company is efficiently managed and that dividends are annually

[1] F. R. Harris, *Life of J. N. Tata*, 1925, p. 203.

declared. But he is able to get paid in a number of other ways, and receives commission on purchase and sale, on insurance, and thus is in a position to make money even when the company is unable to declare any profit. Managing agency by itself tends, therefore, to secure a certain value because of its rights and privileges, apart from its ability to show profit in the concerns managed. It might happen, although such cases are undoubtedly exceptional, that the managing agents may be able to secure some income from the concerns for a considerable time, although the concerns they manage have been losing. But the nemesis comes ultimately, and the more enlightened among them are not willing to kill the goose that lays the golden eggs.

CONCLUSION

It will be clear from the above that the methods of floating industrial units in India have on the whole been sound and economical, and that the system of promoting concerns by managing agents has yielded fruitful results. It has for one thing kept away the parasitic type of company promoters, who, except in some abnormal years, were given short shrift. The men who pioneered the enterprise were persons with considerable financial resources, able and willing to command expert assistance for investigating and prospecting thoroughly any projects before trying to float them.[1] Large sums of money were spent on pioneering schemes which could not ultimately reach the stage of flotation, and the burden of such losses was borne by the managing agents, and the public were relieved of it. Thus managing agents performed services in India which issue houses were doing in other countries. They were, indeed, what may be termed universal providers of industry, being promoters, financiers, and managers

[1] For example, "In regard to the Katni Cement Company, we first started a syndicate putting in 5 or 6 lakhs of rupees and tried and risked money; finding that it was successful we finally started the concern and threw it open for public subscription. We asked our machinery agents to give us different kinds of machinery and got from Germany experts and paid them all at our risk" (Sir Fazulbhoy Currimbhai, *Industrial Commission*, Evidence, Vol. 3, p. 98).

of the venture they established. The name of the managing agent was in itself a guarantee to the public of the soundness of the enterprise in which he was interested, and the absence of it in a public issue a presumption of its untrustworthiness. In this way the public came more and more to realize that they were not to risk their capital in ventures not backed by one or other well-known agency firms. A great deal of waste was thus avoided. True, there was danger even in this. A scheme sound in itself and promoted by a person not belonging to an agency firm might be unable to effect a successful flotation. When to this is added the fact that managing agents were sometimes unenterprising, it is obvious that some desirable ventures might have been crowded out. But on the whole there seems to be little doubt that the public would lose less by putting a brake upon the activities of even able promoters than by encouraging too freely the brilliant but resourceless and opportunist promoters. The system of promotion by managing agents was thus a distinct gain to industry.

Secondly, since managing agents had a deeper interest in the concern than a mere promoter would have had, they were not only interested in successful flotation but their interests were linked up with the fortunes of the concerns they started. They were at least believers in their own offspring, and being endowed with more than average ability there was every chance of their enterprise turning out to be a success. Most of them owned, at least in the early years of the company, the bulk of the shares in the concerns for which they were managing agents. Failure of the ventures meant not merely loss of dividend and agency commission but, what is even more important, it implied loss of credit. This close association of ownership and control has resulted in a unity of aim and motive, and the common defects of joint-stock enterprise arising from diffused authority were obviated by a system in which the managing agents who had the greatest interest were able to work with a single-minded purpose and free from the shackles of control by a Board of Directors. The inertia that sometimes characterizes the management of a joint-stock company because of the unwillingness of the Board to take risks is absent in a system of management in which the management is assured of a long tenure. The "golden rule of capitalism" that "where the risk lies, control must lie" is satisfied in the scheme of organization in India. But the special feature of the system arises when the managing agent ceases to have a majority or even a considerable portion of the shares of the company, and then arises conflict of interest between him and the shareholders. It is the emergence of this conflict in recent years in the system of managing agency as it works in Bombay city that has caused all the difficulty and brought discredit to the system. But further consideration of all this must be deferred to a later chapter dealing with an estimate of the work and future of the Indian managing agency system.

Thirdly, industrial enterprises were nursed for a long time by managing agents until they felt they could be safely launched out and thrown open to public subscription. This has been specially so in regard to concerns floated by British managing agents. The Indian Paper Mill Company was started years ago, and still continues as a private company, because Messrs. Andrew Yule & Co. would not float it as a public company until absolutely assured of success.[1] It has been said that owing to doubts in the mind of the investor about the value and character of any new proposition placed before him there exists a gap between the sources of demand for capital and the sources of supply which constitutes an "economic distance" in every country,[2] and in India this distance is bridged in a fairly effective way by the managing agent, who has proved a helpful intermediary. What is more, since the concern had previously been working successfully in a small way the investors could be certain of a safe and sound investment.

It is not, however, to be understood that the flotation of industria lconcerns was not sometimes attended with waste or that there were not cases of ill-conceived and even fraudulent promo-

[1] *Indian Tariff Board: Paper and Paper Pulp Industries*, Evidence tendered by applicants for protection, 1925, p. 311. Also Report, 1931, p. 99.

[2] F. Lavington, *British Capital Market*, 1921, p. 103.

tion. The number of companies that were wound up within a year of their starting is some measure of the amount of capital running to waste each year.[1] There have been cases where unscrupulous promoters organized themselves into so-called managing agents with a view to hoodwinking the investors; but the only resemblance between them and the old and well-known agency firms was the name "managing agents." Fortunately, such people have never had a long innings. Again, in the hectic years of 1920 and 1921, some cases of mill reorganization occurred where the promoters made enormous profit at the expense of the investors. An instance of this character is given in the Report of the Bombay Stock Exchange Enquiry Committee, p. 52, and it reveals the fact that managing agents were not wholly immune from the charge of wasteful promotion and reorganization.

Further, while the fullest credit may be given to the pioneering work of managing agents there is increasing justification for the view that in recent years they have been rather unwilling to pioneer and risk in new enterprises[2] where the profits might neither be large nor certain. It must be admitted, of course, that whether a new business is to be started or not is a matter which must really be left to the discretion of the managing agents. But the point is that in a country where the public look for leadership to the managing agents, any conservatism and narrow-mindedness in the latter may have serious effects on the economic development of the country. While from their personal point of view there may be justification for their concentrating attention on routine lines of business activity, and on pursuit of certain gains, it may be that the country would have been better served if its industrial leaders had been more adventurous, and if they had not shown a tendency to rest on their oars and to be content to earn from old investments rather than embark on new and uncertain ventures. However successful the managing agency system of promotion might have been in the past, it cannot be concluded that it is so at present, or will continue to be so in the future. The past was the golden

[1] See Chapter IV for the number of liquidations each year since 1915–16.

[2] *Report of the Indian Industrial Commission*, p. 13.

age of Indian industrial development. There was such a vast, unexplored field that the way was very smooth, and men of ordinary ability and initiative were able to pioneer in those years. Now that the task is less easy because of the greater obstacles to encounter, one is not so certain that the managing agents will justify their permanent existence. Since the country is largely dependent upon the agency system for its industrial development, the extent to which it is capable of fulfilling its functions by continuously supplying itself with fresh talents and new blood is not a mere private matter but an important social problem on which some light must be thrown.

Again, there has not been enough co-operative endeavour among managing agents in floating concerns which may be either too big or too risky for any one individual firm to undertake. The only way of overcoming the existing defect is for them to co-operate with one another in floating big enterprises. Further, it is also unfortunate that the Indian and European managing agents have been working on parallel and often in separate fields. They have not fully co-operated in the common purpose of advancing industrial development. The differences in methods and organization between the Indian and British managing agents will engage our attention later.

APPENDIX I

Holdings of Messrs. Tata, Sons & Co., Ltd., in the Tata Iron and Steel Co., Ltd.

	Par Value
3efore 1914, 32,800 ordinary shares and 3,000 deferred shares	Rs. 25,50,000
:n 1924, 32,600 ordinary shares, 4,500 deferred, and 2,800 second preference shares ..	Rs. 28,60,000

out of a total called capital in March 1922 of 946.80 lakhs amounts to less than 3 per cent (*India 3oard: Steel Industry*, 1924, Vol. 1, Evidence, p. 219).

Percentage Holdings of F. W. Heilgers & Co., Managing Agents of Titaghur Paper Mills

	Per cent
Ordinary Shares ..	11·5
Preference, old issue ..	0·3
Preference, new issue ..	0·6
Deferred	60·8

percentage of total capital held by managing agents is 13·1 (*Indian Tariff Board: Paper and Paper Pul es*, 1932, Vol. 1, p. 325).

Holdings of the Managing Agents of Deccan Paper Mills, Ltd.

hold 5 to 6 lakhs of rupees out of a total paid-up capital of Rs. 9.25 lakhs, i.e. nearly 60 per cer nares (Ibid., p. 580).

TAKEN FROM THE "MIRROR OF INVESTMENT," BY PAT LOVETT, 1927

[N]ame of the Mill or Company	Managing Agents	Total Number of Paid-up Shares	Holdings of the Managing Agen[ts]
edabad Advance Mills	Messrs. Tata, Sons & Co.	10,000 shares of Rs. 100	Sir D. J. Tata, 1,038
al Nagpur Cotton Mills	Messrs. Shaw, Wallace & Co.	90,000 ordinary of Rs. 10. 3,000 preference of Rs. 100	Agents' holdings, 4,330
Cotton Spinning and eaving Mills, Ltd.	Messrs. Birla Bros., Ltd.	100,000 of Rs. 10 ordinary. 50,000 of Rs. 10 preference	G. D. Birla, 106,020; K tan, 33,997; B. M. R. K. Birla, 1,400. T 141,417
bay Dyeing and Manu- turing Co., Ltd.	Messrs. Nowrosjee Wadia & Sons	25,098 of Rs. 250	Wadia family, 2,450
eah Cotton Mills, Ltd.	Messrs. Kettlewell, Bullen & Co.	6,000 of Rs. 100 ordinary. 12,000 Rs. 100 preference	Agents, 532
bury Mills, Ltd.	Messrs. Currimbhai Ebra- him & Sons, Ltd.	4,000 of Rs. 250 ordinary. 6,000 of Rs. 250 preference	Agents, 624
ral India Spinning, eaving, and Manufac- ing Co., Ltd.	Messrs. Tata, Sons & Co.	46,875 of Rs. 100 ordinary. 10,000 of Rs. 500 preference	Sir D. J. Tata and R. Tata, 3,750
ury Spinning and Manu- turing Co., Ltd.	Messrs. C. N. Wadia & Co.	18,500 of Rs. 100	Wadias, 8,050
a Land and Mill Co., d.	Messrs. W. H. Brady & Co., Ltd.	28,000 shares of Rs. 100	Agents, 100
la Spinning and Weav- Co., Ltd.	Messrs. Cowasjee Jehangir & Co., Ltd.	13,000 of Rs. 100	Jehangir, 4,450
ent Mills Co., Ltd.	Messrs. Currimbhai Ebra- him & Sons, Ltd.	15,000 of Rs. 100	Agents, 1,293

mbhai Mills Co., Ltd.	Messrs. Currimbhai Ebrahim & Sons, Ltd.	8,800 of Rs. 250	Agents, 4,202
a Mills Co., Ltd.	Messrs. Sassoon, J. David & Co., Ltd.	3,200 of Rs. 250.	Agents, 924; Sir S. Dav 50
l Mills Co., Ltd.	Messrs. E. D. Sassoon & Co., Ltd.	1,800 of Rs. 500 6,000 of Rs. 250 ordinary	Sir V. Sassoon, 1,331
ar Mills, Ltd.	Messrs. Kettlewell, Bullen & Co.	14,000 of Rs. 100 ordinary. 5,000 of Rs. 100 preference	Agents, 2,704
aim Pabaney Mills Co., l.	Messrs. Currimbhai Ebrahim & Sons, Ltd.	8,000 of Rs. 250	Agents, 484; Currimb Ebrahim, 640; Tot 1,124
rd Sassoon Mills, Ltd.	Messrs. E. D. Sassoon & Co., Ltd.	8,500 of Rs. 200	Agents, 1,452
bhoi Mills, Ltd.	Messrs. Currimbhai Ebrahim & Sons, Ltd.	7,200 of Rs. 250	Agents, 810
ji Petit Mills Co., Ltd.	D. M. Petit, Sons & Co.	1,400 of Rs. 1,000	Petits, 804
e Manufacturing Co., l.	Messrs. Turner, Morison & Co., Ltd.	10,000 of Rs. 100	Agents, 1,885
k Mills, Ltd.	Messrs. Forbes, Forbes, Campbell & Co.	39,047 of Rs. 100	A. Scott, 12,651
asthan Spinning and aving Mills	Damoder Thackersey, Mooljee & Co.	1,184 of Rs. 1,000	Agents, 174
eshi Mills Co., Ltd.	Messrs. Tata, Sons & Co.	20,000 of Rs. 100	Agents, 2,039
Mills Co., Ltd.	Messrs. Tata, Sons & Co.	6,000 of Rs. 500 ordinary. 7,000 of Rs. 500 preference	Agents, 1,007
u Cotton Mill, Ltd.	Bombay Co., Ltd.	3,200 of Rs. 500	Agents, 474

Vide also Statements 2 and 3 in Appendix I of Chapter IV.

APPENDIX II

1. Mr. Currimbhai Ebrahim, whose sons controlled up till 1933 as many as eleven cotton mills in Bombay and elsewhere, was born in 1840 and was engaged in the yarn trade with China. The profits in the trade enabled him to project successfully the Currimbhai Mills in 1886, and in 1888 they actually started work. Later the Mahomad and Ebrahim Mills were started, and in 1900 the agency of a mill was transferred to him by Lukshindas Khijir & Co. The experience he had gained as a merchant and his great administrative talent were responsible for his success as mill agent (*Indian Textile Journal*, April 1904).

2. Manilal, Marsden & Co., Ltd., managing agents of the Monogram Mills, Ahmedabad. Mr. Charles Marsden before he came out to India in 1906 as weaving-master had a thorough practical training, serving his apprenticeship in a mill in Blackburn. In 1908 he went to Ahmedabad as weaving-master to the new Maneckchowk Mills, and later became manager of the New Cotton Mills. His brother, Ben Marsden, was weaving-master of Finlay Mills after 1907, and in 1913 became manager of Becherdas Mills at Ahmedabad. In 1921 the brothers built and started an entirely new mill of their own called the Marsden Mills. For six years they worked in it. In view of the success of this enterprise they were induced to start another mill with up-to-date machinery in 1924, and formed a partnership with Manilal Mulchand under the name of Manilal, Marsden & Co., Ltd. (*Indian Textile Journal*, October 1929).

3. Mr. J. F. Bradbury came out from Lancashire as manager of a mill in Bombay. He next became a machinery importer, and his business as machinery importer and agent of machine manufacturers in partnership with W. H. Brady was very successful. The partnership concern became also agents for the management of cotton mills. After retiring from machinery business, he started a new partnership with Mr. Knowles under the name of Messrs. Bradbury & Knowles, and became agent of nearly half a dozen mill companies. Some time before his death he also took as partner Mr. J. Hall, a gentleman who had great knowledge of the trade of Bombay (*Indian Textile Journal*, March 1916).

4. "Prominent among the pioneers of the Bombay cotton industry was Mr. John R. Greaves, the present head of Messrs. Greaves, Cotton & Co. Mr. Greaves had spent several years in the well-known works of Platt Bros. & Co., Oldham, before coming over to India in 1874. With such an intimate knowledge of the mechanical side he came out and joined the firm founded by his father in partnership with Sir George Cotton. Their chief business activities were the manufacturing, ginning and pressing factories and importing of cotton-mill machinery. The agents soon started mills of their own and had a few others brought under their agency, and thus eight mills with over 300,000 spindles were under their control and management. Mr. Greaves is now assisted by A. K. Leslie and his two brothers, Messrs. Herbert and Septimus Greaves" (*Indian Textile Journal*, February 1904, p. 149).

HISTORY OF MARTIN & CO.

In 1874 Mr. T. A. Martin came to India to form a branch of Messrs. Walsh, Lovett & Co., a firm of merchants with large interests in South America and headquarters in Birmingham and London. In 1875 an office was opened in Calcutta. Their main business was trade in general stores and metal; besides large contract such as the building of an aqueduct. Martin associated with R. N. Mukerjee. Waterworks and drainage schemes which absorbed the partners' attention did not appeal to Messrs. Walsh, Lovett & Co., and they subsequently withdrew from the Indian trade. In 1892 the firm of Martin & Co. was established, the parties being Sir Acquin Martin, Sir Rajendra Nath Mukerjee, Mr. Harold Martin, and Mr. C. W. Walsh. The first feeder railways were constructed by them. They got the Indian agency of the Bengal Iron and Steel Co. They started and managed some collieries, docks, engineering works, manganese mines, tea, timber, and electricity supply companies, cement and allied workshops—all following a clear and well-defined policy of developing the resources of India chiefly so far as they related to engineering in all its branches.

Martin & Co. are now managing agents of a number of collieries, Indian Manganese Co., Hooghly Docking and Engineering Co., Natal Insurance Co., Sonne Valley Portland Cement Co., Borooch Timber Co., Ltd., and agents for four tea companies. They have recently floated the Sonapur Tea Co., Ltd.

BURN & CO.

Burn & Currie were doing engineering work in India. Currie retired, and his place was taken by William Burn and James Mackintosh: the firm then became known as Burn & Co. At a later date Mr. James Mackintosh retired and founded the rival firm of Mackintosh, Burn & Co.

In 1879 the name was changed to Burn & Co., with offices in Calcutta. In 1895 the business was converted into a joint-stock limited liability company, the partners retaining the old firm's name of Burn & Co., and became managing agents of the new limited liability company (Burn & Co., Ltd.). This step was necessitated by the tremendous growth of the firm in the iron and steel business, etc. The similarity of name has caused some confusion, but the relation has become better known in recent years, since the firm (limited company) became in addition managing agents of Indian Iron and Steel Co., Ltd., and the Indian Standard Wagon Co., Ltd.

SAMNUGGUR floated in 1873 was a concern of great efficiency. This was promoted by Mr. Thos. Duff, who had retired after leaving the Borneo Company's service and who was managing the Barking Mills near London. But he could not rest. In conjunction with the brothers Nicol, of A. J. Nicol, and Mr. J. J. Barrie of Dundee, he floated the Samnuggur Co. They were particularly fortunate in their selection of an expert to conduct their business in the agents' (Messrs. Schoene, Kilburn & Co.) office. He was W. Smith, who rose from the position of office boy in Messrs. Cox & Brothers, to a confidential position with the firm. He was so successful in his work that another company, Titaghur, was floated in 1883, in which 40 per cent bonus shares were allotted to the holders of the Samnuggur. In 1883 the firm of Thos. Duff & Co., Ltd., came into existence and took over the agency.

Here was a case of a company floated in England with the co-operation of two other people; had an agency firm to work it in Calcutta; had a home Board in London; a new mill started and the agency taken over by Thos. Duff & Co., whose original partner had floated the Samnuggur.

APPENDIX III

The following is from the "Replies to the Tariff Board Questionnaire" sent by the Bombay Shareholders' Association.

THE AJIT MILLS, LTD., AHMEDABAD, 1931. AGENCY AGREEMENT

Clause 1: Agents' firm to be the sole managing, non-changeable, non-removable, and permanent Secretaries, Treasurers, and Agents.

No transfer to take place unless Agents appointed Agents of the transferee Company.

In case of winding up, Agents entitled to recover in priority over all other claims ten times the average annual commission accrued during the preceding five years, and if the Company shall not have so long existed then a sum equivalent to ten times the commission accrued during the previous year.

In the event of the Company requesting the Agents to cease working as such and the Agents consenting, then the Agents shall, before handing over the charge of the Company's property and business, be paid as compensation a sum equivalent to twelve times the commission accrued from the Company during the preceding year.

THE NEW NATIONAL MILLS, LTD., AHMEDABAD, 1931

Appointment of Agents not liable to be revoked or cancelled on any other ground except their voluntary resignation in writing.

No sale or transfer of the Company can take place if the Agents are not appointed Agents of the transferee Company (Clause 11).

THE KALYAN MILLS, LTD., AHMEDABAD

Clause 9 of the Agreement contains the following stipulation: (Limitation of the Powers of Directors) "Except where a particular act is required by statute to be performed only by the Board of Directors or a General Meeting, whenever same or similar powers appear to have been given to the Company in general meeting or to the Directors on the one hand and the Agents on the other, they are to be exercised only by the Managing Agent till he happens to cease to be such Agent."

BRADBURY MILLS, BOMBAY. AGENTS: CURRIMBHAI EBRAHIM & SONS, LTD. (Managing Agents expressly authorized to work for and contract with the Companies)

"Under Article 97 the Agents' firm is expressly allowed generally to work for or contract with the Company and also to do the work of shipping, landing, and commission Agents for the Company and any other work for the Company upon such terms and conditions and under such remuneration as may from time to time be agreed upon between them and the Directors."

MODEL MILLS, BOMBAY. AGENTS: BANSILAL ABIRCHAND DADABHOY & CO.

"Clause 8 of the Agreement provides that if the Agents' firm shall at any time act as muccadams or brokers of the Company or selling Agents they shall be paid such additional remuneration as shall be agreed upon between them and the Directors. Under Article 109 the Agents are expressly allowed to work for and contract with the Company and also to do the work of shipping, landing and commission Agents, maccadams and cotton brokers of the Company, and to do any other work of the Company upon such terms and conditions and with such remuneration as may from time to time be agreed upon between them and the Directors of the Company.

EDWARD SASSOON MILLS. AGENTS: E. D. SASSOON & CO., LTD., BOMBAY

Clause 6 of the Agreement runs as follows:

"The said firm and its branches in India, Hong-Kong, China, Europe, America, and elsewhere are also hereby appointed the selling agents of the Company for the sale of yarn, cloth, or other fabrics, goods or articles manufactured or produced by the Company and all other products of the Company and are also appointed the buying Agents of the Company at all the aforesaid places for the purchase of machinery, stores, and all other articles and things required for the purposes of the Company for the period during which they are entitled to act as the Agents of the Company pursuant to this Agreement at such rates of commission on all sales effected by them for and on behalf of the Company as may from time to time be agreed upon between the said firm and the Directors, such remuneration to be paid to the said firm in addition to the Agency commission payable to them under the provision of clause 2 hereinabove contained, provided that nothing herein contained shall prevent the said firm from themselves purchasing the yarn, cloth, or other fabrics or goods or articles manufactured or produced by the Company upon such terms and at such prices as may from time to time be fixed by the Board of Directors and in the event charge any commission as selling agents on the quantity of such purchases by the said firm themselves; but the said firm shall not be entitled to sales to themselves."

KOHINOOR MILLS. AGENTS: KILLICK, NIXON & CO., BOMBAY

"Under Article 131 the Agents are with the previous consent of the Directors given generally or in each separate case entitled to contract with the Company either as vendors of cotton, coal stores, or other articles required for the business or purposes of the Company or as purchasers of the manufactures or products of the Company."

See also page 19*n*. of Chapter I, where extracts from the Articles of Association relating to some jute mills are given.

APPENDIX IV

ATEMENT SHOWING THE NAMES OF SOME MANAGING AGENTS AND THE VARIETY OF BUSINESSES UNDERTAKE BY THEM, PREPARED FROM THE "INVESTORS' INDIA YEAR BOOK," AND FROM THE REPORT OF THE INDIAN BANKING ENQUIRY COMMITTEE

Name of Managing Agent	Number of Companies Managed	Jute	Tea	Coal	Electricity and Engineering	Transport	Sugar	Othe Indust
ew Yule & Co.	54	10	18	14	—	3	1	8
an Bros. & Co.	25	1	24	—	—	—	—	—
n & Co.	22	—	—	7	6	8	—	1
ius Steel & Co.	20	—	13	1	5	1	—	—
Dunlop & Co.	19	4	13	—	1	—	1	—
& Co.	20	8	—	3	2	5	—	2
od & Co.	17	5	6	—	—	6	—	—
aders, Arbuthnot & Co.	17	2	5	3	—	6	—	1
mson, Magor & Co.	17	—	16	1	—	—	—	—
, Wallace & Co.	16	—	7	6	—	—	—	3
ie, Skinner & Co.	16	4	6	4	—	—	—	2
rn & Co.	15	—	9	3	2	1	—	—

ıport & Co.	14	—	14	—	—	—	—	—
Low & Co.	13	—	—	12	—	—	—	1
er, Lawrie & Co...	12	—	—	2	5	—	—	5
Heilgers & Co...	11	2	—	8	—	—	—	1
eill & Co.	10	1	—	8	—	—	—	1
Sutherland & Co.	8	—	—	—	1	—	5	2
s, Ltd.	6	—	3	3	—	—	—	—
well, Bullen & Co.	6	2	1	—	—	—	—	3
Henderson & Co.	5	2	3	—	—	—	—	—
Bros. & Co.	4	1	—	—	—	—	—	3
Finlay & Co.	4	1	3	—	—	—	—	—
as Duff & Co.	3	3	—	—	—	—	—	—
Brady & Co.	6	—	—	—	—	—	1	5 cott
nbhai Ebrahim & Sons, Ltd. ..	14	—	—	—	—	—	—	13 cott 1 dyei
Sons & Co.	13	—	—	—	4	—	—	5 texti 3
, Nixon & Co.	17	—	—	—	2	8	—	7
Sassoon & Co.	12	—	—	—	—	—	—	12 textil

CHAPTER II

LOCALIZATION OF INDUSTRY IN INDIA[1]

I

CONCENTRATION OF INDUSTRY

In the last chapter we traced the origin and development of the managing agency system. The managing agents whose activities in trade and commerce were naturally concentrated in the chief port towns of India found that these cities were equally well adapted for the location of industries. The "agglomerating" tendencies that favour concentration of industry in a locality were found to operate with full force in cities like Bombay and Calcutta. These latter were not only great ports but junctions of railways. They had favourable transport relations both for natural resources and finished products, and in so far as localization depends upon the distribution of productive powers they offered the only suitable location; for therein were to be found all the factors of production in suitable forms. Such capital as existed was available only in these towns, and the presence of merchants and traders increased the "agglomerating" tendency. The distribution of managing agents mainly in the two important cities of Bombay and Calcutta influenced the location of industries to such an extent that even to-day the distribution of industries in India is characterized by its unevenness and by the excessive concentration in and around Calcutta, Bombay, and a few other big towns. In Calcutta and in the three districts next to it, Howrah, Hooghly, and 24 Parganas, the factory population is well over 450,000. Bombay city and island has about 190,000 workers, so that these two small areas contain between them more than half the factory workers of India. With the exception of Ahmedabad, where there are nearly 70,000 workers, there is no other centre with as many as

[1] The writer is particularly indebted to the *Theory of Industrial Location* by Alfred Weber, and *Inter-regional and International Trade* by B. Ohlin, for the theoretical background of this chapter.

30,000 workers. When a few other centres of secondary importance with some concentration of industries are mentioned, e.g. Cawnpore, Jamshedpur, Madras, and Rangoon, one has nearly exhausted the list of industrial centres in India. The two staple trades, cotton and jute, are located mostly in Bombay and in Calcutta respectively, although Ahmedabad has now become an important centre of the cotton industry.

The reasons for this early concentration in ports are obvious. Until the country was covered with a network of railways there were no opportunities for any modern industry to be established in any internal area. Indeed, when the late Jamsetjee Tata established a cotton mill, the now famous Empress Mills, in Nagpur, an inland place at the time not well connected by railways, it was felt that he was taking a great risk, because at that time no site other than Bombay or Ahmedabad was thought of for the cotton industry. An industry which looked to the overseas market, as the early Bombay cotton industry did, was ideally located in a seaport town like Bombay, and thus for a long time Bombay was a convenient industrial centre which had excellent transport relations and enjoyed the advantage of a large consumers' market which, of course, is governed by the distribution of productive power, i.e. labour, capital, and organization. The fact that Bombay was also the great centre of the raw cotton market for export was another factor. The policy of the railways which stimulated traffic to and from the ports increased the "transport" advantages of the port towns and incidentally led to that congestion of industries to which the Industrial Commission drew pointed attention.

In the same way Calcutta enjoyed similar advantages. Further, it possessed certain exceptional facilities, such as cheap water transport and proximity to coal and jute. It had the same favourable "transport" relations as Bombay in regard to raw materials, and if it had a comparative disadvantage in overland freightage for the transport of products, it was more favourably situated in respect of power resources than Bombay. Its advantage in capital and organization-location was even greater than that of Bombay.

The managing agents of most important industrial concerns had their head offices in Calcutta, and even industries like tea and coal, which utilized goods of the first order and were thus dominated by natural factors in their localization, were intimately bound up in their financial, marketing, and administrative functions with Calcutta.

In recent years, however, owing to the operation of a number of factors, there is a tendency for this excessive concentration to break up. New centres are springing up which find that owing to the improvement of communications, of railways and motor transport, they can command good "transport" relations with materials and product, and are therefore setting up new industries. The establishment of the paper, cement, match, and several other new industries, the rise of chemical industries, the expansion in the development of industries like sugar and iron and steel, have not merely created new centres of activity but invested the problem of industrial location with peculiar interest. These new centres find their transport relations relatively improving in respect of markets within the country, owing to the fact that in a large country like India the greater costs of transport must bring about a more even spread of industrial activities, each centre supplying wholly or partly a limited market. Bombay and Calcutta cannot expect to supply the needs of all the various consuming markets in India, as their transport relations must be inferior to those of other centres which are nearer the markets. Further, the advantage which the distribution of productive factors conferred on Bombay and Calcutta is now tending to diminish as capital and business ability, formerly scarce, are becoming more abundant in other places.

This drift of industry which is seen in India is noticeable in other countries as well. In Great Britain the centre of industrial life is shifting from the north to the south, and the south-east districts of England have gained at the expense of the north and north-east.[1] In the United States of America, too, the cotton

[1] *Ministry of Labour, Annual Report* 1933, also *Economic Journal*, June 1930, p. 247.

industry is migrating from the north to the south.[1] Under the influence of a more even supply of capital, certain American industries have in recent years shown a tendency to move southward, evidently attracted by the lower wage-rates prevailing there. In India, Bombay city is fast ceasing to occupy that predominant position in the cotton industry which it once held, and "deglomerating" tendencies, such as high rents, high rates of wages, and relatively high costs of transporting goods to distant inland markets, are counteracting the former tendency towards concentration. This breaking down of local concentration, the relative decline of the highly developed areas and the development of formerly backward centres are not without compensating advantages, whatever may be the temporary inconveniences of such adjustments. There is certainly a growing feeling that the advantages of local concentration of industry have been overrated, and that, on the whole, it is desirable to secure for each country a more equal geographical distribution of economic life. No one who is aware of the extraordinarily grave social problems to which the concentration of industry in Calcutta and Bombay has given rise will have any doubt that anything that breaks down this excessive specialization and promotes industrial life in other less congested centres is wholly to be desired.

Even from a purely economic point of view it is felt that excessive specialization and dependence on one or two industries carry with them great risks which the present protracted depression has fully illustrated,[2] both in England and India. That Bombay and Lancashire have been greatly handicapped owing to their dependence upon single types of livelihood is too well known to be stressed.

Diversification of industrial activity means less violent depressions and less excited booms since the various industries will not all move in exact accord.[3] Birmingham affords an example of the ability of an industrial centre to survive depression owing to the varied nature of its industrial activities.

[1] *Recent Economic Changes, U.S.A.*, Vol. 1, 1929, p. 206.

[2] *Economic Journal*, 1930, p. 247.

[3] *Recent Economic Changes, U.S.A.*, Vol. 1, 1929, p. 215.

II

A study of the factors that affect localization in India is of great importance not merely because of the changing conditions of production and transport referred to above, but also because some industries like paper, matches, and particularly sugar are growing up fast under the shelter of high protective duties, and it is important that they should be suitably located with reference to primary geographical and economic factors. It is no part of the duty of the State to come to the aid of an industry which suffers from wrong location and has no hope of consolidating its position owing to the competition of energetic young rivals from more favourable areas. A country like India, which has adopted discriminating protection as its definite policy, will have to ensure that industries, whether already protected or seeking protection, are located suitably, and with this end in view may justifiably control industrial location. The importance of this consideration will be brought out in examining the location of the quickly developing sugar industry of the country. Secondly, in a comparatively undeveloped country like India, a great amount of waste can be avoided if haphazard methods of choosing sites are replaced by deliberate and carefully worked-out plans for the future development of industrial locations. The importance of this aspect is enhanced in the special circumstances of India where a very difficult and nicely balanced set of "transport" relations are brought into play owing to the distances between the raw materials, power resources, and marketing centres. Owing to the concentration of all the best coal deposits in a single locality, from which so far the bulk of industrial power has been obtained, places near the coal areas have the best "transport" relations, but raw materials and markets tend to draw industries away from the coal areas. If, therefore, suitable alternatives to coal can be developed nearer the sources of raw materials and markets, certain localities now labouring under a handicap will have superior "transport" relations. These factors are of such importance to the future industrial development of India that the problems of localization deserve close examination.

THEORY OF LOCALIZATION

By localization is meant the concentration of different industries in different localities which in its international aspect is usually termed territorial division of labour. It is, however, best studied from a national aspect, for there alone physical factors are allowed free scope, and not impeded by those elements of economic friction, such as national prejudice, tariffs, and other legislative restraints. The manufacturing industries result from a combination of conditions largely geographic in their origin, and depend for their success upon such factors as raw materials, labour, market, power, etc. Natural resources are much more important for the production of goods of the first order, e.g. wheat, tea, timber, and coal, than for the later stages of production.[1] Paper and wheat flour may be manufactured almost anywhere, and the location depends entirely upon the economics of transport costs. Cotton-spinning is favourably affected by a moist climate; but if additional expenses may be incurred, it is possible to provide moisture in a dry climate. Localization of industry depends upon the distance relations of all places with reference to natural resources and consumers' markets, and the transportability of various goods. The Twelfth Census of the United States of America has summarized the main causes of localization in these terms: Nearness to materials, nearness to markets, water power, favourable climate, supply of labour, capital available for investment in manufactures and the momentum of an early start (due to the presence of some enterprising leaders). In terms of economic language these can be expressed thus. Localization of industry depends upon the transport relations of each place and product with regard to natural resources, and upon the distribution of productive powers, such as labour, capital, and organization, which govern the distribution of consumers' markets.[2] For it is

[1] B. Ohlin, *Inter-regional and International Trade*, 1933, p. 191.
[2] Ibid.

necessary to note that nearness to materials and nearness to markets mean more than geographical distances, and are largely a matter

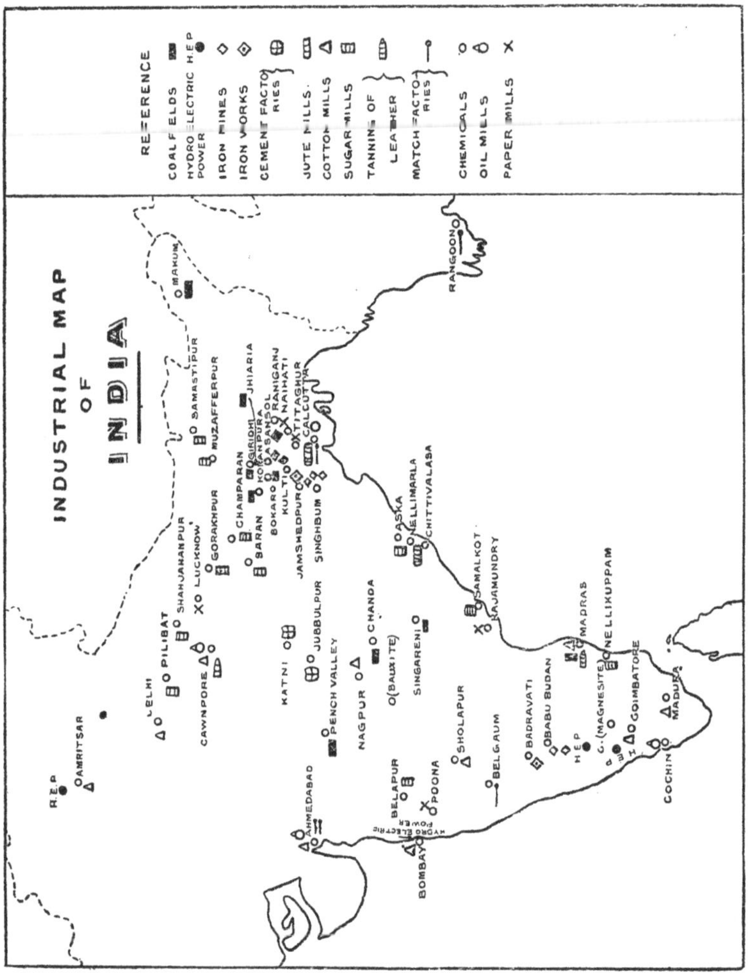

of costs. Further, with reference to the ideal location in regard to raw material, "the test is not the cost of a unit of material, but the material cost of a unit of completed product."[1] Moreover, the progress of industrial invention is perpetually changing the

[1] E.D. Jones, *The Administration of Industrial Enterprises*, 1925, p. 45.

economic import of physical conditions. Everyone knows how the iron industry, which was first located near the forests and water power, had to shift to coal areas when coal took the place of wood as fuel and steam power replaced water power. In the same manner better facilities for supplying regions without access to cheap coal with other power resources have contributed much, and in India will soon tend, to a changed localization of industry. "The utilization of new forms of power, such as petroleum or hydro-electric energy, and the new possibilities of electric transmission of power have made possible the use of machinery in localities not supplied with coal."[1] At every period similar technical changes are occurring which completely change the relative significance of the various elements that affect localization. Each industry has its location determined by the transport relation in respect of all materials and goods required for production and in respect of the market. It is the "transport" relations and not the mere geographical distance relations that have economic significance. But the various circumstances affecting localization of industry cannot all be regarded as basic elements or as known and unchangeable economic data. They are not only changing but greatly influenced by localization itself. Some of these considerations can best be studied in the light of the localization of a few specific industries in India with the help of the map opposite.

OLD INDIAN HANDICRAFTS

The factors that led to the localization of industries in India up to the end of the eighteenth century and the middle of the nineteenth were fairly clear and definite. The simple articles needed to clothe and house the population and to supply them with tools were widely scattered over the country, and were sufficient to meet local needs. But there was some degree of localization in the manufacture of specialities and luxuries for export and for consumption at the large urban centres. While some of these towns had a diversified industrial activity, there were others which became famous as centres of certain specialized industrial

[1] L. D. Edie, *Economics, Principles and Problems*, 1926, p. 660.

products. The patronage of courts, the concentration of population in towns providing a market for goods, and the traditional skill of the artisans were the chief determining factors in those days. The inherited skill of the carpet-weavers of Kashmir, of the marble-laying workers of Agra, of the muslin weavers of Dacca had not a little to do with the prosperity of those urban centres.

III

THE COTTON INDUSTRY

It is, however, with the growth of the modern factory industries that the complex considerations affecting localization come into play. The cotton industry affords a striking illustration of the truth of the statement that the production of raw material in a country or centre is no reason why we should expect the industry to flourish therein. In the United States of America, while the southern states grow cotton, the manufacturing was carried on till recently almost exclusively in the north. Neither Lancashire nor Japan grows any cotton, and yet they are great world-centres of production of cotton goods. While there is a very wide distribution of raw cotton in India, and while cotton ginning and pressing factories lie scattered all over the country in the Bombay Presidency, Central Provinces and Berar, Madras, the Punjab, the United Provinces, Ajmer, and Merwara, the manufacturing industry is located principally in four or five centres in the Bombay Presidency. Out of 295 cotton-spinning and weaving mills in 1929, 203 mills were located in the Bombay Presidency,[1] and of these Bombay City and Ahmedabad together accounted for 174 mills; the other centres being Sholapur, Surat, and Broach. By the side of Bombay city and Ahmedabad the other centres pale into insignificance. There were 21 factories in Madras Presidency, chiefly in the towns of Madras and Coimbatore; 22 in United Provinces, of which Cawnpore accounted for 10; and about 15 in the Central Provinces with Nagpur and Wardha

[1] In 1931, out of 302 cotton-spinning and weaving mills actually at work in India, 178 were located in Bombay Presidency.

as leading centres. There are vast cotton-growing tracts with no cotton-spinning and weaving factory, and some explanation is required for this lack of correlation between the sources of raw material and places of manufacture. Particularly when it is borne in mind that in the spinning of yarn the cost of raw material accounts for about four-fifths of the total costs, the present localization does strike one as strange.

But it is here that the theory of localization, properly understood, is found to be of great value. For, as already pointed out, it is not the distance relations so much as the transport relations that are important. In the textile industries generally the cost of transportation is so small that raw material and finished product can go very great distances with very little addition to total cost. Ocean transport is cheaper than land transport. It costs no more to bring cotton from Galveston to Lancashire than to take it to the chief manufacturing areas in the United States itself. Japan is able to take cotton from India at nearly the same cost as the Bombay mills because of the exceptionally cheap ocean freights. The cost of carrying cotton from Bombay, Calcutta, or Tuticorin to Japan is only 4.56 yen per bale of 400 lb., of which about 1.40 yen is returned by the shipping company as rebate.[1] The cost of bringing cotton from New Orleans to Liverpool was 43 cents in 1913, and 51¾ cents per pound in 1929.[2] Secondly, there is no great difference in weight between the raw material and finished product made from it, with the result that there is no compelling motive to manufacture the cotton in the producing centres, which are less favourably situated in other respects. In general it may be stated that "raw materials tend to attach industries to their place of production in inverse proportion to the amount of the raw material that enters into the finished product."[3] Conversely, the presence of a raw material of which a large proportion is waste, or in other words weight-losing material, will attract manufacture to it. Thus

[1] Arno Pearse, *The Cotton Industry of Japan and China*, 1929, p. 49.
[2] *Journal of the Royal Statistical Society*, January 1930.
[3] G. G. Chisholm, *Handbook of Commercial Geography*, 1922, p. 100.

the saw mill, the manufacture of wood pulp, coconut oil, and other such industries must necessarily be located near the place of material, whereas there is not the same need to economize in freight in the textile industry. Thirdly, the advantages of reliability of supply and of a wide choice of selection are so great that a factory will prosper better in a great raw material assembling centre than in the region of production of any particular variety of cotton.[1] The grading of cotton so essential to secure uniformity in spinning can be more easily done in big markets like Liverpool or Bombay than in the up-country, cotton-growing areas in India.

In the light of the theory of location enunciated above it will be seen that Bombay was admirably located in respect of the cotton industry owing to its favourable "transport" relations with the raw material and markets, and owing to the availability of productive factors and the presence of its enterprising merchants and managing agents. Railway freights favoured Bombay, because rates from and to the ports were always cheaper than for inland towns. Whether an industry should be located near the material or near the market is more or less decided by the respective rates on raw materials and manufactured product. Not long ago Punjab wheat was sent to Calcutta to be turned into flour and returned to the Punjab, but now most of the wheat is milled into flour locally.[2] In all this the relative freights on raw material and finished products come into play. If the rate on raw material is low, the remoter area will be favoured; if it is high, manufacture will take place near the source of the material.[3]

Bombay was favoured not less by her cheap sea transport, which is always cheaper than land transport. All places close to the sea have relatively favourable transport relations with all other places similarly situated, and Bombay can always import cotton

[1] *Vide* Statement of the Bombay Millowners' Association before the Indian Tariff Board: Cotton Industry, 1932.

[2] K. C. Srinivasan, *Railway Freight Rates*, 1928, p. 35.

[3] W. Z. Ripley, *Railway Roads*, 1924, p. 134.

and all stores and other accessories of production from other countries more cheaply than inland centres. What is more, the location of the cotton industry was greatly influenced by the fact that she was serving a foreign market in China and Hong-Kong, and therefore enjoyed special "transport" relations in regard to the marketing of products.

But since 1920 considerable changes have taken place, and the cotton industry is getting more widely scattered all over the country. Whilst after 1920 there has been a decrease in the number of mills in Bombay city, the number of mills in the rest of India has increased by about 79 in the period 1921–30. The factors that had favoured concentration in Bombay city are apparently wearing themselves out and new factors are exerting a contrary influence. Three sets of circumstances may be pointed out by way of explaining this drift of industry from Bombay to other centres. In the first place, Bombay is now faced with certain "deglomerating" tendencies which have the effect of breaking down excessive concentration. The very "agglomerating" tendencies which formerly helped local concentration have, by raising the prices of natural resources, cost of land, internal costs of transport and of labour, brought about counteracting influences checking this process of concentration. The high rents of land in Bombay, high taxation, and high local rates for water and other services are making it increasingly difficult for Bombay to hold its ground against new rivals. In the second place, it is losing its advantage in respect of its transport relations owing to the change in the character of its production. It is now supplying an internal market, and not so much for a foreign market. This means that when a group of factories have to supply a large country like India with its enormous distances, the average distance to the consumer will be much longer and transport costs increase. It is true that Bombay can still import raw cotton more cheaply, but in so far as it relies on Indian cotton it has no advantage over other centres, and in the marketing of cotton goods has to meet higher transport costs. Thirdly, inter-regional differences in wages have been affecting Bombay very adversely in recent years. The advantage which it enjoyed in the matter of capital and labour has disappeared both because other centres are now able to raise capital for the development of industry and also because the advantages of lower wages in those centres are not wholly lost in differences in efficiency. On the contrary, wage differences between Bombay and other centres in the Bombay Presidency and elsewhere are such as cannot be explained wholly by the differences in the cost of living or differences in efficiency.[1]

Further, the earlier policy of the railways to favour unduly the port towns is giving way to more uniform rates based on distances, and the work of the Railway Rates Advisory Committee has been in the direction of securing more equitable arrangements.[2] This has the effect of reducing Bombay's advantage in respect of transport relations and of increasing that of other centres. In India, owing to the vast size of the country, transport costs will have to be reckoned as a dominating factor in location. The greater the costs of transport the more evenly each industry will be spread over the whole country, and the smaller the areas supplied wholly or partly by each industrial unit. In other words, a wider distribution of the cotton industry in India is only to be expected. The future position of the Bombay section of the cotton industry will depend upon the extent to which, by a process of grouping and large-scale production, and concentration on the turning out of special kinds of finer goods, it is able to secure the economies of concentration. For the greater the superiority of the large-scale producing units the more will be the advantages of concentration. By specializing in the production of superior varieties of cloths and of non-competitive goods where the economies of large-scale production may be realized, Bombay may still be able to maintain her ground.

[1] For a further account of this matter, refer to Chapter X.

[2] For example, the higher rates charged by railways between Sholapur and Delhi than between Bombay and Delhi have been reduced. Railway Rates Advisory Committee, Case Nos. 14 and 16 (*Report with the Orders of the Government of India*, 1930, p. 11).

The distribution of the cotton mills of all kinds in India in 1931 may be seen from the following table:

Bombay	70
Ahmedabad	65
Other Centres in the Bombay Presidency	44
Madras Presidency	28
United Provinces	18
Central Provinces, Berar	17
Rajputana	—
Central India	16
Bengal	11
Others	9

Although Bengal had only eleven cotton mills in 1931, there is no reason why the cotton industry should not develop there to an increasing extent. Calcutta is favourably situated both in respect of power and market, and can import cotton and stores cheaply. The main reason why the cotton industry did not develop was probably the concentration of the jute industry. For some years past it may be said that the jute industry has shown signs of over-development as its chronic short-time working indicates. It is possible, therefore, that Bengal might turn its attention to the cotton industry in the near future, and in 1931 four new mills were projected. In the United Provinces, Cawnpore is the great centre of the cotton industry. It is situated in the cotton district and has a big cloth market at the spot, and thus saves double freight.[1] Madras Presidency, which is already a region of some importance, is likely to set up more cotton mills, and especially the north and north-western parts of the Presidency may be expected to become important centres in the next few years. In any case a certain breakdown of the present concentration is inevitable in the future. The future of the Bombay section of the cotton industry is itself in doubt. It is faced with unprecedented labour troubles; its labour is costly and inefficient. Its industrialists are partly losing their resilience and the spirit of earlier enterprise owing to continued depression. It began to use electric power with considerable advantage for some time, and

[1] *Indian Tariff Board: Cotton Industry*, 1927, Vol. 2, p. 165.

though it finds that at the level of prices obtaining for the last five or six years coal is cheaper, it is unable to get back to coal. High cost of land and heavy local taxation affect the industry adversely. In the circumstances its relative position over a period of time will certainly be weakened; but whether even absolutely it will begin to take a secondary place or continue to be an important centre of the cotton industry will depend upon the ability of the entrepreneurs to rationalize their productive units and to secure great economies in costs of production and marketing, partly by amalgamation and grouping of factories, but mainly by organized co-operative methods in buying and selling and research.

THE JUTE INDUSTRY

The jute industry seems, however, to be an exception to the general theory of location of the textile industries. Its raw material is cheap and it cannot therefore afford much transportation cost. Bengal is the world's jute-producing centre, and its position is not likely to be challenged except under very extraordinary circumstances, for no other place affords such exceptional facilities for the growing of jute. "It is in the great stretches of fertile land in Bengal where clay and sand are mixed with decayed vegetable matter, and where the overflow of the rivers leaves deposits which renew the soil year by year that the world's jute fields lie."[1] The raw material is transported very cheaply by the many waterways with which Bengal abounds, and thus in every way the unique and unrivalled position of that province continues to be maintained. Of the 95 jute factories in India, nearly all are in Bengal, with the exception of four which are in the Madras Presidency where a fibre (known as Bimilipatam jute) different from the true jute is grown, and one in Bihar; and they all lie in a small strip of country about 60 miles long and 2 miles broad, along both banks of the Hooghly above and below Calcutta. There is, therefore, a great concentration of the industry in and around Calcutta, and it is not likely that Calcutta's position

[1] *Royal Commission on Labour*, Report, 1931, p. 8.

will ever be seriously threatened. The jute industry with its 95 mills employs slightly more workers than the cotton industry with its 295 mills, and raises very grave social problems of overcrowding, sex disparity, and so on

IV

COAL AND POWER

Before examining the location of other industries it is necessary to consider the transport relations of various industrial centres in India in respect of power resources. This is of great practical importance, for cheap power is one of the essential conditions of industrial progress. Up to the present moment coal has been the main source of industrial power in the country, with the exception of the Bombay section of the cotton industry which has utilized electric power supplied by the Tata and Andhra Valley Power Companies. Unfortunately, coal deposits are very unevenly distributed. The best coal deposits and the great bulk of the collieries of India are concentrated in a comparatively small area, the outlying fields being of much less importance. The Raniganj, Jharia, and Bokaro fields, which together produce 90 per cent of the total coal output of the country, lie in a narrow strip running roughly from Raniganj in Bengal (about 160 miles north-west of Calcutta) westwards for about 100 miles. The greater part of the Raniganj coalfield lies in Bengal; the remainder of it, and all other fields, are in Bihar and Orissa. Out of a total estimated coal reserve of nearly 54,000 million tons, nearly 52,359 million tons are accounted for by the deposits in Bengal and Bihar and Orissa.[1] High-grade coal being confined to the north-eastern parts of India, any industry which has its raw material (other than coal) in places far from this region will find its cost of coal (and therefore of power) very unfavourable, and be compelled to make a difficult choice. The supply of cheap power to these regions away from coal

[1] Report by Dr. Fox of the Geological Survey Department, submitted to the Tariff Board, vide *Report of the Tariff Board on Steel Industry*, 1924, p. 96.

is a prime necessity if industry is to develop successfully. The development and use of hydro-electric power may be expected to improve the "transport" relations of those areas in respect of power.

According to the *Report on the Water-Power Resources of India*,[1] although estimates of the total water-power resources must be conjectural in the absence of detailed examination of the various sites, the total amount of power in 1919 actually in use and estimated from "known" sites amounted to 1·78 million electrical horse-power. In 1921 about 213,150 kilowatts was the amount of power actually developed, about 55,640 kilowatts was the amount of power likely to be obtained from the plants under construction, and about 1·2 million kilowatts was estimated to be the amount available from investigated sites.[2] A preliminary forecast of the water-power resources was made in 1921 by the Hydro-Electric Survey Department, showing a total of 5·58 million kilowatts, or 7·44 million electrical horse-power.[3] At present it is in Mysore, Bombay, Madras, and the Punjab that hydro-electric power resources have been developed. There is scope for further development in these areas, and also in the United Provinces, Assam, and part of Central Provinces. Bombay, the Punjab, Madras, Mysore, and Burma have the greatest potentialities.[4] So far, hydro-electric power has not attracted any great industry of the old type; nor has it given rise to any new industry demanding cheap power in large quantities, like paper mills, electro-metallurgical or electro-chemical industries. It has gone to the rescue of the Kolar goldfields, Mysore, whose working might have been unprofitable otherwise, as the depth had increased considerably, and it has also been utilized by the Bombay cotton mills. It has attracted a number of small industries like flour mills and small weaving sheds and oil mills, which without cheap power

[1] *Preliminary Report on the Water Power Resources of India*, 1919, p. 48, and *Indian Year Book*, 1933, p. 326.

[2] *Triennial Report*, 1919–21, *Hydro-Electric Survey of India*, pp. 56, 57, 61.

[3] Ibid., p. 55. One kilowatt is equal to 1·3 electric horse-power.

[4] *Triennial Report, Hydro-Electric Survey of India*, p. 52.

might not have been set up. It will possibly be used with advantage in agriculture, for lifting water, etc. Hydro-electric power has been used (like other electric power generated from coal or oil) mostly for street and house lighting. This is not unimportant from the point of view of new industries as cheaper rates might be offered by power companies to industries with a view to obtaining day load. It is also to be noted that hydro-electric power is not very cheap in India owing to the seasonal flow in rivers, costliness of storage, long transport and transmission lines, etc. The popular assumption that "water power costs nothing" is entirely mistaken, and in the conditions of India especially so. On the other hand, improvements are effected in the generation of electric power from steam turbines. That is why Ahmedabad is getting electric power cheaper than Bombay.

However, from the point of view of industries seeking location outside the coal area, any reduction in the present cost of power will be of advantage, and the development of hydro-electric power in the north, west, and southern parts of India may be expected to improve the "transport" relations of those places. But relatively to the coal area, these centres will perhaps continue to occupy less favourable transport relations to power as, owing to the possibility of producing electricity more cheaply from coal, regions near the coalfields will still be able to command cheaper power. But any change in the relative prices of electricity from coal and from water power will bring about a change in the conditions of localization. The cost of coal in different parts of India has great bearing upon the advantages or otherwise of hydro-electric power. "With coal under Rs. 10 per ton it is doubtful if water power could ever compete unless (rare combination) it existed right on the spot and could be developed exceptionally cheaply. On the other hand, with coal at Rs. 30 a ton, water power would generally prove cheaper and for a well-sustained industrial load invariably. Between these limits proper estimating would be necessary."[1] Thus the future location of industry in India depends upon the extent to which water-power resources are

[1] *Preliminary Report on the Water Power Resources of India*, 1919.

developed, electricity from coal is generated, and the relative costs of both. There are, of course, industries like iron and steel and engineering which cannot dispense with coal, and will therefore always tend to be established not far from the coalfields. On the other hand, industries like aluminium, soda, and soda compounds may be located near the water-power zone, provided electricity at very low cost can be produced. But within these limits there is a fairly wide area over which location of industries will depend upon the transport relations of various centres in respect of raw materials, including power, and of markets.

V

IRON AND STEEL INDUSTRY

The Indian Iron Works at Asansol, the Bengal Iron Works at Kulti, and the Mysore Iron Works at Badravati are producers of pig-iron; but pig and steel are both produced only at Tatanagar in Bihar. The iron industry is entirely dominated by the locating force of raw materials, iron ore, coal, and limestone. To make a ton of pig-iron, $1\frac{2}{3}$ tons of coking coal and nearly 2 tons of iron ore are required,[1] and it is therefore necessary to avoid long transport and to save freight. The localized raw materials are costly to transport. Both coal and iron are weight-losing materials, and hence the iron and steel industry is raw-material-localized rather than market-localized. As between coal and iron ore, if they are at some distance from one another, the ore goes to the fuel because it is a less weight-losing material than coal. Rather it will be more correct to say that the best location will be at the point of minimum transportation cost in regard to both coal and ore.

In recent years, however, owing to the economies in the utilization and consumption of coal, the locating force of coal has been reduced relatively to that of the iron ore, and partly

[1] Russel Smith, *Principles of Industrial Management*, 1915, p. 102, and also *Report of the Tariff Board regarding Protection to Steel Industry*, 1924, p. 7.

owing to a desire to take advantage of the market[1] the tendency has been for the fuel to go to the ore, for thereby the minimum transport costs can be secured. This is seen in the United States where the movement of the iron industry from Eastern to Western Pennsylvania has become marked since 1890. It came about because of the obvious economy of locating the industry in regions where the combined transportation costs of bringing coking coal and ore to the furnaces and of delivering the finished products in their markets would be at a minimum.[2] Again the iron and steel industry in the Chicago district is an example of localization in a place which has excellent transport relations with raw material sources even though the latter are at a distance. Other places in the Chicago district have equally good or better access to coal and ore, but Chicago city profits from a large local market and sells products to the agricultural machinery industry. Thus iron manufacture on a huge scale is undertaken at points distant alike from ore and from coal.[3] Similarly the heavy British steel industries have been moving to the sea coast or the lower reaches of deep rivers,[4] for they obtain easily imported ore and "can put much of their product on board ship for exportation, or even into the frame of a ship itself, which is even more greedy of steel."[5]

In India the most important iron ores lie in the so-called iron belt extending over the district of Singbhum and the adjoining feudatory states of Orissa. These ores are very rich, the proportion of metallic iron frequently rising to over 60 per cent. Besides being rich, they lie close to the coalfields, the distance separating them being less than 200 miles. This is a very important consideration as the freight on raw materials is a very heavy item in the cost of manufacture. India occupies, then, a unique position in regard to the iron industry. The Tata Iron and Steel Co., Ltd., is able

[1] A. Marshall, *Industry and Trade*, 1919, p. 283; also Russel Smith, *Principles of Industrial Management*, p. 104.

[2] F. W. Taussig, *Some Aspects of the Tariff Question*, 1915, pp. 124-5.

[3] Ibid., p. 125.

[4] Marshall, *Industry and Trade* (Marketing Influences on Localization) p. 283.

[5] Ibid., p. 283.

to bring its iron ore from a distance of 50 miles, and its coal from about 100 miles. Comparing this with Europe or America, where we find that coal or iron ore has got to come from a distance of 200 or 300 miles, and often from longer distances, we realize its unrivalled position. India, therefore, is able to produce pig-iron at less than half the cost in America, England, and Wales, and export it at half the British price from Calcutta.

But the economics of the steel industry are somewhat different. Sheffield is the centre of an immense steel industry, but not of the iron trade. Trades requiring minute delicacy of handling, and trades requiring the production of huge weights of metal both flourish in Sheffield, which is an inland town dependent on costly railway carriage for the transport of its wares for the production of which most of the material is brought from the coast. Swedish iron is imported for cutlery. Iron from Spain is used for the heavy finished products which are sent forward to the coast in turn. All this is due to the extraordinary skill of the worker, which has descended through generations of handicraftsmen, and to the best kind of technical training. Again, the greatest steel manufacture of the world is in the western district of Pennsylvania, which brings its ores from Lake Superior more than 1,000 miles away, the journey involving a double transference from rail to water carriage and vice versa, and its coal by rail from 60 miles. It is thus clear that while the iron industry is almost entirely dependent upon raw materials, the steel industry depends upon a highly trained and technically efficient class of labour and upon organization. Incidentally it may be pointed out that one reason for granting protection to the steel industry in India is to give time to enable the industry to train a body of skilled workers. Although it may be stated with confidence that this great iron belt will continue to be the region of India's iron and steel industry, it is doubtful in view of the very large amount of capital required whether more works will be established at all, unless production costs are reduced much more than has been possible so far. Climate also affects steel production in India, and there is an unmistakable fall in output per worker in summer as compared with winter,[1] and temperate regions have thus a slight advantage over the tropics.

VI

Location of Other Industries

THE SUGAR INDUSTRY

Unlike that of the cotton industry the location of the sugar industry is dominated by accessibility to raw material, and the industry must be established in relation to the transportability of sugar-cane irrespective of the cost of fuel and power. The location of the sugar industry in India presents some interesting features, and under the high protection guaranteed to it for fifteen years, from 1932, a large number of new factories have been established, most of which are in North India. It is necessary to examine whether the distribution of the industry at present, and in the near future, has regard to sound theories of localization.

For the manufacture of sugar directly from cane it is essential that there should be not merely a sufficient quantity of sugar-cane in existence, but that the cane should be fresh when it arrives, since the sugar content of cane deteriorates rapidly after the stalks have been cut. A 16-mile radius of canes round about the factory is the utmost that can be satisfactorily managed in India.[2] The successful working of a sugar factory depends upon the concentration of sugar-cane in proximity to it, and such concentration of sugar-cane areas is to be found only in the United Provinces, Bihar and Orissa, and the Punjab, but not in Bombay or Madras, except in a few favoured localities. The importance of the raw material will be evident from the fact that in the cost of producing white sugar, the price of sugar-cane represents two-thirds of the total cost. Power is not a dominating factor in the location of the sugar industry as nearly the whole of the fuel required for gener-

[1] *Indian Tariff Board, Statutory Enquiry: Steel Industry*, 1926, Vol. 3, p. 66. The hot weather in India "affects the efficiency of men as well as of the furnace."

[2] *Report of the Tariff Board on the Sugar Industry*, 1931, p. 31.

ating power is provided by the bagasse. The following table explains the distribution of the industry in India in 1931–2:[1]

	Cane Factories	Gur Refined	(1930–1) Area under Sugar-Cane in acres*	Total
Bihar and Orissa	11	2	284,000	13
United Provinces	15	5	1,488,419	20
Madras	3	3	114,877	6
Bombay	1	—	64,687	1
Burma	1	—	20,227	1
Total	31	10	1,972,210	41

* *Statistical Abstract for British India*, 1930–1.

In 1932–3, 27 cane factories were established, of which 20 were in the United Provinces and 7 in Bihar, and none in other parts of India.[2]

Several new factories, numbering about 73, have been established during the last three years, and these are located mostly in North Bihar, the United Provinces, and the Punjab, and a few in South Bihar. Only 4 or 5 factories have been projected in Madras and Mysore.[3] Although there is scope for expansion in Bombay, Bengal, and particularly in Madras and Mysore, judging from the manner in which the industry has been developing during the last three years, it may be stated that over-expansion and congestion in some areas and under-development in other areas seem to be the result. South India, including Mysore, lies entirely within the tropics, and is from the point of view of climate much more favourably situated for the growth of sugar-cane, on tracts irrigated by channels or wells, than any other part of India. According to the Indian Sugar Committee of 1920 "there can be no question that there is no part of India, except, possibly, the

[1] *Indian Finance*, July 21, 1933. Industries Supplement]

[2] Supplement to the *Indian Trade Journal*, May 18, 1933. *Review of the Sugar Industry of India*, a supplement.

[3] *Proceedings of the Sugar Conference*, Simla, 1933.

Deccan canals tract of Bombay, in which cane can be grown with greater profit than in Madras." Another important advantage from the point of view of a big factory industry is that in the southern regions cane can be planted and grown so as to be harvested in different parts of the year, so as to prolong the period of milling well over a hundred days, which is the working season in North India.[1] On the contrary, North India, which has been so rapidly expanding in sugar production, is subject to great heat before the monsoon, which compels close planting of thin canes, resulting in low yields in unirrigated tracts while growth is checked after November when severe cold sets in and lasts till February.[2] Frosts are feared not only in North India but even in western India.

Some explanation is therefore necessary for this uneven distribution of the sugar industry in India. One reason is that for the moment North India has been more favourably situated in respect of production factors, such as capital and business ability, and a large number of rich capitalists were eager to take advantage of the opportunity offered by protective duties to develop the sugar industry. The managing agents' sphere of influence is in North India; but South India has not attracted them to the same extent as northern and western India. But the chief cause for the failure of South India to develop the sugar industry is that owing to the diversity in soil, climate, and irrigation facilities, and consequently in the conditions of cultivation, suitable canes have not been grown in sufficient quantities to attract a sugar factory. Again, the marked preference for rice in South India has militated against the extension in the cultivation of sugar-cane. A concentrated area of about 2,000 acres at a time is required, and so far only in the South Arcot district of Madras has this been found, where a successful factory has been set up.

Although these difficulties explain why the newer factories have all been set up elsewhere than in Madras, there is no reason to think that a better distribution of the industry is not either

[1] F. Noel Paton, *Notes on Sugar in India*, 1911.
[2] A. Howard, *Crop Production in India*, 1924, p. 125.

possible or desirable. The opening of the Irwin Canal in Mysore and the new irrigation schemes of Mettur are likely to add nearly three-quarters of a million acres to the area under cultivation, and some alternative crop to paddy is urgently required. The production of rice has been so unprofitable since 1930 that the ryots are willing to turn to alternative crops. The scope for the cultivation of sugar-cane is great, and it is possible for sugar factories, if established in these regions, to induce planting of canes in concentrated areas. Such a development will be desirable, as it will not be possible for North Indian markets to supply Madras and Mysore with sugar owing to their distance from the South. Considering the vastness of India, there is no doubt that "transport" relations will always demand some diffusion of industry rather than excessive concentration, unless the economies of large-scale production and concentration are overwhelming. Already the conflict of interests between the sugar manufacturers in the north and those in the south has become evident in their respective attitude towards rail freight on sugar. While the manufacturer in the United Provinces has been able successfully to press for a reduction in freight from Rs. 2.8.0 to Rs. 1.4.0 a maund from Cawnpore to Madras, the manufacturers in Madras, Bombay, and the Punjab have been pressing for an increase in freight with a view to getting the advantage of proximity to their natural markets.[1] Madras consumes 100,000 tons of sugar per annum, of which less than one-tenth is produced within the province. It is almost certain that within the next few years the sugar industry would develop rapidly in Madras, with the result that the factories that have grown up in such haste in United Provinces and Bihar might be adversely affected.[2]

The need for some form of public control in the location of sugar factories is urgent for various reasons. In the first place, the new factories in the north have no organization as in other countries to ensure an adequate supply of cane to them. They do

[1] *Proceedings of the Sugar Conference*, Simla, 1933.

[2] Since this was written the terrible earthquake in Bihar has wrought great damage both to sugar-cane lands and to cane factories.

not own the lands or plantations, and although some of them have entered into leases with the sugar-cane growers, the supply is uncertain. There is bound to be excessive competition among the factories in some places for a limited supply of cane, and in others it is possible that the growers are entirely at the mercy of the manufacturer. Overlapping and overcrowding of factories in a small area must be avoided. The proper line of action will be to secure to the manufacturer an assured supply of cane and to the grower a fair selling-price. These objects can be secured only by some method of control, either by a system of licensing the factories or by owning them. Each system has its difficulties, and the choice of the one or the other must depend upon conditions in each province. But some control of location in United Provinces and Bihar is overdue, and in other provinces, too, it is desirable to take legislative power to control the location of factories before the problem becomes acute. It is fortunate that these questions have been fully discussed at the recent Sugar Conference in Simla and that the Governments are alive to them.

THE PAPER INDUSTRY

No industry provides better illustration of the complex elements that enter into the problem of localization than the paper industry of India. The principal seat of the paper industry is in Bengal and in the neighbourhood of the Hooghly in Raniganj. The Titaghur Paper Mills and the Bengal Paper Mill at Raniganj together produce more than three-fourths of the total output of paper in India. The Upper India Paper Mill at Lucknow in the United Provinces, the Indian Paper Pulp Company at Naihati (Bengal), and the Deccan Paper Mills in Poona (Bombay) are the other important paper mills in India. The Punjab Paper Mill Company has been started recently at Saharanpur (Punjab) and uses hydro-electric power. The Carnatic Paper Mill established in North Madras has not been working successfully, partly owing to its very bad location.

In examining the factors that influence the location of the paper industry we come across the changing economic import of physical conditions and processes of production. The paper industry must be located in centres which enjoy favourable transport relations in respect of (*a*) raw materials, (*b*) power, and (*c*) market. When Sabai grass was the chief raw material, although it influenced location to some extent, the industry was drawn to a place nearer the source of power and market. Thus the Titaghur Mills and the Bengal Paper Mill which used Sabai grass were getting it from a distance of 900 miles because they found it more economical to pay freight on 2½ tons of grass rather than pay freight on 5 tons of coal for nearly the same distance, and on the finished product. Thus power (in this case coal) and market were the chief considerations. But if it were possible to find cheap power near the source of raw material as the new Punjab Paper Mill has done, then the advantage of that centre becomes great, and the industry will be attracted to it.

But the future of the Indian paper industry is largely bound up with the use of bamboo pulp owing to the excessive cost of Sabai grass, and owing to the limited extent of market for paper made out of Sabai grass. This change in the nature of the raw material required alters the original forces of the location, and the location of the industry will now have to be determined by good transport relations in respect of bamboo-growing, cheap power, and markets. But unfortunately the raw-material areas, with the exception of one important centre, Cuttack in Orissa, are remote from the coalfields, and have not developed cheap power resources. Thus the Indian Paper Mill Company at Naihati, which makes paper out of bamboo pulp, gets its raw material from Chittagong and rails it to Naihati, a distance of 300 miles. If the mill had tried to save freight on this raw material and established itself at Chittagong, it would have lost the advantage of cheap coal and proximity to markets. Nor does it seem possible in India to establish a bamboo pulp industry separately from the paper industry. The English paper industry depends for its wood pulp on Scandinavia and the Baltic countries. The United States imports pulp from Canada, Norway, and Sweden. If it were possible in India to make bamboo pulp near the source of the material and manufacture paper near the markets it would be a distinct advantage. But in the conditions of India the demand for pulp would not enable mass production to be carried on; and what is even more unfavourable is the lack of cheap sources of power near the raw-material areas. Most pulp factories will have to depend on coal brought from long distances. In the circumstances the future of the Indian industry and of its localization will depend upon the discovery and utilization of local sources of hydro-electric power in close proximity to the bamboo-growing tracts, upon the reduction in coal consumption by using wood fuel and by securing the highest steam efficiency, and upon a reduction in the freight on coal.[1] The bamboo-growing tracts are, apart from those in Burma, chiefly Chittagong and Cuttack. The development of hydro-electric power in the Chittagong area may be expected to improve the transport relations of that area and attract the paper industry to it. The industry will locate itself in centres which have the cheapest transportation costs in relation to material, power, and finished product.

At present while the Bengal Paper Mill has the advantage of cheap coal it has been unable to command the markets in all parts of India owing to the heavy railway freight on paper. It may also be pointed out that the development of chemical industry is essential for the success and prosperity of the paper mills as a large quantity of chemicals has to be used in the process of manufacture. Bleaching powder, caustic soda, rosin, china clay must all be available at cheap costs.

The Carnatic Paper Mill at Rajamundry affords a striking illustration of the dangers of unfavourable location. Despite the assistance it has received under the State Aid to Industries Act, the mill has not been working successfully. While most of the mills have the advantage either of cheap raw material or coal, it has none at all. Being near a bamboo-growing area, the mill expected to get the raw material cheaply; but the bamboo is in great demand

[1] *Indian Tariff Board: Paper and Paper Pulp Industries*, Report, 1925, p. 75.

as fuel in the neighbourhood, and can therefore be had only at high cost. Situated as it is, 627 miles off Calcutta, it gets its coal very dearly, and has no advantage of location. Its only hope must rest in the manufacture of special paper for use in the Madras market.

THE CEMENT INDUSTRY

The cement industry in India has grown enormously in recent years, owing to her great natural advantages. Limestone of excellent quality exists abundantly in many parts of the country and close to the railway lines. It has been found possible, therefore, to establish factories in the immediate vicinity of the quarries. The longest distance between the quarry and the factory is nowhere more than 20 to 30 miles. Suitable clay is invariably to be found near the works, and there are ample supplies of it. But as in other industries it is the freight on coal that forms a serious item of cost, and in this the cement industry has no advantage. The cost of power and coal is at least 40 per cent of the total works cost, and often a great deal more. Theoretically, half a ton of coal is required for one ton of cement; but Indian firms use more, partly owing to a lower output, but mainly owing to the higher percentage of ash in Indian coal. Thus in this industry, too, the concentration of coal within a limited area imposes a serious handicap. Existing cement factories are also badly located from the point of view of markets. There is no cement works anywhere within 300 miles of Bombay or Calcutta which are the principal markets for cement. Although, therefore, the industry has a protected internal market, it is unable to compete successfully in the chief Presidency towns. Katni and Jubbulpore in Central Provinces are the chief cement-producing centres; Dwarka in Kathiawar and Gwalior are the other main centres. There is one cement company in Washermanpet (Madras) whose maximum capacity is 10,000 tons per annum. The existing factories are able to satisfy nearly all the requirements of the country. If more factories are to be established, they should be located near markets not served by existing factories, and near hydro-electric power zones.

THE TANNING AND LEATHER INDUSTRIES

The tanning industry is so much dependent for its success on cheap supplies of tanning material that it has been changing its location as the supplies of tan bark get exhausted. Madras is the biggest centre in India for the tanning of hides and skins because the *avaram* bark is available cheaply and in plenty. Elsewhere the cost of railway freights makes tanning with the bark commercially unprofitable. The establishment of the tanning industry in northern and Central India is essentially a problem of finding cheap substitutes for *avaram*[1] bark. At present the North India hides and skins are sent to Madras, where they are tanned, and partly exported out of the country as leather and returned in part in the tanned state to Agra and Cawnpore, and this has been possible because of the freight policy of railways. A subsidiary factor in the location of the tanning industry is the supply of local labour in Madras, where large numbers belonging to certain castes are pursuing this trade.

On the other hand the development of leather goods manufacture in contradistinction to the light tannage of Madras and Bombay is almost entirely the outcome of military efforts to obtain supplies for boots and accoutrements. Where arsenals were established there came into existence both a demand for boots and leather goods and a supply of hides and skins. Cawnpore's reputation as a big leather manufacturing centre was originally built upon the Government Harness and Saddlery factory which became a great success. The market which the army provided was an important factor in the localization of this industry. Moreover, Cawnpore possesses certain additional advantages; it is a convenient centre for the collection of hides from North India and for distributing goods to other places, and at the outset there was available cheap *babul* bark, an excellent tanning material. Although Madras is not unsuited for leather manufacture and for the making of boots and shoes, the market is very much narrower in the south than in the north, and a market is a major factor in the successful development of this industry.

[1] *Avaram* (*cassia auriculata*) is a shrub, commonly found in southern India, whose thin bark is considered to be an excellent tan material.

VII

Some Observations on the Future Localization of Industry in India

It is not necessary to consider other industries in detail. The development of the heavy chemical industry, which comprises a large group of chemical products of which sulphuric acid, hydrochloric acid, nitric acid, magnesium sulphate, potash, alum, aluminium sulphate, zinc chloride are the most important, is vital to the future development of the textile, leather, paper, glass, porcelain, rubber, artificial silk, and other industries. The most important factors affecting the location of the chemical industries are accessibility to cheap coal and power, to raw materials, and to market. The industries are located at present in Calcutta and Bombay, but are not able to work economically as their output has to be limited to the narrow market within their own respective areas. If the industry is to establish itself firmly and face foreign competition successfully, the scale of production must be on a vaster scale, and the products must reach other parts of the country as well. Bengal is a promising centre for the development of chemical industries owing to its cheaper coal, but the industry can expand rapidly in Bombay if cheaper power can be made available there, for the market for chemicals is greater there.

Thus in the localization of industry the dominating factor is the "transport" relation of a centre in regard to raw materials, power, and market. The availability of factors of production is also very important. In general, where capital is abundant, labour can be attracted to it, but after a time wages tend to increase more than in proportion to increases in efficiency. In the meanwhile, other centres might be able to get access to capital resources and find that owing to cheaper labour they have better advantages than old-established centres. In such inter-local differences in wages, not fully compensated for by differences in efficiency, is to be found the chief explanation for the dispersion of industrial activity noticeable in India, particularly in the cotton industry.

The concentration of coal within a small area in Bengal and Bihar has naturally brought about concentration of industrial enterprises near that area, as other distant centres could not enjoy similar transport relations. But despite the pull which coal gives to industrial location, some industries, like sugar, cotton, cement, matches, etc., have established themselves away from coal owing to the importance of other factors. The centres away from coal will all gain if hydro-electric power is developed and supplied at lower cost. The future location of industries will depend upon the extent to which electricity from water power is made available in areas away from coal. Even if by improved methods of using coal and by converting it to electricity, regions nearer the coal area get power more cheaply than those getting power from hydro-electric installations, the latter will gain in transport relations generally as some of them are already nearer the sources of raw material. Further, as has been pointed out already, owing to the vast size of India, transport costs of marketing will always be considerable, and a better distribution of industrial activities will always be more economical as no centre by itself will be in a position to supply all parts of India. The iron and steel industry and the bigger engineering industries are, of course, an exception to the above statement, both because they have to be located near the coal and iron regions, and also because the economies of large-scale production are so great that the costs of marketing may easily be counteracted.

But speaking generally, of all the factors determining location, the influence of the market has been relatively gaining ground in recent years. The advantages to be derived from personal contact between consumer and trader and producer have caused capital cities in each country to become the homes of miscellaneous industries of all grades, and especially of those requiring labour of high quality. Further, new industries like the luxury trades and food industries which have grown enormously in recent years in most countries have favoured the capital cities where large numbers of people live. In so far as the market forms a dominating factor of industrial location, India is favourably placed. It is under the influence of this factor that during the last decade industries like matches, cement, paper, and sugar have been able to establish themselves firmly despite certain handicaps.

APPENDIX

Power Capacity Installed in India

Province	Total Installed Capacity (kw.)					Maximum Demand on Feeders (kw.)	Units sol[d] (In Millio[ns] of Units)
	Water	Steam	Oil	Gas	Total		
Assam	300	—	738	—	1,038	620	0·85
Baluchistan	—	—	760·7	—	760·7	495	0·87
Bengal	1,130	164,859	1,696	—	167,685	71,890	196·5
Bihar and Orissa	—	56,200	4,510·5	—	60,710·5	7,315	27·0
Bombay Presidency ..	183,500	1,141	16,763	—	201,404	112,530	409·8
Burma	—	15,236	4,255·5	350	19,841·5	8,970	29·5
Central Provinces	—	4,600	2,028	—	6,628	2,145	4·6
Delhi	—	3,400	2,992	—	6,392	5,590	12·8
Madras	1,750	21,500	4,392·5	—	27,642·5	11,890	28·3
Military Engineer's Services	—	1,922·5	4,038	—	5,960·5	3,365	9·1
N.W.F. Province	290	800	693	—	1,783	620	0·7
Punjab	2,850	16,145	3,765	135	22,895	11,835	30·3
Railways	—	19,400·5	2,331·5	—	21,732	10,610	28·7
United Province	9,500	24,625	8,800	—	42,925	20,150	70·5
Indian States*	34,300	1,100	—	—	35,400	26,820	123·0
Total	233,620	330,929	57,763·7	485	622,797·7	294,845	972·5

* Exclusive of Kashmir and Jammu. Figures for Sivasamudram are up to the end of 1927–8.

[Not]e.—The above table is extracted from the Second Supplement to the *List of Electrical Undertakings in Ind[ia]* compiled by the Electrical Inspector to Government, Punjab, up till the years 1931–2.

CHAPTER III

FACTORS AFFECTING THE SIZE OF INDUSTRIAL UNITS IN INDIA

I

DEFINITION OF A FIRM

In studying the efficiency of industrial organization in India the question whether in each class of industry the individual units are of a size that is capable of securing the maximum efficiency is of great practical importance. For unless in each industry the representative firms are of such a size that the cost of production per unit of output is as low as possible, the efficiency of the industry within the country and its competitive power outside will be seriously affected. Unfortunately, however, although theoretical considerations can point to certain broad conclusions, the difficulty of finding a correlation between the size of industrial units and their efficiency is increased by the existence of many complicating factors that render the task extremely hazardous.

At the outset one is faced with the problem of defining a firm or industrial unit,[1] and while several possible definitions may be valid, the choice must depend upon the purpose in view. From the point of view of the technique of production it would be best to regard "any plant or productive group which is confined within and completely fills one factory"[2] as an industrial unit. But where two adjacent factories or mills are owned by a single employer or company, and are separated off from each other either because the old mill had no space to expand or because it was convenient to have another factory instead of expanding the older one, they may be regarded for all purposes as constituting a single firm or in-

[1] The difficulties of defining and delimiting an industry are not examined here, but the reader who is interested is referred to Mr. Robinson's *Structure of Competitive Industry*, Nisbet, and Cambridge University Press, 1931.

[2] *Journal of the Royal Statistical Society*, April 1914.

which were operated under a common ownership or for which one set of books of account was kept. If, however, the plants constituting an establishment as thus defined were not all located within the same city, county, or state, separate reports were secured in order that the figures for each plant might be included in the statistics for the city, county, or state in which it was located." This is a workable plan to adopt, and where there exist certain factors such as some combination or other organization within an industry designed to bring about economies of buying and selling, or other influences tending to counteract the disadvantages of smaller size, these will be noted separately and their effects on size studied.

The idea of a "representative" firm has been made familiar to students of economics by Marshall; but the "representative" firm in one industry may be of a scale very different from that in another, and in the case of any particular industry the "representative" firms may differ very much as between countries. It is necessary to consider first of all what has been the dominant type in each industry in India and what changes are noticeable in recent years. But it has also to be examined whether this dominant type has been of a size which is economical in working and conducive to the maximum of efficiency.

THE OPTIMUM UNIT

It has been for a long time held that for each industry there is a minimum size of individual unit requisite to ensure efficient production, and that smaller units would not be able to produce economically and compete successfully. In recent years the idea of a minimum size or cheapest productive unit has given place to what is known as an "optimum" size of industrial unit, and it is considered that firms smaller or larger than this optimum size will be uneconomic. This development of the theory from the notion of minimum to that of optimum size has been the natural sequence to the growth of industrial units, and to the tendency towards industrial concentration. When industry was carried on by small units, the only important question was whether the units were large enough to ensure economical working. But when giant businesses have grown, either by expansion or by combination, the question whether they are of the proper size and not too big to be efficiently worked and administered has an intensely practical bearing.

A study of the structure of some of the industries in India reveals the varying influences of different factors on the size of the typical units not merely in different industries but in different centres of the same industry. How far in each industry the typical units are of the optimum size it is difficult to state in the absence of data relating to costs of production of firms of varying scales of output. But such information as is available is sufficient to indicate broadly the reasons why industrial units are on different scales in the different centres where the industry is carried on. Firms continue to prosper or to suffer on widely different scales of output and equipment. If we define an optimum firm as that firm which has the lowest average cost of production, we find that the interaction of the various technical, financial, managerial, and marketing factors in an industry, instead of securing one optimum firm, has often the effect of bringing about a number of optima at various stages in the evolution of that industry and at different centres in the country. Thus a firm which under certain conditions of technique is at the optimum size may become smaller than the optimum firm when those conditions alter.[1] The size of an optimum firm in one country may be very different from that in another country, and vary also as between different districts within the country. Were only one set of forces, say the technical, to determine the structure of an industry, it might be expected that the units in that industry, wherever they are found, will all conform to a uniform type. But the forces governing the size of the optimum firm are various and do not act always in the same direction. The result is that although from some points of view a firm at one scale of output may be at an optimum size, from certain other points of view a smaller firm may be in a position to do better. In such cases the limits of expansion will be reached at

[1] *Recent Economic Changes*, Vol. 1, U.S.A. (1930), p. 190.

that level of output where, taking all costs into account, the lowest cost per unit of output may be obtained. This, in practice, can be reached only by gradual experimentation.

STANDARD BY WHICH SIZE IS MEASURED

It is necessary to have some standards by which size may be measured. Various standards of measurement may be applied, the choice depending partly on the nature of the industry under investigation and partly upon the accuracy of the data available. The amount of capital invested in establishments in the same industry may serve as a test; but accurate data regarding capitalization are difficult to obtain. The paid-up capital of industrial units, even when it is known for each case, is no measure of the size of the units. For the methods of financing the industries may vary much—some firms being content with small owned capital and willing to borrow a great deal. The total block value of each firm will be a better measure of the size; but the methods of valuation of the capital invested in buildings, equipment, and material are so various that the figures do not have the same significance in respect of each firm. In industries like the cotton and jute textiles the amount of capital per spindle or loom is considered to afford a useful basis of measurement. But even here it is unsafe to draw any inference. The amount of capitalization per spindle is affected by many factors, including location, availability of labour, methods of financing, etc. Where power is supplied to the mill by the municipality or other power company, where labourers have not to be brought into the centre and housing facilities provided for them, the amount of capital needed may not be very great. But where banking facilities do not exist and the mills have to provide working funds from out of their own capital, the amount of capitalization will be high. Hence the amount of tool equipment, e.g. spindles and looms in the textile industry, may be a better and safer measure. In iron and steel works, for example, the number of blast furnaces, together with their capacity, may be a reliable index of the size.[1]

[1] D. S. Kimball, *Industrial Economics*, 1929, p. 158.

A second measure of size is the number of workers per establishment. This is often used to compare establishments of similar character, but when applied to those in industries that differ widely in the nature of their products, the results are likely to be misleading. Thus it has been said that factories dependent on handwork (e.g. where artificial flowers are made) have to employ workers proportionate to the output, whereas in factories where the product is turned out by automatic machines the number of workers will depend upon the number of machines.[1] Another measure of size is the amount of power that is used per establishment, and this serves as a useful index of the size and growth of manufacturing plants and can be advantageously used for some purposes. A further method applicable to some industries, like coal-mining, is the annual output of each unit, and the larger the output the bigger (it may be inferred) the individual unit.

II

THE COTTON INDUSTRY

The technical advantages of division of labour were clearly illustrated early enough in the cotton industry, which was practically the first industry to be organized on factory lines. Hand-spinning and hand-loom weaving have given place to the spinning factory and the power loom nearly all over the world. But it is significant that even to-day in the Western world the average (and presumably also the optimum) weaving firm is smaller than the average spinning firm. In some countries like India, side by side with the weaving power factories there exist hand-loom weavers who not merely pursue their old trade, may be in poverty, but taken together are responsible for the supply of nearly a third of India's domestic consumption. It has been calculated that out of about 6,000 million yards of cloth consumed in India in 1929–30, 2,420 million yards were produced by the mills, 1,910 millions imported, and 1,670 millions supplied by hand-

[1] D. S. Kimball, *Industrial Economics*, 1929, p. 159.

looms.[1] Although the proportion between mill production and imports has varied since then, the production of the hand-loom industry has been fairly steady. Even in the case of the spinning industry the typical British firm has not recently grown very much, and the industry does not lend itself on the technical side to a further division of processes beyond what existed a hundred years ago.[2] In this respect the cotton industry is unlike the motor industry or the steel works, where, apart from the ample scope for greater subdivision of processes, certain special technical and economical factors have tended to bring about a great increase in the size of the average industrial unit. The representative spinning mill in England in 1911 was, according to a study made by Sir Sydney Chapman, of a size of 100,000 spindles; and although there were fourteen mills having 200,000 spindles and over, 185 firms out of 408 joint-stock spinning firms were within the range of 80,000 to 120,000 spindles.[3] Whether at that date the bigger firms of 200,000 spindles were the optimum ones, or those of 100,000 spindles were at the optimum size, we have no means of knowing, as costs of production were not available for those firms. All that can be said is that at that time the firms having 80,000 to 100,000 spindles were the most typical units in Lancashire and were able to realize the economies of division of labour and integration of processes in a manner which enabled them to get normal profits.

In India, at the same period, the average spinning mill was very much smaller than the average British mill. There were, indeed, two types noticeable if spinning mills were classified according to size. A large number of firms, 33 out of 84, belonged to a class having a range of 10,000 to 20,000 spindles, and 22 out of 84 were of a size of 40,000 to 50,000 spindles. But a great

[1] *Statistics Relating to Production in the Cotton Piece Goods Industry in India* (1932), *Report of the Bombay Millowners' Association for 1932*. See also Utley, *Lancashire and the Far East*, p. 280; *Textile (Cotton) Tariff Board Report*, Appendix. In Appendix I to the *Industrial Commission Report* it was estimated that the total quantity of yarn available for hand-loom producers was 253 million lb. of yarn, equal to 287 million lb. of cloth in 1913–14 (Appendix I, p. 395).

[2] *Journal of the Royal Statistical Society*, April 1914.

[3] Ibid.

change in the character of the industry had already taken place, the effects of which became more and more visible as years passed on. The Indian cotton mill industry, which up to the beginning of this century was essentially a spinning industry, became more and more a combined industry undertaking both spinning and weaving, and the whole structure of the industry has changed. In 1931, for example, the number of mills doing spinning alone had fallen to 48, while the total number of cotton mills had increased from 263 in 1911–12 to 313 in 1931.[1] Table I gives the distribution of the spinning mills according to the number of spindles they possess, and it will be seen therefrom that 28 out of 48 mills have less than 20,000 spindles each, whilst 37 out of 48 have less than 30,000 spindles. The most striking difference between the figures of 1911 and of 1931 is that while the smaller firms have continued to be in the same position, and probably even have become smaller, there has been a distinct tendency for a few mills to increase their equipment very considerably, so that five firms have a spindleage exceeding 50,000, whilst one mill in South India had 223,623 spindles (in 1931). The mills doing spinning only, with the exception of four mills in South India managed by a private limited company, are not of great importance, and need not be further considered here.

It is therefore the mills of the spinning-weaving type with which we must be concerned. The Bombay millowners in their statement to the Tariff Board stated that a mill with at least 30,000 spindles and 1,000 looms was, according to them, the minimum size required to ensure the cheapest cost of production.[2] Their statement was empirical, and they did not adduce any reasons or evidence for this view. On the other hand, the Ahmedabad Millowners' Association[3] gave it as their opinion that a mill with 25,000 spindles and 600 looms would be conducive to efficient and economic working. In suggesting these scales of equipment, each Association was influenced by the prevailing

[1] *Annual Report of the Bombay Millowners' Association*, Bombay, 1932.
[2] *Indian Textile Tariff Board: Cotton Industry*, Vol. 2, 1927, p. 136.
[3] Ibid., p. 396.

type existing in its own centre. Table II[1] gives the distribution of cotton mills of all kinds according to their spindleage in the various centres where the industry is carried on. A glance at the table will show that the majority of the mills, numbering 158 out of 277, have less than 30,000 spindles, and 47 out of those 158 have less than 30,000 spindles; 111 mills out of a total of 277 mills fall within the range of 15,000 to 30,000 spindles. It will be interesting to study the distribution of the firms according to the empirical view of the most economic size suggested by the Bombay Millowners' Association and the Ahmedabad Millowners' Association. If a mill having a minimum of 30,000 spindles is to be considered as the cheapest unit of production, then 158 out of 277 mills fall below the minimum. But only 12 mills in Bombay out of a total of 70 are smaller than this "economic" unit; whilst of the 65 Ahmedabad mills as many as 43 fall below the standard. On the other hand, taking 25,000 spindles as the standard,[2] we find that 127 mills out of 277 are below this standard of equipment, and 34 mills in Ahmedabad would still be smaller than the size required to ensure economical working.

Before proceeding to comment on the significance of these data, it is well to furnish ourselves with such further information as is available. In Bombay city, 81 mills contained in the list of the Bombay Millowners' Association for 1931 had altogether about 3,427,000 spindles, and 76,975 looms, thus giving an average of 42,300 spindles and 900 looms per mill. The proportion of 30,000 spindles to 1,000 looms is not closely kept up, but it may be noted that some mills are included which are purely spinning mills, and there are others which supply the needs of the yarn trade both in and out of the country, and hence it is reasonable to expect a larger spindleage equipment relative to loom equipment in the mills. Apart from the balance between spindles and looms there is no doubt that the units in Bombay

[1] The tables were prepared from the Millowners' Association's list of cotton mills for the year 1931.

[2] These results are arrived at by reclassification of the distribution of spindleage with a class-interval of 5,000.

are considerably larger than the minimum required, in the opinion of the Millowners' Association, to ensure economical working. In China the greatest number of mills fall within the class of 25,000 to 30,000,[1] whereas the greatest number of mills in Bombay are within the class of 40,000 and less than 45,000.[2]

In Ahmedabad the units are smaller and the proportion of spindles to looms is slightly higher than in Bombay. This is due to two causes. The preparatory machinery in the spinning department differs from that in Bombay mills and hence there is less output per spindle, and, secondly, in Ahmedabad finer counts are woven and more spindles are required.[3] The Ahmedabad mills have an average of about 23,000 spindles and 530 looms, thus showing a proportion of 43 to 1. But the difference in the proportion between Bombay and Ahmedabad is in reality greater than the figures suggest, because in Ahmedabad nearly all the spindles are utilized for the production of yarn for consumption within the factory, whilst in Bombay some portion is used for sale both in India and abroad.

The mills in other centres of India are also smaller than the units in Bombay city, and the majority of them (87 out of 142 mills)[4] have less than 25,000 spindles each. The same differences are noticeable when mills are classified according to the number of workers employed and the quantity of cotton consumed. Of course a reduction in the number of workers employed may mean greater efficiency, and a smaller quantity of cotton consumed may mean that finer yarn is spun. To some extent this last fact does slightly affect the position of Ahmedabad as it has been spinning higher counts than Bombay. But its importance is inconsiderable, and the efficiency of the workers in Ahmedabad is by no means higher than that of the workers in

[1] H. D. Fong, *Cotton Industry and Trade in China*, 1932, p. 199.

[2] These results are arrived at by reclassification of the distribution of spindleage with a class-interval of 5,000.

[3] *Indian Tariff Board: Cotton Industry*, Report, 1927, p. 82. Also Evidence, Vol. 2, p. 446.

[4] These results are arrived at by reclassification of the distribution of spindleage with a class-interval of 5,000.

Bombay, and hence does not detract from the utility of the comparison of the numbers employed in different centres. Table III gives the distribution of mills according to the number of workers employed. Whereas both the mode and the median are in the second class-interval (1,000–2,000) for Bombay, they are in the first class-interval (less than 1,000) for the rest of India. While the Bombay mills employ on the average about 1,600 workers each, the Ahmedabad mills employ about 915 per mill. In China the commonest size of a Chinese-owned mill is one employing 1,001 to 1,500 workers, but that of a Japanese-owned mill is lower and varies from 501 to 1,000 workers. This may be explained by greater efficiency in Japanese-owned mills, and by less efficiency in Chinese-owned mills.[1] In India, however, the differences are a measure of the differences in size between the typical unit in Bombay and the typical unit in Ahmedabad and other centres, as the workers in Bombay are certainly not more inefficient than those in Ahmedabad.

REASONS FOR THE DIFFERENCES BETWEEN UNITS IN BOMBAY AND IN AHMEDABAD

Judged by any standard, therefore, the industrial units in Bombay are bigger than those in Ahmedabad and, with a few exceptions, in other centres of India as well. This is due to a number of circumstances arising partly from the different methods by which the industry in Ahmedabad was built up. The Bombay industry was, from the commencement, organized for an export trade in yarn, which for a long time was the most important feature of the industry. An industry organized with a view to extending its influence over foreign markets has necessarily to establish itself on a fairly large scale. Further, the persons who set up the industry in Bombay were cotton merchants who had made fortunes in the cloth trade, and they conceived industrial organization on somewhat bold and large lines. On the other hand the distinctive feature of the industry in Ahmedabad is the peculiarly local character of its organization. The industry grew up

[1] H. D. Fong, *Cotton Industry and Trade in China*, 1932, p. 196.

in that centre in the hope of taking advantage of the local markets, and it afforded scope for the smaller capitalists and for men of average ability but great industry. Proximity to raw cotton and to internal markets which could not so well be reached by Bombay conferred an advantage on Ahmedabad, and the merchants there were not slow to take advantage of that. The industry has, however, been growing, although from small beginnings, and it is possible for the average mill to become larger as time passes.

But perhaps the most important reason for the differences in the scale of organization between the two centres is to be found in the widely differing methods of promoting and financing a mill prevalent in each. Later chapters contain a detailed account of the methods of financing cotton mills. It will suffice here to bring out the fact that in Ahmedabad the cotton mills are organized on lines more or less resembling the private limited liability type, and not on the lines of the public joint-stock companies according to which the Bombay mills are floated and financed. The difficulties of getting the public to invest in the shares of a cotton mill have given rise to a peculiar system of mill promoting and financing in Ahmedabad. The common practice is for the managing agents and a few friends to take up the shares of the company and become joint partners in the enterprise, with a share in the profits of the management. The friends who subscribe to the share-capital not only get the dividend on the shares subscribed by them but also a share in the managing agency commission, and the whole organization is a sort of partnership on a fairly broad basis. The public do come in occasionally as shareholders, but mainly as depositors of funds with the managing agents. Now this method of financing an enterprise obviously sets a limit to the size of the individual unit. In any case the beginnings have to be small, and the industry has to depend upon the financial ability of the managing agents and their friends. An increase in the size of the units will have to wait upon the readiness of the public to take up the shares of the companies and upon the growth of the investment habit. On the other hand, in Bombay there has always been greater activity in the stock-exchange market, and the public have not been unwilling to invest in the shares of the cotton mills. Almost all the mills are joint-stock companies, not merely in name, as in Ahmedabad, but in all essential features. More capital was forthcoming, and there was an assurance of capital coming into the industry. Thus it is possible that in Ahmedabad considerations of finance and methods of organizing the industry have compelled the promoters to be content with mills of smaller size. Just as in England there was in 1911 a dominant type of textile firms of the magnitude of 10,000 to 20,000 spindles, owing largely to the fact that they were mills set up by men who had only moderate capital, but who were versed in the technique of the industry and rose from the higher grade of workers, so in Ahmedabad special conditions are responsible for the prevalence of this dominant type.

RELATION BETWEEN SIZE AND EFFICIENCY

There remains the more difficult question whether either the average Bombay mill or the average Ahmedabad mill is of the optimum size, and whether an increase in size necessarily brings about greater efficiency. It is most difficult to answer this with any degree of certainty in the absence of the necessary data. One might expect that, taking a few selected mills of different sizes in each of the centres over a period of time, and finding out the rates of profits secured by them, it would be possible to establish some correlation between size and efficiency. But we are not warranted in drawing any hasty inferences from the mere study of the amount of profits earned by different concerns. Profit is the result of such a variety of factors, among which size is only one, that it will be unsafe to establish a correlation between those two. The methods of distributing profits as between reserves and dividends also vary, although, over a fairly long period, the average rate of dividends will depend upon the average amount of profits in the period. The relation between "owned" or share capital and borrowed capital will also affect the rate of dividend. There are again difficulties in the selection of the concerns, because often they have either increased their equipment or have changed their management, or increased their capitalization in different ways.

However, an attempt has been made to find out to what extent,

	Number of such Firms	Profits per cent during the Period 1916–30
Group I Firms having less than 30,000 spindles	8	Four went out of business; for the rest, the profits were 19, 23, 10, 25 Average, 19·25 9·8 including failures
Group II 30,000 and less than 45,000	25	Seven closed down or reconstructed. 4, 11, 14, 16, 17, 18, 15, 20, 23, 25, 28, 24, 26, 31, 32, 33, 37, 33 Average 22·6 16·3 including failures
Group III 45,000 and less than 60,000	9	6, 16, 13, 18, 21, 46, 48, 50, 57 Average 30·5
Group IV 60,000 and less than 75,000	2	25,105 Average, 65
Group V 75,000 and less than 100,000	3	26, 13, 11 Average, 16
Group VI 100,000 and over	6	One was reconstructed during the period 5, 24, 46, 52, 61 Average, 31 26 including reconstructed

if any, the larger firms have been able to secure a higher average rate of profits over a given period of time. A fifteen-year period was selected, 1916–30, and only firms which were working since 1914, whose shares were quoted in the Bombay Stock

Exchange, were chosen, and the information was taken from the *Investor's India Year Book*. The statement on page 97 shows the result of the study. In view of the highly complicated and indirect relations between profits and size, one should be cautious in making deductions. But despite the limitations suggested above, the results show that mills having spindles below 30,000 and above 75,000 do not do as well as those within these limits. But one or two very large mills have done very well, even as one or two small concerns show a fair rate of profit.

Those that failed to declare a Dividend for—	Number of Firms	Spindle Equipment in Round Figures
Years		
1	5	42,000, 23,000, 19,460, 40,000, 34,000
2	3	27,800, 44,000, 106,940
3	3	44,000, 52,000, 32,000
4	*nil*	——
5	2	46,000, 65,000
6	3	31,600, 46,400, 82,400
7	3	57,800, 109,000, 31,000
8	4	69,000, 45,100, 35,800, 37,450
9	6	109,700, 41,300, 80,200, 81,600, 32,500, 33,600
10	1	51,800
11	1	32,000

Of the 12 firms which either closed down or were reorganized, 4 fell within the class of 1 to 29,999 spindles, and 7 were those having 30,000 to 44,999 spindles; 31 out of the 53 firms under inquiry failed to declare a dividend for one or more years.

There seems to be some correlation between size and profits up to a certain point, after which size becomes uneconomical and profits show a decline. It is, however, dangerous to press this point far without getting further confirmation from other kinds of evidence.

The most conclusive evidence would be that furnished by costs of production of firms of varying size and output. But such data have not been available even to the Tariff Board.

In the absence of details regarding costs of production of firms of different sizes we are thrown on some of the indirect evidence available to elucidate the relation between size and efficiency. The first kind of evidence is that furnished by the effects of depression on the cotton mills at Ahmedabad. Mills which have been struggling on before the depression set in had to close down, and all of the nine mills which closed down or went into liquidation were small ones having less than 20,000 spindles and looms ranging from 200 to 500.[1] Obviously they were too small to be efficient, and even in normal times had not much chance of prosperous existence. Further, it has been stated that in the case of a mill having 27,000 spindles and 400 looms the concern was compelled to expand with a view to reducing the overhead costs and hence grew up into one of 36,000 spindles and 800 looms.[2] That was considered to be the optimum size for that firm. The evidence of the President of the Ahmedabad Millowners' Association[3] bears out the fact that most of the units in Ahmedabad were smaller than they should have been if overhead charges were to be as low as possible per unit of output. That the more enlightened and conscientious managing agents have always sought to utilize their financial resources on extensions of existing mills with a view to reducing their charges rather than setting up new concerns, although the latter might be more profitable to them in view of the commissions on materials of all kinds and the fixed minimum commission payable to them by each mill, shows that the Ahmedabad mills are below the optimum level.

Again, among the mills in Bombay the cost of power supplied to them is less per unit for those that consume a large quantity in the aggregate, and higher for those consuming less, thus pointing to the comparative advantages possessed by the bigger units.[4] Another piece of evidence which throws some light on

[1] *Indian Tariff Board: Cotton Industry*, 1927, Vol. 2, pp. 413–14.

[2] Ibid., p. 514. [3] Ibid., p. 514.

[4] *Report of the Millowners' Association*, 1930. Speech of the Vice-Chairman of the Millowners' Association. Also *Indian Textile Journal*,

this question is the relative overhead costs for the Bombay and up-country mills respectively. Unfortunately the figures for the Ahmedabad mills are not separated into manufacturing or works costs and overhead costs. While the total works costs are appreciably higher in Bombay than in the up-country centres, the overhead expenses are decidedly lower. The prime costs are often an index of the advantages or otherwise of the location of the mills, while the overhead charges reflect the influence of size. When, therefore, we find that although the manufacturing charges per spindle in Bombay are 8.46 pies, in the up-country centres they amount only to 7.77 pies per spindle per day, yet the overhead charges in Bombay are only 1.51 as against 2.24 elsewhere, we may safely conclude that size has been a distinct factor in efficiency.[1] Production per spindle in both cases is nearly the same,[2] and hence this difference in the relative charges shows the advantages of size in respect of overhead expenses. This result is even more evident when we compare the cost of production of the output per loom per day. Although both manufacturing expenses and the total costs are higher for Bombay than for the up-country mills, including the Ahmedabad mills, the overhead charges are 60.36 for Bombay, and 70.88 for the up-country mills.[3] Although the overhead costs for Ahmedabad are not separately given, there is no reason to think that conditions there are different from those in the up-country centres. As the Textile Tariff Board have pointed out, office expenses are, contrary to the commonly held view, considerably lower in Bombay than in Ahmedabad and other up-country centres. The lower office expenses in Bombay have been rightly explained by the Tariff Board as resulting from "the large average size of the Bombay mills, and from the greater concentration of the managing agency in the same hands."[4]

March 1931, p. 233. A saving of Rs. 10 lakhs to the larger mills thus became possible. The smaller mills could not, by reason of their smaller power requirements, share in this reduction of costs.

[1] *Indian Tariff Board: Cotton Industry*, Report, 1927, p. 119.
[2] Ibid., p. 120. [3] Ibid., p. 120. [4] Ibid., p. 122.

These facts tend to show that the larger Bombay units are perhaps more economical in working than the smaller Ahmedabad units, and that neither the troubles of the Bombay mills in recent years nor the comparative prosperity of the Ahmedabad mills are to be ascribed to the bigness of the Bombay units or to the smallness of the Ahmedabad units. There are other factors which in Bombay neutralize the advantages of size, and in Ahmedabad minimize the disadvantages of size. Other factors, such as management or marketing, may have consequences which outweigh the results of size. Where the managerial optimum is bigger than the technical optimum there will be no difficulty in expanding the business unit, for what is required is only a duplication of plants. Where, however, the technical optimum is higher than the managerial optimum, the former has got to adjust itself to a lower level, viz. that set by the managerial optimum, because otherwise diseconomies will result and costs will increase.[1] It is possible that in Bombay the very concentration of mills among a few managing agents might have a result adverse to economical working. The managing agents have not only more concerns than they can efficiently manage, but are engaged in a variety of trading and commercial activities.[2] This conclusion is strengthened when we find that those mills which have been managed by agents wholly devoted to their industrial enterprise have been working at a profit even during the years of depression. Hence although there is no reason to think that the Bombay mills are too large from the technical point of view, they must either try to secure a better and more earnest class of managing agents for their enterprise or must reduce their scale of operations. Even that will probably not be sufficient. It is not that the individual mills having 70,000 to 80,000 spindles are too big to be managed; rather the combination of several mills under one managing agency firm which is not well equipped for the task of managing

[1] E. A. G. Robinson, *Structure of Competitive Industry*, 1931, p. 114.

[2] Arno Pearse, *The Cotton Industry of India*, p. 12; also evidence tendered by the Shareholders' Association, Bombay, before the Tariff Board in 1932.

all of them causes each individual mill, whatever its size, to suffer as a consequence. It is true that some of the European managing agency firms concerned with the management of the jute mills are also equally engaged in quite a miscellaneous range of duties; but as will be shown later, their case is different.[1] Their methods of recruiting partners for the managing agency firms and their organization for managing various enterprises are generally well adapted to the needs of the situation. On the other hand, despite the disadvantages of the small size which the methods of financing the industry have brought about in Ahmedabad, the mills have been growing in prosperity because at a lower level of output there has been secured a better balancing between management and technique. The very limitations which financial considerations have imposed upon the technical equipment have in this case proved to be not altogether a disadvantage. The men in Ahmedabad found it well within their capacity to manage the smaller concerns under their control and were able to give concentrated attention to them. Thus even the defects of size were partly offset by the detailed care of the management.

If this inference is correct, it suggests another reflection. In a country like India, schemes of rationalization are limited partly by the lack of managerial ability. The men necessary to undertake the task are not readily available. Apart from leadership, there is also a deficiency in the supply of the higher-grade workers capable of doing supervisory work efficiently. It is not without significance that the scheme of rationalization proposed for the cotton industry in Bombay has fizzled out. Of course, vested interests, inertia, and other factors were also responsible for the failure of the scheme. But the difficulty of finding suitable organizers and administrators is not to be ignored. Some grouping of mills will be desirable in view of the need for specialization and large-scale production. But it is doubtful, considering the limitations of managerial ability, if very large units are generally to be welcomed. A Ford or a Carnegie might undertake the management of giant enterprises. Such men are few in any country, and in India

[1] See Chapters VIII and IX.

at the present time there is little doubt that industry can be run more successfully when the industrial units are of a size less than the optimum fixed by managerial ability in other countries. The managerial optimum for a firm in India would be much smaller than elsewhere.

The importance of the raw material in the cotton industry is so great and its cost forms so large a proportion (ranging from 40 to 50 per cent, depending on the ruling price of raw cotton[1]) that it is of the greatest importance that firms should be in a position to buy cotton as cheaply as possible. The small firms may be and often are at some disadvantage in buying the material cheaply and on proper occasions owing to financial difficulties. In most of the centres in India other than Bombay, raw cotton has to be purchased during the cotton season as later in the year cotton of good quality is not available. Financially weaker mills are not in a position to buy it in large quantities, and to that extent the advantages of buying the material economically lie with the larger and financially stronger mills. But even here it has to be stated that in the first place the small buyer, provided he has the necessary financial resources, can get the raw material as cheaply as the large firm, and that in the second place the relation between size and efficiency is not direct but works out through the financial strength or weakness of the firms. It may therefore happen that a firm which has a bigger equipment but is financially weak may be worse off than a smaller one which is able to command sufficient working capital. In times of depression it sometimes happens that firms are unable to obtain credit from the banks, and on such occasions big firms may be at a disadvantage compared with smaller ones. On the whole, it may be said that in regard to the buying of raw material, while very small firms may be at some disadvantage, those of moderate size will be able to realize the economies of buying as fully as the bigger ones, and the marketing organization for the buying of cotton in Bombay and other centres does not in any way penalize the smaller firms provided they have the knowledge and the financial resources to buy at the

[1] *Indian Tariff Board: Cotton Industry*, Report, 1927, p. 31.

proper time. Indeed, they have a wide range of choice offered in the Bombay cotton market, and owing to the extreme keenness of competition among the dealers, the middlemen's profits have been cut down to a minimum, and mills are able to buy at the lowest possible cost.

It is, however, difficult to speak with any degree of certainty as to the relation between size and marketing economies. Such a variety of methods is in vogue in different centres that it is possible for firms of very different sizes to carry on equally efficiently. When, as in the Lancashire cotton industry, the business of marketing was taken over by a distinct, separate organization, it was possible for firms of moderate size to utilize it for the purpose of selling their goods efficiently. On the other hand, where we have an integrated system of manufacturing and marketing, the optimum firm must necessarily be larger.

SALES ORGANIZATION

Sales organization differs from place to place. In Bombay the mills have commission agents who have to deal exclusively with the goods of particular firms, and the commission agents guarantee that the merchants take up the goods sold to them and are solvent.[1] The units in Bombay are larger and turn out for a wider market goods whose aggregate value is greater than in Ahmedabad and employ methods different from those elsewhere, where local needs are understood and catered for. Sales are made in the market, and there is not the same chance of establishing contact with small customers. In recent years, however, some of the more enterprising mills of Bombay have taken to selling their goods directly, and in such cases the firms have to be on a much larger scale. It seems to be still an open question whether it would not be preferable for the mills to confine themselves to manufacturing and to leave the sales to a separate organization. Sufficient time and experience have not been available in India to judge of the relative merits of direct selling, which has been resorted to only recently, and selling by commission

[1] *Indian Tariff Board: Cotton Industry*, Evidence, Vol. 2, p. 478.

agents, which has been the practice so far. All that can be said is that while the bigger firms may realize some economies by integrating the selling process, the risks attending such expansion in the case of mistakes are very great. The moderate-size firm, if it does not gain as much profit by its system of selling through commission agents as by direct sale, may not also have to lose as much. In Ahmedabad the brokers do a lot of useful work by bringing the customers directly into touch with the mills. In consultation with the mills they cause new designs to be made and new varieties to be introduced. The smaller units in Ahmedabad are able to keep in close touch with the markets; and thus even in the case of marketing economies it is difficult to state how far an increase in size is necessary to ensure greater profit. But it is significant that the system of mill-shops has been adopted "by some of the largest, most efficient, and most successful up-country mills, who appear on the whole to be well satisfied with the results."[1] It would appear that in Bombay, and most certainly in Ahmedabad and other centres, the units are not at the present moment at the optimum marketing level. But it would be wrong to conclude that therefore the units must become larger. For in view of the risks of growth leading to diseconomies of management and lack of co-ordination, the better way of securing marketing economies would be by promoting a special organization which would undertake the marketing of the goods of all the member mills. By this plan of what Mr. E. A. G. Robinson calls vertical disintegration, the disadvantages of growth may be avoided and the advantages of large-scale marketing ensured.

One final factor remains to be noticed. In the cotton industry, where two or three mills are managed by one managing agency firm, the disadvantages of smaller size arising from their inability to face a critical period of prolonged depression are considerably reduced by the practice[2] of the managing agents in using the funds

[1] *Indian Tariff Board: Cotton Industry*, Report, 1927, Vol. I, p. 162.

[2] Although the practice was denied by the representatives of the Bombay Millowners' Association in 1925 when they gave evidence before

of the more prosperous concerns to rehabilitate the weaker ones. This course is not altogether an unmixed gain to the cotton industry as a whole. For it would be better in the long run that the weaker and really inefficient mills should close down or become merged in the larger concerns than that they should be propped up by the support of the managing agents at the expense of the shareholders of the stronger mills. It is also, perhaps, not necessary to consider at this stage how far it is right to sacrifice the interests of one set of shareholders for the benefit of another. Neglecting the other consequences of such a practice, it is sufficient to point out here that the method by which managing agents come to the rescue of the weaker mills, even by utilizing the funds of other concerns, undoubtedly enables moderate-size firms to face industrial fluctuations with greater confidence than would be the case had they remained as independent mills managed by separate Boards of Directors. This point is illustrated by recent experience in regard to the tea industry which, from 1928 till 1931, passed through critical times. The individual units might not have survived but for their being controlled by a managing agency firm which was able to support them with credit. Banks in India would not have been able to avert the inevitable liquidation of some of the concerns, and this the financing by managing agents has been able to do.[1]

In another aspect, too, there is a striking contrast between the Ahmedabad section of the cotton industry and the Bombay section. Some of the managing agents in Bombay have a considerable number of units under their management; in Ahmedabad, with a few exceptions, each mill is under a separate managing agency firm. This has some interesting results both from the point of view of financial and managerial optima. While a strong managing agent brings strength to the units under his control and is able to help them considerably in periods of stress and depression,

the Tariff Board, it would appear from the evidence given before the Tariff Board in its second inquiry that the practice obtains and is fairly general. (*Vide* Statement of the Bombay Shareholders' Association.)

[1] Refer to Chapter VI.

TABLE I—*Spinning mills in 1931 classified according to the number of spindles*

Number of Spindles	Bombay	Ahmeda-bad	Rest of Bombay Presi-dency	Central Provinces, Berar, Hyderabad	Rajpu-tana, Central India	Bengal	United Provinces	Madras Presi-dency, Mysore	Punjab	Burma	Tota
an 10,000	1	—	2	—	—	—	1	5	—	—	9
and less than 15,000 ..	—	1	4	—	—	1	2	2	1	1	12
and less than 20,000 ..	—	1	3	—	1	—	1	1	—	—	7
nd less than 25,000 ..	1	—	—	—	—	—	1	4	—	—	6
and less than 30,000 ..	—	—	—	—	—	1	1	1	—	—	3
and less than 35,000 ..	—	1	—	—	—	—	—	—	—	—	1
nd less than 40,000 ..	—	—	—	—	—	—	—	—	—	—	—
nd less than 45,000 ..	2	—	—	—	—	1	—	—	—	—	3
nd less than 50,000 ..	1	—	—	—	—	1	—	—	—	—	2
nd over	—	—	1	—	—	—	1	3	—	—	5
Total	5	3	10	—	1	4	7	16	1	1	48

)f the five mills having 50,000 spindles and over, two mills fall within the class 60,000 and under 70,000, on
n the class 80,000 and under 90,000, and one has 223,623 spindles, and is in the southern part of Madras.

TABLE II

n textile mills of all kinds in India in 1931 classified according to the number of spindles in them. Fig do not include those of mills not working or in course of erection.

Number of Spindles	Bombay	Ahmeda-bad	Rest of Bombay Presidency	Madras	United Provinces	Central Provinces, Berar, Hyderabad	Rajputana, Central India	Bengal	Rest of India	All In
than 15,000	3	7	16	8	3	2	3	2	3	47
and less than 30,000 ..	9	36	21	8	8	11	10	4	4	11
and less than 45,000 ..	32	17	2	3	—	2	2	2	—	6
and less than 60,000 ..	14	2	2	5	5	1	1	2	1	3
and less than 80,000 ..	9	3	2	2	—	—	—	1	—	1
and less than 100,000	2	—	—	1	1	—	—	—	—	
100,000	1	—	1	1	1	1	—	—	—	
Total	70	65	44	28	18	17	16	11	8	27

TABLE III

Cotton mills of all kinds in India in 1931 classified according to the average number of workers employed therein

Number of Workers	Bombay	Ahmeda-bad	Rest of Bombay Presi-dency	Central Provinces, Berar, Hyderabad	Rajpu-tana, Central India	Bengal	United Provinces	Madras Presi-dency, Mysore	Punjab	Burma	To
han 1,000	8	36	29	7	7	6	11	14	5	1	12
nd less than 2,000 ..	40	24	8	7	4	4	2	7	1	—	9
nd less than 3,000 ..	15	3	3	1	4	—	3	2	—	—	3
nd less than 4,000 ..	6	1	3	1	1	1	1	2	1	—	1
nd over	1	1	1	1	—	—	1	3	—	—	
Total	70	65	44	17	16	11	18	28	7	1	27

TABLE IV

Cotton mills in India classified according to the amount of cotton consumed during the year 1930

at of Cotton Candies of 784 lb.	Bombay	Ahmeda-bad	Rest of Bombay Presidency	Central Provinces, Berar, Hyderabad	Rajputana, Central India	Bengal	United Provinces	Madras Presidency, Mysore	Punjab	Burma	Tota
.. ..	—	4	1	1	1	—	—	3	1	—	11
.. ..	1	6	11	3	2	2	1	4	2	—	32
.. ..	6	19	11	3	1	2	3	4	1	—	50
.. ..	9	21	7	3	1	2	2	2	1	—	48
.. ..	12	7	4	3	2	2	4	4	—	1	39
.. ..	14	5	1	1	4	1	—	2	—	—	28
.. ..	5	—	1	1	1	—	1	2	—	—	11
.. ..	7	1	—	—	—	—	1	1	—	—	10
.. ..	3	—	2	—	1	1	—	1	—	—	8
.. ..	2	1	1	—	—	—	—	1	—	—	5
0,000 ..	10	—	2	2	3	1	6	4	2	—	30
Total ..	69*	64†	41	17	16	11	18	28	7	1	272

mill (Bombay Industrials) did no spinning in 1931. † One mill in Ahmedabad did no spinning in 19

a weak managing agent would bring disaster to all the concerns under his control. Thus if the chances of profit are greater in the case of mills managed by one and the same agency firm than in the case of mills like those of Ahmedabad which are managed singly, the chances of failure, too, are greater in

TABLE V

Statement showing the paid-up capital of the cotton mills in Bombay city, Ahmedabad, and a few selected centres in India

Total Paid-up Capital	Bombay	Ahmedabad	Rest of Bombay Presidency	Bengal	Madras
Not over 5 lakhs of Rs.	3	28†	8	2	4
Over 5 lakhs but under 10	17	30	13	1	9
Over 10 lakhs but under 15	17	6	8	1	4
Over 15 lakhs but under 20	13	—	4	3	1
Over 20 lakhs but under 30	8	1	4	1	—
Over 30 lakhs but under 40	4	—	2	2	—
Over 40 lakhs but under 50	2	—	—	—	—
Over 50 lakhs	—	—	—	—	—
Total	64*	65†	39‡	10§	18‖

* These do not include the Sassoon group of mills for which capital is given in a single figure, and five other mills for which no separate figures are available.

† Includes one new mill just commencing work.

‡ Excludes mills which are owned by individuals.

§ Excludes proprietary concerns and includes mills just started work.

‖ Excludes the group of Madras mills for which no separate figures are given.

the former. This has been confirmed by the recent collapse of the several concerns managed by Messrs. Currimbhai Ebrahim & Sons in Bombay, and the critical position of certain other mills.

III

THE JUTE INDUSTRY

The jute industry presents some striking differences compared with the cotton industry. Judged either by the average number of workers employed per productive unit or by the average paid-up capital per firm, the industry would seem to comprise units considerably larger than those in the cotton industry. While the average number of workers employed in the cotton industry is about 1,150 per establishment in 1929, the average employed in the jute industry per establishment is nearly 3,635 in the same year. The 96 jute mills noted in the publication *Large Industrial Establishments* employed 348,982 persons in 1929, only slightly less than the 387,159 employed by the 341 cotton mills listed in the same publication.[1] But the true comparison should be not between the cotton mills and jute mills, as given in the above-mentioned publication, but between the units as defined in the beginning of this chapter. Thus two or more productive units situated close to one another and owned and controlled by one and the same company must be regarded according to our definition as comprising one firm or establishment. From this point of view we find that the 76 jute firms employed in 1929 about 4,600 workers on the average, whilst the 278 cotton firms employed about 1,400 workers each.[2] Again, while the total paid-up capital and reserve was Rs. 24.31 crores for the 74 cotton mill companies in the city of Bombay for 1929, the total paid-up capital and reserve of the 59 jute companies in Bengal was £31,000,000, which at 1s. 6d. per rupee was equal to Rs. 41.35 crores, thus showing an average capitalization of 70 lakhs of rupees per unit as against 31 lakhs per unit in the cotton industry. The mill industry in Ahmedabad has only about Rs. 15 lakhs of paid-up capital and reserve on the average.

When, however, a comparison is made regarding the spindle

[1] *Large Industrial Establishments in 1929* (1932). In 1931 there were 98 jute mills employing on the average about 343,200 workers daily.

[2] Statement issued by the Bombay Millowners' Association, 1930.

and loom equipment, we find that a jute firm has on the average only about 17,900 spindles as against 26,000 spindles of a cotton textile establishment, thus showing a smaller spindleage equipment. But the number of looms owned by a jute establishment is larger than in the cotton industry, the figures being 1,400 and 500 respectively. This significant difference in equipment in respect of the number of looms in an average cotton and in an average jute firm is due, of course, to the relative proportion between spindles and looms in each industry. In the cotton industry the proportion of spindles to looms is of the order of 40 to 60 spindles to one loom.[1] In the jute industry the proportion is 20 to 1, the reason being that for the kind of output turned out by a jute mill, a smaller number of spindles will be sufficient. But the individual units in the jute industry have also expanded greatly in recent years, and the expansion has been, not as in the cotton industry by the formation of small new units, but by adding more plant to the same unit. The average jute firm is, therefore, in every way bigger than the average cotton firm, a result due in part to the differences in the nature of the industry and in part to the differences in the manner of growth. That the average jute firm has increased greatly in recent years will be evident from the fact that between 1900 and 1927, while the number of firms increased from 31 to 59, the number of plants increased from 31 to 84, the number of spindles from 334,000 to 1,083,800, and the number of looms from 15,000 to 50,000.[2] In other words, assuming 100 to be the index number at the beginning of the century, we find that in 1927 the index number of firms rose to 190, that of plants to 270, that of spindles to 327, and that of looms to 330.

Tables VI and VII classify the jute establishments in Bengal according to their loom equipment and the number of workers employed.

It will be seen from the tables that the majority of the concerns, 33 out of 63, have from 250 to 749 looms. Of these, 16 fall within

[1] *Indian Tariff Board: Cotton Industry*, Report, 1927, Vol. 1, p. 13.

[2] *Indian Year Book*, 1931, and also D. R. Wallace, *The Romance of Jute*, p. 95. For an idea of the size of jute firms in Great Britain, see the *Final Report of the Census of Production*, 1930, Part I.

the range of 250 to 499 looms, and 17 within the range of 500 to 749. The number of workers employed in each plant and in each concern is far larger than in any similar industry, 21 concerns employing more than 6,000 workers each. This is partly because more men are required to look after jute sacking and hessian looms than to mind cotton looms, and partly because the workers are less efficient than the cotton weavers. Labour in the jute industry is also cheap compared to the cotton industry, and there is no incentive to economize it.

RELATION BETWEEN SIZE AND EFFICIENCY

As in other industries, the lack of data relating to cost of production prevents us from establishing any direct relation between size and efficiency. But the jute industry has been organized on such a uniform plan that if any relation could be established between the profits of the concerns and their size, we can conclude that size and efficiency can be correlated. For this purpose the rates of profits declared by the jute concerns that are quoted in the Calcutta Stock Exchange have been analysed for 36 firms, and the results of this study have been shown in the annexed table.[1] A fifteen-year period has been selected (1914 to 1928 inclusive), and only those firms which were working continuously from 1914 were chosen. Subject to the same caution as in the cotton industry, some very tentative conclusions may be drawn. Of the six firms having less than 500 looms, only one failed to declare a dividend in any year, and that firm apparently passed through difficult times in 1920–1. The smallest firm having only 175 looms showed also the smallest rate of profit, that is 24 per cent, but one of the largest firms having 1,744 looms had an average profit of only 28 per cent, and did not give a dividend for one year. Firms falling within the limits of 500 to 999 looms have done exceedingly well in this period, and 9 out of 14 show an average profit of 70 per cent and over. Among the firms falling within the next group, having looms ranging from 1,000 to 1,499, are to be found those having the highest rates of profit on the average. The biggest

[1] See Table VIII.

mills do not show the highest profits; indeed, the two biggest concerns, having 1,952 looms and 1,744 looms respectively, show the least average rates of profits, 33 per cent and 28 per cent respectively, which are the lowest of the rates of profits of the firms included in the inquiry, with the exception of that of the smallest mill. Further, three out of the seven in this group have rather low average profits, while the remaining four show a high average rate, although in no case is it close to the maximum rate obtained by the firms in the previous group. On the whole it may be said that in the jute industry concerns having looms over 500 and less than 1,500 have at least as good a chance of carrying on efficiently as those which are larger. Perhaps one may go further and state that concerns smaller and larger than those of this group do not do nearly as well as those which are of the size represented by the 500 to 1,500 group.[1]

[1] In a letter to the writer, Sir Thomas Catto, the present head of the firm of Morgan, Grenfell & Co., who control Andrew Yule & Co., stated that units of anything up to 1,000 looms are a handy size for efficient supervision; but there are firms having very much larger units which they manage with success.

In regard to the size of jute concerns, although small concerns having less than 500 or 750 looms would certainly be uneconomical, the reasons why the majority of the Andrew Yule mills are of the size 500–1,000 are that the late Sir David Yule, the leading captain of the jute industry, was a believer in starting in a small way and held that from the purely technical and productive point of view a mill having 500 to 1,000 looms was a reasonable size, and that 3 or 4 mills situated close to one another, and having similar equipment and plant and buying raw material from a central office in the managing agency firm would be a check on one another in regard to cost. Finally, the economy of management and supervision, of central buying and selling and of finance is secured by the system of several mills being managed by one agency firm. Thus the firm of Andrew Yule & Co. manages 10 jute mills, Bird & Co. 8, Jardine & Skinner 4, McLeod Co. 5, Begg, Dunlop 4, and Thomas Duff 3. While Jardine & Skinner manage big units of over 1,000 looms (3 out of 4 being over 1,500 looms), Andrew Yule's units are 500-loom units, and both have been successful.

The General Motors (U.S.A.) is organized in a number of medium-size plants; this is explained by its President on grounds similar to those suggested by Andrew Yule, viz. the relative advantages of several plants serving as checks on one another (H. A. Marquand, *The Dynamics of Industrial Combination*, 1931, p. 138).

Tables VI and VII classify the jute establishments in Bengal according to the number of workers employed, and according to their loom equipment respectively.

TABLE VI*

Number of Workers Employed	Number of Firms
Less than 500	4
500 to 1,000	3
1,000 to 1,500	1
1,500 to 2,000	5
2,000 to 2,500	4
2,500 to 3,000	7
3,000 to 3,500	9
3,500 to 4,000	3
4,000 to 4,500	9
4,500 to 5,000	4
5,000 to 5,500	3
5,500 to 6,000	3
6,000 and over	21
Total	76

* *Large Industrial Establishments in 1929* (1931).

TABLE VII*

Number of Looms	Number of Firms
Less than 250	2
250 and less than 500	16
500 and less than 750	17
750 and less than 1,000	7
1,000 and less than 1,500	12
1,500 and less than 2,000	8
2,000 and less than 2,500	—
2,500 and over	1

* *Indian Year Book* (1931).

TABLE VIII

	Number of Firms	Average rate of profit per cent declared between 1914 and 1928 inclusive
Group I		
Firms with less than 500 looms	6	90, 74, 65, 50, 40, 24
Group II		
500 to 999 looms	14	112, 112, 98, 85, 76, 74, 72, 70, 70, 66, 58, 45, 38, 38
Group III		
1,000 to 1,499 looms ..	9	160, 120, 100, 83, 72, 70, 42, 32, 26
Group IV		
1,500 to 1,999 looms ..	7	107, 93, 93, 88, 34, 33, 29

Figures taken from the quotations found in the issues of *Capital*, from 1914 to 1932.

IV

THE COAL-MINING INDUSTRY

The coal-mining industry of India, like that of Britain, reveals distinctly the adverse effects of small size on economical working. There are, broadly speaking, two types within the industry, mines raising coal of high quality (usually known in India as first-class coal) and those raising coal of rather inferior kind (known as second-class coal). The distinction is so well marked that each type has organized itself separately, so that the Indian Mining Association is an organization comprising mostly the first type of collieries, whilst the Indian Mining Federation represents the second type of collieries. Whilst in each type there are units of varying size, the average coal unit is distinctly smaller in the second type than in the first. The combination of smaller units and inferior quality has rendered the position of the second type of coal companies extremely precarious, and the first effects of any adverse factors fall wholly on them.

Of the 548 coal companies which were working in 1929, 134

belonged to the first type and produced about 14,000,000 tons of coal, while the remaining 404 units produced only 7,000,000 tons.[1] Thus two-thirds of the total output was raised by one-fourth of the number of units. Even here were to be found some small units raising less than 10,000 tons a year. In 1926, for example, 21 out of the 134 concerns raised each less than 10,000 tons per annum. The following table classifies according to their output the coal companies raising a superior variety of coal.

11 units, each with less than 5,000 tons per annum.
10 units, each with from 5 to 10,000 tons per annum.
6 units, each with from 10 to 20,000 tons per annum.
45 units, each with from 20 to 50,000 tons per annum.
62 units, each with 50,000 tons and over per annum.

In 1920, of the collieries then in existence, 50 per cent of the total number had a total production of only 6·3 per cent of the total output, and on the average produced less than 12,000 tons per annum. About 36 per cent of the number raised between 12,000 tons and 60,000 tons each, and were responsible for 35 per cent of the output, and the remaining 14 per cent of the number of collieries produced nearly 59 per cent of the total output. Some of the smaller collieries have since gone out of existence. Although the smaller concerns, even among those raising coal of high quality, do suffer on account of higher costs of raising coal, it is not the size so much as the quality of the coal raised that appears to be the most important factor. In times of depression poorer mines of whatever size have to close down, whilst those raising coal of better quality and higher grade struggle on. Most of these units were established during the boom years in 1919 and 1920, and since then have had to face a continuous period of depression. Each year found a number of these mines shutting down, and between 1925 and 1929 the number of colliery units at work was reduced from 810 to 548. Another factor that affects the position is the level at which the mining operations are carried on. Where we have a small colliery working "first-class" coal at a high level and a large one

[1] *Indian Coal Statistics*, 1931.

working the same class of coal at a lower level, the disadvantage that the small mine has on account of its working on a small scale is neutralized by the fact that it is raising coal at a higher level, and therefore its raising costs are lower. Thus in the coal-mining industry it is not merely the size but the kind of coal that is raised and the level at which the mine is worked that are equally important factors. A large colliery unit working second-class coal has often to close down, whilst a smaller unit may continue its operations if it raises better class coal. Depression hits the larger collieries of the second class more than the smaller ones raising first-class coal.

However, it is still true to say that the larger ones in each class have a better chance of surviving than the smaller ones of the same class. There is no doubt that the smallness of the colliery units prevents economic working and the introduction of electric power. The excessive number of separate steam-raising plants of wasteful design, together with the unskilled feeding of the boilers, has caused a great increase in the consumption of fuel for power. "Small units are unable to have steam plants of proper efficiency, and in the majority of cases each of these little units, raising only small outputs, has its own steam plant, consisting usually of one or more vertical boilers, and occasionally horizontal boilers of the Lancashire type. Very little insulation is used to prevent radiation, and the steam used is generally at a low pressure, while the stoking is unskilled and wasteful."[1] It may be noted that in 1925, out of 810 colliery units, 336 did not utilize mechanical power, whereas in 1929, when most of the smaller units had closed down, as many as 382 utilized mechanical power, and only 156 did not use mechanical power—thus showing that small units are unable to employ mechanical power. If the units combined, it would be possible to get concentrated and intensive working within a narrower area leading up to diminished cost owing to the use of machinery and plant, and a reduction in the cost of

[1] Report of Mr. Treharne Rees on the methods of coal-mining in India, 1919, included in the *Report of the Coal-Fields Committee*, 1920, p. 41.

maintenance and supervision. It would also be possible to secure economy in the purchase of supplies, the maintenance of stocks of stores, etc. That the individual units in the coal-mining industry are very small will also be clear from the fact that the average output per unit is only 38,000 tons per annum. It has been said that in England the difference between the smaller and larger collieries was seen in the output per worker (the extent of the difference being 3 cwts. per man shift), a less difference of costs (about 1s. 6d. in place of 3s. per ton for smaller collieries), and an even greater difference of profits (over 2s. in favour of the larger undertakings).[1] All the heavy losses were confined to the smaller undertakings. Similarly in India, in times of depression and uneconomic prices, it is the smaller collieries among those raising superior coal that close down first, and this lends support to the view that production costs are higher for the smaller units than for the larger. It is unfortunate that we have no means of knowing the extent of the difference in the costs of mining coal between the smaller and the larger units. But there is no doubt that small collieries not only cannot use electric power, but sometimes do not reach the stage of steam power. Their work is carried on intermittently at comparatively shallow depths. Sometimes the areas leased for mining have been "of such small dimensions and fantastic shapes that it is quite impossible to work the coal satisfactorily."[2] The quantity of coal estimated to be destroyed or lost by present methods was estimated in 1920 to be one-third of the total coal raised.[3] Amalgamation of small units, supply of power from a common source, and prevention of waste in all forms are necessary if production costs are to be lowered. The high annual consumption of fuel can be reduced if the excessive number of separate steam raising-plants of wasteful design are reduced, and power got more and more from fewer generating stations.

The following table[4] gives a classification of the coal companies

[1] *Report of the Royal Commission on the Coal Industry*, Cmd. 2600, 1926, p. 55.

[2] *Report of the Coal-Fields Committee*, 1920, p. 4.

[3] Ibid.

[4] Compiled from *Indian Coal Statistics*, 1931, pp. 63–70.

Joint-Stock Coal Companies (including private and public) at work on March 31, 1932.

Paid-up Capital	Number of Companies
Under 1 lakh of Rs. ..	30
Over 1 under 2½ lakhs ..	36
Over 2½ under 5 lakhs ..	48
Over 5 under 7½ lakhs ..	20
Over 7½ under 15 lakhs ..	15
Over 15 lakhs	17

Output of Coal (long tons 2,240 *lb.), British Possessions and Foreign Countries.**

	In Millions of Tons		Number of Persons Employed	Output per Head
	1930	1931	1928	1928
				Tons
United Kingdom	243·86	219·43	—	—
South Wales	45·10	37·08	—	—
British India	23·79	23·81	179,600	131
Canada	10·20	8·31	28,800	504 (1927)
Australia and New Zealand	11·73	11·21	36,300	—
South Africa and Rhodesia	12·95	11·28	32,800	444
U.S.A.	479·28	390·66	682,800	707 (1927)
Germany	153·43	127·91	517,600	—
France	53·02	49·23	286,900	161
Belgium	26·97	26·60	163,300	—
Russia	39·31	48·90	—	—
Japan	32·86	32·46	237,900	138
China	24·35	—	—	—

* *The Coal-Mining Industry of the United Kingdom, the various coal-fields thereof, and the principal foreign countries of the world,* Finlay A. Gibson, Cardiff.

working in 1931, according to their paid-up capital. There were 206 joint-stock companies (private and public) working in 1931 in Bengal and Bihar and Orissa, but figures relating to paid-up capital are available only for 166 of them. It will be seen from the table on page 121 that 30 companies had less than 1 lakh of rupees of paid-up capital, and only 17 companies had a paid-up capital of 15 lakhs of rupees and over; 114 companies out of 166 had a paid-up capital of less than 5 lakhs of rupees, i.e. £37,000.

V

THE PAPER INDUSTRY

According to expert opinion, a complete four-machine-mill fitted with plants for undertaking all processes for converting raw material into paper is the smallest economic unit possible.[1] Judged by this standard there were in 1931 out of the eight then working only three mills which possessed four machines and had a complete equipment for the various processes involved. The Titaghur Paper Mills Company owned two of them, one at Titaghur and the other at Kinkinarah, and the third mill having four machines was the Bengal Paper Mill Co. at Raniganj. Each of them had a capacity of over 10,000 tons annually, and from the point of view of size was sufficiently large to ensure economic production. There were also three mills with two machines each, having a total capacity of 11,000 tons, and two mills with only one machine each, and these last were undoubtedly too small to ensure economic working. In Great Britain the usual size of a mill producing similar kinds of paper is one varying from two to four machines each, and it cannot be said therefore that the three mills having only two machines each are necessarily uneconomic units of production. But it should be noted that the capital cost of a British mill is considerably less than that of an Indian mill of the same size because more than 50 per cent of the cost of a mill erected in India represents the cost of machinery and plant

[1] *Indian Tariff Board: Paper and Paper Pulp Industries*, 1925, Vol. 1, p. 254.

in which the English mill has a decided advantage amounting to a third of the machine cost.[1] And this disadvantage is likely to be a permanent one and cannot be reduced merely by increasing the size of the paper mill. Further, in England they do not have to provide a very expensive water plant or huge walls round the mills, or build assistant's quarters as they have to do in India. Cheaper raw material, cheaper labour, and reduction in other costs can be the only sources from which economy may be looked for.

How big should a paper mill be in India in order that it may produce as cheaply as possible? Fortunately we have some data regarding costs of production for three firms producing paper of varying output, and it is possible to draw some conclusions regarding the relations between size and efficiency. But even here there are grave difficulties in comparing the costs of production of one mill with those of another. As the Tariff Board have pointed out, there is in the first place a great disparity in the proportion in which the primary materials are used, and the costs of these materials vary greatly owing to local conditions.[2] Secondly, the processes of manufacture are not the same in all the mills. The methods of mechanical treatment and digestion adopted in the manufacture of bamboo pulp vary from mill to mill. The proportion between the imported auxiliary materials and those produced within the mills also varies. Further, the classes and qualities of paper manufactured by the mills show marked differences, although it may be held that the writing and printing papers commonly made in India do not differ much either in cost or selling price. For all these reasons it would be dangerous to make any definite correlation between size and costs based merely on the costs of production of the mills. On the other hand, we have for the same mills the figures of costs at different scales of output between 1924–5 and 1930–1, and are in a position to find out how far increased economies are possible at increased output. The difficulty here, however, is to separate the reduction in cost

[1] *Indian Tariff Board: Paper and Paper Pulp Industries*, 1925, Vol. 1, p. 512.

[2] Ibid., Report, 1931, p. 56.

due to the fall in prices from a reduction due to economies of increased output, and again to distinguish between economies due to working at full capacity from those realized owing to increased equipment and increased output. But despite all these difficulties, some conclusions seem to be possible. First, taking the Indian Paper Pulp Co. at Naihati, we find that in 1924–5, when it had only one machine, although the cost of cutting and rafting bamboo and crushing it was the same whatever the output, there was considerable saving in respect of miscellaneous charges for a larger output. This was due to the fact that the amount of royalty to be paid was a minimum of Rs. 10,000, whatever be the quantity of bamboo cut up to 10,000 tons, and was one rupee a ton above that minimum. The incidence of cost was Rs. 3.5 in 1923–4, while with an extraction of 10,000 tons there would be an immediate saving of Rs. 2.5 per ton.[1] A great saving on the special establishment employed to handle the raw material could also be effected by increasing the extractions to 10,000 tons, the extent of the saving being estimated at Rs. 11 a ton.[2] A saving on the raw material would be possible with increased size.

In respect of power and fuel, if the capacity of the mill were increased from 2,500 to 5,000 tons of paper, it would be possible to reduce the coal consumption from 5 tons to 4½ tons of coal per ton of output.[3] But this is because the mill has a power unit designed for a mill of double the size, more coal being used per ton of paper now than would be necessary if a second machine were added. The expenditure under the heading of general and miscellaneous, which included supervision charges and cost of local management, was highest in the one machine mill at Naihati, and lowest at the biggest mill in Titaghur, thus showing the advantages of increased size.[4] When the quantity of paper produced was increased after 1925 in all the three mills under study, the costs in every case fell considerably.

[1] *Indian Tariff Board: Paper and Paper Pulp Industries*, 1925, p. 37.
[2] Ibid., 1925, p. 37. [3] Ibid., 1925, p. 43.
[4] See Appendix II, 1925 (*Tariff Board Report*), pp. 17, 23, 33.

The statement below shows that the increase in output has brought about in all cases a great reduction in cost. Although the Bengal Paper Mill Co. shows the highest percentage of reduction, this is only because the cost in 1924–5 was excessive. The increase of output of the Indian Paper Mill Co. has certainly resulted in a considerable diminution in cost, and the fact that a second machine was added which has brought down the costs to the lowest among the three paper mills shows that a two-machine mill is able to carry on at least as well as a four-machine mill. How far a further increase in the equipment of the mill from two to four will bring about further reductions in cost we cannot tell, although the fact that the Titaghur Mills No. 1 and No. 2, each having four machines,

	Output in 1924–5 in Tons	Output in 1930–1 in Tons	Percentage Increase of Output	Percentage Decrease in Costs of Manufacture per Ton between 1924–5, 1930–1
Titaghur Mills Co. ..	15,556	19,260	23·8	2·3
Bengal Paper Mill Co. ..	6,349	9,218	45·2	43·8
Indian Paper Mill Co. ..	2,545	6,188	143·1	34·6

do not show lower costs might lead one to give a negative answer. But such a conclusion is not warranted, for other factors besides size might explain the difference. It is only when a mill located in the same centre and using the same raw material and processes of production as the Indian Paper Mill Co. sets up four machines that comparisons of real value in respect of costs can be made. But that a one-machine mill is smaller than the optimum unit is proved by the lack of success of such mills. Of the nine mills in existence in 1924–5, five had only one machine each. Since that period two mills have increased their equipment to two machines. Of the other three mills having only one machine each, two were in Bombay, of which one had to close down, and the other was sold and acquired by another paper mill. The third mill has not been working for some years past. Thus the career of the single-machine mills has been unfortunate. Indeed, two new mills erected since 1925 each having only one machine have not been working properly; one of these has gone into liquidation, and the other is in a state of suspended animation. A small mill is not merely technically ill-equipped for production, but is always in financial straits. The capital that it raises is insufficient for its working expenses, and the mill is compelled to resort to borrowing at ruinous rates. Hence financial breakdown sets in even before technical difficulties occur.

A return submitted by the Deccan Paper Mills in 1924 contained, besides actual figures of cost on the basis of the then available output, a statement showing what the costs would have been had production increased to 3,600 tons annually. The figures showed that while the costs of materials would remain nearly the same, there were great economies possible in the case of labour, coal, and repairs. Administration and supervision charges and the cost of agents' remuneration would be decidedly lower. But there was no economy in packing, in railway freight, and in one or two other items.

The advantage of large-scale production in the saving of labour consists in the reduction in the cost of supervisory and foremen staff. The incidence of overhead charges and depreciation per unit of production is less as production is increased, and this is particularly so in the paper industry (unlike, for instance, in the cotton industry) where the larger "beaters" are relatively cheaper than the smaller machines and the smaller beaters.

VI

THE PIG-IRON INDUSTRY AND THE STEEL INDUSTRY

Pig-iron is produced by four companies in India. The blast furnaces of the Tata Iron & Steel Co., Ltd., and of the Indian Iron & Steel Co., Ltd., are of the largest and most modern type. Indeed, Indian equipment in this industry is in no way inferior to that of any other country. Substantial progress has been made in blast-furnace practice in recent years, and Jamshedpur is fully abreast of the times. The two blast furnaces which were originally installed had a capacity for making only 250 tons a day; in 1919 a third was added, and between 1922 and 1924 two additional furnaces of approximately 500 tons capacity per day were put into operation. Although these two were quite up to date at the time, one of them has been re-designed and re-equipped, and can now turn out 1,200 tons of pig-iron in twenty-four hours. As now designed and equipped, the three largest blast furnaces have a producing capacity of nearly one million tons of pig-iron annually.[1] The plant in the Indian Iron & Steel Co. consists of two blast furnaces designed to turn out 350 tons each. One was turning out 450 tons a day in 1923, and it was hoped to have soon a production of 850 to 900 tons a day.[2] In 1930–1 the annual production was 331,000 tons, and in 1931–2 it was 250,000 tons. The Bengal Iron Co. has also two blast furnaces, but they are of smaller capacity, and the equipment is not satisfactory, as one of them has only a capacity of 100 tons a day.[3]

The Mysore Iron Works at Badravati (Mysore State) has a plant consisting of a single blast furnace of a capacity which has been estimated at 60 tons per day, and of a wood distillation plant for the production of charcoal. This furnace is the only charcoal blast furnace in the world which has been erected in recent years.[4] The annual production was 25,000 tons in 1931–2.

THE STEEL INDUSTRY

The only steel works in India, the Tata iron and steel works at Jamshedpur, has an annual capacity of 600,000 tons of finished steel, although the actual output has been ranging from 400,000 to 450,000 tons.[5] According to the Balfour Committee on Industry and Trade, a modern steel plant must have a minimum capacity of 300,000 tons of finished steel annually if it is to work econo-

[1] *Capital, Trade and Engineering Supplement*, 1931.
[2] *Indian Tariff Board: Steel Industry*, Evidence, Vol. 3, 1924.
[3] Ibid.
[4] *Capital, Trade and Engineering Supplement*, 1928.
[5] Production in 1930 was 427,000 tons.

mically.[1] The old steel plant at Jamshedpur was capable of producing only 126,000 tons, and obviously was too small to be economical. The Tariff Board considered that at an annual output of 400,000 tons the firm would be in a position to secure the lowest average cost per ton.[2] That would be so if their plant had been planned properly and carefully laid out. But, actually, the Tata Iron & Steel Co. found in 1927 that their plant was ill balanced and ill proportioned, some sections having larger capacities than others. The capacities of the coke ovens and steel furnaces proved too small, while those of the blast furnaces and rolling mills turned out to be too large. To restore a proper balance between coke ovens, blast furnaces, steel furnaces, and rolling mills the company had to increase the size of the plant with a view to getting an annual output of 600,000 tons. But this extension of the plant to restore a proper balance has possibly made the plant too large. It is true that some of the most modern continental plants are designed for an output far in excess of that possible in the Jamshedpur works. But as has been pointed out with reference to Great Britain, having regard to the complications of large units, to the necessarily increased difficulty of exercising adequate control, and to considerations of capital cost, a somewhat smaller plant, if well-balanced and operated with every attention to detail, may be more successful.[3] This applies particularly to India, where the difficulties of detailed control have already become apparent.

Further, while the capacity of the plant is now 600,000 tons per annum, the actual output has not exceeded 450,000 tons. This results in waste. "The most efficient method of producing a small quantity of steel is to produce it in a small furnace and not in an underworked or overstaffed large furnace. The plant which is designed for a larger output requires as a rule its full team of

[1] *Balfour Committee on Industry and Trade: Survey of Metal Industries*, p. 8.

[2] *Indian Tariff Board: Steel Industry*, Report, 1924, p. 42.

[3] *Balfour Committee on Industry and Trade: Survey of Metal Industries*, p. 29.

workers to make it work at all, but that team will be larger than it would have been had it been designed for the reduced output. . . . For these reasons a plant which is more efficient than others at full capacity may yet have a higher prime cost than the others at output below its capacity."[1]

Thirdly, in times of depression, a medium-sized plant, if well-balanced, may not have to diminish production and to work at reduced capacity to the same extent as a big plant. The Tata works has been faced with difficult times necessitating a curtailment of production, and therefore producing at higher cost. Considering all these factors, if its size had been restricted to a capacity of 400,000 to 450,000 tons of steel annually, and if it had secured a proper balance at that level of output, better results would have been possible.

VII

THE CEMENT INDUSTRY

The Cement Industry is one in which the advantages of large-scale production can be achieved and in which increased output would mean increased economy of production. The cheapest unit of production may be said to be a factory with a two-kiln plant,[2] capable of producing 40,000 tons of cement a year. In England a three-kiln plant is considered to be a reasonably large factory, but in America, where many of the factories have as many as 16 to 20 kilns, the minimum size of a cheap and efficient unit of production is regarded to be one with a large number of kilns, between 10 and 15.[3] In India the number of factories has increased to such an extent that the maximum productive capacity is far in excess of the present needs of the country, and thus many of them are turning out only a fraction of their maximum output. Provided a factory is located properly and has an up-to-date plant and adopts the latest practice, it may be said that even a

[1] E. A. G. Robinson, *Structure of Competitive Industry*, p. 95.
[2] *Indian Tariff Board: Cement Industry*, Evidence, 1925, p. 80.
[3] Ibid.

single kiln plant producing 150 to 200 tons a day and a capacity of about 50 to 60,000 tons per annum will be capable of economical working. Of the ten factories working in 1925, five had a capacity of 60,000 tons or more, and five of less. Like the paper industry, the cement industry finds that much of the capital cost (varying

	Year 1930*	
	Capacity in Tons	Number of Kilns
Indian Cement Co.	40,000	2
Gwalior Cement Co.	45,000	2
Bundi Portland Cement Co., Ltd. ..	160,000	3
Punjab Portland Cement Co., Ltd. ..	80,000	2
Katni Cement & Industrial Co., Ltd.	85,000	2
Central Provinces Cement Co., Ltd.	180,000	3
United Cement Co. of India, Ltd. ..	45–50,000	1
Sahabad Cement Co., Ltd.	120,000	2

* *Capital, Trade and Engineering Supplement*, 1931, p. 42.

from 60 to 70 per cent) is incurred in machinery and plant, and thus the average Indian firm is at a great disadvantage compared with the British firm which has an advantage of nearly 20 per cent in capital cost. The capital cost of a good cement factory with a capacity of 60,000 tons comes to about Rs. 54 lakhs, and thus it is an industry which requires a large amount of capital.

VIII

THE SUGAR INDUSTRY

In view of the large number of factories growing up under the shelter of the substantial protection granted to the sugar industry for a period of fifteen years from 1932, it is necessary to inquire if they are of a size conducive to efficient and economical production. Within a year of the grant of protection, 27 new cane sugar factories were established, and although the estimated capacity of each factory is available, there is bound to be a gap between the estimates and actuals as sufficient time has not elapsed for the factories to find out their actual output. So far as factories existing before 1932 are concerned, out of 28 cane sugar factories for which details are available, 5 had a capacity of crushing only 250 tons or less a day, 9 had a capacity of 251 to 400 tons, 5 had a capacity of 401 to 600 tons a day, and 9 had a capacity of over 600 tons a day. The Industrial Commission estimated that a factory having a minimum capacity of crushing 250 tons a day would be able to produce at the lowest cost.[1] But the Tariff Board, with the advantage of the report of an expert committee (the Indian Sugar Committee, 1920), considered that for the running of an economic factory the scale of output must be about 4,000 tons of white sugar, crushing about 50,000 tons of cane per season of 100 days. A crushing capacity of 500 tons of cane daily was considered to be the proper size. Most of the new factories have been planned to crush 400 tons of cane daily, and provided other conditions are satisfactory may be expected to produce sugar economically. Of the 27 new factories established in 1932–3, 3 are small ones with a crushing capacity of less than 250 tons a day, 17 have a capacity of 251–400, of which 13 have a 400-ton capacity, and the remaining 7 are big ones having a crushing capacity of over 400 and up to a maximum of 600 tons. There are only 7 factories, having a capacity of less than 400 tons of cane daily, which may be regarded as likely to be too small. Provided estimates and actuals do not vary, it may be stated that the majority of the sugar factories are planned on proper lines. But very much depends upon their ability to get sugar-cane fresh and at cheap transport cost. Although some increase in the number of sugar factories since 1931 is justified owing to the grant of protection, the development of the industry may be checked by a want of proportion between the development of the industry in its agricultural aspect and in its industrial aspect. Too many factories have been suddenly established in a limited area, and all of them will be seeking for supplies of good cane. Unless there is an equal improvement in the quantity and quality of the cane

[1] Appendices to the Industrial Commission.

required by the factories, the latter would find themselves unable to produce up to their capacity, and part of the plant would always be idle. Unused capacity leads to increased costs and renders economic working difficult. Without further data, which would become available only after a few years, it is not possible to state how far in practice the capacities of the new sugar plants would be fully utilized.

IX

CONCLUSION

A study of the size of industrial establishments in India shows that as in other countries industry is carried on in units of varying size. Although there are to be found in each of the industries examined a number of units which are too small to produce economically and to realize all the economies of production, and which, therefore, may increase their scale of production with advantage, it cannot be maintained that the larger the unit the greater will be the profits, or the lower the costs. For size by itself does not ensure economy after a certain point. It is true that in every industry, and for every method of production within each industry, there is more or less a fixed minimum size of plants below which production is technically impossible or economically unprofitable. "The minimum size of plants with mechanized productive processes is determined by the smallest mechanical aggregate able to enter competition."[1] Thus in a paper factory the minimum is at least one set of paper machines. In some cases the minimum-sized plant will be one which can reasonably utilize the energy of one entrepreneur, or in an enterprise comprising several plants of a salaried manager who must be provided with sufficient executive tasks. Thus factories employing foreign experts must necessarily be on a bigger scale than those that can be operated by the natives of the country.

But when we pass away from this minimum "technical" size and consider the "optimum" size, we come across the personal

[1] Von Beckerath, *Industrial Organization*, 1933, p. 92.

element among other factors, and the growth of a factory may bring about diseconomies owing to the lack of ability on the part of the executive. The size of a firm comes to be limited by the administrative ability of the industrial leaders of the country. The small firm and the medium-sized undertakings, even if they may be technically deficient, may do better because it is more easy to get suitable leadership for smaller firms than for the larger ones. A study of the profits of 1,130 companies in the United States resulted in the conclusion that it was not the largest firms that gave the best average profits. Mr. H. B. Summers, writing in the *Quarterly Journal of Economics*, May 1932, concludes thus after analysing the earnings of the small and large companies included in the above study:[1] "With respect to any positive advantages accruing to large-scale production the study offers nothing whatever in support of the idea that size in itself brings greater earning power." The fact that in Ahmedabad the mills, although smaller than in Bombay, show better results would seem to suggest that factors other than size may be even more important. The fact is that the capacity for management is a very important factor in organization, and that as long as that is limited it would be better for industry to be organized on only moderate lines. It is possible to find two fields of industry in India well marked out from each other. Industry in the hands of the less experienced leaders can thrive better when it is organized in smaller units than when it is organized in large units. Exceptions there may be, but broadly speaking it would be correct to state that better results may be achieved when industry is established on a small scale to start with, and allowed to grow slowly. Medium-sized undertakings also serve as a training-ground for executive leadership. The disadvantages arising from the smallness of size can be offset by co-operative organization for buying and selling established by and for each industry. But in a country where industrial

[1] Also according to the Federal Trade Commission (U.S.A.), in the flour-milling industry in the United States "companies of medium size show slightly higher rates of profit than either the larger or the smaller companies" (*Recent Economic Changes*, 1929, Vol. 1, p. 191).

leadership is of a high order the "optimum" firm can be comparatively larger. The establishment and successful working over a period of time of big businesses is in itself an outward manifestation of high executive capacity. The scale of business in each country is thus connected, both as cause and effect, with the level of industrial leadership.

CHAPTER IV

METHODS OF RAISING CAPITAL FOR INDUSTRY

I

ESSENTIAL CONDITIONS OF INDUSTRIAL GROWTH

How far industrial development has been retarded in India by lack of indigenous capital, and how much it has owed to foreign, especially British, capital has been dealt with by many students of Indian economic conditions. It may be admitted that lack of indigenous capital has not merely meant slow industrial expansion, but implies also a rather limited share in the development, such as it has been for Indians. For in the early stages of capitalistic industry control and ownership went together and lack of capital was a serious handicap to the establishment of industry. Even to-day, when the principle of joint-stock limited liability has made it possible for the entrepreneur to depend on the outside public for a large portion of his capital requirements, the ownership of a certain amount of capital which could be risked in an enterprise before the latter reaches the stage at which it can be thrown open to public subscription lies at the root of all pioneering enterprise. Industrial development therefore implies two essential factors: (*a*) the combination of initiative and managerial ability with control and ownership of capital, and (*b*) the existence of a body of persons willing to invest.

It was stated in the last chapter that the cotton industry owed its growth to the enterprise and financial strength of the merchants who had made profits from commerce. But even there development was arrested among other causes by the lack of a wide class of investing public and especially by the absence of a well-developed capital and money market. It has been only since the beginning of this century that the cotton industry came to be organized rapidly in other centres than Bombay, but as was pointed out in the last chapter it was the profits of the small class of moneylenders and private bankers that formed the basis of this new development. The second most important centre of the cotton industry in India, i.e. Ahmedabad, owed its rise to the industrial enterprise of the shroffs and other financiers who put up a portion of their capital for the promotion of cotton mills. While the wealth of the trading class gave rise to the cotton industry in Bombay, the profits of finance and private banking were utilized for the development of the industry in Ahmedabad at a rather later date. Thus in each case a certain reserve of capital in the hands of merchants and bankers was the essential preliminary to the development of the industry. On the other hand the rapid growth of the jute, coal-mining, tea, transport, and other industries in Bengal was the result of their easier access to capital which came to be supplied by the European managing agents both directly by themselves and indirectly by their command of capital in the hands of others. But for the financial facilities placed at India's disposal by the British managing agents, these industries would not have developed at all, at least not as rapidly as they have done. But this was not the only way by which British capital flowed into Indian industry. Nearly the whole of the work of opening out communications in India was done with British capital, which entered India on the guarantee of the Indian Government. The Government had, by taking the responsibility of financing railway enterprise and by having recourse to the British capital market, rendered it easier for the cotton and other industries to finance their requirements from within the country. But even so it cannot be denied that the establishment of other industries and the growth of existing industries have been held in check, among other causes, by the lack of regularity in the flow of capital to industries, and until recently by the inadequacy of the amount.[1] The evidence tendered before the Industrial Com-

[1] In India the problem has often been regarded as a question of the total quantity of capital in the country. But from the point of view of industry what matters is only the capital that will become currently available for investment. From that point of view, for a long time to come there will be need for foreign capital. Sir Basil Blackett stated in 1925 that within a short time India would become a creditor country,

mission is very definite on the point. In almost all cases great difficulties were experienced in finding sufficient capital from the public for the requirements of the business.[1]

It has been estimated that in Great Britain the annual savings before the war were of the order of about £400,000,000, equal to 10 per cent of the annual income.[2] In the United States the estimate is also about 10 per cent of the annual income of the country, which is the total saved and invested.[3] No such estimates are available for India, and since even the estimate of national income is still in the region of speculation, it will be dangerous to draw any inference as to the total savings of the country. For our purposes, however, it will be sufficient to indicate the order of

and that in any case she could dispense with foreign capital. But judging from the needs of the country and the sums annually available for industry, it must be stated that it was far too optimistic a view. Indeed, even in regard to existing businesses additional capital has had to be imported. For instance, Messrs. Tata, Sons, & Co. recently concluded an agreement with an American syndicate with a view to getting better financial facilities for all the power companies under their control. The agreement provided that "the firm of Tatas will share with the syndicate the agency of the three companies, viz. Tata Power, Tata Hydro-Electric, and Andhra Valley Power. The American syndicate will have a half share in the agency and has paid Rs. 37.50 lakhs as consideration for it. The agency will be converted into a private limited liability company consisting of 7 directors, 4 to be nominated by the syndicate and 3 by Tatas. Of the 4 to be nominated by the American syndicate, 2 will be American experts and 2 Indians" (*Indian Textile Journal*, August 1929, p. 421). Accordingly, the new agency has been registered in the name of Tata Hydro-Electric Agencies, Ltd., Bombay, who are the managing agents of the above-mentioned three power companies.

[1] *Indian Industrial Commission*, Evidence, Vol. 5, p. 171; Vol. 2, pp. 374, 482; Vol. 3, pp. 13–14. F. Lavington, *The English Capital Market*, 1921, p. 87.

[2] Mr. Keynes's estimate is £500,000,000 for 1929, and about 12–15 per cent of national income. See *A Treatise on Money*, Vol. 2, p. 112. The annual income of corporations, including undivided profits of joint-stock companies in Great Britain and Northern Ireland, the whole of which is practically to be regarded as savings, was estimated to be £205,000,000 by Dr. Bowley (*The National Income*, 1924, p. 47). See also *Committee on Industry and Trade: Factors in Industrial and Commercial Efficiency*, p. 55.

[3] *Recent Economic Changes, U.S.A.*, Vol. II, 1929, p. 625.

importance of the flow of capital annually to industrial, financial, and other enterprises, and to Government and other public securities.

The following statement gives in a summary form the relevant figures relating to growth of savings.

	1913–14 (in Lakhs of Rupees)	1931–2 (in Lakhs of Rupees)	Annual Average
Rupee Loans	14,569 (Mar. 31, 1914)	42,270 (Mar. 31, 1932)	1,923
Postal Cash Certificates (1917–19) (outstanding)	888	4,459	255
Postal Savings Banks' Deposits	2,316	3,822	83
Deposits with:			
1. Imperial Bank (private deposits)	3,648	6,385	152
2. Exchange Banks (Indian deposits)	3,450	6,700	181
3. Other Joint-Stock Banks	2,410	6,607	233
4. Co-operative Banks (1922–3)	843	3,182	260
Paid-up Capital of Joint-Stock Companies ..	7,656	28,633* (1929–30)	1,165

* Figures for 1930–1 and 1931–2 are still not available, but the monthly returns published by the Government of India give the number of companies registered and their authorized capital, but not the paid up capital. In 1930–1, 731 companies with an authorized capital of 2,176 lakhs and in 1931–2, 768 companies with an authorized capital of 2,997 lakhs had been registered.

Net imports of gold coin and bullion.—Total net imports from 1900–1 to 1929–30 = 68,701 lakhs. Annual average = 2,290 lakhs.

Estimate of profits of joint-stock companies carried to reserve.—Profits of companies and of registered firms subject to income-tax for five years from 1927–8 to 1931–2 (both years inclusive) amounted to Rs. 23,224 lakhs. The most usual practice is to take 20 per cent of the net profits to reserve. Thus the annual average will be $\frac{4,645}{5} = 929$ lakhs.

Dr. Jeidels, in estimating the value of the investment market in India, reached a figure of Rs. 700 crores as the total capital invested in Government, municipal, and other local bodies, loans and securities, and in industrial and joint-stock companies, including deposits with banks but excluding the bulk of foreign capital functioning in the country.[1] Although the total figure looks impressive, it cannot be regarded as adequate, considering the needs of industry and agriculture. There is, however, little doubt that there are large volumes of hoarded wealth in gold and silver coins and ornaments the existence of which has been brought to light by the continuous export of gold since the middle of 1931. From September 1931, when England went off the gold standard, to January 1933 the total value of gold exported came to Rs. 110 crores and the stream has not yet dried up (July 1933).[2] It is quite possible that some of it will go back to the hoard when normal conditions are restored and monetary standards have become stabilized. But the gold exports from India have revealed a source of potential capital wealth which might be available to industry.

It should not be forgotten that even when capital and savings increase in the country the tendency has always been for the public to invest them in real property, and part of the savings goes annually to finance the increased value of such forms of property. Merchants and even certain classes of indigenous bankers invest their funds largely in the purchase and mortgage of land and buildings.[3] Further, even those who are inclined to invest their savings profitably prefer to invest in Government securities and in municipal and port trust loans rather than in industrial securities.[4] It is therefore not merely an increase in the volume of savings and capital that is needed, but a well-balanced distribution of the capital resources among the various needs. The function of organized industry is, therefore, to devise suitable methods for the

[1] *Indian Central Banking Committee*, Report, p. 636, and (discussions with foreign experts), Vol. 4, p. 149.

[2] By October 1934 the figures went up to Rs. 200 crores.

[3] *Indian Industrial Commission*, Report, para. 282; also Evidence, Vol. 3, p. 260. *Indian Central Banking Committee*, Report, pp. 432, 433.

[4] Ibid., p. 299.

attraction of capital from the public in the most economical manner, and to check the tendency which draws capital away to hoarding and to non-economic uses.

II

INDUSTRY AND BANKING

How far has industry succeeded in this task? The first thing to note is that widespread banking development in India came later than industrial development and that therefore in many cases industry had to adopt its own methods of financing without reference to the banking structure.[1] When, however, modern banking organization slowly evolved in the country, it in turn developed on lines familiar in England, and without any conscious reference to the needs of industry. Thus in India there has been little intimate relationship or close link between industry and banking, with the result that industry was deprived of the most beneficent influences born of mutual understanding between it and banking. Indeed, in this respect it is possible to trace a similarity between Indian and English banking. When joint-stock banks began to develop in the middle of the nineteenth century in England, they found the financial mechanism already well adapted to the needs of industry, and hence they grew up without any close contact with, or knowledge of, industrial conditions. In both countries, therefore, a lack of understanding between banking and industry has been the result, although in England, owing to the existence of enormous reserves of capital and the growth of various kinds of financial institutions, this defect was long hidden from view. In India the structure of industry was also greatly influenced by the methods of finance which industry had to develop for its growth. The managing agent became the very centre and life of every important industrial concern because he, and not the industry as such, established contact with the banking system.

[1] Several British managing agency firms had their own banking department.

The later and slower banking development of the country had also another influence on industry. Had there been a well-developed banking organization, interest on the capital needed for industry would have been lower. But the high cost which had to be paid for capital in India has not merely retarded the growth of industry but necessarily confined industrial activity to fields of production yielding high profits. That capital and enterprise will seek the most profitable outlets at first is, of course, true of every country; but what is significant in India is that the lack of an efficient banking system threw the whole burden of industrial finance on a limited class of entrepreneurs (managing agents) who were unwilling to pioneer new enterprises unless the chances of high profit were bright. This was at the root of the complaints made by several witnesses before the Industrial Commission that the managing agents were content to proceed on well known and safe lines.[1] The cotton industry, the jute industry of which India has a monopoly, the tea companies, and the coal companies, these were all yielding fairly high dividends. But there was by no means any rapid extension into other fields of industrial activity. In the opinion of several leading business men, 10 to 15 per cent on invested capital was the minimum return required to draw capital into new fields.[2] The natural inference is that India had, and still has, some disadvantage as regards the development of industries, owing to the high cost of capital; for whatever might be the total stock of wealth in the hands of the people, the amount that can be drawn for industrial investment comes in only at high cost. Although compared to countries in similar stages of industrial development, India is not worse off in this respect, the point is that, owing to the need for assuring larger returns to invested capital, the level of protective duties in India becomes somewhat higher than it might have been if capital could be attracted more cheaply. The Indian Tariff Board includes a minimum of 10 per

[1] *Indian Industrial Commission*, Report, para. 280: "The investment of capital has been upon comparatively restricted lines up to the war, and there has been little enterprise in new directions."

[2] *Indian Tariff Board: Paper and Paper Pulp Industries*, Evidence, 1925, Vol. 1, p. 639.

cent on invested capital in the estimated costs of production in the case of every protected industry.

LACK OF A WIDE BASIS OF INVESTMENT

The dominance of the managing agent in the industrial organization of the country is to be explained not only by the deficiencies of the banking system. In part it is due to the lack of a wide basis for raising industrial capital and the extremely narrow range from which capital could be drawn. The managing agents and their friends who had confidence in them supplied all the finance needed for the industry, both current and fixed capital. The Central Banking Committee has made the statement that "investors for this (industrial) class of securities are drawn from a wide circle, including all classes of people, from princes and millionaires to clerks and shopkeepers." But this is really a post-war phenomenon. In the early years of company promotion in India, and for a considerable time later, the capital was mainly found by the agents, directors, and their friends. "The public was always reluctant to subscribe, since people knew that it would take nearly three years before a mill would begin to earn, and by the time the new mill was in a position to work fully the conditions might change and prosperous times might disappear."[1] It is true that in certain years of prosperity and trade boom like 1913, 1916, 1921, and 1925 the public have taken an interest in industry and freely invested under the excitement of prosperous times, as is shown by the accompanying statement giving the number of companies started each year and their paid-up capital.

But the experience of the boom periods when, in the words of the Bombay Stock Exchange Committee, the public were caught up in a wave of speculative fever and when even the city clerks and shopkeepers had a hand in the game, does not warrant a general and sweeping statement of the nature of the capital market in India. Those that speculated then burnt their fingers and became shy. It cannot be maintained that except in cities and big mofussil centres there has been any direct participation of the

[1] *Indian Industrial Commission*, Vol. 4, p. 135.

people in the financing of industries. There are no stock exchanges except in three cities in India, and of these the one in Madras has not been functioning efficiently.

Statement

Up to 1918–19 the figures relate to British India and Mysore State. In 1919–20 companies registered in other Indian States were also included. Returns from Travancore and Hyderabad have been included only since 1920–1 and 1921–2 respectively. (Taken from the reports of the Registrar of Joint-Stock Companies.)

Year	Number of Companies Registered	Paid-up Capital in Lakhs of Rupees	Number of Companies Liquidated	Paid-up Capital of Company Liquidated
1911–12 ..	334	24	—	—
1912–13 ..	287	19	—	—
1913–14 ..	356	76	—	—
1914–15 ..	112	28	—	—
1915–16 ..	131	67	201	166
1916–17 ..	184	100	147	99
1917–18 ..	276	29	118	124
1918–19 ..	290	25	165	149
1919–20 ..	948	158	117	323
1920–21 ..	1,039	315	137	409
1921–22 ..	717	190	220	198
1922–23 ..	496	147	524	825
1923–24 ..	430	67	411	1,416
1924–25 ..	416	86	427	721
1925–26 ..	470	57	374	681
1926–27 ..	529	44	309	587
1927–28 ..	626	86	335	764
1928–29 ..	726	78	229	549
1929–30 ..	839	238*	264	333*
1930–31 ..	734	2,176	292	3,531
1931–32 ..	768	2,997	220	1,513

* Authorised Capital.

In Madras the persons that take up shares are usually permanent investors, and there are hardly any transfers. The exchange is not very active. The Calcutta Stock Exchange, formed in 1908, is still working on primitive and unbusinesslike lines. Apart from jute and coal shares, the market is by no means a free one, and unless actual buying and selling orders have come from outside, it is generally impossible to do business. Only a fraction of the transactions which take place in a day are actually recorded, and the Stock Exchange official quotations list appearing in the daily papers is often misleading to the public. The Exchange contains many members who "are speculators pure and simple, and act solely as intermediaries between other members,"[1] and these people have undoubtedly contributed to a change in the atmosphere of the Stock Exchange, which has become more and more a field for over-speculation and gambling. There are several other defects, such as the system of blank transfers, the absence of any Settlement days, and unless the Association appoints a strong and efficient committee with sufficient authority and courage to insist on carrying out reforms, and to bring about an improvement in methods, Government would have to intervene. It is unfortunate that the Stock Exchange of such an important city as Calcutta should conduct its business on antiquated and inefficient lines. The Bombay Share Bazaar, as the Bombay Stock Exchange is called, is now regulated by Bombay Act VIII of 1925, and has been working on the whole successfully. In spite of its being subject to periodical attacks of frenzied speculation and cornering, it has maintained its reputation as a responsible body and continues to provide good facilities for investment.

But however much these Stock Exchanges might serve to direct the flow of capital to industry by providing a market for the purchase and sale of recognized shares and debentures they cannot touch the large number of small savers except indirectly. It is not to be concluded that more Stock Exchanges should be established in India; for they ought to follow and not precede industrial development. The point is that investment in India is restricted to a small class of investors, mostly in cities, and that the smaller investors in up-country centres have no chance of getting into touch with any reliable members of the Stock Exchange. The same set of individuals hold the bulk of the shares in all the

[1] "The Calcutta Stock Exchange," by W. P. O'Cock, in Pat Lovett's *Mirror of Investment* (1927).

cotton, jute, and other concerns, as a reference to the names of principal shareholders given in the *Mirror of Investment* will show. It will also be noticed from the table at the end of the chapter that the bigger shareholders all come from the major cities like Bombay and Calcutta.[1] Nor are there any recognized methods by which the public can obtain advice and assistance as regards investments in India.[2] Banks are unwilling to advise their clients about suitable investments because they are held morally responsible if the investments turn out to be unprofitable.[3] On the whole, it may be said that the industrial investor is drawn from the bigger towns of India, and although within that limited field may be found some small investors like "the city clerks, the shopkeepers, and the small professional classes," the bulk of the investments come from the rich merchants and the more prosperous professional classes. Even those who have newly tried to experiment with industrial investments have found their confidence shaken by the failure and lack of success of many of the smaller industries and banks. As long as money-lending is a universal profession and absorbs a large portion of the annual savings as it does in India, the chance of industrial investment from small savers is remote. Further, the public outside the business classes generally prefer Government securities because of the greater stability of their returns.[4] Democratization of ownership which

[1] Industrial enterprise (and industrial investment) is too much confined to Bombay and Calcutta (*Indian Industrial Commission*, Evidence, Vol. 4, p. 327; Mr. A. G. Gray of the Bank of India).

[2] *Indian Central Banking Committee*, Report, p. 273.

[3] Ibid., Evidence, Vol. 4, p. 248.

[4] *Indian Central Banking Committee*, Report, pp. 432–4. The Banking Committee has not been quite clear on this question. Its conclusions are contradictory. Although in one place it states that investment is very widespread, it also states that there are only a few classes willing to invest in industry. "The wealth of the landed aristocracy consisting mainly of land contributed little to the capacity of the capital market of the country. Among the other well-to-do classes the salaried classes are on the whole content with a low but assured income from investments and prefer to invest in Post Office savings banks, postal cash certificates, or Government securities. A considerable section of the well-to-do classes also prefers gilt-edged securities. . . . The commercial community generally prefers

in recent years has become a feature of industrial enterprises in Britain and America is yet a long way off in India. The small investor has preferred postal cash certificates, and in recent years rupee securities,[1] and it is not his fault that he does so. Considering the manner in which capital is mismanaged both by industrialists and the banks, it is surprising how optimistic the investor continues to be in India. The large number of failures of joint-stock industrial enterprises and the enormous bank failures of 1913–17 would be enough to shake the confidence of any investor. The statement opposite, together with that on page 143, giving an account of the number of industrial companies' liquidations, will afford some explanation of the "shyness" of industrial capital in India.

Despite the heavy losses which the investors have incurred, they are still willing to invest by fits and starts. The hope of high profits in the protected sugar industry has led to a regular boom in investment, and the Indian investor, even if shy, is ready to speculate. But what is wanted is intelligent and steady invest-

to invest surplus funds in short-term deposits or Treasury bills when these are available. It also subscribes to the share capital and debenture issues of joint-stock concerns. It appears, however, that numbers of merchants, and even certain classes of indigenous bankers, invest their funds largely in the purchase and mortgage of land and building." Land investment is still popular, although at the present time the funds available for such investments are limited. "To the Muhammadan also investment in land appeals the most." Next to land, jewellery is a form of investment common to both rich and poor. It will thus be seen that the habit of investing in industry can only be of slow growth.

Indian Industrial Commission, Vol. 1, p. 1: "Although the concern (Lahore Electric Supply Co.) was a perfectly sound and promising one, and despite the fact that a competent canvasser was employed to place the position and facts before men of substance, it was not supported by the public until it demonstrated its value in balance sheets" (Mr. James Currie).

Ibid., Vol. 4, p. 82, James Blair (Saw Mills Co., Ltd.): "... Bulk of the capital is provided mainly from European sources. Indian capital is not so easily or readily available. Maharajas, landowners, and bankers have more remunerative uses for their capital."

[1] The large number of applications from small investors for sums of less than Rs. 10,000 was a noticeable feature of the 1930–1 rupee loan, and they formed 85 per cent of the total.

ment, and there is a growing view in the industrial world that direct investment by the public is too risky and too complicated an affair, and that it should be taken out of the hands of the smaller capitalists and that investment should be done by Investment Trust Companies and special financial institutes only.

Bank Failures

Year	Number	Authorized Capital in Lakhs of Rupees	Paid-up Capital in Lakhs of Rupees
1913	12	274	35
1914	42	710	109
1915	11	56	5
1916	13	231	4
1917	9	76	25
1918	7	209	1
1919	4	52	4
1920	3	10	7
1921	7	70	1
1922	15	1,015	3
1923	20	2,187	465
1924	18	630	11
1925	17	190	19
1926	14	71	4
1927	16	69	3
1928	13	82	23
1929	11	150	8
1930	12	627	41
1931	18	160	15

An inquiry into the number of shareholders and the average shareholding of ten leading British industrial concerns has revealed the enormous extent to which ownership has become diffused.[1] The number of shareholders in those concerns runs into tens of thousands, and nearly two-thirds of them are holders of less than 200 shares each of the value of £1 per share. Ninety per cent of the total shareholders own fewer than 500 shares each in concerns each having a paid-up capital of over £150,000,000. It should be noted, however, that owing to the tendency of

[1] H. Parkinson, *Scientific Investment*, 1932, p. 44.

the investors to spread their investments wide, the number of small investors may seem to be larger than in reality. One reason for this diffusion of ownership has been the high rate of taxation which has altered the distribution of the supply of capital which now has to be attracted from the small savings of many.[1] Similarly, in the United States the ownership of joint-stock companies has become democratized to a great extent.[2] In India the investors are still a small class. The fact that 42 jute mills are managed by 10 managing agency firms who own a considerable percentage of the shares in the concerns they manage, one of them controlling as many as 10 companies, is significant of the concentration of ownership. We find similarly 75 coal companies managed by 6 managing agents. In individual cases the managing agents own more than 50 per cent of the total shares and debentures.[3] An exact idea of the extent of managing agents' holdings cannot be obtained because the shares are held in various names, sometimes in the name of their wives and children and other relations or in that of friends. But a general picture of the extent to which ownership in industrial securities in India is diffused or concentrated can be had from the annexed tables (at the end of the chapter) which give the percentage of the shares held by a small number of shareholders in some of the cotton, jute, coal, and other miscellaneous concerns. As regards the jute industry, in recent years there has been a great increase in the number of Indian shareholders, and at present it is estimated that 60 per cent of the shares in the industry are owned by Indians. But these are held mostly by the Marwari Community.[4] The other industries controlled by European managing agents, such as tea, coal, inland transport,

[1] Sir J. C. Stamp, *Present Position of Rationalization.*

[2] *Quarterly Journal of Economics*, August 1930.

[3] "There are cases in which 85 to 90 per cent of the shares are held by them. To strike an average is difficult; but it is probably correct to say that 40 per cent of the shares are held by managing agents" (Evidence of the Ahmedabad Millowners' Association before the Cotton Tariff Board (1932), *Indian Textile Journal* (1932), p. 424). The proportion is rather less in Bengal.

[4] *Indian Fiscal Commission*, 1922, Vol. 2, p. 433.

are in the hands mainly of European shareholders. It is in respect of the smaller industries and the small-sized tea and coal companies started by Indians that a comparatively wide diffusion of ownership has taken place. In the case of concerns which yield a stable income, and which are managed by European managing agents, shares are somewhat widely held because they are considered to be safe *investments*; but this occurs only long after the concerns are established and after dividends are declared for a considerable number of years. As has been observed by the Bengal Chamber of Commerce in their evidence before the Indian Industrial Commission,[1] "in Calcutta, the sources from which capital is drawn for enterprise with which the members of this chamber are connected are twofold: *Europeans in India* and *the United Kingdom.*" Indeed, until recently the statement was true that in India "investors are few, nervous, and suspicious; the average rate of interest is much higher than in other industrial countries, and no local capital is available even for local industries, capital being mainly centralized in a few large cities and among a few wealthy classes."[2]

In the cotton industry the shares themselves ranged from Rs. 500 to Rs. 1,000.[3] Only recently has there been a tendency to split them up into shares of lower denominations. In Bengal industrial shares are also dealt with in lots of 100 in the case of Rs. 10 shares, and of 25 in the case of higher denominations. The investor of modest means has no chance of buying them. The methods of financing the industry were thus influenced greatly by the absence of an organized capital and money market, and they in turn affected the structure of industrial organization. Much of the capital was, to start with, entrepreneur's capital, and even if the concern was converted into a public limited liability company its real structure was for a long time that of a

[1] *Indian Fiscal Commission*, 1922, Vol. 2, p. 929.

[2] *Indian Industrial Commission*, Evidence, Vol. 4, p. 3 (C. N. Wadia).

[3] Out of 48 mills quoted on the Bombay Stock Exchange, only 4 had shares of less than Rs. 500. Eleven had shares of the value of Rs. 500, 5 between 500 and 1,000, and 28 had shares of the value of Rs. 1,000 and above.

private concern. Even in England until the war the majority of the established English firms were one man or family enterprises. Working capital was seldom provided by paid-up shares, but rather by loans of capitalists connected with the industry in question. In the textile industry particularly the system grew up by which a large portion of the capital was raised in the form of deposits from employees and others who took up shares, but paid up only a portion of the share value, and for the unpaid reserve-liability were willing to deposit with the mills. These were all efforts on the part of industry to meet the emergencies of a situation when the capital market was not well developed and when banks were unwilling to contribute to the provision of any kind of permanent capital.

III

RESULT: UNDER-CAPITALIZATION

Somewhat similar circumstances have led to equally interesting methods of industrial finance in India. Since the burden of financing was thrown mainly on the entrepreneurs (Managing Agents), their resources even when combined with those of their friends who subscribed to the capital of the company were insufficient for the needs of the concern. Even in Bombay city where the capital resources were ampler, and the number interested in industrial concerns larger, the cotton industry was established with initial paid-up capital not always sufficient to pay for the block, and totally inadequate for the working capital required.[1] In most cases, therefore, the concerns were under-capitalized. In Ahmedabad, where the system so characteristic of Indian methods of raising capital has been developed, under-capitalization at the start is invariably the rule.

The terms under-capitalization and over-capitalization are used in such different senses that it is necessary to explain the sense in which they are used here. A firm may be said to be

[1] Evidence given by the Bombay Millowners' Association. Vol. 2, *Indian Central Banking Enquiry Committee.*

under-capitalized when the total capital invested in, and available for, the enterprise is inadequate to its total needs, or when the permanent needs of a concern are sought to be met by the fluctuating supply of funds either from the public or from banks. Over-capitalization as the converse of under-capitalization means that there is a redundance of real capital invested in the concern in such a wise that part of it might have been better and more profitably employed elsewhere. In other words, the concern has grown beyond the "optimum" size. While over-capitalization in this sense does occur occasionally, it is not of great significance compared to its use in other senses. Where the total value of the capital is in excess of the surplus assets of a concern, including the value of goodwill, or where the profits of the concern over a period of years are too low in proportion to the amount of nominal capital waiting to earn dividend, we have over-capitalization. This may be brought about either by inflating capital during a period of hectic boom and temporary prosperity by the issuing of bonus shares or may be the result of a changed set of conditions. When at a time of high prices and good demand extension and expansion take place, and machinery and plant bought at high prices, and it is found that the demand falls off and prices go down, the value of the capital therein ceases to have proper relation to the value of the assets of the concern. During the post-war years India was witness to both kinds of over-capitalization, brought about partly by the addition of large bonus shares and by a revaluation of the shares on a new basis, and also by an expansion of investment at very high prices. There are grave dangers of over-capitalization which will be examined in a later chapter, and the solutions to meet cases of over-capitalization must have regard to the particular aspect in which it has presented itself.

But the defects of under-capitalization are more quickly revealed, and the concern which starts with an initial lack of capital is definitely placing itself under a severe handicap. Most of the concerns which have failed to survive for a year in India are those which had a shortage of capital. Under-capitalization is the result of financial weakness, while over-capitalization is the result of an apparent or superficial financial prosperity. While the latter is almost always the concomitant of an industrial boom, the former occurs during the period when industry is not on the upward trend and unable to raise enough capital. One important cause of under-capitalization is the failure of the entrepreneur to estimate accurately the capital needs of a business concern, combined with an insufficient realization of his responsibility in providing himself with adequate current finance.[1]

Although among the major industries under-capitalization is not so common, it must be noted that in the system of industrial finance developed in Ahmedabad there always lurked the dangers of under-capitalization. Even in Bombay the disastrous system of floating cotton mills with a subscribed and paid-up capital of only 10 to 12 lakhs, but with an initial debt of 6 or 7 lakhs, was often adverted to in the *Indian Textile Journal* as a source of weakness. Before the war when a cotton mill was started on a small scale in Ahmedabad, while the capital requirements amounted to about Rs. 12 to 15 lakhs, including the provision of working funds, the capital actually raised was only Rs. 5 lakhs at the start. The balance of the capital needed for block and the whole of the current finance required were obtained from the public in the shape of six monthly or yearly deposits, the public lending the money on the credit and respectability of the owner concerned. The mills in Bombay, too, were originally started on similar lines, though the total capital raised was larger. If such concerns did not go under, as normally they would have done, it was due to two circumstances. In the first place the entrepreneurs were men of substance and had financial resources of their own, and they were trusted by the public. But it was also due to the fact that as soon as the danger-point was passed, and the concern became more and more successful, the supplying of capital became less and less difficult. This becomes clear when the methods of financing a concern after the war are studied. "Out of 20 lakhs required to finance the block capital, 5 lakhs is raised as share capital, and the balance is found in the form of seven-year deposits for 5 lakhs, and the

[1] *Capital*, June 21, 1934, p. 1079.

remaining 10 lakhs is found partly by managing agents and partly by the public in the form of one-year deposits."[1] Thus the success of the older concerns paved the way for the development of long-term deposits; but even so the deposits are likely to be withdrawn as they have been in Bombay and to a less extent in Ahmedabad. Had the mills been faced with an early crisis, the under-capitalization of many of them would have been an effective check to their growth. But, luckily for them, they were on a wave of prosperity, and the reserves they were able to accumulate were now available for the industry and were inter-deposited.

DEFECTS OF UNDER-CAPITALIZATION

But the defects and dangers of under-capitalization are revealed in the case of the smaller enterprises of the major industries, and the smaller or medium-sized businesses generally. The Indian section of the tea industry has always been under-capitalized. "A tea estate requires about 15 lakhs of capital, but is unable to raise more than 10 lakhs whether owned-capital or from the public, and for the rest has to borrow at high rates of interest."[2] Sufficient capital is not raised at the outset to enable the estates to tide over the period during which adequate returns could not be got. Some of the Indian tea companies secure an admission fee of Rs. 20 or 25 per share. No interest is paid on that; but it is refunded to the shareholders from the profits before any dividend is declared. For non-recurring purposes loans are obtained from loan offices, Marwari bankers, and moneylenders on the personal guarantee of the proprietors or Directors or on the mortgage of the gardens. The rate of interest is 9 to 12 per cent from loan offices, and 12 to 21 per cent from Marwari bankers.[3] Again, the fundamental fact about the Indian section of the coal trade of Bengal and Bihar and Orissa is that most of the enterprises are either proprietary or partnership concerns, and even when some of them are registered under the Indian Companies Act the capital

[1] *Indian Central Banking Enquiry Committee*, Vol. 4, p. 161.
[2] Ibid., Vol. 3, p. 675.
[3] *Report of the Bengal Banking Committee*, 1930, Vol. 1, p. 120.

is not open to the public. The capital required for them initially is found by the owners, but not even the full demand for block capital which is continuously increasing (unlike the case of other industries) is met.[1] Expensive borrowing is resorted to, and the heavy interest payments act as a deterrent to growth.[2] In a few years the concerns close down. Similar misfortune has overtaken most of the newer industries like match factories, soap works, etc. "They usually begin as private enterprises; the private financier begins by supplying a portion of the funds; then the amount of money is exhausted and the concern wants some more funds before it reaches the stage of production."[3] Unable to secure them, it winds up. Examples like this can be multiplied. In every case it will be found either that the necessary minimum amount of capital required for the block and current expenditure is not raised[4] or that a proper balance between the two is not maintained.

IV

THEORY OF FINANCING. WORKING NEEDS

Part of the under-capitalization is undoubtedly the result of the difficulties involved in the securing of capital and of the initial miscalculations as to cost of buildings and plant, and as to the amount of working capital needed;[5] but a no less important reason is to be discovered in the theory of the industrialists that the working capital of a business concern is to be met entirely from bank credits. It is necessary to examine this view critically, not merely because of its theoretical importance, but also because of its practical bearing. Had a different view prevailed it is certain that although fewer industrial concerns would have been started at first, they would have succeeded to a greater extent, and their success would have enabled more enterprises to be started, and more capital to be drawn. But the view has long been held by

[1] *Indian Central Banking Enquiry Committee*, Vol. 2, p. 504.

[2] Ibid., Vol. 2, p. 504.

[3] Ibid., Vol. 3, p. 870.

[4] Report of the Registrar of Joint-Stock Companies in Bengal, quoted on p. 43, Vol. 2, *Indian Industrial Commission*.

[5] *Indian Industrial Commission*, Report, para. 286.

industrialists, right from the beginning up to the most recent times when the Central Banking Committee reported, that industry had a claim for the supply of bank credit on the basis of the security of block, or in other words on building, brick and mortar, and plant.[1] Complaint has been made before every important committee or commission of inquiry that the banks were unwilling to lend on the security of plant and buildings, and that working capital, too, had to be raised by industry[2] itself. Their view was that it would be sufficient for industry to raise capital adequate for block expenditure, and that for the rest industry must be in a position to get bank credit for current finance. The stage at which banks ought to undertake industrial financing was in their opinion almost immediately after the buildings and plant had been set up. Even the managing agents who may be expected to possess an intimate knowledge of the working of the banking system, and who did not actually depend upon bank credit, have joined in the complaint. There are still others who have held that banks must also provide finance for fixed capital expenditure and extensions on the security of machinery and plant. If the existing banks would not undertake this function, then a special bank should be created with a network of branches to supply industrial credit for fixed expenditure. As has been pointed out by Mr. K. M. Macdonald, Managing Governor of the Imperial Bank of India,[3] "In the numerous little industries that have been started in India, there has been much too great a tendency to borrow money from the outside public instead of the promoters putting up their own capital, and the idea as far as I can make out is held that investment trusts should be formed in order to supply these embryo industries with the capital which should be provided by the promoters."

These views have held the field for a long time, and the idea that no bank, whatever its financial strength, can permanently provide for the fixed expenditure of industry without sterilizing its own

[1] *Indian Industrial Commission*, 1916–18, Vol. 3, pp. 40, 52, 91.
[2] Ibid.
[3] *Indian Central Banking Enquiry Committee*, Vol. 3, p. 917.

activities in the future had to be continuously pressed on the Banking Committee before the latter grudgingly accepted it.

The question then arises, to what extent should industry find its own finance for its fixed and working capital? And what is the role of the banking system in the financing of industry?

BANKING NEEDS OF INDUSTRY

Every business concern requires capital for "block" expenditure, for current working expenses, and for extension and improvement. The starting and equipment of a factory involves considerable initial outlay, which is more or less permanently fixed on it, and cannot be got back at will. This fixed capital is represented by buildings, works, plant, and machinery, and other goods of a more or less durable character. Working capital is required "for the purchase and working of raw materials into finished products, for financing outstandings in respect of goods supplied, and for providing the necessary funds for meeting day-to-day requirements."[1] The need for working capital arises from the fact that an interval of time occurs between expenditure on production and realization from sale and that during this period the manufacturer has to carry a considerable amount of capital outlay. The relative proportion between block and working capital required in an industry varies with the nature of the industry. In small industries and in handicrafts the proportion of fixed capital is small because the implements are inexpensive and few. But in large-scale enterprises employing large and expensive machinery the proportion is very much larger. But it must be noted that in such cases, although the proportion of fixed to working capital may be great, the actual volume of working capital required in the industry may be very considerable. In an industry like the hydro-electric industry, however, the value of the fixed assets bears a very high proportion of the total capital needs of the industry. The amount of working capital needed in each industry will depend mainly upon the value of the output and the average length of time occupied by the productive process. "If

[1] *Indian Central Banking Enquiry Committee*, Report, p. 267.

the productive process lasts six months on the average, and if the product grows in value at a steady rate so that its average value during the six months is half its final value, then it follows that the working capital required is equal to three months' output."[1] It will be clear, therefore, that the amount of working capital required will vary enormously between different products corresponding to variations in the length of process—from next to nothing in the case of personal services up to the equivalent of a year's output or more in certain cases. Some idea of the order of magnitude of the amount of working capital required in a moderately sized unit in each industry may be had from the evidence tendered by the applicants for protection in India before the Indian Tariff Board. It has been calculated that the working capital needed in the steel industry in India is equal to about the cost of six months' productive output, and this, representing provision for raw materials, outstandings, and stocks of finished goods normally held by the Tata Steel Company, was estimated at Rs. 3½ crores in 1924.[2] In 1927 the works cost of production had fallen, and a sum of Rs. 2.2 crores was held to be sufficient. In the steel works, therefore, both the fixed and working capital required is very large.

The amount of working capital required in any individual industry not merely depends upon the length of the process of production and the cost of output, but also upon the time at which the manufacturer gets paid and the methods of buying raw material and effecting sales. This is illustrated in the textile industry by the differences in the practice between Bombay and Ahmedabad or Nagpur, in regard to the buying of raw cotton. In Nagpur the amount of working capital needed in a cotton mill is greater owing to the need to supply itself with cotton for nearly the whole of the year's requirements at the cotton season,[3] whereas in Bombay the purchase of cotton is spread out through

[1] J. M. Keynes, *A Treatise on Money*, Vol. 2, p. 103.

[2] *Statutory Enquiry, 1926: Steel Industry*, Report, p. 36, and Vol. 2, p. 310.

[3] *Indian Textile Journal*, September 1912, p. 433 (Speech of Ratan Tata).

the whole year. Again, when an industry integrates the business of selling, instead of selling through the merchants, some part of the capital which formerly was supplied by the merchants has now got to be provided by the manufacturer himself. Thus the tendency of some of the cotton companies in India to sell directly by means of their own shops in the market centres[1] adds to the volume of working capital needed. Of course, this does not increase the total volume of working capital required by the country as a whole. It only adds to the needs of the manufacturing firm and correspondingly diminishes the needs of others engaged in merchanting.

In the cotton industry the amount of working capital needed is often in excess of the fixed capital expenditure, owing to the cost of raw cotton and stores, and the time during which the raw material and the finished product have to be held. Thus for a big cotton mill with 100,000 spindles and 2,000 looms like the Central India Spinning, Weaving, & Manufacturing Co., Ltd., with a paid-up capital of Rs. 97 lakhs, nearly the whole of the paid-up capital represents fixed capital outlay, while about 150 lakhs is needed annually by way of working capital.[2] In other industries, too, large sums have to be employed for meeting current expenses. The economic unit of production in the paper industry with four machines and an annual output of about 10,000 tons was estimated to require an outlay of about Rs. 80 lakhs in block at 1930 prices. Its working expenses would come to about 16 lakhs or more corresponding to the cost of about 6 months' output.[3] The capital equipment of an average cement works in India with an annual capacity of 60,000 tons was estimated to cost about 48 lakhs and its working capital at Rs. 9 to 10 lakhs.[4] In respect of the sugar industry in India, the Tariff Board estimated the fixed capital and working capital requirements at Rs. 13½ lakhs and Rs. 3 lakhs respectively for a moderately sized factory

[1] *Indian Textile Journal*, September 1912, p. 433 (Speech of Ratan Tata).

[2] Ibid.

[3] *Indian Tariff Board: Paper and Paper Pulp Industries*, Report, 1931, p. 89.

[4] *Indian Tariff Board: Cement Industry*, Report, 1925, p. 24.

producing about 117,000 maunds of sugar per annum. The amount of working capital required was in this case found to be the equivalent of three months' output.[1] On the other hand, four months' output was considered to be a fair basis for estimating the working capital needs of a match factory, and out of a total capital of 30 lakhs, 23 lakhs would be for block and 7 lakhs for working expenses.[2]

NOTE.—Mr. Keynes, in making a rough estimate of the total amount of working capital employed in Great Britain, has (like the Tariff Board in India) taken six months as the period required to finance the net output of industry and agriculture plus imports, and arrived at a figure of about £1,650,000,000.[3] Dr. Jeidels's estimate of working capital for German industry is rather lower, being about one-quarter of the annual turnover.[4]

"A jute mill company's requirements of working capital are usually mostly for raw material, which is seasonal, and the buying is therefore much heavier at certain seasons of the year than at other times. In the case of an average jute mill in Bengal, and as a rough guess, I should say that the working capital of a mill need not be more than *half* the fixed capital investment, and indeed might well be less if in the hands of a strong managing agency house able and willing to lend money to the mill. This would enable the mill to carry a substantial part of its raw material stock with its own working capital, and if its business was in a sound state it would have little difficulty in borrowing from banks anything in excess of this against the security of raw material."[5] Of course, whosoever supplies the working capital, whether it be the managing agents, or the company itself or banks, the requirements of working capital in a jute concern are about 50 per cent of the value of the fixed capital investment.

The characteristic feature of the tea industry is the long interval

[1] *Indian Tariff Board: Sugar Industry*, Report, 1931, p. 67.

[2] *Indian Tariff Board: Match Industry*, Report, 1928, p. 33.

[3] J. M. Keynes, *A Treatise on Money*, Vol. 2, p. 106.

[4] Discussion with experts. *Indian Central Banking Enquiry Committee*, Vol. 4, p. 181.

[5] Letter from Sir T. Catto to the writer.

between the opening up of the tea garden and the yield of tea. Large permanent capital is therefore required, not only for acquiring lands, laying out gardens, purchase of machinery, construction of buildings, etc., but for enabling the garden to be worked for the four or five years until actual production is realized. Assuming that a minimum size of 500 acres is required to ensure economical production, an initial capital of about 7 to 8 lakhs of rupees is said to be necessary.[1] After the stage of production is reached, the amount of working capital needed is not very much, as banks are willing to lend on the security of the output. But capital will be required for development and improvements. Like the tea industry, the coal-mining industry also requires a continuous supply of permanent capital for some years. Although the capital required initially is usually provided, the demand for block capital, unlike that in other industries, is a recurring one. Much capital has to be sunk, even after the colliery has been brought into working order.[2]

WORKING CAPITAL

It will thus be seen that for most of the industries with which we are concerned, the volume of working capital required bears a very considerable proportion to their total requirements.

Now in capitalizing a concern and framing a financial plan with a view to starting it on a secure foundation, how much of the estimated working capital of the concern should be raised by shares or debentures, and how much of it might the ordinary commercial banks be expected to provide? The answer is that a certain portion of working capital, although used for current expenditure, is in reality of the nature of permanent capital.[3] The stock of raw materials, manufactured and semi-manufactured commodities, never falls below a certain minimum, and the capital required for holding them is of the nature of permanent capital. Even if banks are willing to grant the so-called "revolving" credits,

[1] *Bengal Banking Committee*, Report, 1930, Vol. 1, p. 120.
[2] *Indian Central Banking Enquiry Committee*, Vol. 2, p. 504.
[3] K. Kock, *A Study of Interest Rates*, 1929, p. 9.

a manufacturer is taking a grave risk if he uses them for the permanent minimum working expenses.[1] Only that amount of working capital over and above this minimum falls under the category of short-term finance. The mistake of most of the entrepreneurs in India lay in thinking that the whole of the working capital was in the nature of a fluctuating demand for credit, varying with the demand for the products of industry. Dr. Jeidels, a leading authority in the practice of continental banking, has stated the position in unambiguous language thus: "It has to be made clear that it is not sufficient in itself that an industrial firm should put up its block from its own capital and that having done so the firm can appeal to the banks for loans and assistance. Not only block but also normal working capital has to be furnished out of the firm's own initial capital, and before the firm is fit for industrial banking or industrial finance it must have been in operation for a sufficient period to prove that it is strong enough. It cannot be sufficiently emphasized that these two conditions are essential, and to attempt a different way of financing is not only unwarranted for the bank, but also unsound and dangerous for the industrial enterprise."[2] These are rather strong words coming from a banker of a country where it has been usually supposed that the banks were the promoters, financiers, and controllers of industry. But lack of familiarity with the true working of the German banking system has been partly responsible for the insistence of Indian entrepreneurs upon a more active policy of banking assistance to industry. That the Indian Central Banking Committee was not willing to accept the above view is further evidence of the extent to which the contrary opinion has been held in India. The Committee holds the view that industrial concerns "may reasonably expect to have the *whole* of their working capital supplied by commercial banks,"[3] if adequate security is offered.

Not that there were not persons who took the more conservative

[1] Von Beckerath, *Industrial Organization*, 1933, p. 62.

[2] Discussion with experts. *Indian Central Banking Enquiry Committee*, Vol. 4, p. 146.

[3] *Indian Central Banking Enquiry Committee*, Report, p. 299.

view. Nearly all the British Chambers of Commerce, the European witnesses who gave evidence before the Industrial Commission, 1916–18, and before the Indian Central Banking Committee, 1929–31, the Exchange Banks' Association, and the representatives of the Imperial Bank were all of the view that it was the function of industry to provide itself with the whole of the capital for block and normal working capital.[1] Mr. Ratan Tata recognized the need for financing the minimum current requirements of industry by the issue of debenture or preference capital as early as 1912. In his speech at an extraordinary meeting of the shareholders of the Central India Spinning, Weaving, & Manufacturing Co., Ltd., he said that "the working capital required was a minimum of 60 lakhs and a maximum of Rs. 106 lakhs over and above the company's reserve funds. This enormous capital was raised by deposits and by loans and advances from bankers under the personal guarantee of the agents or by mortgaging the company's goods. This created not only constant dependence upon the fluctuations of the money market, but involved the personal liability of the agents to an enormous extent. In good times there would be no difficulty in raising the maximum of a crore of rupees required for the purpose of the mill, but what your Directors have for a long time felt is that a provision should be made to place the *minimum* requirement of our working capital upon a permanent basis and independent of the fluctuations of the money market. They therefore came to the conclusion that a debenture loan at 5 per cent, or preference shares at 5½ per cent, will be suitable."[2] But such a view was exceptional, the average Indian industrialist always holding the view that working capital may be got by way of deposits or bank credit. But the difference between the European view and the prevailing Indian criticism of the banks was partly a difference in conception, but partly also the result of the former's

[1] *Indian Central Banking Enquiry Committee*, Report, Vols. 2 and 3 (Evidence of the Exchange Banks, the Managing Governor of the Imperial Bank of India, the Bengal Chamber of Commerce).

[2] *Indian Textile Journal*, September 1912.

better access to bank credit.[1] The closer contact with the British merchants and the greater knowledge of their credit-worthiness had enabled banks to supply them with financial facilities to the fullest possible extent, within the existing framework of the banking machinery. Their experiences being different, the British industrialists found no great fault in the working of the Indian banking system.

But whatever the explanation, the failure on the part of the medium-sized industrial units to recognize their responsibility in the matter of providing themselves with sufficient funds has had adverse effects on their prosperity. Instead of concentrating attention on the best and most effective means of raising capital from investors of different types whose motives range all the way from absolute security to speculative gains, the entrepreneur had been content to raise by way of his own or paid-up capital just enough for block expenditure and to depend for the balance of his requirements either upon deposits from the public or on loans from moneylenders, Shroffs, and banks. Nor were attempts made to start special types of financial institutions for the purpose of granting mortgage credit or taking up the debentures of industrial concerns, a need which has come to be more and more keenly felt. All this has had the incidental result of perpetuating the system of managing agency control. Had the share and permanent capital raised at the start been sufficient to cover the needs

[1] Some idea of the easier access to bank credit enjoyed by European managing agents may be formed from the fact that on the directorate of the old Bank of Bengal the nominees of some of the managing agents had been continuously represented. The following was quoted from *Capital*, Calcutta: "The Directorate of the Bank of Bengal has always been a close borough, confined to certain managing agency firms, some 16 in number. Some of them have had members of their firms as directors during the past 50 years at least. Even if a director went on leave, another partner got into his place." Again, "Shares were held by the firm (and not by the persons in their individual capacity) so that as soon as one partner left or went on leave, the shares were transferred to another member of the firm" (Quoted in the Legislative Assembly Debates, September 11, 1933). Messrs. Jardine, Skinner & Co., Messrs. George Henderson & Co., Gillanders, Arbuthnot & Co., Begg, Dunlop & Co., Turner, Morrison & Co. have had seats on the bank's Board continuously.

of working expenses, there would not have been the same need for the continuance of an institution like the managing agent to finance industrial concerns. As it happened, however, companies managed by weak managing agents soon closed down, and those managed by strong agents found themselves in their grips.

Although in regard to the jute, tea, coal, and light-railway companies controlled by the European managing agents, and the cotton industry of Bombay and other centres, it has not been difficult to find the necessary capital from the public, much difficulty has been experienced in raising capital for new enterprises involving heavy outlay, and of a somewhat risky nature. There are many even in India who contend that a good proposition would always command enough capital,[1] but this is not true probably of any country in the world, least of all of India where the public are conservative in their investments and unwilling to take risks in pioneer and unknown ventures. It is true that in industries like cotton, jute, tea, and others where the investor was assured of success or in a protected industry like sugar there has been no check to the flow of funds. Indeed, the over-investment in some industries, e.g. in rice milling, oil crushing, and in the more recently protected industries like sugar and matches, is evidence of the willingness of the public to invest in what they regard as successful and promising concerns. But there is no doubt that for businesses outside the usual lines there has always been a gap between the demand for and supply of capital, and this is partly due to the doubt in the mind of the investor about the value and character of the proposition placed before him. Even the reputation of a managing agency firm has not been quite sufficient to attract sufficient capital in all cases. It was not without considerable difficulty that capital was raised for the great steel works in India, and for the hydro-electric power companies floated by Messrs. Tata, Sons, & Co., Ltd. In all these instances, the Tata Iron & Steel Co., Ltd., the Hydro-

[1] *Indian Central Banking Enquiry Committee*, Vol. 3 (Evidence of the Bengal Chamber of Commerce).

Electric Co., the Tata Power Co., the excellence and thoroughness of planning and investigation could not be doubted. The explanation of the difficulties in securing capital is less a general deficiency of the Indian capital available for such purposes than a legitimate feeling of caution on the part of the investors due to the frequent losses to which they have been subjected. But the absence of financial institutions or agencies to underwrite industrial securities and shares, or otherwise assist the company in the floating of shares and debentures, is undoubtedly a gap in the financial and banking organization of the country and an obstacle to industrial advance. The investing public have also no institution or body of persons to guide them in their investments.

Before examining some of these deficiencies in greater detail,[1] it is necessary to explain and criticize the actual methods adopted by organized industry in India to raise capital for its needs.

V

SHARES AND DEBENTURES

Although Indian industry illustrates within itself all methods of raising capital known to the industrial world, by means of ordinary shares, preference shares and debentures, there are some distinguishing characteristics both in the proportion in which the different classes of capital are secured and the manner of securing them. It is a well-recognized fact that industries should not be content merely with raising capital by means of shares. Not only would the adoption of a single method lead to poor results and serve to raise but little capital, but it would also not meet the needs of different types of investors.[2] Both from the point of view of the industrial concerns and of the investors, different devices must be adopted. By attracting different classes of investors and by raising part of the capital at fixed and lower rates of interest, capital will be raised not only in larger amounts but with greater economy. The provision of money can be had

[1] See Chapter VII.

[2] E. S. Mead, *Corporation Finance*, Sixth Edition, pp. 105–6.

on easier terms. The investors willing to take some risk will be in a position to realize larger returns than would have been possible if all the capital were in one form.[1]

The capital that is raised by shares is of course very different from that raised by debentures. Although expressed in money it represents in fact the acquisition of a fraction of ownership in the undertaking which entitles the subscriber only to a given proportion of such profits as may be earned whilst the company is a going concern, and of its "surplus assets" when it is dissolved. That is the reason why in America shares having no par value are issued. On the other hand, capital provided by debenture-holders, depositors, banks, and other financial institutions is money borrowed and repayable as such by the undertaking; and the lenders of such capital are entitled only to receive the stipulated interest. The shareholders are proprietors whilst the debenture-holders and others who have contributed to the financing of the company are creditors with rights of varying degree.

PREFERENCE SHARES

Among the proprietors or owners of the concern there are to be found two classes, the preferred shareholder, who is entitled to a fixed preferential dividend *after* the claims of the creditors are met and before the ordinary shareholder gets any dividend. This preference may be only in respect of each year's dividend or may be cumulative, i.e. the arrears of dividend due in any year may be carried forward to other years. Several types of preference shares are issued by industrial companies in India with varying rights, but the most common type is the cumulative preference with preferential rights as to repayment of capital, but with no further right to participate in surplus assets. Although the cotton, coal, and tea companies have all raised some capital by way of preference shares, it is the jute industry which has raised a large percentage of its share capital in the form of preference shares. Out of a total of 52 jute mills given in the *Investor's India Year Book* (1932–3) as many as 48 have issued preference shares, and the

[1] E. S. Mead, *Corporation Finance*, Sixth Edition, pp. 105–6.

amount raised in this way forms about 42 per cent of the capital of all the 52 mills. All excepting two, which have only cumulative rights to dividend, are cumulative preference shares with a preferential claim to the repayment of capital. The preference shares of the jute mills are very popular and regarded as an extremely sound investment. Preference shares have equal voting rights,[1] and although the managing agents may just as well retain preferential shares as ordinary shares, a jute mill in which the managing agents are known to have ordinary shares will find its preferential shares more popular with the investing public because of the knowledge that in order to get a dividend for themselves the managing agents will have to provide a dividend for the preference holders.

Out of 67 cotton mills given in the *Investor's Year Book* (1932–3), 21 have issued preference shares, but the bulk of the mills which have issued them are outside Bombay city. The Bombay cotton mills, excepting 7, have only ordinary share capital. While about 42 per cent of the total paid-up capital in the jute industry is supplied by preference shareholders, in the cotton industry the preference capital is only about 15 per cent of the total paid-up capital. The bulk of the preference shares enjoy both cumulative rights to dividend and preferential rights to repayment of capital. In a few cases it is provided that the preference shares will have a right to cumulative dividend of, say, 5 or 6 per cent, and to a non-cumulative dividend of 2 or 3 per cent in addition. In regard to coal companies, only 9 companies out of a total of 70 given in the list have preference shares. In some cases, provision exists for converting the preferred shares into ordinary shares on certain terms. In the smaller railway companies promoted by private enterprise, though with a Government guarantee,

[1] Preference shareholders have in most cases the same voting rights as ordinary shareholders, but there are instances in some industries where their powers of voting are restricted. Sometimes they have no power of voting on general matters except when their interests as preference shareholders are distinctly affected. (Evidence by Applicants for Protection, *Indian Tariff Board: Paper and Paper Pulp Industries*, 1931, Vol. 1, p. 162.)

preference shares are not common; for the guarantee of a certain minimum interest by Government makes all the shares virtually preferential.

In respect of the iron and steel companies, the Tata Iron & Steel Co., Ltd., has raised over 70 per cent of its share capital by way of cumulative preference, which, in the opinion of many, is an excessive proportion. The wisdom of raising such a large percentage of share capital in the form of preference shares is questionable, as it interferes with the safe and prudent financial management of the concern on the one hand, and, on the other, reduces the security to the preference shareholder himself. The security of the preference shareholder lies in the certainty that however poor the profits in any year might be they would be sufficient to pay him the dividend. Where 70 per cent of the capital is raised in this form, however, the fall in earnings is sure to affect his dividend, and in practice the cumulative right does not amount to much. Over a period of continuously diminishing profits it is impossible for the preference shareholder to insist upon his claim. In all such cases reorganization has to be effected, arrears of dividend have to be written off, and fresh rights of a diminished nature conferred on the preference shareholder.[1] From the point of view of the company, too, the fact that the ordinary shareholder gets no dividend at all for years, lowers the prestige of the company and reduces its credit. It finds itself unable to attract fresh capital, and even to raise loans from banks or from the public. It is therefore of the utmost importance that a proper proportion should be maintained between the amount raised by ordinary

[1] But such reorganization is beset with difficulties. Thus when the Tata Iron & Steel Co. desired to secure a reorganization of capital with a view to reducing the burden of the higher interest payments to first and second preference shareholders, they could not secure the necessary majority required under the Articles of Association and experienced great difficulty in finally achieving their object (*Statutory Enquiry*, 1926, *Tariff Board: Steel Industry*, Vol. 2, p. 340).

The Government of India also wrote that "an arrangement of capital whereby 74 per cent of capital consists of cumulative preference shares, 90 per cent of which bearing the high rate of 7½ per cent cannot be regarded as satisfactory" (Ibid., p. 336).

shares and that raised by preference. The 21 per cent of the total capital which is in the form of preference shares in the Bengal Iron & Steel Co. seems to be a more reasonable proportion. The proportion, however, need not be a rigid one, and must necessarily vary with each industry and even in respect of individual concerns within an industry.

Although preference shares are issued with a view to attracting the cautious investor who wants a certain minimum dividend guaranteed to him, it is often true that they are neither as safe as the debenture (where the security is greater) nor so profitable as the ordinary shares (where there are chances of great though uncertain gain).[1] Where, however, as in the case of the jute industry, or steamer or light-railway companies, the certainty of some earnings is almost assured, or where the percentage of preference shares to the total is only small, about one-quarter, preference shares become attractive. Their popularity will increase if industry in India offers the further incentive of letting the preference shares participate in the further profits of the concern after they and the ordinary shares have received an equal dividend. Although one or two such instances exist, this arrangement is not common and needs to be extended. Again, Indian industry might usefully adopt the device so common in the United States of issuing preferred shares which may be converted into bonds with fixed interest.[2] In these and several other ways greater variety and more attraction should be offered to the investor.

ORDINARY SHARES AND DEFERRED SHARES

Where deferred shares are issued the ordinary become preferred, but this arrangement is not quite common in respect of

[1] "Too often the rights of preferential capital are violated, with the result that preference capital has come to be regarded with increasing suspicion by a growing body of investors who have learnt from experience that if a company does well they get no more than their fixed dividend, while if it does badly their capital may be raided" (*Financial Times*, December 10, 1925).

[2] Von Beckerath, *Industrial Organization*, 1933, p. 149.

the major industries in India. There are instances, however, where deferred shares are issued in addition to the ordinary and preference shares. In such cases the arrangement often is that after the ordinary shares receive a certain minimum dividend, the deferred shares also get an equal and sometimes a higher rate of dividend, and surplus profits remaining thereafter are divided into two equal *amounts*: one half distributed among the large number of ordinary shares and the other half given away to the deferred shares, which, being few in number, receive a very large percentage dividend. The importance of this arrangement is not very great as there are not more than about a dozen instances over the whole range of Indian industry where deferred shares are issued. Some of the instances are the Katni Cement & Industrial Co., the Titaghur Paper Mills, and Tata Iron & Steel Co. In the jute and cotton industries the system of issuing deferred shares or founders' shares does not exist. In some instances deferred shares have only limited rights, and may only vote on matters relating to the distribution of the company's profits.[1]

DEBENTURES

The raising of some part of the permanent capital required for an industry by debentures is a very desirable step as it ensures economy, but not all industries admit of the floating of debentures. When a concern possesses real estate and property it can issue debentures easily; but even so, if its earnings are likely to fluctuate greatly from year to year it cannot afford to raise much capital by way of debentures or bonds. Jute concerns, because of their monopoly, are assured of large and on the whole certain earnings, and their debentures are popular in the Calcutta market, whereas very few coal companies in India are able to float debentures because of the nature of the industry. Speaking generally, mining companies can furnish a basis for bond issues only when the extent of their resources is definitely known. But even so the

[1] Evidence given by the Titaghur Paper Mills before the *Indian Tariff Board*, 1931, Vol. 1, p. 162.

amount issued should be strictly limited to the earning power of the concerns in the most difficult conditions, for otherwise there might be foreclosure and bankruptcy.

There are two kinds of industry which lend themselves to the issue of debentures. Where the property of a concern is of a non-specialized character and can be put to a variety of uses, then the property itself will furnish the security for the loan. Most agricultural lands and certain kinds of manufacturing industries are of this type. But even where the property is specialized, if the concern belongs to an industry which can be reasonably certain of relatively stable earnings, as most of the monopolies are, then it can furnish the security for bonds and debentures. Railway and tramway companies belong to this class and their debentures are taken up in the market because of their earning power. In India, apart from the chief railway systems which have been all financed by debenture stocks issued by the Government of India or the Secretary of State, about 50 per cent of the smaller railway concerns have issued debentures successfully. But care must be taken lest too much capital should be raised by way of debentures. Indeed, one authority holds[1] that in railway companies not more than 20 per cent of the gross earnings should be absorbed by the interest payable on debentures or mortgage debts. This is the limit beyond which no company may go in pledging its earnings for the payment of interest charges without imperilling its position in the future. As Von Beckerath observes,[2] "constant interest-credit which does not share in business losses, i.e. bonds, mortgages, and short-term loans become a danger to the existence of all legal forms of industrial enterprise; for several years in depression will eat away the capital stock if interest payments have to be continued. The transformation of a fixed-interest indebtedness into a dividend-bearing indebtedness encounters great difficulties, as experience has proved in Lancashire."

However, a comparison with British methods of industrial finance will show that Indian industry has on the whole not

[1] Mead, *Corporation Finance*, p. 117.
[2] Von Beckerath, *Industrial Organization*, 1933, p. 62.

raised sufficient capital by way of debentures. In 1925–6, over the whole range of British industry, it was estimated that out of a total capital of 100 units, ordinary capital accounted for 47, preference 33, and debentures 20.[1] In India in 1927–8 the corresponding figures were 75 ordinary, 16 preference, and only 9 debentures.[2] (The actual figures were for 1927–8, estimated total of paid-up capital in industry, Rs. 126 crores: Ordinary shares, Rs. 95 crores; preferred, Rs. 20 crores; and debentures, Rs. 11 crores.) A return submitted by the Bombay Millowners' Association showed that out of 74 cotton mills working on October 1, 1930, the 64 which had submitted returns had a paid-up capital of Rs. 12.14 crores, including preference shares. The debentures amounted to Rs. 2.38 crores, i.e. 16 per cent of the total available capital. But this is actually even a smaller percentage if to the available capital we add the public deposits of Rs. 2.73 crores. Including this, the percentage of debentures to the total capital comes to only 13·8 per cent.[3]

In the jute industry the percentage of debenture capital to the total capital was 14 in 1930–1. Out of 52 mills given in the *Investor's Year Book*, 27 had debenture capital, and the amount raised by these concerns was substantial, being £2·4 millions. In respect of coal companies, out of 70 coal companies in the list only 5 had debenture capital, and although one would expect larger mortgage debt in regard to tea companies floated in India, there are only 9 tea companies (out of a total of 128 listed in the *Investor's Year Book*) which have issued debentures. Among the smaller railway companies floated by private enterprise, 17 out of 35 in the list had debenture capital, but only 2 had preference shares. Of the other industries like cement and paper, it may be stated

[1] *Committee on Industry and Trade, Factors in Industrial and Commercial Efficiency*, p. 50.

[2] *Indian Central Banking Enquiry Committee*, Vol. 4, p. 156.

[3] The debentures were taken partly by the managing agents and banks but mainly by the public, the shares being 45.5 lakhs held by managing agents, 52.7 lakhs by banks, and 139.5 lakhs by the public. Besides the total funds of Rs. 17.25 crores, the companies had Rs. 5.32 crores from managing agents and Rs. 2.26 crores from banks.

that while most of them have issued debentures the proportion of debenture is higher in the cement than in any other industry, being as much as one-third of the total capital. In regard to the iron and steel industry the Tata Iron & Steel Co. issued debentures in 1922 to the value of £2·16 millions. The Indian Iron & Steel Co. and the Bengal Iron & Steel Co. work under an agreed arrangement in close co-operation with each other. The latter, registered in England with sterling capital, has debentures equal to 29 per cent of the total capital, while the Indian Iron Co., registered in rupee capital, has a small issue of sterling debentures of the value of £550,000.

On the whole, it must be admitted that industries in India have not raised sufficient capital by way of debentures or mortgage debt, and had the system of industrial mortgages been developed, most of the smaller organized industries which suffered on account of lack of capital would have had a better career. Mortgage banking offers, perhaps, the most hopeful line of advance in the future, and is a useful means of supplying the smaller concerns with long-term capital. But the difficulties of raising large sums by industrial debentures are considerable. In the first place, small concerns cannot issue debentures which will be taken up by the public. They require special institutions which will lend capital on the security of their real estate and machinery for a definite period of time. But even these institutions will be faced with a certain amount of risk; for the possibility of mortgaging real industrial estate is always limited, because the value of the building sinks to the mere worth of stone and scrap if manufacturing is stopped. Secondly, in the case of all manufacturing concerns, only after they have worked for some time with profit will their debentures be acceptable to the public. Still, despite these difficulties, more might have been raised had industrialists and banks put their heads together to make debentures a success. Instead, industries have depended for their working capital and for extensions on the deposits of the public and on the funds of the managing agents. Even the debentures that have been issued have been raised on rather costly terms and under severe handicaps. Not only has the interest been not less than 7 to 8 per cent, but the additional cost involved by way of commissions, stamp fees, underwriting commission or brokerage, often amounting to 2–5 per cent, has been disproportionate.[1]

It has also been stated that the market for debentures in India has been rather limited. The Indian investor, if he wants safety, still plumps for agricultural landed property and is unwilling to take up industrial ventures unless there is a chance of capital appreciation. Hence debenture loans with fixed yield of interest and with no prospect of capital appreciation do not attract him.[2] Insurance companies which could afford to take up industrial debentures have so far refrained from doing so, and this is, perhaps, a measure of their confidence in Indian industry. The initial stamp duty of Rs. 7.8.0 per 1,000 on debentures which are transferable by endorsement and Rs. 15 on bearer debentures incurred by the company which issues them, is felt to be a burden, although in reality it is negligible,[3] and the costs of transfer which fall on the investor are considered to be a handicap to effecting easy transfers.

Further, the small size of most of the debentures militates against the creation of a real market for these issues. The jute debentures are an exception. Not only are they popular, but they are considered to be so safe an investment that very few transactions are reported on the Stock Exchange.[4] In regard to some of the debentures floated in Bombay, most of them have been taken up by limited groups of financiers, and for reasons different from those applying to jute debentures, they, too, do not come to the market. Hence the public in Bombay have not become accustomed to the buying and selling of industrial debentures. Although from the point of view of the particular concern that issues debentures it does not matter whether its debentures are taken up by one or many persons, the market becomes narrow when a

[1] *Indian Central Banking Enquiry Committee*, Report, p. 273.

[2] Ibid., Evidence of M. K. Macdonald, Vol. 3.

[3] Ibid., Evidence of the Calcutta Stock Exchange, Vol. 3.

[4] In Calcutta these debentures are bought by investors rather than speculators and do not pass from hand to hand as shares.

small group holds the debentures. When the Tata Iron & Steel Co. floated debentures to provide itself with working capital, the entire sum of £400,000 (60 lakhs of Rs.) was subscribed by one Indian Prince, the Maharajah of Gwalior.[1]

Perhaps the most severe handicap to the development of debentures in India has been the attitude of the banks. A company which issues debentures finds its credit weakened in the eyes of the banks. Its shares cease to be acceptable as collateral, and a cotton or other factory which is "encumbered" with a debenture loan has not the same full credit with them as one without it.[2] While shares are taken as collateral security, a person who holds debentures of a factory is unable to use them as collateral security. The reason for this attitude is that since debentures are a first charge on the property of the concern, it is supposed that the security for bank credit is necessarily less. But this attitude of the banks should change. Indeed, the banks must take a more active part in helping the industrial concern with advice and by co-operating with it in the issuing of debentures. Such co-operation and friendly assistance will have the effect of making debentures really popular. At present debentures are not issued in the most attractive way with a view to tempting the investors.[3] There has been little variety in the nature of the industrial bonds offered to the market; 6 per cent and 7 per cent bonds, and occasionally 8 per cent bonds, with no special attractive features have been offered to the public, and these do not compare favourably with Government securities, which in the years 1921 to 1931 also yielded from 5½ to 6½ per cent interest. Other countries have known a great many forms of debenture issues, such as convertible debentures, i.e. debentures convertible into shares under certain terms, debentures with a comparatively high premium at maturity, and so on. Similarly, Indian industries must also issue bonds possessing as many attractive features as possible, and must compete more successfully than they have so far done with Government, who have

[1] F. R. Harris, *Life of J. N. Tata*, p. 202.

[2] *Indian Central Banking Enquiry Committee*, Evidence, Vol. 4, p. 163.

[3] Ibid., Dr. Jeidels's Evidence, Vol. 4, p. 222.

shown greater imagination in appealing to the investor. It is true that in a country like India, industry will have to offer much more liberal terms than Government if it is to raise capital successfully.

Unfortunately for industry, the Government of India has been a serious rival in the Indian capital market since 1920, and has raised loans at rates of interest which, however justified from their own point of view, have affected industry adversely. In the Appendix to this chapter is given the list of loans raised since 1920, and the rates of interest at which they were raised. It would be seen therefrom that the 7 per cent or 8 per cent interest which industry has had to pay for its debentures is the inevitable consequence of the high interest which Government has been prepared to pay for the capital in the same market. Not until Government is in a position to borrow more cheaply can industry raise capital at more easy rates of interest.

It should, however, not be forgotten that in India part of the loans floated by Government is as much industrial capital as the capital raised by private industry. If it be contended that the cost of the capital raised by Government has been excessive, the answer is that high cost is just a measure of the dearness of capital. It is arguable that Government's machinery for the raising of capital both at home and abroad must be reorganized, and that had it been more efficient the cost might have been less. This, however, is a different question. With the establishment of the Reserve Bank and the assistance of a Board of National Investment if one were set up, it may be hoped that better methods of raising and distributing loans will be adopted. But all that need be said here is that, given the conditions under which the Government of India had to work, it has probably done as well as it could, and it will be an unwarranted inference to conclude that when Government could have actually raised capital more economically, it deliberately failed to do so. On the other hand, it has to be considered whether the existence of a separate machinery for raising capital for the railways and other schemes of public outlay would have resulted in the more economical raising of capital. In every country the effects of public finance on the cost of industrial capital are great, and India is no exception to the general rule. Not unless it is proved that the cost of the capital raised by Government was much more than in other countries in similar circumstances can it be held that industry has unjustly or unfairly suffered. The truth is that, owing to the general financial and economic conditions, Government no less than industry has suffered, and the high cost of industrial finance in India in recent years is to be explained not so much in relation to the defects of the financial policy of Government, but in relation to the economic and financial conditions of the country, and indeed, of the whole world. Despite this, there are sound jute mill debentures carrying even smaller return than the yields of Government securities.

Debentures in Indian industry are issued chiefly in the following forms: (*a*) registered debentures which are transferable only by deed; these are not very common, and there are only about six issues in all of registered debentures; (*b*) bearer bonds, and (*c*) bonds transferable by endorsement only. All the debenture issues are redeemable and a cumulative sinking fund is applied annually to redeem the stock. Bearer bonds are more easily held, and hence are more popular.

In conclusion, it may be stated that efforts should be made to popularize debenture issues, (*a*) by making them more attractive and holding out redemption at a premium, (*b*) by offering more freely than at present the right of converting them into shares, (*c*) by removing the prejudice of the banks against companies which have issued debentures, and (*d*) finally by greater co-operation between banks and industry. The Stock Exchange can help in this direction by the more energetic work of the "listing committees" whose recommendation for inclusion of debenture issues on the Stock Exchange would carry great weight with the public and with the banks.

The period of the debentures, i.e. whether they should be issued for a long or short period, is also a question to be carefully considered. Generally, it may be stated that 15 to 20 years would be a proper period, but the difficulty is that a comparatively new concern cannot afford to float debentures redeemable in 15 or 20 years as the period will be insufficient to redeem the loan. On the other hand, if the prevailing rate of interest is high, and if there is reasonable ground for thinking that long-term interest will fall, there is justification for short-term bonds.[1]

Jute mills have issued debentures for a longer period than cotton mills, the reason partly being that cotton mills are unable to raise long-term debentures successfully. Debenture capital is usually additional to share capital; it is in the nature of a permanent issue of capital. It is highly improbable that companies which float them would be able to pay them off under 20 or 25 years. But the difficulty is that the investors in Bombay Presidency would not take up debentures of a longer period than 10 or 15 years. Further, in the opinion of the investors, jute mill company debentures have greater security because of their superior earning power than cotton mill debentures, although the latter are secured by a lien on the property of the cotton mills.[2]

Another point to be considered is the amount of debenture issue. Care must be taken in issuing a right amount of them, as when once they are issued further debentures cannot be placed on the market unless the first issue was very small and the company itself was extremely sound and strong.[3] In the circumstances

[1] "Business corporations choose short-term indebtedness either if a gradual increase in the demand for capital makes its temporary satisfaction by short-term credit seem good policy or if the stock market in business depressions does not allow the sale of stocks at favourable quotations" (Von Beckerath, *Industrial Organization*, p. 61).

[2] In some cases the company which has issued debentures is required before paying any dividend to the shareholder to allow for depreciation on the buildings, plant, and machinery comprised in the security of the debenture-holders and to set apart specified sums from a fund to be applied for the redemption of debentures. In most cases provision is made for a sinking fund to be applied annually for the repayment of debentures.

[3] When the Tata Hydro-Electric Co. took up the development of the new power scheme, i.e. the Andhra Valley Power, it was found necessary to float a separate company as Rs. 85 lakhs of capital in the Tata Hydro-Electric was represented by first mortgage debentures and as no further

the prudent course for every concern to adopt is to have an authorized issue larger than that needed for the moment, and issue the balance as circumstances require. In such cases, however, it is necessary, as has been stated by one writer, that the amount to be issued in any single year should be limited, and that at no time should the total amount exceed 50 per cent of the value of the property as represented by its total assets.

VI

PUBLIC DEPOSITS AS SOURCE OF WORKING CAPITAL AND CAPITAL FOR EXTENSIONS

The system by which the cotton factories of Bombay and Ahmedabad and, to a lesser extent, Sholapur and other centres provided themselves with capital for current expenditure and for extensions by means of deposits received from the public has some analogy to the methods of finance adopted by the Lancashire cotton industry. In both cases such loans came to be in excess of the ordinary paid-up capital of the concerns, and this form of financing had a great advantage as it enabled a company by keeping its capital low and by borrowing at cheap rates to pay higher dividends than would have been possible if the whole of their money had been in the form of share capital. But the disadvantage of this form of financing came to be felt in both cases during the recent depression in 1925–6, when public confidence was shaken and deposits were withdrawn, and when there could be no expectation of their coming back. What was considered to be a distinct merit in normal times proved to be a source of weakness and embarrassment when industry was on the downward grade. Again, as in England so in India, this form of borrowing was most characteristic of the cotton industry. But there are some important dissimilarities in the two methods worth noticing. In the first place the system so common in Lancashire of issuing

debentures ranking equally with them could be issued. It was not possible to place an issue of second debentures (Speech of Sir D. B. Tata quoted in the *Indian Textile Journal*, September 1916, p. 372).

shares which are not fully paid up, and utilizing the uncalled share capital as security for the purpose of getting bank credit, does not exist in the Bombay Presidency. In Lancashire a person who subscribed for the shares of the cotton mill paid partly in cash and left the balance due on the shares as deposits with the company. Often the employees of the concerns took up these shares, and in course of time were able to pay off the full value of these shares. There is nothing corresponding to this in the Bombay cotton industry. The "unpaid" margin was not by any means a source of strength to the Lancashire mills, as they discovered to their cost in 1922–3. When their financial position became so serious that they found it necessary to call up the unpaid part of the shares, shareholders who were required to meet the calls could in many cases do so only by withdrawing loan capital from the same or other mills, and this left the position of the mills as a whole in no better position than before.[1] Secondly, Indian cotton mills have not been financed to any extent by cotton merchants and brokers, or by yarn agents and dealers. They have only depended for their current finance on the managing agents, and thus, unlike some of the Lancashire mills, have not been "tied" to their creditors with the inevitable dangers of being in debt to trade creditors.

"In its origin, the system of deposits with industrial concerns was undoubtedly a reflex and a transformation of the old system of money being kept for safe custody with the Mahajan."[2] In Bombay and in Ahmedabad the men who established the mill companies were either merchants or shroffs in whom the public had confidence, and hence their savings were entrusted to them. The sums thus deposited with the mill companies became a very important source of industrial capital for the cotton industry in both the centres, but more especially in Ahmedabad, where the amount loaned by banks is inconsiderable.[3] The following table[4]

[1] *Survey of Textile Industries* (1928)*: Committee on Industry and Trade*, p. 36.

[2] *Minority Report, Indian Central Banking Enquiry Committee*, p. 329.

[3] Ibid.

[4] Ibid., p. 278.

shows the relative shares of the various agencies in the financing of the cotton industry.

As on October 1, 1930.

(*In Lakhs of Rupees*)

	Bombay (Figures are for 64 Mills)		Ahmedabad (Figures are for 56 Mills)	
	Rupees	Percentage of Total Finance	Rupees	Percentage of Total Finance
Amount loaned by the Managing Agents	532	21	264	24
Amount loaned by the Banks ..	226	9	42	4
Amount of Public Deposits ..	273	11	426	39
Amount of Share Capital ..	1,214	49	340	32
Amount of Debentures issued..	238	10	8	1

Of these debentures, Rs. 45.5 lakhs, 52.7 lakhs, and 139.5 lakhs were taken up by managing agents, banks, and the public respectively.

It will be seen from the above that in Ahmedabad public deposits are the most important single source of industrial finance for the cotton industry, and they are considerably in excess of the amount raised by share capital and debentures. The figures for Bombay do not bring out the full value of the role of deposits in the financing of the cotton industry as during the years since 1921 there has been a continuous withdrawal of deposits owing to the loss of confidence in the Bombay cotton companies.[1] Bombay had enjoyed the full effects of this system up to about fifteen years ago. Before it struck these difficult times the industry financed itself like Ahmedabad through the medium of public deposits. The deposits were in Bombay mostly short-period deposits for six or twelve months, and were available at low rates of interest, ranging from 4½ to 6½ per cent, the rate of interest being governed partly by the conditions of the money market, but mainly by the

[1] For instance, in March 1924 the total unsecured loans (mostly in the form of deposits) was Rs. 11.19 crores; in March 1929 it was only Rs. 6.91 crores (*Indian Central Banking Enquiry Committee*, Vol. 3, p. 777). (Bank loans were mostly secured loans.)

personal position of the managing agents. The six monthly deposits were considered by the Bombay millowners to be "more than ordinarily sound"[1] because during the season when cotton was purchased for the whole year the mills required far more working capital than during the latter part of the year when stocks were getting hard. But this view does not have regard to the fact that it is possible for banks to finance on the security of stocks, and the same result would have been achieved had these deposits gone to the banks and the latter financed the mills. The greater dependence of the Bombay mills on bank credit in recent years when the deposits have fallen off shows the possibility of banks financing the industry to an increasing extent. At the same time it has to be noted that public deposits cannot be replaced by ordinary banking credit. So far they have done for industry what debentures are doing. The withdrawal of deposits has brought to the forefront the urgency of finding some substitute for them.

In Ahmedabad, however, even at the present time, deposits continue to play a large part in the financing of the industry, and there is no immediate danger of their falling off. An important reason for this is that the character of these deposits has altered in two directions in recent years. In the first place, Ahmedabad has developed the system of seven-year deposits, and all the new mills have been financed on the basis of long-term deposits. They are, therefore, the nearest approach to debenture bonds, and perhaps from the point of view of the mill companies even better than debentures, as depositors have no lien on the properties or assets of the companies. Although serving the purpose of debentures, they rank *pari passu* with other deposits, and have no more rights than other short-term deposits. The inducement to such deposits is the right to a share in the agency commission, but for which these would not have been attracted. Nearly a quarter of the financial requirements of a new concern in Ahmedabad is met by these long-term deposits, and these funds are utilized for block expenditure.[2]

[1] *Indian Tariff Board: Cotton Industry*, 1927, Vol. 2, p. 136.

[2] *Indian Central Banking Enquiry Committee*, Vol. 3, p. 478.

In the second place, while before the war all the deposits came from the public both in the city and in the rural areas, the high profits of the mill industry have facilitated the building-up of reserves, and it is these reserves that are now deposited with the mill.[1] Inter-deposits, i.e. deposits as between one mill and another, have now largely replaced public deposits. Hence the Ahmedabad mill industry has developed a system by which the industry is increasingly financing itself out of its own reserves and profits.

But even so the system is not free from defects. There are still large volumes of short-term deposits in the Ahmedabad mill industry which in times of depression and adversity would be withdrawn by the public in the same manner as in Bombay. Public deposits are, after all, a "fair weather" friend, as aptly characterized by the Managing Governor of the Imperial Bank; and the twenty-five or thirty years' experience in Ahmedabad, successful as it has been, does not get over the fact that when hard times come, as come they must, the deposits will be a source of weakness and embarrassment.[2] In so far as they at present deter the creation of banking and debenture capital, the mill industry would be left with no alternative source of finance when the deposits are withdrawn. As Sir Basil Blackett put it in his speech at the opening of the Calcutta branch of the Central Bank of India, "The habit of using short deposits to provide capital for industrial concerns has the further disadvantage that it restricts the supply of good industrial securities, shares, debentures, etc., available for the ordinary investor, and unduly narrows the market for such investment. An industrial concern which is taking considerable sums on deposit is really doing good business of a kind for which it is not equipped, and in which it is not experienced. . . . Finally, the losses which must occur in a crisis or panic owing to money lent on short deposits being locked up in fixed capital assets must tend to frighten many Indians both from investing in industrial shares and from putting their money on deposit with a bank or anyone else at all." Again, the success of the public-

[1] *Indian Central Banking Enquiry Committee*, Vol. 3, p. 479.
[2] Ibid., p. 867.

deposits system had its root in the primitive banking organization of the country when the public had no choice except to deposit with rich merchants and big capitalists. In the early years of banking development in India, the public had greater confidence in the prosperous cotton industry than in banks, the failure of some of which had shaken public trust in them. Now that confidence in banks is increasing, industry cannot hope to draw a continuous stream of deposits. Lastly, there was then no alternative investment available to the small savers. The establishment of the Postal Cash Certificate system has drawn away a large number of such depositors from industry, and the statement of the Ahmedabad millowners that the popularity of the cash certificates adversely affected their deposits is a warning of the unreliability of deposits as a permanent factor of industrial finance.

Thus we have now reached a stage when the problem of financing industry has become very pressing. An increase in the supply of capital is required for the purpose of meeting the requirements of all industries. But within the limits of available supplies, industry has to devise the right methods of attracting industrial capital in proper proportions and in suitable forms. The machinery for drawing such capital has also to be considered in the light of the existing banking and financial structure.

Statement showing the percentage of shares held by a small number of shareholders in the cotton, jute, and miscellaneous industries.

The following have been taken from the *Mirror of Investment* (1927), edited by Pat Lovett. Before drawing any valid inference it is necessary to note that owing to the vogue of "blank transfers" it is unsafe to assume that the shares purchased by the registered shareholders are still held by them. Hence the information recorded below may not be accurate; but it indicates the standing and prestige of the managing agents and their friends who constitute the chief owners of the concern.

Cotton Industry

Number given to each Concern as it appears in the *Mirror of Investment*	Percentage of Shares	Number of Share-holders	Residence		
			Bombay	Calcutta	Ahmedabad
1	30	21	9	—	9
2	9	21	18	—	—
3	37	15	—	—	—
4	99	15	—	—	—
5	—	—	—	—	—
6	29	19	—	—	—
7	14	15	—	—	—
8	72	20	20	—	—
9	—	—	—	—	—
10	33	23	22	—	—
11	63	21	15	—	—
12	28	20	18	—	—
13	70	19	19	—	—
14	29	22	22	—	—
15	96	20	19	—	—
16	95	11	9	—	—
17	58	20	19	—	—
18	31	15	—	13	—
19	28	20	18	—	—
20	61	23	20	—	—
21	55	21	18	—	—
22	—	—	—	—	—
23	40	21	21	—	—
24	—	—	—	—	—

Cotton Industry—continued

Number given to each Concern as it appears in the *Mirror of Investment*	Percentage of Shares	Number of Share-holders	Residence		
			Bombay	Calcutta	Ahmedabad
25	90	19	19	—	—
26	70	9	9	—	—
27	28	20	18	—	—
28	31	19	4	(12 Surat)	—
29	11	8	8	—	—
30	27	22	10	—	—
31	50	20	19	—	—
32	50	20	—	20	—
33	54	20	18	—	—
34	81	15	10	2	—
35	19	13	12	—	—
36	—	—	—	—	—
37	—	—	—	—	—
38	80	19	17	—	—
39	75	17	16	—	—
40	56	20	17	1	—
41	—	—	—	—	—
42	38	10	8	—	1
43	—	—	—	—	—
44	39	20	17	—	—
45	64	21	17	—	2
46	29	16	1	14	—
47	—	—	—	—	—
48	45	23	23	—	—
49	59	22	18	1	1
50	—	—	—	—	—
51	—	—	—	—	—
52	51	23	11	(11 London)	—
53	31	8	6	—	—
54	21	17	12	—	—
55	60	11	10	—	1
56	89	21	17	—	3
57	53	22	18	—	—
58	59	21	19	—	—
59	17	20	16	—	—
60	—	—	—	—	—
61	74	14	10	(4 London)	—
62	29	20	10	—	—
63	59	10	9	—	—

In the jute industry the shares are rather widely held. The following table giving the amount of shares held in each case by fifteen persons brings this out clearly

Managing Agents	Number of Mills Managed	Number of Shareholders	Percentage of Shares in each Concern
Andrew Yule & Co. ..	8	15	29, 24, 14, 30, 43, 21, 26, 7
Begg, Dunlop & Co. ..	4	15	35, 30, 10, 13
Bird & Co.	7	15	23, 16, 13, 15, 17, 15, 16
Kettlewell, Bullen & Co.	2	15	15, 38
Jardine & Skinner & Co.	4	15	6, 21, 13, 47
Mackinnon, Mackenzie ..	2	15	15, 38
McLeod & Co.	4	15	9, 18, 1, 72
Barry & Co.	2	15	18, 47

Coal Companies

Managing Agents	Number of Mills Controlled	Number of Share-holders	Percentage of Shares in each Concern
Andrew Yule & Co.	15	15	43, 30, 31, 27, 25, 22, 55, 26, 46, 38, 22, 34, 40, 30, 51
Heilgers & Co. ..	7	15	44, 31, 68, 57, 44, 25, 28
Martin & Co. ..	7	15	19, 22, 31, 79, 18, 73, 74
Shaw, Wallace ..	6	15	37, 47, 34, 24, 56, 42
H. V. Low & Co. ..	5	15	68, 17, 33, 28, 26
McNeill & Co. ..	7	15	27, 99, 30, 56, 81, 38, 65

In one company the managing agents hold 25 per cent of the shares.

Coal shares are more concentrated than jute shares. The individuals whose holdings are available are, with the exception of English investors, capitalists from Bombay, Calcutta, Ahmedabad, and other important industrial centres.

Statement showing the borrowings of the Government of India, together with the rates at which they were borrowed from 1921–2 *to* 1932–3. (*From the Reports of the Controller of Currency.*)

	Description	Terms and Rate
1921–2	Five year bonds at par	6 per cent free of income-tax
	Ten-year bonds at par	6 per cent free of income-tax
1922–3	Five-year bonds at par	6 per cent free of income-tax
	Ten-year bonds at par	6 per cent free of income-tax
1923–4	Ten-year bonds at Rs. 97	5 per cent, giving a yield of 5·39 per cent
	Long-term loan issued at Rs. 95 and repayable in 1945–55	5 per cent free of income-tax, giving a yield of 5·31 per cent
1924–5	5 per cent bonds issued at Rs. 98.4.0, giving a yield of 5·25 per cent	
	Long-term loan issued at Rs. 99 per cent	5 per cent tax free, giving a yield of 5·1 per cent
1925–6	Ten-year bonds	5 per cent
	1945–55 long-term loan issued at Rs. 96	5 per cent tax free
1926–7	Taxable loan 1960–70 issued at Rs. 88 per cent	4 per cent, giving a yield of 4·75 per cent
1927–8	Taxable loan 1934–7 issued at Rs. 94½ per cent	4 per cent, giving a yield of 5 per cent
1928–9	1955–60 loan issued at Rs. 94 per cent	4½ per cent, giving a yield of 4·9 per cent
	Five-year bonds at Rs. 97½ per cent	4½ per cent, giving a yield of 5 per cent
1929–30	Taxable loan of 1939–44 at Rs. 96½ per cent	5 per cent, giving a yield of 5·45 per cent
	Five-year bonds	5 per cent, giving a yield of 5·395 per cent
1930–1	Tax-bearing loan 1933–6	6 per cent
1931–2		
1932–3	Taxable loan issued at Rs. 98 per cent, 1938–40	5½ per cent
	Taxable loan issued at Rs. 98, 1940–3	5 per cent
	Ten-year bonds taxable	4 per cent
	4 per cent conversion loan, 1960–70	

Of these loans amounting to Rs. 387 crores, only Rs. 211 crores was in cash, and the balance represented conversion of old debt.

CHAPTER V

BANKS AND INDUSTRIAL FINANCE

I

JOINT-STOCK BANKS

We have examined in the last chapter the methods by which industry raised capital for its fixed and working needs. It was pointed out how, owing to the slow growth of the investment habit, the managing agents became not merely the link between the investing public and the industrial enterprises which were established, but were also the chief providers of capital. For a fairly long time their strong financial position, combined with the resources of their friends and other rich capitalists, enabled them to carry on independently of the banking system. Gradually, however, the changed economic conditions of the country, the growth of newer and additional enterprises, and the inevitable ebb of industry threw on them a burden which they were unable to bear unassisted by banks. But even up to 1916–18, when the Indian Industrial Commission instituted an inquiry into the adequacy of finance for industry, the major industries controlled and managed by the Bombay and Calcutta managing agents had no great complaint about the adequacy of available facilities for the supply of fixed and working capital for industry. Although there were some who complained about the rigidity of the conditions under which banks worked, the bulk of the managing agents were on the whole satisfied that "no industrial company, supported by reputed managing agents and with good prospects, found any difficulty in getting the required finance." But a change of considerable importance has occurred since then, and particularly after 1921–2. Industry struck on hard times, and the flow of capital even to the major industries has been checked. The system by which the deposits of the public were utilized for current expenses and for extension and improvement and which enabled the managing agents of Bombay Presidency to carry on independently of the banking organization, except in respect of the financing of the purchase of raw materials and sales of goods, proved to be a distinct weakness when depression set in and public confidence was shaken. In Bengal, where both on account of the greater financial resources at the command of the European managing agents and the better facilities of credit they enjoyed at the hands of the banks, there has been no serious dissatisfaction with the banking system, the view is still held that "where an industrial venture is sound the facilities available are fully equal to the actual requirements" and that "banks in India have freely financed industries, large and small."[1] But the Bengal National Chamber of Commerce, representing the Indian section of the managing agents, has stated that in respect of the industries like rice mills, oil mills, hosiery factories, soap factories, and smaller tea gardens, great difficulties are experienced in getting the required finance, and the demand on the part of those representing smaller industries for a more liberal policy on the part of the banks has grown more and more insistent. It is therefore necessary, in view of the change of opinion and of industrial conditions, to review the work and functions of the Indian banking system, and to examine how far the task which it had set itself to do was done efficiently, and in what respects if any it should modify its structure with a view to meeting the legitimate requirements of industry.[2]

Commercial banking organization in India comprises several loosely linked units which are not integrated into an organic whole. The Exchange Banks, of which there were eighteen in 1933, although essentially concerned with the financing of foreign trade, play some part in the financing of inland trade. They compete with the ordinary joint-stock banks in the receiving of deposits, both on current and time, and on savings-bank account. These deposits amounted to £53·35 millions in 1928 in India, and enable the Exchange Banks to carry on most of their business in India

[1] *Indian Central Banking Enquiry Committee*, Vol. 2, pp. 472-3.

[2] The present position and future needs of Indian Joint-Stock Banking have been examined by the Indian Central Banking Enquiry Committee, and its report may be referred to with advantage.

without having recourse to the English money market, except in certain parts of the year. As R. W. Beaumont Peace, Chairman of Lloyds Bank, observed, "the total of the deposits received in India [by that bank] largely exceeds the amount of the bank's advances, and no portion of the bank's deposits at home is used for the purpose of making loans in India." But this is not quite true of all the Exchange Banks, and there is no doubt that in the busy season they draw funds from their Head Office in England and compete for available deposits by offering rates which induce Indian banks to lend to them. Since the primary function of the Exchange Banks is to finance foreign trade, we may pass at once to consider the position of the Indian joint-stock banks.

The orthodox practice of English banks and the limitations under which the Imperial Bank of India was allowed to work have had enormous influence on the development of modern Indian joint-stock banking. Indian joint-stock banks are deposit banks, and since their liabilities are short-term, their advances, too, can be for short periods only. The deposits are liable to be withdrawn either on demand or at short notice, and hence the assets have to be kept liquid. The Imperial Bank of India, which grew out of the three Presidency Banks of Madras, Bombay, and Bengal, is a commercial bank, like other joint-stock banks in India, but combines with it some of the functions appertaining to a Bankers' Bank. But it has to work under many restrictions; for instance, it should not make a loan for a period longer than six months, nor on the original security of immovable property, nor upon the security of any negotiable instrument of any individual or partnership firm which does not carry with it the several responsibilities of at least two persons or firms unconnected with each other in general partnership. Although the ordinary joint-stock banks have no such restrictions, they have all been dominated by the practice of the Imperial Bank to such an extent that for all practical purposes they may be regarded equally with the Imperial Bank as purveyors of credit for short terms and against certain forms of security only. As in England, so in India the distinction between short-term and long-term operations is rather rigid, and commercial banks confine themselves to certain kinds of tangible and easily realizable security. It is obvious that in a country like India, where banking has only been slowly developing, and where the paid-up capital and reserve is rather small, liquidity of assets must be a prime consideration. Especially where the proportion of deposits to total resources is high, the banks will have to be careful to keep their assets liquid, i.e. of such a kind that they could be readily converted into cash without losing heavily. In 1928 the capital and reserve of the Imperial Bank amounted to Rs. 11.01 crores; deposits, including those of Government, Rs. 79.25 crores; and cash balances Rs. 10.57 crores. The capital and reserve of 74 banks amounted to Rs. 12.30 crores; deposits, Rs. 66.35 crores; cash balances, Rs. 8.71 crores. Although the proportion of liquid resources to deposits may seem to be high compared to other countries, it has to be remembered that owing to a lack of concentration of resources, the position of the individual banks is always risky, and the failure of many banks in India is a warning that safety must still be a prime consideration.

It was pointed out in the last chapter that the provision of the minimum working capital was no part of the duty of a commercial banking system, and that we cannot condemn the Indian joint-stock banks because of their unwillingness and unreadiness to provide this. But it is necessary to examine how far they have been successful in providing the fluctuating needs of industry in regard to its current requirements, in enabling it to buy materials and to hold stock temporarily till it may be used up or sold off, and in enabling it to tide over the period between production and sale. In other words, have the banks been efficiently performing their function of providing that part of the "circulating" capital which represents the excess over the minimum working capital?[1]

[1] The terms "circulating" capital and "working" capital are often used interchangeably in one and the same sense. For our purpose we may distinguish that part of the circulating capital which represents the excess of current assets over current liabilities from the whole of the current assets. The latter will be circulating capital, and the excess of current assets over current liabilities will represent the minimum working capital.

II

COSTLY AND INADEQUATE FINANCE

There are those who hold the view that the development of Indian banking on the lines of English joint-stock banking was a great mistake. They urge that the conditions in the two countries were entirely different. English industry was so well supplied with permanent and minimum working capital by industrialists themselves that the tendency of British banks to concentrate their activities upon short-term lending resulted in their providing the circulating capital at the cheapest possible cost, but that in India the needs of industry required the provision by banks of long-term finance to industry. Without seeking an answer to this aspect of the matter, it is necessary to note that if there be any implicit assumption that Indian banks already supplied short-term loans cheaply and sufficiently, and that the only remaining problem is to provide long-term credit, that assumption is entirely wrong. The defect of the banking organization in India is not so much that it has specialized itself in a limited field, but that even within the field of its specialization it has not been performing its functions efficiently and cheaply. The larger joint-stock banks made advances usually at the Imperial Bank rate, or 1 per cent higher; but the smaller ones charge 2 to 3 per cent higher. As the Central Banking Committee has pointed out in summarizing the evidence on the subject, "the rates of interest charged to industries for loans and advances are said to be generally higher than the industries can bear."[1] Even when the rate of interest charged is that of the Imperial Bank rate, it must be noted that that rate advances with reference to seasonal market conditions, and therefore industries are penalized by higher interest charges.

The smaller banks charge very much higher rates. The Chotanagpur Banking Association stated in their evidence before the Central Banking Committee that they charged 12 per cent per annum to small colliery proprietors.[2] The Puri Bank, Ltd. advanced

[1] *Indian Central Banking Enquiry Committee*, Report, p. 272.

[2] Ibid., Vol. 2, p. 61.

loans at 16 per cent per annum on sums above Rs. 5,000, and at 18 per cent on amounts less than Rs. 5,000 on the security of mortgage bonds.

The efficiency of a country's banking system is not to be judged merely by the interest charged by banks on advances. Many of the medium-sized industries resort to indigenous bankers who charge very much higher rates. "Coal companies have to borrow money from indigenous bankers for the periodical development of their collieries at so high a rate as 12 to 18 per cent. In some years 24 per cent had to be given."[1] Industries like leather and tanning, oil mills, rice mills, smaller tea gardens, have had to pay as high as 24 per cent, even when they borrow on the security of their assets.[2]

The dependence of industry on the costly finance supplied by the indigenous banking system is a reflection on the efficiency of the Indian joint-stock banking organization. Had the banks been developed more fully, industry would not have had to resort to such expensive borrowings. Further, the indirect effect of bringing about a general reduction of interest rates all over the country can only come about by better banking development. At present only a portion of the needs of industry is met by joint-stock banks and that not as cheaply as in other countries; but industry has to resort to other institutions for the remaining part of its needs, which are satisfied only on very expensive terms.

The number of principal towns which possessed a bank or a branch office or agency of a bank increased from 185 in 1919 to 339 in 1928, and this is by no means a negligible progress. But still 85 per cent of the towns are not served by a bank. Even some of the smaller industrial towns which need the services of a bank are not served by one, and industries suffer from lack of remittance facilities. The result is that several small industrial concerns in Bengal, Bihar and Orissa, and United Provinces depend on moneylenders for the short-term capital which they need, and it

[1] *Indian Central Banking Enquiry Committee*, Report, Vol. 2, p. 504.
[2] Ibid., Vol. 2, p. 529.

can be had only at a very high cost. Some of the smaller collieries have had to borrow at rates of interest varying from 18 to 36 per cent. The position of the smaller tea estates is worse. The inadequacy of capital for industrial needs and the high cost of such as is available are the essential features of industrial finance in India. Contrary to the popular notion that assistance in the provision of initial capital is the most urgent need, it may be stated that the provision of part of the working capital at cheap cost is the more pressing problem in India. It is in this respect that the contrast between India and other countries is seen to the disadvantage of the former. No country has perhaps solved successfully the problem of supplying long-term credit needed by industry by evolving a sound scheme of financial and banking organization; but Western countries have, on the whole, evolved an efficient system of providing short-term capital. India has still to solve the problem of cheap working capital for industry. The crying need of industry in India is therefore an extension of banking facilities. In a recent book on *Indian Industry and its Problems*,[1] it has been stated that "it is difficult to see what useful purpose the mobilization of money through the extension of banking facilities would serve," and that "the extension of ordinary banking facilities will prove to be a totally useless expedient" as far as the supply of finance for fixed capital expenditure is concerned. In the opinion of the present writer, the supply of "initial" finance is not more urgent than the provision of short-term capital. The mobilization of money through the extension of banking facilities would have the effect of bringing about a reduction in the rate of interest, not so much on the capital supplied by joint-stock banks themselves, but on that amount of capital which is now provided at an exorbitant rate by the indigenous bankers and moneylenders. The most serious handicap to Indian industry is, among others, the high cost of capital, and anything that contributes towards a reduction of that cost is a welcome step. Further, the indirect influence of banking development on the supply of initial finance cannot also be neglected. Banks can and do offer facilities

[1] H. R. Soni, *Indian Industry and its Problems*, 1932, p. 234.

to their customers for investment. At present these facilities are provided in connection with Government securities; but it is no less possible for them to offer facilities for the taking up of industrial securities and debentures, and in this way the supply of initial finance may also be facilitated indirectly by the extension of banking facilities.

It is true that in India the joint-stock banks are not the only agency for the supply of industrial or commercial credit. Nor would it be correct to measure the extent of the banking habit by the number of people who have banking accounts and who possess cheque books. The volume of "Hundi" transactions is very considerable, and far in excess of the volume of transactions by cheques.[1] "The indigenous banking system provides still the bulk of the capital provided by all the credit agencies put together."[2] It fulfils valuable functions in affording credit facilities of some kind, but it is doubtful how far it is in itself capable of development to an extent that would satisfy the banking requirements of the country. Further, modern industry cannot develop alongside of a banking system which works on antiquated lines and supplies credit only on very onerous terms. Part of the difficulties of industrialists is due to their mediaeval methods of doing business and their inability or unwillingness to exhibit their financial position in a manner which can be readily understood by the joint-stock banks. They are thus compelled to throw themselves on the mercy of the indigenous bankers. The only way by which the

[1] *Indian Central Banking Enquiry Committee*, Vol. 4, p. 17. While the number of banks and branches and agencies including Provincial and Central Co-operative Banks was only 750 in 1924, the number of indigenous bankers and moneylenders has been estimated at 264,000.

[2] Ibid., Report, p. 107.

The financing of agriculture is almost entirely controlled by the indigenous banking agencies. The same can be said in regard to Indian cottage and small-scale industries. "The bulk of the work of financing the internal trade of the country is in the hands of the indigenous bankers outside the sphere of joint-stock banking." "The part which the Indian joint-stock banks play in the financial life of the country pales into insignificance when contrasted with that of the indigenous bankers" (L. C. Jain, *Indigenous Banking in India*, p. 175).

situation may be improved is for both banking and industry to be modernized. Various proposals have been made from time to time with a view to linking the indigenous banking system to the organized banking system of the country. That something must be done to secure this cannot be doubted. It will be a long time before India will have a network of joint-stock banks or branches of such banks. For banking facilities outside the 400 centres which are now served by a joint-stock bank or branch of it, "agriculturists, traders, merchants, and small industrialists, have to depend largely on indigenous bankers and moneylenders."[1] One of the most hopeful lines of strengthening and improving the position of the indigenous bankers will be by bringing them into direct relations with the Reserve Bank, and providing them with rediscounting facilities, as suggested by the Indian Central Banking Committee.[2] Such indigenous bankers as are willing to shed their outside activities should be eligible to be placed on the approved list of the Reserve Bank in the same manner as joint-stock banks, and the bills offered by them should be rediscountable at the bank. In the proposed scheme of Reserve Bank for India, provision has been made to review the position of indigenous bankers *vis-à-vis* the Bank at the end of three years, and it may be hoped that the link which will be established will not only strengthen the indigenous banker but will also have the effect of reforming his practices and methods and removing the temptation to charge excessive rates. Another desirable step will be to recognize the indigenous bankers as agents for collection of cheques and bills both on behalf of the Reserve Bank and the bigger commercial banks. At present they are allowed by the Imperial Bank to cash cheques and bills and collect them on its behalf, but are not granted the same concessions given to joint-stock banks in regard to remittance facilities. When the Reserve Bank begins to function, the privileges which may be granted to joint-stock banks in regard to facilities for remittance of funds should also be extended to those indigenous bankers who are included in the approved list.

[1] *Indian Central Banking Enquiry Committee*, Report, p. 106.

[2] Ibid., p. 107.

In these and other ways the banking organization of India may be strengthened by making the indigenous banker an integral part of it. But time will be needed to secure this end, and until then organized industry will have to depend upon the growth and development of banking on modern lines, and it is to this aspect of the matter that we now turn.

It will be observed from the tables given at the end of the chapter that the progress of banking judged by the amount of deposits has not been as rapid during the last decade as in the previous decade. Indeed, the total deposits at the end of 1931 were lower than those in 1919, despite the increase in the number of banks, and this must be regarded as somewhat unsatisfactory. From these data the "experts" who came to assist the Indian Central Banking Committee concluded that the country did not abound "in untapped banking facilities," and implied that, whatever the need for extending banking facilities, the scope was rather limited. But this view fails to make allowance for the exceptional nature of the period under consideration. Some of the most important industries in India like cotton, jute, and tea passed through very difficult times, and the purchasing power of the masses fell considerably at first owing to the deflation of values from the peak prices of 1919–20, and later owing to the depression of agricultural prices. The failure of a large number of banks in 1922–3, involving a total paid-up capital of Rs. 469 lakhs, must necessarily have affected deposits both directly and indirectly. If we took a longer period into consideration, i.e. from 1900 to 1930, we find that progress was not unsatisfactory. The deposits of all banks increased from Rs. 32 crores in 1903 to Rs. 213 crores in 1930, an increase of over 565 per cent in thirty years. Even taking 1913 to 1930, we find that deposits of banks other than Exchange Banks increased from Rs. 60 crores to Rs. 145 crores, an increase of over 140 per cent. Further, even in respect of the period 1919–30, the deposits cannot be considered to have diminished if account is taken of the great fall in the general price-level at the end of the period. If we make allowances for the difference in price-level, we find that the real value of deposits is as follows:

	1913	1914	1915	1916	1917	1918	1919	1920	1921
General Index of Price*	100	103	106	129	137	157	193	196	165
Deposits, Nominal ..	24	18	19	26	32	42	61	73	80
Deposits converted into Pre-war Price-level ..	24	17	18	20	23	27	32	37	48

	1922	1923	1924	1925	1926	1927	1928	1929	1930
General Index of Price..	162	150	155	159	151	141	141	142	120
Deposits, Nominal ..	65	48	55	58	63	64	66	66	67
Deposits converted into Pre-war Price-level ..	40	32	35	36	42	46	47	47	56

(*N.B.*—Deposits are in crores of rupees.)

* It is not clear how Mr. Jain arrives at different figures in his *Monetary Problems in India*, p. 92.

These figures indicate that, despite the most unfavourable conditions, some progress has been achieved. In any case there is no justification for taking too pessimistic a view of the situation. The investments of the public in co-operative banks, postal savings banks and cash certificates afford enough evidence of the possibility of an increased flow of savings to banks. The need for consolidating the position of existing banks and for extending branch banking is apparent.

A question that inevitably arises in a large country like India is whether progress in banking should be by an increase in the number of independent bank units or by the method of branch banking. It would be some time before this problem can ever become pressing in India, for considering the vast size of the country, even if the number of independent banks doubles itself within the next twenty years there is no need for alarm. But the trend of banking developments all over the world has been towards concentration and amalgamation with extensive branch banking. As Parker Willis and Beckhart have pointed out, the tendency is world wide and not a phenomenon whose appearance is due to the type of banking system existing in a country. The movement towards bank amalgamations was before the war noticeable only in comparatively few countries. But during and after the war it became more general. The movement is parallel with, and a consequence of, the organization of industry into big combines with larger individual credit needs. In the economic development of Canada and Australia, the ramifying influence of their big banks has been very pronounced. In England "the general trend of the evidence was that on the whole industry is better served by the banks than before amalgamations. . . . Indeed, the evidence before us gives a good deal of support to the view that without amalgamation the power of the banks to give support to industry would have been considerably less than at present in view of the increased size of the average business unit."[1] There is no reason to think that amalgamation and concentration of banking must necessarily bring about any lack of touch with the industrialists and their needs. Up to a certain point, substantial services may result from such mergers. It is true that in India local independent units would give the local big men a chance to play a useful role and to engage their capital in the task. The proper line of advance is consolidation and branch banking. The collapse of the American banking system in 1933 is a warning that the "unit banking principle" has great weaknesses in certain times.[2] In India the large number of banking failures is to be explained in part at least by the multiplication of small banks with insignificant paid-up capital. Provided large banking units are started, the increase in the number of banks in India would not altogether be a disadvantage, but the hopeful line of advance lies in the strengthening of existing banks by the building up of large resources and the increase of bank branches. At present the 159 joint-stock banks (the Imperial Bank of India not being

[1] *Final Report of the Committee on Industry and Trade*, p. 48.

[2] "The existence of a heterogeneous banking structure in which there have been more than 10,000 bank failures during the past twelve years constitutes a burden upon commerce" (*Federal Reserve Bulletin*, March 1933).

included) have only 492 branches, i.e. about three branches each; the Imperial Bank of India has 162 branches and the Exchange Banks 80. All these were located in about 389 towns in 1931. The number of principal towns which possessed a bank or branch or agency of a bank was only 339 in 1929, and 389 in 1931, although the total number of towns is about 2,300. It is, of course, to be remembered that the towns are served by the indigenous bankers to some extent, but for reasons already stated, modern industrial development is linked up with the development of modern banking.

The relative inferiority of the position of India in respect of banking may be judged by several other tests. The number of banks, or branches of banks, per 10,000 persons of the country affords some evidence of banking development. In 1925 there was one banking office for every 2,450 of the population in Canada; 3,900 in the United States; 4,600 in England and Wales; 3,100 in Scotland; and 2,108 in Australia. In India there was a banking office only for every 500,000 persons (440,000 according to the Minority Report of the Banking Committee), excluding, of course, the indigenous bankers whose numbers have been variously estimated; for except in Bombay, Madras, and Burma, the latter are more of the type of moneylenders than bankers.

So much has been said above of the need for extension of banking facilities because not until commercial banking is able to fulfil its main purpose, i.e. of supplying short-term credit, can advance be made in other directions. The cost of short-term credit must be reduced, and it will be reduced only if banks develop on such a scale as to tap all the savings of the people.[1]

[1] For example, the tanning industry, a very important one in Madras, is carried on partly with owned funds and partly with funds borrowed from the exporters and *mandi* or commission merchants. The interest charged by the exporting firms is 9 to 12 per cent and that by the *mandi* merchants is much higher, sometimes as much as 24 to 30 per cent.

In the Punjab, again, the tanners borrow on the security of ornaments, and are charged 12 per cent, and if on personal security 18 to 36 per cent.

Refer also to pp. 100–1 of the *Report of the Indian Central Banking Enquiry Committee*.

III

CONDITIONS AND METHODS OF ADVANCES BY BANKS

It is not merely the deficiency of banking facilities that hinders industrial advance. Owing to a multitude of causes, the methods of granting credit by banks have been marked by a rigidity characteristic of primitive banking. The prominent position held amongst banks' loans by those given against actual merchandise, deposited whether in the banks' godowns or in those of the borrower under letters of hypothecation, is a sign of the comparatively undeveloped banking system. Personal and unsecured credit finds little place in the portfolios of the Indian joint-stock banks. Advances that are given by commercial banks are either (1) advances against tangible and marketable security lodged or pledged with the lender, or (2) clean advances against personal credit but with a second signature to the note of hand. Both these methods of advances have great limitations. The Ahmedabad millowners would rather not go to a bank than apply for a loan which would require them to pledge their stocks as the mills thereby lose prestige, and as the public deposits may be withdrawn. Secondly, the second-name rule has perpetuated the system of managing agents who by guaranteeing the loans granted by the banks to the companies under their management have inevitably regarded themselves as indispensable to the very existence of those companies. Industrial units have thus been rendered unable to stand on their own feet and to develop an independent method of financing themselves.

Industrial concerns obtain their credits from banks in the shape of overdraft or cash credit, on the security of letters of hypothecation on goods. This practice is not generally agreeable to the banks as the goods are in the possession of the borrowers, whilst such loans are not a quick asset; and naturally banks restrict such credits within a narrow circle of highly reliable customers.[1]

Traders could raise credits on the security of produce, but banks insist on such produce being deposited in their own go-

[1] *Indian Journal of Economics*, January 1931.

downs (warehouses) under the control of their own staff, and as this is regarded as derogatory by substantial merchants, they have often to sell their goods at unprofitable prices and in a depressed market.

So long as sales are on the "open account" and notes and drafts are not discounted, monetary supply will remain inelastic. All borrowings for business purposes must be through some negotiable instrument which may be rediscounted in case the lender wants to transfer his claim to someone else.[1]

The general practice of granting advances by means of a cash credit account (under which the advance is allowed against a promissory note signed by the borrower and secured by hypothecation of stocks) has hindered the development of trade bills which are the most suitable instruments of short-term credits. There are, of course, obvious advantages of the cash credit system, which explain its popularity in India. In the first place, "interest is paid by the borrower only to the extent to which the credit is availed of from day to day," subject, of course, to a certain minimum interest which would have to be paid in any case. The bank can curtail or withdraw the facilities at any time, and unfortunately some banks do this often without regard to the difficulties of the industry. Thus both parties have a sneaking regard for a system which is admitted to be inelastic and needs reform. In England, too, although in the past industry and agriculture were financed by bills, in recent years for one reason or another British industrialists have to a large extent given up the use of bills as far as internal trade is concerned in spite of the fact that bankers would like to see some return to the old methods. Industrial credit is now given almost entirely through loans and overdrafts. Governor Strong, in his evidence before the Royal Commission on Indian Currency, has explained how the United States sought to develop the use of trade bills to a greater extent than before. The stamp duty on these bills was found to interfere greatly with the operation of the Federal Reserve Banks, and had

[1] Governor Strong's Evidence, *Royal Commission on Indian Currency*, 1926, Vol. 5, p. 313.

the effect of restricting the development and use of the type of paper upon which a money market must depend for its functioning. It was considered to be "a nuisance tax," and was removed. Similarly, in India, too, in Governor Strong's words, "a stamp tax upon bills is possibly quite a mistake," and must therefore be abolished.

In order to enable banks to grant advances on the personal credit of the borrowers, the provision of the Indian Companies Act requiring the balance sheet to show separately a bank's secured advances from unsecured advances should be abrogated. Further, not until a closer contact and a more intimate knowledge exist between borrowers and banks would it be possible for such clean advances to be made. To secure this end, two steps are essential. In the first place, business men must be both willing and able to show their trade and industrial position in an intelligible form to the bankers, and secondly, the practice common elsewhere of "one man, one bank," must be cultivated. "The drift towards the use of secured paper as against unsecured or credit paper and the growth of paper protected by collateral" have become more universal since the war.

But even in the granting of secured credits, some hindrances exist. Banks might show a more liberal policy in regard to lending on stocks of goods and material in course of manufacture. The practice of keeping goods under the lock and key of the banks without giving suitable facilities for sale should be done away with, and independent warehouses should be established under legal safeguards, whose warrants could be used as collateral security, thus dispensing with the need to hand over the goods to the banker. Provision should also be made for the independent valuation of goods so that the banks may be able to dispose of the present arbitrary methods of valuation, and to advance on smaller margins.

For smaller concerns, and in regard to temporary loans, mortgages created by a single deposit or documents (without any mortgage instrument or registration) would be a great convenience to the commercial community as well as to banks. The practice should grow, and the existence of many legal impediments against easy and free transfer of property owing to the Hindu and Mohammedan laws of property has been a great obstacle to the use of property as security for bank credit. If these legal hindrances could be removed, a most useful instrument of credit would be available for bank advances.

IV

The Indian Money Market

BANKS' INVESTMENTS

One of the most outstanding features of the Indian banking system is the large proportion of investments in Government securities and the unimportant position of bill holdings among the assets of the banks. The following table[1] brings out the difference between the position in England and that in India.

British Banks, 1928 (*in Million £*)

Capital and Reserve	133	Cheques in transit	48
Current and Deposit Accounts	1,769	Investments	259
		Bills Discounted	246
		Advances	945
		Money at call	145
		Cash	197

Indian Banks (*in Crores of Rupees*)

	Imperial Bank	Joint-Stock Banks
Liabilities		
Capital and Reserve	10·85	6·66
Current and Deposit Accounts	79·25	52·20
Assets		
Investments	19·04	20·06
Bills	12·47	1·23
Advances	51·85	33·42
Cash	10·65	6·83

[1] *Indian Central Banking Enquiry Committee*, Report, p. 395.

But, as has been observed by Parker Willis and Beckhart,[1] there has been since the war a great change in the degree of liquidity of the portfolios of banks all over the world. This is seen from the fact that there has been an increase in the quantity of public or Government paper carried, a general invasion of assets by paper obviously of long-term or of somewhat "frozen" character, e.g. advances made to Government, etc., and an increase in the proportion of time deposits. These are the results of changed conditions which required the nursing of weak concerns by commercial banks. The large investment in Government securities takes partly the place of marketable bills which may be rediscounted with a central banking institution. At present, although it is possible for joint-stock banks to discount their bills, they are unwilling to do so because they regard the Imperial Bank as a rival which should not know their bill portfolios, and also because if they borrow on Government securities they have the advantage of clearing off their debt at any time. In the words of Mr. Macdonald, Managing Governor of the Imperial Bank of India, "the real reason for the preference of joint-stock banks for borrowing against Government securities to rediscounting bills with the Imperial Bank is that the banks desire to benefit by reducing the interest they pay to the Imperial Bank and that it is more difficult to do this if they obtain the accommodation by rediscount than by loans against Government securities." The lack of any definite standard as to what constitutes an approved bill has made the position of joint-stock banks uncertain, thus preventing them from going to the Imperial Bank for rediscount. Whatever the cause, the large investments in Government securities have restricted the supply and the turnover of available funds for industry.

Closely connected with this question has been the difficulty of supplying sufficient credit in times of seasonal pressure, owing to the absence of abundant trade bills. For a long time it was thought that the seasonal stringency of monetary purchasing power was inevitable, and although attempts have been made to relieve this stringency by various measures, there still remains a

[1] *Foreign Banking Systems*, Pitman, 1929, p. 22.

very wide divergence between the rate in the busy season and that in the slack season as Table VI below will show. The Indian Central Banking Committee has done well in placing on record its opinion "that the present conception that the seasonal monetary stringency in India is inevitable, and that this stringency must bring about a wide range of interest rates is *erroneous* and can be traced to the existing defective system of control of currency and credit." Something has been done to introduce more elasticity into the system of credit control by section 20 of the Indian Paper Currency Act of 1923, whereby power has been taken to issue currency notes to an amount not exceeding Rs. 12 crores against bills of exchange maturing within 90 days of the date of such issue. But "no issue can be made until the bank rate rises to 6 per cent, and the entire amount outstanding at any time bears interest at bank rate, subject to a minimum limit of 6 per cent for the first 4 crores, and 7 per cent for the subsequent Rs. 8 crores." The fixing of the minimum rate, the supply of the extra currency only at 7 per cent, and the fixing of the arbitrary limit of Rs. 12 crores are all makeshifts which are really an anachronism in any up-to-date money market. But no permanent solution of these problems can be found until the Reserve Bank is established.

DIVERGENCE OF RATES IN THE VARIOUS MONEY MARKETS

There is a wide disparity between the bank rate and the market rates, and the central problem of banking in India is to bridge the gulf that separates the two. One of the important reasons for this divergence is that there is no central bank to control both currency and credit. As the Royal Commission on Currency has pointed out, "The Government controls the currency. The credit situation is controlled as far as it is controlled at all by the Imperial Bank. With divided control there is likelihood of divided counsels and failure to co-operate." But the Imperial Bank not being a proper central bank, but an ordinary commercial bank doing banking business for the State, is dependent on Government policy in respect of the credit that it can supply. It has, further, no means of controlling the operations of the indigenous bankers and shroffs.

Thus there are in the country two money markets, the Indian money market or the bazaar, and the money market controlled by banking institutions working on Western lines. "The natural link between the two markets would appear to be a steady supply of trade bills endorsed by reliable firms or discount houses which are in touch with both markets, and are able to meet the needs at one end of the merchant who prefers the elastic methods of bazaar finance and to take advantage at the other end of entry into the central money and discount markets."[1] But this implies a mobilization of the whole of the floating resources of the country into one large pool into which bills can find their way with as little delay, and with the intervention of as few intermediaries as possible. "At present the resources more closely resemble a stream which is constantly being blocked by obstacles preventing a flow of bills." The establishment of a central bank is the only solution to all these difficulties, and the only method by which a properly functioning money market can be established.

BANKS AND TREASURY BILLS

Although Treasury bills were first introduced in India in 1917, with a view to raising funds for the temporary needs of the Government of India and for supplementing the Ways and Means programme, they have become in recent years, and especially since 1926, the instrument by which Government has assumed control of the credit situation in the country. They are issued in amounts of Rs. 5,000 and over, and normally only banks and financial houses can participate in their purchase. But for several years they had the effect of reducing deposits and of competing with banks for available deposits.[2] This had a double consequence. Owing to the high rates at which Government was borrowing on long-dated Treasury bills, the ability of the cotton mills to

[1] *Indian Central Banking Enquiry Committee*, Report, p. 401.

[2] Ibid., Vol. 1, p. 405; Vol. 2, p. 750. When Government issues Treasury bills, some Indian deposits are actually withdrawn from banks and invested in them. It is not merely the banks that take up the Treasury bills (Lala Harkishan Lal).

attract public deposits was seriously curtailed.[1] Secondly, in so far as part of the available deposits went from the banks to Government, the resources of the banks were reduced and they had sometimes to refuse to advance money to mill companies or to do so at enhanced rates of interest. Even if banks were the only institution that subscribed to the Treasury bills, the indirect effects on industry were no less serious. By investing largely in bills, the capacity of the banks to make advances was diminished, and industry felt the restriction of credit. Even when the proceeds of Treasury bills were disbursed into the money market, and contraction of credit counteracted, advances to industry were made only at a higher rate of interest. The fact that "Government paid 1 to 1½ per cent higher than the rate at which banks could secure deposits for a like period"[2] was some indication of the unsatisfactory method of Government's operations. By raising the general rate of interest on gilt-edged investment, Government's Treasury-bill operations had the effect of reacting adversely on all investments. This depreciation in gilt-edged securities injuriously affected the value of the banks' investments, and many banks found their financial position very critical. While the net borrowings of the Government of India since 1925–6 (up to 1930) in the form of loans, Treasury bills and cash certificates amounted to Rs. 140 crores, the amount of bank deposits remained stationary during the last ten years.[3] The conclusion is almost irresistible that industry must have been injuriously affected by lack of credit. Bank investments in gilt-edged securities in India form a very high percentage of their investments compared with such percentages in other countries. Industrial credit can be increased only if such investments are largely replaced by commercial bills as early as possible. Again, the time at which loans and Treasury bills have been issued has not always been happy. Contraction of credit has taken place at a time when industry could not afford to do with less credit. Unlike the British banks, which in similar circumstances when the Bank of England pursued a deflationary

[1] *Indian Central Banking Enquiry Committee*, Report, Vol. 2, p. 594.
[2] Ibid., Vol. 3, p. 496.
[3] Ibid., p. 406.

policy counteracted the possible reduction in deposits by lowering the cash ratio,[1] Indian banks restricted advances to industry on such occasions. But the whole series of reforms proposed in this chapter depend for their success upon the establishment and working of a suitable Reserve Bank, which should be the spear-head of the banking system.

Figures taken from the Statistical Tables relating to Banks (1931):

TABLE I

Number of head offices and branches of banks

	Head Offices	Branches
Imperial Bank of India ..	3	163
Exchange Banks	—	89
Indian Joint-Stock Banks ..	159	492

TABLE II

Deposits of the Imperial Bank, Exchange Bank, and Indian Joint-Stock Banks since 1919 (in Crores of Rupees).

	Imperial Bank (Private Deposits)	Exchange Banks	Joint-Stock Banks	Total
1919	68	74	61	203
1920	78	75	73	226
1921	66	75	80	221
1922	57	73	65	195
1923	74	68	48	190
1924	77	71	55	203
1925	78	71	58	207
1926	74	72	63	209
1927	72	69	64	205
1928	71	71	66	208
1929	72	67	66	205
1930	77	68	68	213
1931	64	67	66	197

[1] *Report of the Committee on Finance and Industry (Macmillan Committee)*, 1931, p. 76.

TABLE III

Clearing-House Returns (in Lakhs of Rupees).

1924 ..	.. 177,824
1925 ..	.. 177,[illegible]
1926 ..	.. 159,158
1927 ..	.. 164,933
1928 ..	.. 185,683
1929 ..	.. 203,807
1930 ..	.. 180,423
1931 ..	.. 156,150

TABLE IV

Proportion per cent of cash to liabilities on deposits of the several classes of banks on December 31st

	1921	1922	1923	1924	1925	1926
Imperial Bank	19	21	18	18	21	26
Indian Joint-Stock Banks:						
(*a*) Large	20	20	17	21	19	15
(*b*) Small	13	17	19	13	20	24

	1927	1928	1929	1930	1931
Imperial Bank	14	13	18	16	15
Indian Joint-Stock Banks:					
(*a*) Large	13	13	14	12	12
(*b*) Small	15	15	13	12	12

TABLE V

Imperial Bank of India. Average Bank Rate from 1921 for each half-year.

	Half-Year ended June 30th	Half-Year ended December 31st	Annual Average
1921	6·04	5·11	5·57
1922	7·13	4·51	5·81
1923	7·42	4·50	5·96
1924	8·05	5·32	6·68
1925	6·58	4·70	5·64
1926	5·65	4·70	5·17
1927	6·51	4·96	5·73
1928	6·94	5·46	6·20
1929	6·88	5·79	6·33
1930	6·51	5·28	5·89
1931	6·74	7·35	7·04

TABLE VI

Seasonal stringency for money will be seen from the following variations in the Bank Rate

1921	per cent
January ..	7
March ..	6
June ..	5
December ..	6
December 29	7

1922	per cent	
February ..	8	
April ..	7	
June ..	6	
June 15 ..	5	
July ..	4	From July to March variations from 4–8 %
October ..	5	
December ..	6	
December 28	7	

1923	per cent
January ..	8

1924	per cent
March ..	9
April ..	8
May ..	7
June ..	6
July ..	5
July 31 ..	4
August ..	5
October ..	6

1925	per cent
January ..	7
June ..	6
July ..	5
August ..	4
October ..	5

1926	per cent
January ..	6
June ..	5
July ..	4

TABLE VI—(*continued*)

1927	per cent	1928	per cent	1929	per cent
January	5	January	7	January	7
February	6	July	6	March	8
March	7	August	5	April	7
July	5	December	6	May	6
August	4			June	5
October	5			October	6
				October 31	7
1930	per cent	1931	per cen		
March	6	January	7		
July	5				
November	6				

CHAPTER VI

MANAGING AGENTS AND INDUSTRIAL FINANCE

I

THE ROLE OF THE MANAGING AGENTS

We have described in the last two chapters the methods employed by organized industry to raise capital for fixed and current requirements and the part played by Indian joint-stock banks and the Imperial Bank of India in the provision of the capital needs of industry. We saw in the first place how most of the industries, not excluding the Bombay and Ahmedabad cotton-mill industry, started with a low amount of share capital and borrowed from other agencies and institutions the balance of their requirements. It was also seen how the banks were not prepared to finance the long-term needs of industry, and were unable to provide more than the "circulating" capital for short periods to industry. Even in providing this credit on the security of materials and stocks of goods, banks insisted upon the signature of two persons, and this in the case of an industrial company meant the signature not only of the company as such, but also of the managing agents in their personal capacity. In these two sets of factors, i.e. in the general under-capitalization of business units and the growth and character of Indian commercial banking, is to be found the explanation for the general prevalence and the continuance of the managing agency system in India. In the words of the Bombay Millowners' Association, "it should be remembered that the managing agents have a double function to perform in India against the single function of the Managing Director in England (and other countries). In England the Managing Director or Manager is a paid servant and only looks after the working of the mills; the managing agents in India have not only to look to the satisfactory working of the mills but to *finance* them, and have frequently suffered very severely by doing so. Banks in India will not lend money as they do in England to the mill company itself. They require not only the signature of the mill company for any loan made to the mill, but also require in addition the guarantee of the managing agents."[1] Again, "the necessity [for the managing agency system] arises from the fact that it is impossible in the present state of banking in this country to find either the share capital at the start or the other finance necessary to run a particular concern unless it is backed by a firm of substantial resources." In the opinion of the Bombay Chamber of Commerce, representing European opinion, "the Bombay mills are under-capitalized; the old school of thought in industrial finance in Bombay was in favour of loan capital" and an insufficient paid-up capital. The theory that was held was that it was better to borrow at 5 per cent than to have to issue debentures at 6½ per cent and to get a lower dividend on the capital employed.[2] One more quotation from the evidence of a person who is not a managing agent himself, but is an investor and a Director in a large number of industrial concerns, will serve to emphasize the role of the managing agents in the industrial life of India. "It is well known that banks at present are unwilling to advance moneys on the security of the assets of a limited concern unless the same is backed by the personal security of the agents themselves. As no practical banker in India would be prepared to make a departure from the practice, it is no use proposing an alternative system unless the whole organization of commercial and banking credit is changed."[3]

Industrial financing in India is so intimately connected with the system of managing agents that it is necessary to examine the nature of the financial assistance rendered by managing agents, the merits of such financing and its drawbacks. In all the quotations given above, only one aspect has been emphasized: viz. the rigidity of the conditions under which bank

[1] *Indian Tariff Board: Cotton Industry*, 1927, Vol. 2. Written evidence of the Bombay Millowners' Association.

[2] Ibid., Vol. 3, p. 239 (Bombay Chamber of Commerce).

[3] Ibid., Vol. 4, p. 4, Evidence of Sir P. Thakurdas.

advances were made to industrial concerns. But this hardly serves to explain why the managing agency system of industrial finance should have taken such deep root in the country, or even why the banks should have imposed such apparently severe conditions in granting credit. Further, it would be altogether too simplified a view of the problem to imply, as the above quotations do, that if the banks were to change their credit practice the managing agency system of industrial finance could at once be altered.

The system by which managing agents came to fulfil a role different from that of an ordinary Board of Directors of a limited company can only be explained by the general economic conditions that prevailed when industries were started as public limited companies. As has been pointed out already, since there were no large classes of investors, the capital had to be provided by them and their friends. The assistance available being limited, the minimum absolutely essential just to start an industrial concern was made the basis for capitalization. It was to them an internal problem whether they should put all their capital in the form of shares, or put in a portion of their capital as shares and the rest to be utilized when and as required. Indeed, there were sufficient reasons why in many cases they chose to start with a fairly small paid-up capital, just enough to meet block expenditure, and reserved the remaining funds to be utilized for working expenses. In the first place the managing agents had greater freedom in the use of their funds than when all their funds were locked up in fixed assets. They could borrow from the rich capitalists or other financiers on account of their own strength, and the interest on this capital would be less than the rate to be given to the shareholders. When managing agents came to control more than one concern it was always useful for them to have control over a certain amount of "free" resources so that they could be transferred from one to another. The advances to each company may suitably be varied with the requirements of each.

But this was not the only reason. The cotton, jute, tea, and other industries grew entirely independent of the banks for the reason that banking development came later, and that in any case the banks would not be able to meet the current capital needs of industry. There was practically no choice for industry except to depend on the managing agents. These were not mere trading and industrial firms. They were inheritors of the tradition of the earlier agency firms who combined a large amount of banking business as subsidiary to their other activities. "The great Agency Houses of Calcutta added banking to their businesses."[1] Sometimes a bank with an independent name, but essentially a department of the Agency House, was started, and the fortunes of the bank or banking department were linked up with those of the agency firm. Thus the Bank of Hindusthan was just "a department of the firm of Alexander & Co.,"[2] and failed when the latter became bankrupt. This fusion of functions of every managing agency firm may be seen from the nature of the business organization of Messrs. Arbuthnot & Co., Madras, whose banking business at one time reached enormous proportions. According to the Official Liquidator of the firm the business transacted by the company was under the following heads:

1. The Banking Department.
2. A General Agency Department.
3. Import and Export Department.
4. Skins and Hides Department.
5. Indigo, Cotton, and Timber Department.
6. General Shipping Department.
7. Estates and West Coast Agencies Department.

The Arbuthnot Bank had invested Rs. 25 lakhs in Arbuthnot Industrials, Ltd., which was directly connected with several industrial concerns, a jute mill, a cement works, rice mills, sugar mills, etc.[3] Although the present managing agents in Bengal have not started separate banking institutions, several of them have banking departments with ample resources to finance their varied activities. Thus the firm of Andrew Yule & Co., one of the leading

[1] H Sinha, *Early European Banking in India*, 1927, p. 4.
[2] Ibid., p. 5. [3] *Madras Mail*, October 22, 1906.

agency firms at the present time, does not have to borrow from any joint-stock or exchange bank for their enormous financing operations.[1] Had the basis of capitalization been different, it might have been expected that industry could have financed itself with the small assistance which banks would have been able to provide by financing the stock of goods, etc. But under-capitalization meant that some agency or institution was needed to provide the minimum working capital and other funds which may be required over and above what the banks could provide. In the cotton industry, public deposits fulfilled this function for a long time, and even now occupy an important place. But these deposits depended more on the solvency and reputation of managing agents, and were not, in any case, sufficient to meet the full needs, and hence the managing agents became very important purveyors of advances to industry. As has been pointed out by the present head of Andrew Yule & Co. in a letter to the author, "certain managing agency firms do the whole of the financing of their companies themselves and are not dependent on joint-stock or exchange banks for raising the finance to provide their companies with working capital; on the other hand, there are other managing agency firms who have not the necessary funds to finance their companies, and they, of course, are dependent on loans which they obtain from the banks." The fact that Andrew Yule & Co. manage 54 industrial companies (excluding certain special classes of enterprise) and yet are altogether independent of bank credit is highly significant.

Again, the methods adopted by the Imperial Bank and the joint-stock banks in granting advances to industry directly led to the establishment of the managing agents as the inevitable link between the banking system and the industrial concerns. The Imperial Bank of India Act of 1920 prohibits the bank from discounting or advancing "on the security of any negotiable instrument of any individual or partnership firm payable at the town or place where it is presented for discount, which does not carry with it the *several responsibilities of at least two persons or*

[1] Letter to the author from the head of Andrew Yule & Co.

firms unconnected with each other in general partnership." This has led to the practice of getting the signature of the managing agents on notes of hand in addition to the signature of a Director of the company who signs on its behalf. Although other banks have not to work under the same restrictions, they have more or less followed the lead of the Imperial Bank in this matter and have been unwilling to advance money on the security of the assets of a limited concern unless it is backed by the personal security of the agents themselves. It is true that where loans are granted on the security of goods which are pledged to the bank, the guarantee of the managing agents is not insisted upon. But the practice seems to vary. In Calcutta the Imperial Bank allows credit on the hypothecation of goods without the personal guarantee of the managing agents.[1] On the other hand, in all other places, including Bombay, even where goods are hypothecated, the signature of the managing agents is insisted upon,[2] and the practice is justified on the ground that if the cotton yarn and piece goods fall in price and a deficit arises, there should be someone on whom the bank may rely to make it up. The explanation is not satisfying, and there is no reason why banks should not take reasonable margins as they often do elsewhere. The real difficulty lies elsewhere, and the present practice is the result partly of accident and partly of evolution. When a mill company applied for credit to the Imperial Bank, the person who applied for it was, of course, the managing agent or agency firm. The bank was perfectly willing to grant credit, but owing to the restrictions under which it works it wanted a second name to the credit instrument. The managing agent got a Director to sign on behalf of the company, thus satisfying the requirements of the bank. It will be observed that in India under the system of industrial management by managing agents, the signature of the managing agents was the most essential thing and that of a Director or Directors signing for the company was a practice which grew entirely out of legal difficulties. Further, the relation of managing agents to the industrial concerns they

[1] *Indian Tariff Board: Cotton Industry*, 1927, Vol. 4, p. 23.
[2] Ibid.

manage is unique and entirely different from the practice in other countries. They put in their funds and take them out at their discretion, and use them in other concerns, often in some of their own subsidiary businesses. The banker cannot know at any given time what the exact financial position of the company is; on the other hand he has greater confidence in the agency firm and therefore is willing to advance on the guarantee of the agents. Thus the system has grown owing to law and the peculiarity of the managing agency system of industrial administration. But whatever the explanation, the grip of the agents on industrial companies has tightened as a result of their being the necessary intermediary in obtaining credit, and the dependence of industry on managing agents for its finance directly and indirectly is very great.

II

FORMS OF FINANCIAL ASSISTANCE BY MANAGING AGENTS

The managing agents, besides being singly the most important shareholders of industrial companies, are also the most considerable creditors. The table on p. 181 shows that in the cotton industry the amount of working funds they placed at its disposal in Bombay and Ahmedabad amounted to Rs. 7·96 crores in 1929, and this compared to the Rs. 2.68 crores lent by banks reveals the preponderance of the credit supplied by the managing agents. Even the public deposits rank only next in importance, being 6.99 crores of rupees. Again, the managing agents hold a fair amount of debentures in their hands, and in the case of Bombay mills about 46 lakhs of rupees out of a total of Rs. 238 lakhs was held by managing agents. But the importance of their financing function is not to be judged by the amount of working capital on loan supplied to the company. Both bank credit and public deposits depend on the guarantee or the good name of the managing agents. In the years immediately following the establishment of an industrial company, the financial backing of the managing agents is often required to save the concern from ruin. The amount of capital which they have lost is some indication of the extent to which industry has benefited by its being supported in times of difficulty by managing agents. Some of the managing agents have such a high sense of their self-respect and pride that they have been prepared to stake their whole fortunes in seeing that an enterprise started by them does not collapse.[1] They would not allow their name, standing, or credit to be easily shaken or impaired. Some of them have rendered a service to industry by taking on their own shoulders the losses inevitable in the initial stages of the career of an industrial concern. The continuous provision of capital to pioneer concerns to enable them to tide over the period during which adequate returns could not be produced is an essential task which in existing conditions the managing agents alone can perform. Some idea of the amount of advances made by managing agents to some concerns may be had from the statements at the end of the chapter. In Ahmedabad, apart from the funds directly provided by the managing agents, a great deal of the deposits was in the first instance provided by the commission partners who shared in the agency commission, in return for which they put in a certain amount of deposits. Altogether, in the cotton industry in western India the role of the managing agents as financiers is very considerable.

In respect of the tea industry, nearly the same tendency is noticeable. But there are differences. The requirements of the tea industry in regard to current expenditure form relatively a smaller percentage of the fixed expenditure than in many other industries, and the managing agents have no great need to undertake the financing from their own funds in normal times. Their financial service to the tea industry becomes very important in times of depression and falling prices. The European section of the tea industry being established with sufficient initial capital does not suffer for want of funds. Such resources as it requires are easily available on the guarantee of the agents from the banks

[1] This holds true only of the more important and reputable agency firms. Tata, Sons & Co., Currimbhais in relation to Kastoorchand Mills are instances in point (*Indian Tariff Board: Cotton Industry*, 1927, Vol. 4, p. 4).

with or without the pledging of the crops. But the grossly under-capitalized gardens, mostly under the control of the Indian managing agents, suffer even in normal times, and more particularly in times of depression. But these are not controlled by managing agents of any great standing. So far as the more important managing agents, British and Indian, are concerned, they finance the tea industry in just the same manner as they finance cotton or jute mills, but as the working capital needs are less and can be had from the banks, it is more their name and guarantee rather than the actual funds directly loaned by them that are important. Further, the establishment and growth of certain financial and sales agents in Calcutta who, while not participating in the actual management of gardens, are able and willing to provide the finance for the tea industry and arrange sales of the produce has partly lightened the burden of the managing agents in financing the industry. Thus Martin & Co. act as financial and sales agents for eighteen tea gardens in Jalpaiguri, and grant advances to them. Most of the funds are granted against mortgage of gardens, buildings and machinery, in the case of new concerns, and against hypothecation of crops in established gardens.[1] Besides interest payments, the tea gardens have to sell their produce through these agents who charge 2½ per cent on gross sales and thus are "tied" to them.

In regard to the jute industry there has been no difficulty in the way of financing the jute concerns by managing agents. The jute preference shares and debentures being very much sought after, the normal requirements of the concern both in respect of fixed and working capital were easily raised from the public. On the guarantee of the managing agents, additional credit could always be raised from the banks, even for the financing of the purchase of raw material, and thus the extent of direct financing by the managing agents in jute concerns has become less and less as each company became well established. In the early years of the starting of a jute mill company the mill agent was certainly required to find a considerable amount of

[1] *Bengal Banking Committee*, Report, 1930, para. 213.

resources himself, but after it worked for some years more permanent financing became possible, and debentures on the one hand and bank advances on the other were found to be adequate for the financial needs of the company. But some managing agents are entirely independent of banks, as has already been pointed out.

When managing agents lend funds to the companies, the interest that is charged is generally 1 to 2 per cent above the bank rate. But this is not universal. In the cotton industry there have been several instances where large funds have been placed at the disposal of industrial concerns at 6 per cent at a time when money could not be had at anything less than 8 per cent.[1] Since control is in their hands, and none can know better the actual financial condition of the mill, they do not need to get security for their advances, and do not take any. But there have been cases where the mill's debentures are placed as security against the overdraft secured directly or indirectly by the managing agents (as in the case of the Bengal Paper Mill Co.). In cotton mills, jute mills, and other concerns, it has sometimes happened that the continuous indebtedness of the company to the agents has led to the issuing of debentures to the agents, and when the concern does not go well and is unable to pay interest on the debentures, the managing agents have themselves foreclosed. Again, both in Bengal and in Bombay, some managing agents have kept the surplus funds of one concern in their hands as deposits at 2 or 3 per cent, and loaned them out at 1 per cent above the bank rate, and pocketed the difference.[2] But such cases are exceptional rather than general. It would be wrong to condemn the managing agents as a class for the shortcomings of a few. On the whole, it may be stated that

[1] *Indian Tariff Board: Cotton Industry*, 1927, Vol. 4, p. 87: "A certain firm of managing agents made Rs. 9,000 in four years by way of commission, but had to undertake financing to the extent of 1 crore of rupees, 70 lakhs of which was its own money lent to the company at 6 per cent."

[2] At an interview with Sir C. Rhodes: The practice of lending the money of one company to another is not unknown in Bengal. In one case a managing agent used the funds of one concern which he held as deposit by paying the bank rate on deposits (2 per cent) and loaned it at 1 per cent above the bank rate for advances.

the financial services rendered by the managing agents are most important in the earlier stages of the career of an industrial concern, and become less and less (or at least ought to become less and less if the concern is properly managed) as the company is firmly established, except in periods of depression. In a country where banking development has been very slow, where difficulties of raising permanent capital from investors are great in the initial stages, and where at any rate during the period of the inevitable handicaps to the growth of a new concern some financial assistance of a kind which the commercial banking system cannot render is necessary, it is obvious that managing agents can fulfil a very useful function.

THEIR SERVICE IN TIME OF DEPRESSION

In another direction, too, they have fulfilled a very essential and highly important function which, in the existing commercial and financial mechanism of the country, could not be performed by anyone else. The managing agents have been the bulwark preventing the industrial concerns from collapsing in times of industrial depression. This aspect of the matter has not been sufficiently recognized in assessing the value of the financial services rendered to industry by managing agents, and while it is possible to exaggerate it, it is equally necessary to note its significance in the industrial development of India. When the tea industry of India passed through difficult times in 1920–1, and again in 1927–8, it was the financial strength of the managing agents that saved them from collapse and liquidation.[1] The continual losses of the industry dissuaded the banks from renewing the advances, and had the industry had no other agency to fall back on, many of the concerns would almost certainly have had to close down. The same thing happened in the jute and coal-mining industry and in the cotton industry. In the years when the Bombay cotton industry was in a critical condition, many more mills would have gone into liquidation than those that actually closed down but for the capacity of the agents to bear the losses them-

[1] Letter to the author from Sir T. Catto.

selves and their willingness or ability to finance at those times.[1] In the existing state of banking organization it was hardly surprising that banks were unwilling to lock up their funds in the cotton industry, and the managing agents carried the burden as well as they could. To this extent the problem of industrial financing has been better solved in India than in England, and this particularly holds good of the industry controlled by the European managing agents. In the cotton industry in Bombay the managing agents have been unable to finance the industry in this period of continual losses, and their ability to undertake financing has been seriously impaired. In regard to the jute and tea industries, owing to the monopolistic position of the former and the relative importance of Indian tea in the world's market, the managing agents have every inducement to persevere and to continue financing, inspired by the knowledge that recovery is only a matter of time. But the crisis lasted sufficiently long to inflict serious damage on the industries and only the ability of the managing agents and their independence of banking credit enabled them to survive.

III

DEFECTS OF THE MANAGING AGENCY SYSTEM OF FINANCE

But the system of managing agency finance reveals certain characteristic defects. In the first place, industry has come to be too much dominated by financial considerations, and too little by industrial factors. Finance, instead of being the servant of industry, has become its master, with injurious consequences. The result of a system by which an industrial concern is handed over to the management of a certain body of individuals, not because they are the most qualified directing heads of the concern, but because they have the financial resources to help industry, inevitably leads to the subordination of industrial to financial

[1] See Evidence of Sir P. Thakurdas, *Indian Tariff Board: Cotton Industry*, Vol. 4, p. 24: "But for the managing agency system, you would have had 30 mills in liquidation to-day."

considerations. In the numerous transfers of agency from one firm to another that have taken place during the last twenty-three or thirty years, it will be found that one set of managing agents gave up their agency because of their financial difficulties, and another took them up because they could for the moment supply the required finance. In neither case does industrial capacity ever enter into the matter. In the cotton industry where transfers of agency are more common, this has led to a certain degree of inferior administration, and in any case such constant changes in managing agencies have brought about a certain amount of restlessness and flux in the industry.

Secondly, the burden thrown on managing agents has sometimes been so heavy that many of them sink, bringing down their businesses, too, with them. This has happened in many cases, and where one managing agency firm manages a very large number of concerns either in the same or allied industries, the difficulties of some concerns have reacted unfavourably on all, and the sound as well as unsound concerns suffer equally and unjustly. In Bombay two managing agency firms have between them about 23 mills, having nearly one-third of the total paid-up capital, and two-fifths of the spindleage, and it is almost inevitable that the weaknesses of one or two concerns should react on others and perhaps bring all of them into great difficulties. Thus the concentration of management of several mills in the hands of a few agency firms has obviously a limit set by the financial resources of the agents; and even the most powerful managing agency firms cannot afford to take up more than a certain number of concerns under their management.

Again, owing to the managing agency system of industrial finance, no mill company has been able to develop its own system of financing independently of the managing agents. This has led to a double consequence. In the first place, instances have occurred when, owing to the deterioration in the financial position of the managing agents on account of their other activities, the mill company suffers, although its own position may remain quite sound. Most of the managing agency firms have other important subsidiary activities, and these sometimes land them in difficulties. Banks withdraw their cash credit whatever be the condition of the mill, for they have no knowledge of the intrinsic soundness of the concerns whose financial position is somehow so much mixed up with that of the managing agent. The earning capacity of the mill and its power of repayment are not the tests applied by the banks, because these tests are difficult of application. In the second place, the transfer of funds from the more successful to a weaker and needy concern, both managed by the same agency firm, even if it helps the weaker firm has the unfortunate effect of reducing the incentive to investment. The stimulus to investment which large dividends afford is removed by the reduction in profits which imprudent loans to allied concerns inevitably bring about. It has been contended with some justification that the shareholders of the stronger mill companies would have benefited both by capital appreciation and larger dividends; and the stimulus to investment, if successful concerns were allowed to declare larger dividends, would more than compensate any check to investment arising from the losses of the weaker companies. In other words, although the failure of weak concerns might scare away some investors, the knowledge that investment in strong and efficient mills is still highly profitable will induce more investment in the industry as a whole, and on balance it may not be undesirable to let the unsound mills wind up rather than allow them to bring about a general deterioration in the industry as a whole. The force of the above argument is weakened if the investment in allied concerns does not bring about any loss. Nor can it hold good in a period of general depression when even a well-managed concern may suffer temporarily. But in any case there is some ground for thinking that the dependence on the managing agency system of finance has had the effect of taking away from the bank its responsibility for looking more closely into the internal financial and economic condition of a concern and preventing the business from getting financial aid on its own assets and goodwill.

But the most injurious result of this system, at least as it works in Bombay, is the enormous speculation in the shares of cotton-mill companies that the managing agency system has brought about. Few persons have understood the significance of the "cornering" activity on the Bombay Stock Exchange and its disastrous consequences. Since the management of a cotton-mill company is in the hands of agents who at the start controlled a majority of shares, any weakness in their position leads to speculative activity on the part of a small group of persons who want to drive them away and get control of the company in their hands by becoming holders of a majority of shares and to earn the agency commission. The financial embarrassment of the agents may have resulted from their speculation in outside business, in trade and commerce. The knowledge of their weakness, which has little to do with the internal position of the mills they manage, causes speculation in the shares of those concerns. Many of the "corners" which have disgraced the Bombay Stock Exchange since 1900 have been the result of the interdependence between the managing agents' external activities and their functions as financial agents of the companies they manage. A body of speculative capitalists are always ready to take the initiative at the first touch of adversity, and it is the existence of this element that supplies the key to the cornering of cotton mill shares in Bombay.[1] Had the mills been less dependent on managing agents for their finance, such situations would not be possible, and the losses to investors owing to the enormous fluctuations brought about by speculation would have been avoided.

IV

SUGGESTIONS FOR REFORM

These grave defects in the system of industrial finance notwithstanding, it would be hasty to conclude that the system of managing agents must go and a different system of financing should be adopted. For one thing, the system is too deep rooted in the country to disappear merely because of the desire of some critics that it should. An institution that has slowly evolved as a result of certain economic circumstances cannot suddenly vanish until the conditions that gave rise to it themselves alter. But even

[1] *Report of the Bombay Stock Exchange Enquiry Committee*, p. 25.

if circumstances change, it is possible for the institution to adjust itself to the changed situation and to reform itself. Further, it is only in Bombay and to a lesser extent in Ahmedabad that the agency system has come in for serious criticism; but some of the dissatisfaction with its working is due to the depression in the Bombay section of the cotton industry. The managing agency system is working still in its full vigour in Bengal and other places. Hence, whatever may be the view one takes of the need for changing the existing method of industrial financing by managing agents, the fact remains that for a long time yet it will continue to prevail and will only change in some of its details. One has to stress this aspect a little because in recent years criticism of the managing agents, perfectly legitimate in itself, has often led to absolutely impracticable proposals of reform. No new institution can be "suddenly" and "newly" created to take the place of an existing agency, and the only possible line of reform is readaptation and readjustment to changed economic and social conditions. This readjustment can be the more easily brought about if certain measures are undertaken. We have seen above how the banking system in India has been working on too conservative lines, and has not merely insisted upon the guaranteeing of the loans and advances by the managing agents, but has based its credits more on the reputation and worth of the agents than on the financial position of the mill companies under their management. This has led to a vicious circle which should be broken.

"The banks are spoiled by the managing agency system and the managing agents are spoiled by the banks, because the banks force the joint-stock companies practically to take managing agents; the banks are quite happy that companies are managed by managing agents, as it gives the banks two signatures for the loans."[1] "The banker is thus not interested in developing other methods of financing industry; he has two signatures and has no reason why he should favour another system which may be quite good for industry but deprives the banker of another signature."[2]

[1] Dr. Jeidels's Evidence, *Indian Central Banking Enquiry Committee*, Vol. 4, p. 244.

[2] Ibid.

If this vicious circle is to be broken, it is necessary for banks to assume greater responsibility in the larger interests of industry, and to rely less on the credit-worthiness of managing agents and more on that of the industrial companies. From the banks' own point of view this will be an advantage, for, owing to the non-registration of managing agency partnerships,[1] it is extremely difficult to assess the credit-worthiness of some managing agents. By granting loans only on the assets of the companies the banks can protect themselves no less than by granting them on the uncertain financial position of the agents. Each industry should have its own credit according to its standing. On the other hand, managing agents should make a clearer distinction between their industrial activities and other commercial or trade activities, and develop a system by which on the assets and soundness of each of their industrial companies they may raise bank loans. The most effective way of bringing about some change is for managing agents to adopt certain common codes, regulations, and practices; and the development of internal rules of conduct will be the most fruitful line of reform. Such concerted action will have the great advantage that while it will strengthen the position of the really strong and reputable agency firms it will have the no less desirable result of weeding out those who have grown like mushrooms and whose existence is a danger and embarrassment to the others.

A no less important step is the need for industry to secure more permanent capital. The whole methods of capitalization must be subjected to greater scrutiny, and no company should be started without an amount of capital which would be sufficient for its fixed expenditure as well as for its minimum working needs. If this be done, it would be possible in normal times for industry to get its current requirements from banks. It would relieve the enormous burden now thrown on the managing agents and diminish the dependence of industrial companies on managing agents. Here again it is up to the managing agents to come to an under-

[1] The effects of unregistered partnerships have been dealt with in a later chapter.

standing. It may be difficult to raise sufficient share capital at the very start of a joint-stock company. But it should be the avowed aim and policy of the managing agents to raise additional capital to the fullest extent of the company's needs as soon as market conditions make it feasible. This would be easy when the company has been in existence for some years and declared dividends. In view of the fact that the failure of a large number of industrial concerns has been due to under-capitalization, the importance of raising sufficient permanent capital at the earliest possible moment cannot be exaggerated.

BUILDING UP OF RESERVES

Equally essential is the building up, by each individual unit, of reserves which may be used as working capital and have the effect of dispensing with the finance supplied by managing agents. This, of course, cannot be done until the concern is well established and has been on a profit-earning basis for some years. But a wise policy of taking annually a fair percentage of profits to reserve will enable the company to face a crisis with greater ease and provide the necessary working capital in normal times. Thus even in the worst periods of depression a few cotton mills were able by drawing on their reserves, which they had carefully built up, to show some dividend. The Textile Tariff Board has given an instance of a mill with a capital of Rs. 8 lakhs, of which 2 lakhs were ordinary shares and Rs. 6 lakhs preference, which, by utilizing part of its profits during the period of the boom to pay off its preference shares, was enabled in the years 1925 and 1926 to pay dividends of 150 and 130 per cent respectively. Further, the reserves may also be utilized partly for extensions and improvement of the industrial concern. In the building up and expansion of British and American companies, the utilization of reserves of profits has been a great factor. The automatic savings of the public accruing to the companies every year have enabled them to make extensions without resort to the public market for capital. In the United States one-third of the net earned income of business is taken to reserves.[1] A similar plan would prove fruitful in India, too.

This method of self-financing is not without its defects, and when carried to excess has serious drawbacks. It might lead to over-investment in the industry, and over-expansion would lead to one-sided consumption. From the point of view of industrial organization as a whole, it might have the effect of an ill-balanced distribution of available capital resources. There is a great deal to be said for declaring a dividend which the profits of an industry would justify and not to depress the security markets by declaring low dividends to shareholders. If the security market is injured by a continual neglect of the shareholders' interest, new enterprises would be unable to procure sufficient capital. Lack of consideration to the shareholder would discourage the public from investing in industrial securities, and new industries might experience great difficulty in getting capital from the public. Above all, it is arguable that the public would make a better choice of investments and distribute available resources among different industries better than managing agents or other entrepreneurs who, in their anxiety to look to their own immediate interest, might bring about over-expansion and over-investment in their own industries. In a country where the capital market is well organized and the investor has a wide choice of investments, he may be able, with the assistance of Investment Trust Companies, Issue Houses, etc., to contribute to more balanced investment than the entrepreneurs who will be interested only in their own individual concerns. From the social point of view it would be preferable if investment had been made in other industries. Although owing to these reasons the policy of "ploughing in" of earnings, as it is called, should be pursued with caution, there is no doubt that in the present circumstances of Indian industry, when there is great need of its developing a system of internal finance without depending on the managing agents, the dangers resulting from the application of such a policy are a long way off and may be practically neglected.

[1] Von Beckerath, *Industrial Organization*, 1933, p. 69.

On the contrary, the injury to the investor has arisen in some cases in a different manner. The remuneration to the managing agents in India includes necessarily the payment for their work of financing the concern, and there is little doubt that excessive dependence on managing agency firms leaves very much less to the shareholders than would have been the case if better methods of financing had prevailed.[1] Hence anything that will release industry from its excessive dependence on managing agents must be considered to be a welcome measure.

The steps suggested above would secure an improvement in the existing system. But as long as there is an absence of other suitable financial machinery to provide industry with capital in times of stress and strain there will be need for the continuance of the managing agency system. The reformation and not the extinction of the agency system of industrial finance must be our objective. To take steps to weed out the incompetent and unsound firms, to improve the position of the well-established and sound ones, to relieve them of the excessive burden now thrown upon them with a view to enabling them to perform the reduced task more efficiently—these are some of the most desirable reforms for the future.

[1] For a further discussion of this point, refer to Chapter IX.

APPENDIX

Fiscal Commission Report, Vol. 3, pp. 910–12.

Statement showing the extent to which some cotton mills depend on managing agents for their financial needs. The information relates to the year 1921.

1. *Meyer Sassoon Mills.*—Out of Rs. 40.8 lakhs of total funds including capital and reserve, the funds loaned by managing agents were 2.8 lakhs.
2. *Tata Mills, Ltd.*—Out of a total of Rs. 342.58 lakhs, the funds supplied by managing agents together with deposits from the public amounted to Rs. 261.28 lakhs.
3. *Swadeshi Mills, Ltd.*—Out of a total of Rs. 139.66 lakhs, Rs. 21.8 lakhs contributed by managing agents, including deposits from the public.
4. *Pearl Mills, Ltd.*—Out of a total of Rs. 57 lakhs, Rs. 10 lakhs contributed by managing agents, including deposits.
5. *E. D. Sassoon United Mills.*—Out of a total capital employed of the value of Rs. 733 lakhs, the working capital borrowed from the managing agents amounted to Rs. 96 lakhs.
6. *Edward Sassoon Mill.*—Out of a total of Rs. 51.21 lakhs, working capital borrowed from managing agents amounted to Rs. 1.5 lakhs.

Tariff Board: Paper and Paper Pulp Industries, 1925, Vol. 1, pp. 113–30.

Bengal Paper Mill Co., Ltd., managed by Balmer, Lawrie & Co., had issued a debenture loan of Rs. 7 lakhs repayable in 1926. Against this there is a debenture redemption fund amounting (in 1924) to Rs. 357,165, and Rs. 192,300 of debentures has not been issued but has been lodged as *security for overdraft with the managing agents.*

Tariff Board: Cement Industry, Evidence of Applicants for Protection, p. 123.

Managing agents of Gwalior Cement Co. had lent Rs. 6 lakhs to the company at 1 per cent above the bank rate.

CHAPTER VII

INDUSTRIAL BANKS AND SPECIAL FINANCIAL INSTITUTIONS

I

PROBLEMS OF INDUSTRIAL FINANCE

The last three chapters have revealed the gaps and deficiencies in the existing system of industrial finance. While some of the defects are undoubtedly capable of being remedied within the framework of the existing banking and financial structure there are others which may need more radical solution or require the establishment of special machinery to remove them. Before examining the possible lines of reform, it is necessary to re-state the essential elements of the problem of industrial finance as it reveals itself in Indian conditions. Apart from the defects in the existing system of deposit banking, the most serious handicap to industry at the present time is the absence of some agency or institution of an organized character which would do for Indian industry what the issue houses and trust and financial companies do for England or what the German banks do for Germany. Industry lacks the assistance of an institution which would help in the formation of the industrial company, and in placing its shares and other securities on the market. Until now this service has been done in varying degrees of efficiency by the managing agents in India, who were able to obtain the additional capital which they needed from parties associated with them by business or personal relations. Owing to a series of adverse circumstances the managing agency system has, especially in western India, and more particularly in the Indian section of it, greatly diminished in prestige and popularity, and will not be in a position to perform this function efficiently. No longer is the name of an Indian managing agent either a guarantee of the soundness of the venture or an inducement to the investor to put his capital into the concern. The investor all over the world is getting increasingly nervous of direct investment in industrial undertakings. As has been pointed out, "owing to the rapidity of post-war industrial and economic changes, owing to the rapid growth of a multitude of minor miscellaneous industries, owing to the losses incurred in previous years, the public is less willing to invest directly in industrial undertakings by the purchase of shares or lend to such undertakings in exchange for bonds."[1] This apathy on the part of the investor, although to some extent the result of the depression in industries in recent times, is likely to remain more or less permanent.[2] The only way of overcoming this natural, and in the circumstances justifiable, shyness is to establish an intermediary between him and the industry, who will be able by his expert knowledge and financial strength to inspire the confidence of the investor in the ultimate success of the concern whose shares he seeks to place on the market. Such an intermediary must also be in a position to underwrite the shares in the first instance, so that the industrial company may not have to wait for the public subscription. The need for the underwriting of industrial securities arises from the inevitable delay to the industrial company which direct appeal to the investing public will involve and the trouble and expense which will have to be incurred in direct sale. Underwriting not only insures the company against the risk of the failure of a public issue, but enables it to get the most valuable advice from an expert agent who generally has great experience of the investing public, and the conditions of the market for securities. Further, in India after the unfortunate experience of the public with the large number of fraudulent promotions in 1920–2, it is doubtful if even legitimate and sound promotions will ever be able to enthuse the investing public by appealing to it directly. An industrial company can assure itself of capital in right quantities and at the right time only if there is a guarantor who can relieve the concern of the financial burden and release its energies for industrial work.

[1] *Memorandum on Commercial Banks* (*League of Nations*), 1931, p. 48.

[2] There is a growing feeling in most of the industrial countries that direct investment is too dangerous a thing for the inexperienced investor, and that it would be better for him to purchase only old securities or to invest through the machinery of an investment trust.

In India the practice of getting the shares underwritten is not very common. Promoters of new concerns usually consult their brokers as to the probability of the success or otherwise of the new issue before offering it to the public, and are guided by their advice.[1] But the brokers have no definite clientele, and their capacity to fulfil this task is limited. Managing agents were usually able to go ahead with their plans because of their own resources, and partly because of the confidence that they would be able to secure, in addition to the subscribed share capital, a considerable volume of public deposits. Occasionally certain firms of managing agents, notably Messrs. Tata, Sons & Co., have preferred to make sure of the success of a new issue by getting it underwritten. Paradoxically enough, the firms of managing agents whose reputation was sufficient to ensure success by direct appeal were those who actually got their issues underwritten. Thus when the Tata (cotton) mills were projected in 1913 with a capital of one crore of rupees, of which 65 lakhs was required at the start, the capital was issued partly in preference shares and partly in ordinary. The whole of the 35 lakhs of rupees of $5\frac{1}{2}$ per cent cumulative preference shares were underwritten by a Dr. Chunilal Saraya of the Specie (Industrial) Bank, Bombay,[2] "while the whole of the ordinary shares were taken up among the friends and acquaintances of the promoters before the company was registered in February 1913."[3] In 1912 a firm of brokers agreed to underwrite for a 2 per cent commission the 5 per cent cumulative preference shares of the Central India Spinning, Weaving, & Manufacturing Co., Ltd., of the value of Rs. 50 lakhs.[4] The commission ranges from 2 to 5 per cent, the larger figure being the more usual.[5] Underwriters are usually either rich capitalists[6] or firms

[1] *Indian Central Banking Enquiry Committee*, Vol. 2, p. 613.

[2] *Indian Textile Journal*, March 1913. [3] Ibid. [4] Ibid.

[5] The Hospet Sugar Mills paid an underwriting commission of 5 per cent to the Eastern Underwriters' Syndicate (*Indian Finance*, June 30, 1933).

[6] Like Sir Shapurji Broacha, for instance, who was a great financier and underwriter of shares. "There has scarcely been any industrial undertaking of importance in which he did not invest a substantial

of brokers, or in some cases private financial institutions doing a certain amount of investment banking.[1] A few joint-stock banks have occasionally helped in the placing of industrial securities by directly investing in them and by lending their name, often resulting in their own serious loss, even involving bankruptcy. Thus the People's Bank, Punjab, which took a large amount of investment banking, came to grief.

Anyhow, the organization for issuing securities and underwriting them is very loose, and none of the agencies mentioned above makes a regular business of it. Thus it has been said that in Calcutta there have been several cases in recent years when the promoters of even the most promising public utility concerns have failed to get their capital underwritten on any terms.[2] There is thus a gap in the banking and financial system in India in respect of the cultivation of industrial relations, and this defect is likely to become more and more visible as, on the one hand, managing agents lose their prestige, and, on the other, newer industrial companies are started by persons of moderate means who cannot with any certainty of success make a direct appeal to the public.

A second group of problems is that connected with the question of long-term credit to industrial concerns, on terms more elastic than are possible at the present time. In certain circumstances it should be possible for industry to get advances on the security of its fixed assets and for a fairly long period. This does not necessarily imply a permanent dependence upon any banking or financial institution, but only until the enterprise is in a position to supply itself with permanent capital drawn from the public. Even a strict adherence on the part of an industrial concern to the principle of funding its fixed and working capital needs is consistent with its temporary dependence upon bank credit at times when the

amount. Railway and tramway companies, cotton mills, flour mills, tile and cement works all claimed his attention" (*Indian Textile Journal*, March 1913).

[1] The Specie Bank and the Karnani Industrial Bank are instances of this type.

[2] *Indian Central Banking Enquiry Committee*, Vol. 2, p. 613.

market may not be favourable for a public issue, but the need for expenditure on expansion and improvement may be pressing.

Thirdly, during a trade slump and industrial depression, when the confidence of the investor is gone and capital will not flow to industry, but when without further capital investment industry cannot set itself upon its feet once again, financial assistance of a kind which at present is not available is required. More especially when schemes of reorganization and amalgamation are proposed, some institution is required which will not only afford advice and financial assistance to the reconstructing industry, but may assure the public of the soundness of such schemes by its impartial investigation and considered judgment.

These, then, are some of the major problems of industrial finance in India, and before examining the various proposals put forward it may be useful to bear in mind that in no country have the relations between banking and industry been satisfactorily settled. Opinion in India has long favoured the starting of industrial banks on the lines of the German Gross Banken with a view to providing industry with initial capital, apparently in the belief that the great German banks are "industrial" banks whose main concern is the permanent provision of fixed capital to industry. Most of the witnesses who advocated the establishment of industrial banks in India both before the Industrial Commission and the Central Banking Enquiry Committee had the idea in mind that the banks should permanently hold the shares and securities of industrial concerns, and in addition grant short-term and long-term advances on the security of goods and of the fixed assets of the company. Even the Indian Industrial Commission were themselves not free from a wholly misconceived notion of the nature and functions of the German banks. In their report dealing with the financing of industry they stated as follows: "What is required, then, is a bank which can keep in touch with small industrialists, is able to estimate the prospects of a fairly extensive range of industries, and possesses funds which it can afford to *lock up* for a time in securities not readily realizable. A bank which is so equipped will often be able, even if it has in the last resort to take over a factory, to avoid much of the loss which such a course would usually entail on an ordinary bank."[1] On the lines of the German "industrial" banks as they regarded them, they proposed that an industrial bank should be started which "should assist in the provision of initial capital either by examining proposals for starting new concerns and allowing their prospectuses to issue with its imprimatur, or simply by providing them with money. This again may be done either by loan or by purchase of shares."[2] Again, the Central Banking Committee, after pointing out that "most of the witnesses who have advocated the scheme of an industrial bank, have done so with a view to provide finance for a part of the initial block capital of industries and for the capital required for any future extensions, such finance being provided, whether in the form of a direct loan to the industrial concern, or by underwriting the capital issue of the concern" has given expression to the prevalent confusion in the following terms: "We are aware that in the various proposals put forward by Provincial Committees and by witnesses before us, they have been influenced by what they conceive to be the relation between banks and industry in Germany."[3]

Misconception of the true nature and functions of the German banking system has persisted to this day,[4] not alone in India, but in other countries as well. Both those who praised the German system and those who condemned it have done so for exactly those features which do not actually exist. Thus, in India, the view has been held that German industry depends upon the banks for a part of its block capital, without realizing the fact that the German banks are only intermediaries between the investing public and industrial companies, and that they do not and cannot furnish to the industrial company what the investing public is not prepared to

[1] *Report of the Indian Industrial Commission*, p. 216. [2] Ibid.

[3] *Indian Central Banking Enquiry Committee*, Report, p. 293.

[4] To what extent misconception still exists among Indian students of economics may be seen from an account given in a recently published book, *Indian Industry and its Problems*, by H. R. Soni, pp. 236–7.

offer.[1] On the contrary, those who have criticized the German system have done so on the assumption that the banks hold industrial shares permanently, and have usurped the function of industrialists and quote as evidence the large number of companies on whose Boards the banks are represented. Professor Foxwell, quoting the words of Pownall, a former President of the Institute of Bankers, that "a banker ought never to be a partner," states, "this is exactly what the German bank is."[2] Nothing has contributed to this misunderstanding of the true relation between German banks and industry so much as the use of the English term "Board of Directors" for what is really a very different thing. There is no English equivalent for the German Aufsichtsrat,[3] which is not identical with the British Board of Directors. It is a Board of Supervision, and not of Direction. Although in 1913 the Deutsche bank was represented on 134 Aufsichtsrat, the Disconto on 114, and the Dresdner on 112, the administration of industrial companies was entirely in the hands of the Executive, and the banks through their representatives only gave financial advice and general counsel. As has been pointed out by Dr. Goldschmidt, "in the exercise of these functions (on the Aufsichtsrat) the banks on the Board of an industrial enterprise nearly always tend to become its confidential advisers," but "the German *banker is not an industrialist.*"[4] Part of the confusion is due to the failure to distinguish between the early German banking system up to the nineties and its later development when the banks, led by the Deutsche group, introduced considerable modifications in their policy and methods.[5]

[1] *Indian Central Banking Enquiry Committee*, Report, p. 634. Dr. Jeidels's statement.

[2] H. S. Foxwell, *Papers on Current Finance*, 1919, p. 117.

[3] *(Macmillan) Committee on Finance and Industry*, Vol. 2, p. 147. Dr. Goldschmidt's Evidence.

[4] Ibid.

[5] English and Continental Banking, Lecture 3, P. B. Whale, *Journal of the Institute of Bankers*, June 1931.

II

THE GERMAN BANKING SYSTEM

In view of the repeated references to the German banks made by witnesses in India, it is necessary to have a clear understanding of the working of the German banking system, and to examine its distinctive features, which differentiate it from the British or the Indian system. Fortunately for our purposes, new and authoritative material has been made available to us by persons who either possess intimate acquaintance with its working or have made a special study of it. Among the former the evidence of Dr. Jeidels (managing partner of the Berliner Handels Gesellschaft, Berlin) given before the Indian Central Banking Enquiry Committee, and that of Dr. Jacob Goldschmidt, a partner of Darmstadter u. National Bank, before the Committee on Finance and Industry, are the most valuable. Of the latter may be mentioned the work of Mr. P. B. Whale, whose *Joint-Stock Banking in Germany* has been commended by Dr. Jeidels as "the only comprehensive and neutral study on the subject giving the facts with careful comment and cautious conclusions."[1]

The distinctive character of joint-stock banking in Germany is "the integration of branches of finance which elsewhere are often separated."[2] Owing to the presence in London of several large international issue houses and other financial institutions, the English banks left the functions of industrial finance to issue houses and stock brokers, whereas in Germany the banks combined financial functions with ordinary commercial banking. In the circumstances in which German credit banks were established, this many-sidedness was not surprising. In the first half of the nineteenth century, before the rise of the credit banks, German industry suffered from lack of capital "not so much because of the actual dearth of savings as of the fact that savings were misdirected."[3] It was with the direct object of assisting industry that

[1] *Report of the Indian Central Banking Enquiry Committee*, Vol. 1, p. 633.

[2] P. B. Whale, *Joint-Stock Banking in Germany*, 1930, p. 326.

[3] Ibid., p. 11.

the first credit banks were founded, and the country owes the great industrial development of the sixties and nineties of the last century and of the first decade of this century to the "entrepreneur" spirit which the banks displayed. From the beginning the banks gave a prominent place in their programme to the promotion of joint-stock companies, and the original statutes of some of the banks empowering them to issue or take over on their own account the shares and debentures of companies newly created afford evidence of this feature. But they were fully alive to the dangers of extensive and permanent participation on their own account in the concerns which they brought into existence, and went on the principle that it was their function[1] "not so much to call great branches of industry into existence through large-scale participation on their own account as to induce the capitalists of the country, by the authority of their recommendations, to apply idle capital to undertakings which, properly planned according to real needs and equipped with expert management, offer prospects of reasonable profits." Their ability to assist in the promotion of new undertakings, or in the conversion of private into public limited companies, was always subject ultimately to the responsiveness of the capital market. In the words of Dr. Jeidels, "if the public were unwilling to put up the new capital required by the industrial company, and which is offered to the market in suitable shape, then the banks under the German system would not take the place of the public; they would not themselves furnish to the industrial company what the investing public was not prepared to take."[2] The banks are always anxious to place their securities with the public as quickly as possible, and not to hold them in their own hands. Contrary to the common belief, lasting participation in industrial enterprises has not been part of the general policy of German credit banks, although there have been occasions when deliberate participations of a permanent character occurred in a number of special cases, or when securities remained

[1] P. B. Whale, *Joint-Stock Banking in Germany*, 1930, p. 11.

[2] *Report of the Indian Central Banking Enquiry Committee*, Vol. 1, p. 634.

in their hands because of the difficulty of placing them in the market. On the whole it has been possible for them to play a considerable part in the promotion of industrial companies without locking up their own resources, and they have been able to manage promoting operations on a large scale because the capital invested in these operations is constantly changed from one investment to another and a considerable amount of diversification of investments exists. This has been possible because the banks are members of the Stock Exchange and deal directly in securities. Thus in 1913 only 13 per cent of the assets of the big Berlin banks were in securities, and this figure fell as low as 4 per cent in 1928. As Mr. Whale has put it, "the object of deliberate participation has been to extend the banks' influence or acquire new connections, but never to enlarge bank dividends by industrial profits."[1] The sympathetic attitude of banks towards industry in Germany and the intimate relationship between the two are the essential features of the German banking system.

But in Germany, as in England and India, the ordinary banking business in which deposits from the general public are employed, is decidedly the most important business. The discounting of bills, the granting of advances with and without security, the re-imbursement credits and acceptance credits are the principal lines of business done by them. The connection between banks and industry has its beginnings as a rule not in an act of promotion, but in what is known as a current-account relation, which is distinct from the current account as used in relation to banks and their clients in India. Each customer in Germany deals exclusively with one bank, and there then arises an industrial current account relation which is the pivot of all transactions between the industry and the bank, and in which the industry is sometimes in debt and sometimes in credit to the bank. Many claims thus arise on both sides which are not settled individually, but are settled periodically, usually once every six months. The current account credits are in most cases for short periods only, although occasionally credits are granted for more or less long

[1] P. B. Whale, *Joint-Stock Banking in Germany*, p. 48.

periods.[1] These are generally preparatory for future loans and are granted chiefly to larger enterprises and represent advances for supplying block for extensions in anticipation of recourse to the investment market. Thus German industry frequently makes use of current account advances for fixed capital charges in anticipation of raising long-term issues, as well as for working capital.

The link between industry and banks is strengthened by the banks' representation on the firm's Aufsichtsrat or Board of Supervision. The proper place of the Aufsichtsrat in the German scheme of company organization can be understood only in relation to the other governing organs of an industrial company. There are three governing organs: (1) the Executive corresponding to the Managing Directors and the Board of Directors; (2) the Board of Supervisors (Aufsichtsrat); and (3) the Shareholders' meeting. The function of the Board of Supervision is very important and valuable. It watches over the conduct of the Company's business in all its branches, and for this purpose it has to keep itself informed of the Company's affairs. It examines the yearly balance sheet, and any proposals brought before the general meeting and reports on them. But it has no powers of direct intervention, and the Aufsichtsrat does not *manage* industry. The banks' representatives perform useful service, and assist the company by concentrating on the financial problems and possibilities which present themselves from time to time. They tend to become the company's confidential financial advisers.

On the other hand, on the Bank's Board of Supervision are to be found important leaders of industry and commerce. The exchange of such representation is a valuable link between banking and industry in Germany. In the development of industry in Germany, the personality of the bankers has been very important and success has been due to leadership. Thus in Germany are seen the fruits of the intimate co-operation over a continuous period during which banks get an insight into the problems and

[1] Evidence of Dr. Goldschmidt, (*Macmillan*) *Committee of Finance and Industry*, Vol. 2, p. 150.

requirements of industry, and industry in turn learns the value of the support which banks can give.

To sum up: banks in Germany perform services to industry which in India are not done at all, or are done to some extent by managing agents. But they are commercial banks in which the discounting of bills and the provision of short-term credits are their most important functions. In addition, they undertake financial operations which in England are left to other special institutions. By co-operating among themselves and by joining together in what is called a Konsortium, they not only reduce the risk borne by any one bank in industrial issues, but are enabled to avoid undue competition among themselves and to undertake operations not possible for any single bank. Although even before the war their holdings of industrial securities were by no means as high as was popularly supposed, in the post-war period, owing to the comparative unresponsiveness of the capital market and the banks' cautious policy, the percentage of their investment portfolio is actually less than that of the English banks, which in reality are more tied to industry than the German banks. But whatever be the proportion of their actual holdings at any given time, the most significant thing is the intimate relationship existing between them and industry, and the sympathetic attitude which they display towards the needs of industry.

THE CONTINENTAL SYSTEM OF INDUSTRIAL BANKING

The German system is more or less typical of the banking system on the Continent. Indeed, in some of the Continental countries the banks have to a much greater extent than in Germany identified themselves with the fortunes of industry, and sometimes with unhappy results. In Austria, the relation between banks and industry had been from the start very close. In the pre-war period the banks formed underwriting syndicates for the issue of shares; but they also retained or were obliged in many cases to retain some part of the stock so issued. Hence the Austrian banks began to have a controlling, or at least an important, interest in very many industrial enterprises. They became, on the one hand, creditors advancing funds on current account "basis," or on some sort of security and, on the other, shareholders of these companies.[1] In the post-war period industry and commerce had to lean even to a larger extent on the banks whose hold on them became still firmer. Savings did not find their way to industry, and there was no alternative except for the national financial institutes to foster industry.

The principal Hungarian banks have from the beginning taken a leading part in the industrial life of the country. This is due "above all to the fact that Hungary was always short of funds, and that private individuals with adequate supplies of capital were not forthcoming in sufficient numbers to take the lead in establishing industrial undertakings."[2] In consequence, the larger Hungarian banks became both shareholders and creditors, a combination which implied a very wide measure of influence and control in the nascent industrial undertakings of the country. The Hungarian credit bank, one of the leading banks in Hungary in 1929, had 84,815,246 pengoes[3] locked up in investments, but all except 11,593,496 pengoes were supplied out of capital and their own funds and not out of deposits.[4] It has invested its entire paid-up capital in the development of industry and agriculture, and there does not seem to be any tendency to regard this as an incorrect or unwise policy.

The same type of mixed banking and the current account relation are characteristic of Belgian banks which have participated in the formation of industrial companies. In the same manner the big Swiss banks are mixed deposit and industrial banks.[5] They undertake every form of current commercial banking; they issue five-year bonds bearing a fixed interest. They finance industry by means of long-term credits on a large scale,

[1] Parker Willis, and Beckhart, *Foreign Banking Systems*, 1929, p. 172.

[2] *Economist*, December 20, 1930, Article by Dr. Tibor de Scitovszky, General Manager of the Hungarian Credit Board.

[3] The par of exchange is 27·82 pengoes to a £.

[4] *Indian Central Banking Enquiry Committee*, Vol. 2, p. 314, Evidence of Dr. L. Nemenyi.

[5] *Memorandum on Commercial Banks* (*League of Nations*), 1931.

but generally without taking direct control of industrial undertakings, though they have representatives acting as financial advisers on the Boards of these undertakings. They also conduct investment banking and underwrite public issues.[1] The Italian commercial banking system combines the characteristics of deposit banks and investment banks, most of the leading banks being closely connected with industrial and commercial enterprises.[2] In Sweden, as in other Scandinavian countries, it was the habit of the investing public to leave a considerable portion of their capital in the form of deposits in banks in preference to investing it directly in the shares of companies. Industrial companies had therefore to be largely financed by bank credits. In the post-war reconstruction of industry, the banks actively assisted in their reorganization and provided a sound basis for the industrial and commercial expansion in recent years.[3]

THE ENGLISH BANKING SYSTEM

In striking contrast to the Continental system of mixed banking was the pre-war English deposit banking (and the Indian banking system) which almost exclusively specialized in the provision of short-term credit and left the other needs of industry to be met by special institutions. In general, advances were made for two kinds of purposes: firstly to provide "circulating" capital to industry for the production and marketing of goods, and secondly, though more rarely, to provide temporary funds pending the issue of long-term capital. In the second case, the proceeds of the capital issue were used to repay the bank.

But since the war a change of some significance has occurred in the banking practice of England. The banks have now become the permanent creditors of large sections of British industry, and their funds have been tied up with them. "In coal, cotton, iron and steel, shipbuilding, in fact, in most of the heavy industries which have more or less been continuously depressed since 1920, the banks have large amounts of 'frozen' advances," and

[1] *Memorandum on Commercial Banks* (*League of Nations*), 1931.
[2] Ibid. [3] Ibid.

have a first claim on the earnings of large sections of these industries. British banks are just as much and as firmly in industry as the German banks. The English banks have now become investors not by choice but by necessity; all the Big Five have considerable investments in industrial shares and debentures,[1] and although they are still unwilling to be drawn into a too-intimate relationship with industry, the connection which the post-war slump has brought about is likely to survive in the future. Although Governor Norman's view[2] is against any definite and incorporated form of liason between banks and industry, it is generally recognized that there has been insufficient contact between industry and banks, and it is felt that the banks should be at hand as advisers on the financial aspects of industry. The (Macmillan) Committee on Finance and Industry has put forth a powerful plea for closer co-operation of industry and finance, and considers that the most beneficial kind of relationship between finance and industry would be one where bankers (and financial leaders) are able by their confidential and continuous relationship with industrialists not only to supplement the information at the disposal of the industrialists themselves but also to give aid of very great value in all financial problems.[3] It is, therefore, highly probable that the present "forced" contact between industry and finance in England will soon become part of an organized and generally accepted plan of co-operation, and that appropriate machinery will be devised to strengthen methods of co-operation.

At the same time for reasons somewhat different, the German banking system is also undergoing changes of a character that will soon bring it into a form more resembling the English system. Not only are the German banks actually less bound up with industry than the English banks are, but there has been a growing feeling that direct financial assistance is not so desirable, and this has expressed itself in the tendency to promote special financial companies which will afford financial assistance to industry. In post-war Europe the contrast between pure deposit banking and

[1] *(Macmillan) Committee on Finance and Industry*, Vol. 1, Question 2251. [2] Ibid., Question 9162. [3] Ibid., Report, p. 165.

industrial banking has been considerably weakened. The systems of the former type have extended their operations over a considerably wider range of activities, and have entered into much closer relations with industry. Furthermore, in England and elsewhere, owing to the fact that issues of industrial shares and bonds (especially those of older industries) are less easily marketed, industry has had to rely upon bank credits to a greater extent. On the European continent, "even the big banks are now devoting more attention to deposit banking. Their holdings of shares in industrial undertakings have been reduced both relatively to other investments and advances and absolutely."[1] Through financial, trust, and holding companies operating chiefly with funds raised by the issue of debentures, the banks now exercise influence on industrial concerns without being too closely identified with them.

Thus two types of banking systems, starting apparently with different ends in view, have by force of circumstances been brought closer and closer to each other. What is more significant is that, however much one may regret the circumstances that have compelled them to change their former practices and methods, the resulting adaptation to a modified system, in which what is most valuable and vital is sought to be preserved is universally approved. The co-operation and sympathetic understanding between industry and finance have been recognized to be the most essential elements in every sound banking and financial system.

Thus conceived, world experience cannot but have value for India. The Indian banking system must seek to cultivate friendly and intimate relationship with Indian industry. The dominant characteristic of the Indian banking system has so far been not merely specialization but even exclusiveness. It is out of touch with the needs and difficulties of industry, and is working on certain rules and practices, rigid and not suited to the requirements of industry. India needs the services which the continental banks are able to render to industry in Europe. Such services include assistance in the issuing of shares and debentures and placing

[1] *Memorandum on Commercial Banks* (*League of Nations*), 1931.

them on the market, the granting of credit in advance of a public issue, and generally all forms of co-operation which would enable industry and banks to understand one another.

III

HOW FAR CAN INDIAN COMMERCIAL BANKING BE CONVERTED INTO MIXED BANKING OF THE CONTINENTAL TYPE?

But the adaptation of Indian banks to a broadening of their functions and activities is beset with considerable difficulties, and it would be unwise to ignore them. The large number of banking failures in 1913–17 in India was partly the result of the attempts on the part of the banks in the Punjab, U.P., and western India to combine investment banking with commercial banking. In a previous chapter the extent of banking failures in the period 1913–17, and again in 1922–7, has been examined, and it has revealed the need for consolidation even more than for an extension of new banking facilities. Most of the joint-stock banks in India are small, with inadequate resources both by way of paid-up capital and reserve and are not in a position to undertake new functions which might even temporarily result in a locking-up of funds. The People's Bank with its paid-up capital of only 12½ lakhs of rupees invested in spinning and weaving mills and other industrial concerns and also in industries controlled by its own Managing Director. The result was disastrous. Similarly, in the case of the Amritsar Bank, 66 per cent of its assets was invested in ten companies, which were the clients of the People's Bank. When the latter failed, the Amritsar Bank had also to stop payment. Experience in the management of banking has been limited, and the reports of the accountants and official liquidators of the banks which failed, show an inconceivably low level of understanding and integrity. In many cases accounts were not properly kept and were not kept up to date. "It is extremely disappointing to have to relate what can only be described as a miserable tale of the lowest form of fraud, the creation of fictitious debtors and the preparation of demand promissory notes in support of these."[1] The directors had in some cases lent to themselves and to companies in which they were directors or partners, large sums out of the bank's funds. Thus the Managing Director of the Indian Specie Bank used the funds of the bank in his silver speculation and brought great losses to the bank. In view of what has been stated above, there should be complete agreement with the view that it is not to the advantage "either of the commercial banking system or Indian industries that any of the weaker banks should participate in such industrial financing. This new class of business requires much experience and an established policy of sound banking. It also demands considerable capital and a firm resistance to the speculation temptations which easily arise in a line of business where securities are created and sold. *The bulk of the joint-stock banks in India are at present not ready for this activity*, and even the larger ones can cultivate it only slowly, with great caution, and preferably under competent guidance as participants in strong syndicates."[2]

THE IMPERIAL BANK, THE ONLY SUITABLE ONE FOR EMBARKING ON THIS NEW ACTIVITY

The Imperial Bank of India is the only institution strong enough to enter into this enlarged field of activities. It has a large paid-up capital and reserve which in 1931 amounted to 11 crores of rupees. Its staff contains men who are trained and efficient. By its knowledge of the general industrial position, by its unrivalled experience in the financing of all the important agricultural and industrial products,[3] and by its ramifications through its net-work of branches

[1] Quoted from the Report of the Accountants appointed in connection with the Specie Bank failure in *Indian Finance and Banking*, by Findlay Shirras, 1919, p. 366.

[2] *Indian Central Banking Enquiry Committee*, Vol. 1, p. 635, Dr. Jeidel's *Memorandum*.

[3] For the range of its industrial banking activities (in the sense of doing banking business with industrial firms) refer to the evidence of Mr. K. M. Macdonald, Managing Governor of the Imperial Bank, and the statement appended to it giving a list of industries which get "advances" from the bank. Ibid., Vol. 3, pp. 968–70.

it is eminently fitted to fulfil this new role. It has also special departments in its local head offices for the purpose of knowing the financial position of industries. The proposed Reserve Bank of India will in any case require the Imperial Bank of India to shed some of the functions pertaining to central banking and will release it from the restraints under which it has been working. The time, therefore, is opportune for the Imperial Bank to reconsider its functions and devise suitable machinery for the purpose of carrying on industrial banking to a larger extent. Such a widening of its activities need not cause alarm. In the first place, the bank has already been supplying working funds in the form of cash credit and overdraft to industries, and these advances have been utilized as general working capital by many industrial companies. Secondly, the change does not imply any *permanent* locking-up of capital; all that it does imply is that the bank would be animated by a new spirit of assistance to and co-operation with industry, and recognize its obligations towards the industrial development of the country.

It is true that the question as to whether the bank should convert itself into the mixed banking type of Germany is essentially a matter for the bank itself to decide. But if in its choice public, as opposed to the bank's private, considerations are given due weight, its acceptance of this new policy is inevitable. If it is too risky for the Imperial Bank of India to take to a certain amount of investment banking, it will be more so for any institution newly created for this purpose; for the latter would lack what the Imperial Bank has already gained, i.e. industrial experience. Those who have suggested the starting of an Industrial Bank or banks for India with Government guarantee of interest for the purpose of financing industry have to meet two important arguments against it, namely, that the new bank would have no industrial experience and be wholly out of touch with industrial needs; and, secondly, that it would work only in one or two big centres and leave the medium-sized industries of the smaller towns and centres absolutely alone. The large number of the branches of the Imperial Bank of India would enable the Bank to keep itself in touch with industrial proposals coming from men of moderate means outside the big cities. There can be thus no effective substitute for the adaptation of the Imperial Bank into the mixed banking type, doing both commercial and industrial banking. To neglect the existence of an organization which is admirably fitted to fulfil this role and to start something new will be not merely wrong in policy, but disastrous in its result.

The Imperial Bank is not, of course, to work all alone. It should, by virtue of its pre-eminent position, take the lead and let the other banks which are in a strong position follow its example. As in Germany, the banks may work in co-operation and form special syndicates for the purpose of assisting in the flotation of new concerns. There are, besides the Imperial Bank, nine major banks with a paid-up capital and total reserve of about 7·5 crores of rupees which, without undue risk, can enter into industrial banking on a modest scale. What the country requires is greater co-operation and concerted action, and good leadership both among banking institutions and industrial firms. So far, Indian banks have been lacking in *esprit de corps*, and a spirit of mutual co-operation. If they can come together for such common purposes as the issuing and marketing of industrial securities, they will not merely be reducing their risks but find that each step in co-operation will strengthen their position.

INDUSTRIAL BANKS NO ALTERNATIVE

Since the days of the inquiry by the Indian Industrial Commission, opinion amongst the Indian section of the commercial and industrial community has been unanimous that the only solution of all the difficulties of industrial finance in India is the establishment of an Industrial Bank. The Commission also endorsed this view, and recommended the starting of an industrial bank, but left the details to be investigated by an expert committee. They stated "we have shown that the lack of financial facilities is at present one of the most serious difficulties in the way of extension of Indian industries, and we believe that industrial banks, especially under the improved conditions towards which the measures proposed by us are intended to lead, would be a potent means of removing these difficulties, and of affording help to industrialists. The Tata Industrial Bank has recently started without Government assistance, but we think there is still ample room for other institutions especially of a type designed to afford assistance to smaller industrial undertakings. . . . We consider that the establishment of industrial banks working on approved lines is of sufficient national importance to justify Government assistance, but we do not feel that we have sufficient material before us to enable us to formulate a definite scheme for industrial banks whether of provincial or imperial scope."[1] At the time when it made this recommendation, the Presidency Banks were working independently and the Imperial Bank of India had not come into existence as an amalgamated bank. Whether the Imperial Bank of India should be allowed to develop into a bankers' bank or a new central bank should be created was much discussed. But now that the controversy is at rest and the Imperial Bank having definitely become an ordinary commercial bank, the whole proposal for the establishment of a new industrial bank must be reconsidered. There is one serious objection, almost fatal to the establishment of an industrial bank, unless it is started privately by persons who know the business and are willing to take the risk. An institution newly created by Government would lack that industrial spirit and practical experience so necessary for success. Industrial banks to be successful require first a staff of administrators who are acquainted with the business world thoroughly, who know the individual businesses and the conditions of each industry, and secondly, a body of experts who can judge new schemes, offer advice, and do the other work peculiar to industrial banks. Government cannot create a staff all at once. The number of qualified men required for the staff of the Reserve Bank of India can only be obtained with some difficulty. There is not an abundance of able men trained for the purpose of carrying on the work of the proposed industrial bank. Even if the men were trained for the purpose and became available, the new

[1] *Report of the Indian Industrial Commission*, p. 217.

institution would lack an essential element, i.e. the practical business element, an element of caution, which the banks with large experience can alone supply.

Secondly, it is possible to exaggerate the value and utility of an industrial bank in India. What is required in India is an institution which will instil confidence in the investing public as to the soundness of the ventures to which it is called upon to subscribe. The Managing Agents have been performing this function to a limited extent. Something is now required to supplement this work. The Tata Industrial Bank, started in 1917 with an authorized capital of 12 crores of rupees, was a venture which, if it had succeeded, would have marked the beginning of a fair number of similar institutions. But it suffered not merely because it was established in a year of boom, but because it committed the fatal blunder of becoming more or less the promoter and financier of concerns associated with one firm of managing agents. On the other hand, its failure provides a valuable lesson to the future promoters of an industrial bank, and it is therefore necessary to review its short career in some detail.

IV

THE TATA INDUSTRIAL BANK[1]

The Bank started business actually in 1918 with a paid-up capital of Rs. 70 lakhs, but enjoyed such reputation and popularity that in 1921 its paid-up capital rose to Rs. 226.69 lakhs. Messrs. Tata, Sons & Co. were the managing agents, and they deliberately raised the large capital with a view to dealing with business that was less liquid. An intelligence section was constituted, composed of technical experts and commercial men, and from the commencement the bank had an ambitious plan of assisting industry both with current and fixed finance. "We look upon the bank's operations in a broader spirit than pure gain, and mean

[1] For part of the information relating to the Tata Industrial Bank the writer is indebted to Mr. P. P. Kallukaran's unpublished thesis on *Industrial Banking in India*, 1922.

to apply its financial power to increase the national wealth of India through industrial grants. That spirit, I hope and believe, equally animates a large number of the shareholders." In these words Sir Dorab Tata described the aim of the Tata Industrial Bank.

But within ten years these expectations failed to materialize, and the bank became amalgamated with the Central Bank of India, which is entirely a commercial bank. The reasons for the failure are twofold. The economic conditions since 1918 were not favourable to the growth of industrial banking. Many new businesses were started on the basis of the high level of prices ruling at the time, but soon collapsed with the turn of the tide. The bank felt that on the one hand it would be imprudent to finance unsound ventures; on the other hand, some outlet for its resources was urgently required. This resulted in a lack of definite policy, and the aims and purposes of the bank had been constantly shifting from year to year. In 1918 the chairman, at the Shareholders' Meeting of the bank, stated: "We believe that the public will readily absorb perhaps the whole of the shares and debentures of the companies which it assists to the stage of flotation, thus enabling the bank to utilize its freed resources in other enterprises."[1] The bank, therefore, pursued a cautious policy, and cultivated ordinary banking, and contented itself with supplying some working capital to a few industrial companies. The industrial side of the business was overshadowed by the volume of ordinary commercial banking business. This continued up to 1920, and industrial finance was not undertaken, "owing to the want of necessary new and industrial propositions." As was stated by Billimoria at a meeting of the shareholders in 1920: "The more highly specialized work which we have undertaken to finance can only come to us with the creation of industrial conditions which it is our object to support." But the feeling that the bank was not fulfilling the purpose for which it was started, combined with the large amount of resources waiting to be utilized,

[1] Speech of Sir R. N. Mookerjee reported in the *Times of India*, May 20, 1918.

rendered a change of policy inevitable, and after 1920 the bank set out not merely to finance industries seeking financial help, but to take a more active part in the promotion of new enterprises. In the words of Sir Dorab Tata, "The bank would not merely wait in future for propositions to turn up but would take the initiative to find out profitable channels for the employment of its resources in industrial investments," and again, speaking in 1923 at the Annual Meeting of the shareholders, he said: "We felt as an industrial bank that not only should we promote industrial companies and support them by underwriting their shares, but that we should also be prepared to retain a considerable holding of shares in such companies as an earnest of our belief in the prospects of the companies concerned."[1] Thus a cautious policy of financing deserving industrial concerns gave place to a bold, almost rash, policy of linking up its fortunes permanently with those of the concerns which it set out to float and finance. The result was unfortunate.

In the choice of the industrial companies to which help was rendered a safe and prudent course was not adopted. The late Sir William Meyer, even at the opening of the bank, gave a shrewd warning in the following words: "I hope you will not tie up all the bank's resources with your own firms (the concerns controlled by Tatas) but be a real and general Industrial Bank of India."[2] Unfortunately, exactly that which was feared happened. In 1920 the Tatas organized a giant sugar corporation with the help of the Tata Industrial Bank. A company was floated with the object of producing sugar by acquiring its own plantations, but within a year it went into liquidation. The other investments of the bank were in the following concerns: (*a*) British Indian Corporation, Ltd., London; (*b*) The Tata Iron & Steel Co., Ltd., managed by Messrs. Tata, Sons & Co.; (*c*) The Industrial Finance, Ltd., a subsidiary of the bank to which, after 1922, all the industrial holdings of the bank were transferred, and through which further investments were made to industries;

[1] *Times of India*, May 2, 1923.
[2] Ibid., mail edition, April 8, 1918.

(*d*) The Tata Power Co., Ltd., managed by Messrs. Tata, Sons & Co; (*e*) The Tata Oil Co., Ltd., also managed by Tatas; (*f*) The New India Assurance Co., Ltd., in which the managing agents were interested; (*g*) The Bombay Electric Supply and Tramways Co. It is difficult to resist the conclusion that the investments were all too much bound up with the businesses floated and controlled by the managing agents of the Industrial Bank.

Finally, but for the fact that it was started in boom, and had an extraordinarily difficult period to face, it might have done better. Circumstances were too much for it. Public opinion compelled the bank to adopt a very forward programme of industrial development, and the funds at their disposal were so large that some investment had to be made.

But its failure is not without its value. Any similar institution sought to be started must not be too closely identified with any one firm or industry. There is great opportunity for the industrial leaders of India to promote a bank in co-operation with the capitalists of the country. The bank, while it should never become a mere financial agency to a coterie of industrialists, must possess a considerable amount of industrial experience amongst the Directorate. Such a development, if it takes place, will be wholly in keeping with the tendencies in foreign countries in recent times. We shall have something further to say on this aspect of the matter after considering the case for a State Industrial Bank.

V

INDUSTRIAL BANK WITH GOVERNMENT ASSISTANCE

At the present time the chances of starting an industrial bank by private initiative are remote and industry cannot indefinitely wait until private capitalists and industrialists are willing to float an institution. Even the Indian Central Banking Enquiry Committee which has presented a very balanced report has, after commending the proposal to convert the Indian banking system into the mixed German type, made a definite proposal for the establishment of a Provincial Industrial Bank. In this recommendation, the Committee has been influenced by the weight of opinion as expressed in the several Provincial Banking Committee reports. It states that "the reports of the Provincial Committees indicate a general consensus of opinion that efforts should be made to start an industrial bank or banks to supplement the existing facilities for the financing of industries. The Bombay, Bihar and Orissa, and the Central Provinces Committees have recommended the establishment of Provincial Industrial Banks. The Bengal Committee has suggested the organization of a special type of bank to help middle-sized as well as large industries."[1] Again, "the general trend of evidence before us was also in favour of establishing a special type of industrial bank or banks to finance industrial concerns."[2]

That opinion in India favours the establishment of a special institution to provide initial capital to industry is undoubtedly true. But there is much confusion as to the scope and value of the proposed institutions. Some recommend them for the financing of medium-sized and smaller industries; others consider that industrial banks are suited only for large-scale businesses. Again, whilst many emphasize the need for promoting and financing permanently the requirements of industries, there are a few who would limit their activities to the function of assisting industry in the securing of permanent finance. The reason given by the Indian Central Banking Committee for its proposal to establish an industrial corporation is rather curious. "A Provincial Government may in the discharge of *its responsibilities for the development of industries within its territories* find it necessary to ensure the supply of financial facilities to industrial concerns, and in such cases we recommend the establishment of a provincial industrial corporation working with capital initially or permanently supported by the Provincial Government."[3] But surely responsibility for directly organizing industry cannot be taken up by Government which has neither the equipment nor the industrial experience necessary for such purposes. In the words of Dr. Goldschmidt, answering

[1] *Report*, p. 284. [2] Ibid. [3] Ibid., p. 301.

a question before the Macmillan Committee as to how far political pressure was desirable to overcome the inertia of the capitalists, "it is not the province of the Government to make laws of that kind. Certainly I believe it is the task of the Government to see that the development of business in a country remains sound, but it can never in my opinion make executive arrangements, which should develop organically out of the economic evolution of the age, by means of laws and regulations. That is dangerous since it disturbs the living movement of economic development and thus destroys and freezes economic life itself."[1] Government may, in view of their public importance, develop certain public utility industries, like the hydro-electric industries or gas works, and so on. In such cases, some machinery for the financing of such concerns may be justifiably established by Government with the shares subscribed in part by Government. Again, in regard to small industries, Government may justifiably assist certain co-operative or special financial institutions by providing them with a part of the funds to enable them to render assistance to small industries and cottage industries. But the establishment of a financial institution to provide long-term finance for competitive industries seems to be a measure which cannot be defended on ordinary grounds.

Not that there is any objection on principle to the active association of Government in the financing and development of some kinds of industry. Experience, not excluding that of India, has, however, shown that direct financial assistance by Government to industry has not always been a success. The working of the State Aid to Industries Act has proved the failure of a scheme of direct financial assistance to industry, a result which seems to be one common in all cases where a system of extensive state aid in economic life has been introduced. State Aid to Industries Acts have been in operation in Madras, Bihar and Orissa, and the Punjab since 1923, and enabled Government to give financial assistance to industries in various forms, loans, guarantee of cash

[1] *(Macmillan) Committee on Finance and Industry*, Evidence, Vol. 2, p. 160.

credits with banks, taking up shares and debentures, guaranteeing interest on capital, grant on favourable terms of land or raw material and grant of subsidies for research. Actually Government assistance was mainly in the form of loans, and in almost all cases the results have been disappointing. Of 8 lakhs of rupees lent by the Madras Government, a sum of 4 lakhs of rupees had to be written off in addition to the interest on it. Out of the nine cases that received help, five resulted in a loss. The total amount actually paid or guaranteed in Bihar and Orissa was also about 8 lakhs of rupees, of which 3 lakhs became irrecoverable. In the Punjab too, the result was nearly the same. The Departments of Industries which had to recommend assistance were not really competent to judge of the credit-worthiness of the applicants. Even in the judging of the technical conditions of a business, serious mistakes occurred. A match factory in Bihar which had been liberally financed by Government had soon to wind up because of the lack of supply of raw materials.[1] In certain other cases some of the machines recommended to be purchased by the department were found to be unsuitable, and these were handed back to the department, which soon became "a museum of obsolete machines."[2] One cause of the failure of the scheme would, perhaps, not apply in the case of the proposed Industrial Corporation, for much of the failure of the State Aid to Industries Act can be explained by the entire lack of an experienced staff to advise Government as to the soundness of an enterprise that sought assistance. It may be expected that in the proposed industrial corporation there will be found men with the necessary industrial knowledge and financial experience to guide the investments on proper lines. But that is exactly the difficulty. Would the Industrial Corporation be able to secure a trained staff for such purposes? Would the men who administer the new institution not lack the practical knowledge and wise caution generally found only among practical bankers? And again, would they not in judging applications for assistance, give undue consideration

[1] *Report of the Bihar and Orissa Banking Committee*, Vol. 1, p. 100.
[2] Ibid., Vol. 1, p. 101.

to the *general* bearing of an industry on the future economic development of the country and insufficient consideration to the question whether the conditions of business success are to be found in the *individual* concerns that apply for aid. This last danger is almost certain to exist, for if the reason for the establishment of a special financial institution is the "responsibility of Government for the development of industry" as suggested by the Central Banking Committee, it can readily be imagined that the Industrial Corporation will be influenced by general considerations of industrial development and will not inquire (as it should) very carefully into the ability of the promoters and the soundness of their schemes. Another consideration to be borne in mind is how far the proposed institution will be in a position to function without being subjected to political influences.

THE INDUSTRIAL BANK OF JAPAN

The Industrial Bank of Japan has obviously inspired many Indian witnesses and Provincial Banking Committees in their plea for a special institution in India, and it is necessary to examine the circumstances which gave rise to it, and its working. It is almost unique in the sense that in no other country has an institution been established by Government deliberately to foster industrial development. The Japanese banking system has been influenced by the idea enunciated by Prince Matsukata that "in a healthy community there should be distinct groups of banks whose functions should be mutually exclusive,"[1] and that there should be special institutions to facilitate long-term investment in trade or industry. Accordingly, after the foundation of deposit banking was laid, attention was soon turned to the starting of institutions for long-term loans to agriculture and industry. The ordinary deposit banks could not with safety grant such accommodation; while as yet there was no large investing public. So it was decided to establish institutions which would absorb the small funds distributed about the country and which would satisfy the need for long-term loans.

[1] G. C. Allen, *Japan's Banking System*, 1924.

Thus came into existence the Hypothec Bank for agricultural credit, and the Industrial Bank for industrial finance. The Industrial Bank was actually started in 1902 with a Government guarantee of a 5 per cent interest on the share capital limited to a period of five years. It is a joint-stock concern with a capital of 50 million yen (£5 million) and a considerable part of the share capital was subscribed by Government.[1] The business of the bank is controlled by a directorate, and the appointment of the President and Vice-President of the bank is in the hands of the Minister of Finance. It relies for its working funds mainly on the issue of debentures up to ten times its paid-up capital, and in June 1933, the debentures outstanding were 356·67 million yen. With a view to attracting small investors, the minimum denomination of debentures had been fixed at 20 yen. The bye-laws require the sanction of Government, and forbid the loan of an amount exceeding half the bank's paid-up capital on urban land or industrial buildings. Although dealing chiefly with investment business, it does a certain amount of commercial banking and its deposits in 1929 amounted to 49 million yen. It discounts bills of exchange and its holdings in bills in 1929 were 90 millions out of a total of assets of 487 million yen, and in 1933, 100·63 million out of a total of assets valued at 578·48 million yen.[2] The bank has a technical department in which experts investigate as well as inspect the factories and mills before and after investment. It has several branches in provincial towns and correspondents in important places throughout Japan and has established connections with banks operating in China, England, France, and America.[3] It has drawn a considerable part of the share capital (more than one-third in 1914) from foreign correspondents, and played an important part in introducing foreign capital into Japan. A great portion of the advances of the bank was given "to newly established and weaker industries which the

[1] *Indian Industrial Commission 1916–18*, Vol. 5, pp. 796–812. *Memorandum on Banking*, by Findlay Shirras.

[2] *Sixty-third Report of the Industrial Bank of Japan*, June 30, 1933.

[3] *Indian Journal of Economics*, January 1931.

Government itself has either initiated or has been specially interested in for reasons of state."[1] Among the industries financed by the bank, the following are the most important: Shipping, iron and steel, food making, paper, dyeing, pottery, machine-making, and the chemical industry. Advances are usually made for five years, although in the case of advances on ships the loan is repayable in instalments over a period of fifteen years. Some idea of the nature of the business transacted by it may be had from the appended statement.

Business transacted by the Bank[2]

1. Loans secured by pledges of national, prefectural or municipal loan bonds or debentures and shares of companies.
2. Loans secured by mortgages on estates created by laws.
3. Loans secured by mortgages on lands, buildings included in, and comprising factories.
4. Loans secured by mortgages on land and/or buildings in cities and towns designated by Imperial ordinances.
5. Loans secured by mortgages on ships, including those under construction.
6. Loans on the security of shipbuilding materials.
7. Subscribing for or accepting national or municipal loan-bonds or debentures of companies.
8. Subscribing for or accepting shares of companies.
9. Fixed deposits, current and special current accounts.
10. Safe custody of securities and other valuables.
11. Trust business connected with secured debentures.
12. Business connected with invitations to subscribe for national prefectural or municipal loan-bonds, or debentures of companies, receipt of payment therefrom or payment of principal thereof and interest thereon or dividend.
13. Discounting of bills.
14. Buying and selling of internal or foreign bills of exchange.
15. Purchase of national, prefectural or municipal loan-bonds, debentures and shares of companies, or gold or silver bullion.

Since the war the bank has departed from the principle of its founders, which was that it should only provide long-term loans, leaving short-period advances to be given by the commercial banks. Some idea of the extent of short-term advances made by

[1] G. C. Allen, *Japan's Banking System*, 1924.

[2] *Sixty-third Report of the Industrial Bank of Japan*, June 30, 1933.

the bank can be had from the fact that at the end of 1921, while the outstanding loans amounted to 333·75 million yen, the total amount of its advances during the year was no less than 1,101 million yen, or more than three times as much. In recent years the bank has been taking special interest in the financing of small industries. In the words of the Governor of the Bank, "a necessary extension was made in the facilities of this particular department (for financing small industries) and an improvement was attained in the methods of operation, while a very liberal policy has been adopted under which prompt service was afforded, disregarding material security, for those borrowers of reliable character and ability, who have good business records so that we may be able to meet fully the financial need of these enterprising men."[1]

Opinion is much divided as to how far the Japanese Industrial Bank has been a success. That the Government has had to come to its rescue on several occasions is perfectly true; but that was almost inevitable considering the fact that its investment policy was not guided solely by economic considerations of safety. Its avowed purpose has been to afford aid to weak and newly established industries. At the same time Government found in it a suitable instrument by means of which it could assist the promotion of some industries. In 1913, when the bank incurred heavy losses owing to the depreciation of securities held by it and the difficulty of recovering the loans given to gold-mining companies, the Government granted a loan of £1,350,000 at a very low rate of interest,[2] arranged through the Bank of Japan and the Yokohama Specie Bank. Even in Japan there has been growing dissatisfaction with the official control of the Industrial Bank and other official banks, and there is a demand that they should be freed from the control of the Minister of Finance.[3] The connection of Government with official banks has been made use of to placate certain parties and groups and the appointments

[1] Speech of the Governor of the Industrial Bank of Japan at the General Meeting of the Shareholders, August 8, 1933.

[2] *Indian Journal of Economics*, January 1931.

[3] G. C. Allen, *Japan's Banking System*, 1924.

to the chief offices of the bank have been influenced by political considerations. The present time is admittedly a critical one, and it will be difficult to form a definite judgment until greater experience is obtained.

The experience of Japan does not, therefore, afford a conclusive lesson for India, and decision about the desirability or otherwise of a State institution in India must be based on the conditions of the country itself. The one argument in favour of a State-controlled institution is that the public will have greater confidence in a State-aided bank which will therefore be able to attract the savings of the investors. But it is doubtful how far public confidence will survive a real failure, and if it will continue if the bank does not show satisfactory results or if its investments turn out to be mistaken or imprudent. Where so much depends upon the personnel, it is difficult to be dogmatic. What is required is a staff of able men who are given the necessary freedom. The Japanese Industrial Bank has not been free of political influence in regard to its staffing. The danger is always dormant that special interests, political or economic, will be allowed to dominate the policy of the bank.

Further, valuable as an industrial bank may be, it is only one of the needs of industry. The view expressed by the Industrial Commission that "the difficulty in raising capital for industries is mainly the measure even in India, not of the insufficiency or inaccessibility of money, but of the opinion which its possessors hold of the industrial propositions put before them,"[1] remains as true to-day as when it was made about fifteen years ago. The paucity of applications for taking advantage of the State Aid to Industries Act shows that financial handicaps are not the only or even the most serious difficulty in the way of industrial development. On a balance of all considerations, therefore, one is inclined to doubt the desirability of an industrial bank on the lines of the Japanese Industrial Bank.

But even if the idea of a State-aided industrial bank is approved, there are many practical difficulties in the way of establishing one.

[1] *Report of the Indian Industrial Commission*, 1918, p. 214.

While on general grounds it may be desirable to establish an All-India Industrial Bank, with branches in suitable centres. there are several objections against any such step. In the first place medium-sized industries and smaller industries suffer from inadequate finance more than the bigger organized industries, and a central institution is hardly fitted to undertake the financing of such types. Secondly, local industries may be able to draw capital more easily from local areas if there be an institution in a province for the purpose of rendering financial advice to industry. Thirdly, in the new constitution, industry, which is already a provincial subject will continue to be a subject under the '"State" as opposed to the Federal sphere. Any expenditure in connection with financial assistance to industrial banks will have to be incurred by the Provincial Governments who must, therefore, decide the extent to which they are willing to embark on such enterprises.

These important practical considerations leave almost no choice in the matter. But if provincial banks are to be started, the dangers of their being allowed to finance all kinds of industry are very great.

VI

PROVINCIAL INDUSTRIAL CORPORATION TO FINANCE PUBLIC UTILITY INDUSTRIES

Although the establishment of a State-aided industrial bank to finance all kinds of competitive industry cannot be recommended, there is a case for the starting of a financial institution to undertake the financing of several public utility industries. Already the need for such an institution has been felt in some provinces. In Madras, the recent hydro-electric undertakings and power supply schemes and the irrigation works have all been financed by Government; but the machinery for financing the schemes is ill-organized. In the Punjab two important hydro-electric schemes have been undertaken, and more are in contemplation. These public utility undertakings have one thing in common, namely, that the capital invested therein will take some time before yielding returns, and therefore the ordinary methods of company financing are not suitable. They, however, afford a very valuable means of drawing capital from the investors provided a suitable financial machinery is devised. The starting of a public industrial corporation for the purpose of financing all semi-monopolistic industries will be not only desirable but necessary, if financing is to be done efficiently. The "foreign" experts who came to assist the Banking Committee also recommended the establishment of an industrial corporation whose field of operations must be the pioneer enterprise of non-competitive character, such as the development of mineral resources, large public utilities such as electric power schemes, gas works, etc. The capital required for them is so large and the intervening period between the beginning of the scheme and its profit-earning stage so prolonged that special assistance will be required.

In Germany, public banks have been working successfully, and especially in the post-war period have had a rapid development. They carry on all forms of business, and do both deposit and investment banking. While concentrating mainly on the financing of railways and public utilities, their sphere of operations has extended to other industries which have been threatened by ruin owing to the aftermath of the war. "In Saxony and Thuringia particularly, the relations between the State banks and industry have been very close, and in both cases the State bank has also participated in other banks and in insurance companies."[1] Far from persuading the banks to confine themselves to public utilities, they are encouraged to provide "banking facilities for those of moderate means," and this is particularly true in Prussia. It is doubtful, however, if an extension into the financing of such new and competitive fields of industry is either safe or desirable. The weight of banking opinion in Germany is against any widening of their scope.[2] But within certain limits, the banks have a very valuable function to perform.

The experience of Germany and other countries strengthens

[1] P. B. Whale, *Joint-Stock Banking in Germany*, p. 247.

[2] See *Dr. Goldschmidt's Evidence before the Macmillan Committee*, Vol. 2.

the case for the establishment of a corporation or financial institution on similar lines. The experts were of the opinion that only an All-India corporation must be considered, but for reasons stated already, Provincial institutions are more suitable.

We have next to consider whether, besides the financing of pioneer industries and public utilities (harbours, roads, and water works), the work of the corporation may be extended to the financing of ordinary competitive industry and of small- and medium-scale industries. The main point of difference between the Banking Committee and the foreign experts was that while the former would give a free hand and not impose any restrictions, the latter would strictly limit the field of their activities to public utilities. The exclusion of smaller industries from the sphere of the Industrial Corporation was naturally dictated by their preference for an All-India institution. But if the institution is to be provincial in character, then there can be no objection to the financing of medium- and small-scale industries *per se*. The only question is if it be desirable to assist industries other than the semi-monopolistic public utilities.

While normally the field of enterprise of the corporation should be limited, as suggested by the experts, there is need for utilizing the machinery of the Corporation for the purpose of affording financial assistance to small industries. It was pointed out that much of the failure of the State Aid to Industries Act was due to the lack of suitable machinery for the purpose of granting credit and loans. When a Provincial Industrial Corporation is established, it will undoubtedly form the most valuable instrument through which assistance to these industries may be rendered.[1] The Indian Industrial Commission have suggested that in cases where financial assistance was considered to be justified, the method of guaranteeing interest on the cash credit granted by a bank on the recommendation of Government might

[1] In this connection it is relevant to note that the recent tendency of the Industrial Bank of Japan specially to help smaller industrialists is the result of the recognition of the difficulties of small industries to get adequate finance.

suitably be employed, the object being to establish some contact between the lending bank and the industrial firm. It is a pity that the experiment was not tried. In any case it is doubtful if any more suitable agency for the purpose of distributing assistance can be devised.

A certain sum may be annually placed with the industrial corporation which will be empowered to loan it out to firms and individuals who have proved the soundness of their schemes, and made out a case for getting aid.

GOVERNMENT ASSISTANCE TO THE PROPOSED CORPORATION

It will be necessary for Government to back the corporation with their support by taking up a certain amount in the share capital of the institution. Such support will inspire the confidence of the investor who will be willing to follow the lead of Government. But in the conditions of India, a further measure of State assistance will be justified. As proposed by the Central Banking Committee, the debentures of the corporation should be guaranteed for a short period of five or ten years. The guarantee of interest may be further limited to the first issue of debentures. Experience in connection with the debentures of co-operative land-mortgage banks shows that the taking up of some debentures by Government and/or the guaranteeing of interest for a limited period have been very helpful in attracting funds from the public. In the circumstances, Government help of the kind mentioned above will be both desirable and justifiable.

The amount of share capital of the corporation must, of course, depend upon the estimated needs, which will vary with each province; but it should in all cases be fairly large. The share capital should be supplemented by debentures, the amounts of which may suitably be varied from time to time according to the activities of the corporation. As the financing of public utilities will be the most essential task, deposits if received from the public should be for a long period and, following the recommendation of the Central Banking Committee, restricted to those for two years or longer. A State-aided institution should not be allowed to compete with the ordinary joint-stock banks for short-term deposits.

But the primary condition of the success of such an institution is the character of the administration and the chief executive staff. The Board should consist of competent men whose only title to appointment must be their business ability and experience. No private or sectional interests should be permitted to have any voice in its administration. Government must have the right of appointing one or two directors to watch its interests and to ensure that nothing is done which will land the corporation in disaster. But it is not necessary to arm the Government directors with powers of veto. It is highly improbable that the remaining directors will refuse to listen to the advice given by the official directors, and to act upon it if it is in their opinion sound.

VII

MACHINERY FOR MEETING THE LONG-TERM NEEDS OF INDUSTRY

While the proposed Industrial Corporations will, within their own field of operations, fulfil a useful function, there will still remain a gap in the organization for financing the long-term needs of large-scale competitive industry. It is true that in the case of the industries with which we have been primarily concerned, there is no need for any special institution to give long-term advances, as the character of the industries is such that, provided they start with adequate permanent capital there will be no need for long-term advances. But in the case of the steel industry and of certain engineering industries which may be expected to develop in the near future, extensions and improvements of plants may not be possible without advances for a much longer period than can be granted by ordinary banks. The existence of a similar problem in Great Britain was brought into prominence by the Committee on Finance and Industry, which stated that the British financial organization was not as fitted as it might be to supply industry with intermediate credit and with long-dated capital. The Committee therefore recommended the establishment, with the co-operation of the big banks and leading private institutions, of a financial concern with a substantial capital and a competent and expert staff. The functions which would be performed by such a concern have been summarized by the Committee as follows: "Acting as financial advisers to existing industrial companies; advising in particular as to the provision of permanent capital, its amounts and types; securing the underwriting of and issuing the company's securities to the public and, if necessary, assisting previously in arranging for the provision of temporary finance in anticipation of an issue; assisting in financing long contracts at home and abroad or new developments of an existing company; or founding companies for entirely new enterprises; acting as intermediaries and financial advisers in the case of mergers or in the case of negotiations with corresponding international groups; and generally being free to carry out all types of financing business."[1] It is true that not all of these purposes are relevant to Indian conditions; but most of them are. Especially in regard to the acting as financial advisers and the assisting of industry in its efforts at rationalization, a financial institution of the kind proposed above will be equally desirable. The Committee on Finance and Industry referred to already not only expressed itself in favour of the adaptation of the Bankers' Industrial Development Company (created as a subsidiary to the Bank of England for the purpose of advising industry in regard to mergers and rationalization) to serve the objects enunciated above, but also contemplated the starting of several such institutions.

The problem has had to be faced not in Great Britain alone. On the contrary, even in countries where credit banks have had a more intimate contact with industry, recent developments have shown a tendency for the banking organization to make a further adjustment to meet the new demands on it by the altered circumstances of industrial organization. Thus in France, where the banking system has been characterized by a division into two classes (i.e. deposit banks and investment banks) and stands

[1] *Report of the Committee*, p. 172.

intermediate between the specialized English system and the integrated German system, a significant change has been brought about, especially since the war. The increased importance of French industry has called for considerable changes in banking policy. On the one hand, the "banques des affaires" have become even more interested in industrial finance than before. But what is more remarkable, the deposit banks, realizing the need to provide more extensive assistance for their industrial customers, have established subsidiary companies for long-term industrial finance. Thus in 1919 the Crédit Lyonnaise and the Comptair National together set up a new financial company.[1]

The same kind of association of a deposit bank with an affiliated financing and issuing institution has been produced in Italy in another way. On the fusion of Credits Italiano with the "Banco Nationale de Credito" in 1930, it was decided to restrict the former to short-term deposit banking, and use the latter for long-term industrial financing. It may be that in the words of Mr. Whale, "through this intimate association of specialized institutions nominally separate, it will be found possible to secure the advantages to industry of the mixed system without exposing the depositor to any greater risks than he remains under the English system."[2] Again, early in 1933, the Institute for Industrial Reconstruction was created with the object of affording long-term finance to sound industries for the purpose of rationalizing production, and already a few important schemes of reorganization have been carried out, including the large electrical company known as S.I.P.[3] (Società Idro-Elettrica Piemontese).

In the United States, too, considerable changes have taken place in recent years. There has always been a close and continuous contact between banks and industry in America, and all the great industries and the railroads have been affiliated in general to particular banking houses which sponsored the issues of those concerns. "In the building up and in particular in the merging of most of the great American corporations, some house or bank

[1] *Journal of the Institute of Bankers*, September 1931.

[2] Ibid.

[3] *The Times*, London, November 17, 1933.

has played a leading part,"[1] and all industrial issues of well-known companies are sponsored by some responsible issuing institution. Since the big private banks and issuing houses would not, however, handle small issues, local industry had to rely on local banks which did not fail to do for local industry what the bigger banks did for the large railroads and big businesses.

Recently the large banks in New York, Chicago, and other centres have constituted special companies known as Subsidiary Securities Companies through which their investment business is transacted. Some idea of the importance of the investment activity of the commercial banks in United States may be had from the fact that in 1927–9 interest and dividends on investments and profits on securities amounted to 28 per cent of the gross profits. Finally, recent developments in Germany reveal interesting features not without significance to India. While there is no tendency to give up their essential character of mixed banking business, the great credit banks are abstaining from their usual part in financing developments in cases where the risks of immobilizing capital have appeared to them too great. They have, therefore, helped to form special financing companies either in collaboration with German industrialists, as in the case of the electrical industry, or more recently, in conjunction with foreign capitalists.[2] These institutions function largely as holding companies. By participating in the capital and management of these companies, the big banks have been able to exercise indirect control over important industries and at the same time avoid excessive immobilization of their resources.[3] Nor is this the only development. Important branches of industry have formed special banks for the purpose of financing themselves more easily and for reducing their dependence on the banks. Thus the Corn Credit Company, the Timber Tradebank, the Sugar Credit Bank, etc., are all special banks to cater to the needs of the particular industry or trade.

The Swiss Banks have, without establishing too direct relations

[1] *(Macmillan) Committee on Finance and Industry*, Report, p. 164.

[2] P. B. Whale, *Joint-Stock Banking in Germany*, pp. 57 and 303.

[3] *Memorandum on Commercial Banks* (League of Nations), 1931.

with industry, exercised by means of Trust Companies great influence on industrial concerns. The Trust Companies established and controlled by the banks, act as holding companies keeping large blocks of shares of several industrial companies.[1] In this way the banks assist and influence industry and supply long-term credits without becoming too closely identified with them.

This brief survey of recent developments in some important countries of the world indicates a definite trend in the course of banking and financial policy. While the existing banks on the Continent are devoting more and more attention to deposit banking and reducing their holding of shares in industrial undertakings, their financial service to industry has not diminished. For, through financial trust and holding companies and special institutions formed as subsidiaries, and operating chiefly with funds raised by the issue of debentures, the banks exercise a beneficent influence without becoming too closely identified with them. Of less importance is the formation of special banks established by particular branches of industry to provide themselves with long-term credit and to gain better access to financial facilities.

VIII

SPECIAL FINANCIAL INSTITUTIONS

What is the significance of all this to India? It is that however urgent and pressing the problem may be it can only be solved by co-operative action on the part of the bankers and of the industrialists. The establishment of special institutions controlled by the banks or of subsidiaries to do the investment side of banking requires organized co-operation on the part of the banks. At the present moment, the Imperial Bank stands far above, and in isolation from, the ordinary joint-stock banks, and is (or at least has been till very recently) looked upon with jealousy as a "pampered" institution. Between it and the other joint-stock banks there has not been enough goodwill and co-operation. The Imperial Bank itself has been in two minds in the face of an impending crisis

[1] *Memorandum on Commercial Banks* (League of Nations), 1931.

to a joint-stock bank. It has had the feeling common to all when a rival is in difficulty, and often neglected its responsibility as the bankers' bank, or even that of the premier bank. Nor has there been any co-operation among the other joint-stock banks themselves, and no organization exists "which could improve the standard, eliminate elements of weakness, and foster the combination of smaller banks to larger units."[1] The creation of an All-India Banks' Association, which would include the joint-stock banks and the exchange banks and, if possible, the indigenous banks, is an essential preliminary to further advances in banking developments. The working of the Reserve Bank of India might also be expected to result in useful forms of co-operation among the banks. A spirit of professional pride and public service should permeate all the banks, and unhealthy competition and a low and primitive feeling of exultation at the difficulties of fellow-bankers should give place to co-operation and friendliness in the pursuit of a common purpose. The secret of success of German banks has been the method of Konsortium by which in all important fields the active co-operation of all the banks is secured. As one of the witnesses, a Hungarian, put it before the Indian Central Banking Enquiry Committee: "If we compare Indian banking, finance, industry, and trade with those of the Continent, we find that one of the chief differences is that the economic units in India, whether they are banks or industrial undertakings, are standing isolated, whereas in Europe we find that these units are connected with each other in many ways."[2] The different banks on the Continent are connected with one another in various ways, and the "friendly" connections of the directors of the banks with one another and with the leading personalities of the economic life of the country are the most vital part of the banking and financial organizations. It is this difference between conditions in India and elsewhere that makes it unsafe to recommend an institution

[1] *Experts' Memorandum on Commercial Banking to the Indian Central Banking Enquiry Committee.*

[2] *Indian Central Banking Enquiry Committee,* Vol. 2, Evidence of Dr. Nemenyi, p. 296.

which depends for its success on such imponderable qualities difficult to be acquired in a short time. But the aim and goal of banking policy in India is clear. It is that opportunities should be cultivated for the systematic discussion of common subjects and common problems. If the suggestion made in the earlier part of the chapter, that banks should establish more intimate contacts with industry, and for this purpose should themselves come together and assist in the financing of new industrial companies be approved, it follows that in itself it will open out a vast field of useful co-operative endeavour.

After this preliminary stage is passed, it should be easier for them to start an institution similar to that proposed by the British Committee on Finance and Industry to perform nearly the same functions as those contemplated in the recommendation. It will certainly be some time before Indian banks will be in a position to undertake that task. But provided the object is kept steadfastly in view, the end will be achieved sooner than may be hoped for now.

In the meanwhile, some of the financial problems of industry are pressing for solution. In the cotton industry the scheme for a merger has temporarily (or permanently?) been abandoned.[1] But if the Bombay cotton industry is to survive and to stand on its own feet without the crutches supplied by a protective tariff, some kind of rationalization will have to be attempted sooner or later. It is true, as has been already pointed out, that the managerial ability needed for administering successfully a vast combine like the one proposed is not easy to secure. But it may not be impossible to secure just the few able men required for the task. If such a scheme matures, the need for a special financial institution will become increasingly felt. Financial advice, long-dated capital, and temporary help until debentures are taken up by the public will have to be given. But even apart from the merger scheme, the cotton industry requires a large amount of capital expenditure in other directions, such as mercerizing, printing and finishing machinery, and the provision of wider-reed-space looms. Develop-

[1] See next chapter.

ment in fine shirting is also held up owing to the relatively small proportion of looms capable of providing cloth over 40 inches wide.[1] The slender financial resources of the mill agents are holding up progress. Capital will have to be supplied temporarily by a financial institution, with a view to enabling the industry to reorganize itself.

Again, the tea industry also requires in its present economic condition a central buying and packing organization, financed by the growers of tea with a view to selling direct to consumers. But want of finance has been standing in the way. The initial cost of such an organization will be considerable, and in the present circumstances of the industry, it will be unwise to expect the public to put in capital. A strong and powerful financial institution may be of great help.

Thus recovery in depressed industries is held up because without additional capital expenditure the economies necessary for ensuring cheap production cannot be secured; but because of its depressed conditions, the public would not invest in it any more, and thus the usual vicious circle found in depressed industries all over the world is found in India too. In the cotton industry particularly, it is common knowledge that a lot of old machinery exists which leads to low production, and needs to be scrapped. The investments in printing and mercerizing plant, and the expenditure involved in adopting the high draft system of spinning which can reduce spinning costs require a considerable amount of capital for lack of which industry is in a stalemate. The most serious aspect of the matter is that instead of treating it primarily as a problem of internal industrial and financial organization, attention is being diverted to its external aspect, and the solution is sought by way of manipulating the tariff.

In normal times, the most promising line of development will be the establishment of an industrial bank by the leading industrialists and bankers acting in co-operation. Such a bank should not be dominated (as was the case in the Tata Industrial

[1] Memorandum submitted by the Bombay Millowners' Association to the Indian Tariff Board: Cotton Industry, 1932.

Bank) by any group of managing agency firms. A bank whose shares are held by most of the important managing agents and the leading joint-stock banks, having on its directorate bankers and industrialists, will have a variety of experience on its Board, and may be expected to work successfully. It will, indeed, represent a logical method of advance. But at the present time the scheme will not be practicable. The losses incurred by managing agents in recent years have cut into their savings, and deter them from investing in new business. There is yet not sufficient co-operation among themselves, or between them and the banks. But when the tide turns and industry is on the flow, it may be possible for an institution to be established by private initiative on a wide basis, whose primary aim should be to give financial advice to industrial companies, assist in the floating and issuing of securities of industrial concerns, and render them other forms of assistance.

There are some who suggest the starting of Investment Trust Companies which, by taking from the hands of the public the responsibility of investment, would not only supply industry with funds but inspire confidence among the public, by their skilful investments and management. Apart from the fact that the same difficulty which prevents the establishment of a large Industrial Bank in the present depressed state of Indian industry would exist in this case also, one is not certain if Investment Trust Companies are the right sort of organization for the needs of Indian industry. Investment Trust companies, judging from British experience, confine their dealings to established securities, and their primary aim is not industrial, but financial. They are therefore inadequate in a country which is more or less in the early stages of its industrial development. What is actually needed is an organization which will make it one of its primary objects to forward the development of new industry, to assist existing industry to rationalize and generally to afford financial advice. Although at a later stage of industrial development, when a wide basis for investment exists, Investment Trust Companies may play an important part, at present they will not meet the purpose.

The only alternative left is to wait upon events. Until then,

Government can render a limited amount of financial aid. It may ask depressed industries to explore the possibilities of rationalization, and upon proved necessity arrange with the Imperial Bank of India to grant advances for a fairly long period at a reduced rate for purposes to be definitely stated. Such purposes should include the importing of special plant and machinery, the improvement of existing plant, and so on. The Imperial Bank must take the full responsibility for the loans thus made, but the difference between the rate of interest charged on them and the rate which the Imperial Bank would normally charge may be met by Government. This step is not without its dangers. But the exceptional circumstances of industry would justify Governmental assistance. In the case of the cotton industry, the grant of protection obviates the need for any such assistance by Government. But it does seem that, instead of continuously raising tariffs, other avenues of improving the financial position of the cotton industry may be usefully explored.

If this chapter has not led to any positive conclusions it is because, in the present state of banking organization in India, no new development of a startling kind can be expected until the banking system as a whole is inspired by a spirit of co-operation and service, and until the Reserve Bank of India has been in operation for some years. We have suggested the adaptation of the Indian banking system to the mixed Continental system, not in its earlier but in its later aspect. In this task, while the Imperial Bank should take the lead, other strong banks might soon follow and work in co-operation with the Imperial Bank. Such organized co-operation would in course of time lead to developments which we have noticed in other countries of the world. It is also possible for the managing agents, some of whom already possess banking experience and organization, to start a financial institution with the co-operation of the leading banks. But the example of the Tata Industrial Bank is a warning that even a powerful institution should not either in form or in effect be an appendage to any group or groups of industrialists. But all these developments will take, perhaps, some time. Nor need this delay be regretted. Experience in other fields of activity no less than in the industrial or banking fields, confirms the view that a too rapid push in one direction leads to waste and sometimes retards progress. Before seeking to gain new positions, the existing position must be consolidated and strengthened. But provided the goal is kept clear in view, progress, even if slow, will be sure, and the end will ultimately be sooner reached.

CHAPTER VIII

INFLUENCE OF THE MANAGING AGENCY SYSTEM ON THE STRUCTURE OF INDUSTRIAL ORGANIZATION

I

STRUCTURE OF INDUSTRY IN INDIA

Modern industry has known a variety of types of industrial organization and combination, brought about by methods of development on horizontal and vertical lines. Partly under the influence of a desire to secure increased economies in production and distribution, but mainly dominated by the motive to eliminate wasteful competition, industry has organized itself into associations of varying degrees of unification. Two broad lines of development, often overlapping and cutting across one another may be distinguished, the vertical and horizontal forms of expansion and combination. Although the motives, objects, and even the conditions of success are different in each case, they both aim at some reduction in cost and some elimination of competition with a view to increasing profits. Speaking generally, while the aim of horizontal combination is to achieve the economies of rationalization in the true sense of the term, the aim of vertical organization is to attain in some degree a position of self-sufficiency and to avoid being dependent on the vicissitudes of the market as regards raw materials or semi-finished goods. Thus a combination of firms in the same stage of production, as for example, the recently formed Lancashire Cotton Corporation, would aim at the elimination of all waste and the increase of economic power by such methods "as systematic works specialization, the elimination of inefficient and surplus plant, and in general the full realization of the advantages of concentrated management and large-scale production."[1] On the other hand, in the case of a vertical

[1] *Final Report of the Committee on Industry and Trade*, Cmd. 3282 (1929), p. 117.

combination, we have a combination of firms in successive stages of the same industry; a steel-making plant for example, may combine with a coal-mining company or with a shipbuilding firm to secure its supplies of raw material or find a market for its products. But whatever the actual method of expansion and combination, the result is always some kind of association, either loose or well integrated, and involves on the part of the units that combine some surrender of their independence. We have thus various forms of organization, cartels, syndicates, combines, trusts, holding companies and so on.

While these have been the developments abroad, Indian industry has afforded a form of organization, unique in some respects, and presenting features of great interest to students of industrial structure. In an earlier chapter, something has been said of the system by which managing agents came to control and manage first a large number of similar undertakings, and secondly a fair number of enterprises in different industries. Now, when we find 10 jute mills, 18 tea companies, 14 coal companies, 3 transport companies, and a number of units in other different industries all managed by one managing agency firm, these several concerns are all uniquely related to the same management. Appendix IV in Chapter I gave us some idea of the extent to which a number of managing agency firms managed concerns in the same industry, and also concerns in different industries. What is the significance of this relationship between the management and the several firms under its control?

It is clearly not a case of horizontal combination in the ordinary sense of the term. For whatever be the degree of co-ordination and control exercised by the managing agents, each individual company has a separate existence. The shareholders of one may be and are different from those in the other concerns; the accounts of each are maintained separately; the materials that are purchased are specifically indented for and assigned to each; and in a word each has an independent existence. Cases have undoubtedly occurred when as a result of the influence of a managing agent, two similar concerns which formerly existed independently have agreed to combine into one. Of examples of such combination may be mentioned the Buckingham & Carnatic Co., Ltd., Madras, which was the result of a combination of two mill companies which were functioning separately as the Buckingham Mill Co. and the Carnatic Mill Co. until 1920; the E. D. Sassoon United Mills, Ltd., which grew out of an amalgamation of six mills formerly working separately; the British India Corporation, Ltd. (1920) formed to combine and amalgamate the following concerns, which had been working independently: The Cawnpore Woollen Mills Co., Ltd., the Cawnpore Cotton Mills Co., Ltd., the New Egerton Cotton Mills, the North-Western Tannery Co., Ltd. Such cases may justifiably be considered as horizontal combination, or a combination of a mixed variety. Nor may the type of organization described above be regarded as vertical, although there are points of contact between a jute company and a coal company managed by the same managing agent. For it is not the case that the jute company was stimulated to expand with a view to acquiring coal for its steam power or driven to acquire tea companies so that its products may be used for packing tea.

Yet there are interesting features in this type of organization which have received insufficient attention among Indian economists. To elucidate the position, we have to examine the degree of control exercised by the managing agents in respect of each firm, the extent to which co-ordination and control by the central office of the Management has affected the economy of each concern, the relation between the allied concerns controlled by the same management, and the extent to which common marketing, financial, administrative, and other economies are secured. We must also further inquire if as a result of several concerns being brought together under one management, there has resulted any noticeable tendency for the profits of each to be more or less the same. Above all, we must examine what are the consequences of a system in which, while a small group of shareholders, represented by the managing agency firms, are part-owners in several concerns with varying interests in each, the other shareholders are interested primarily each in the business in which he has invested. The conflict of interest between managing agents and shareholders, if it does exist, must be explained and its effects examined.

II

ADMINISTRATIVE INTEGRATION

The most striking thing that emerges from a study of the organization of the offices of the leading managing agencies' firms is that industry in India is integrated in its administrative aspect as opposed to mere technical management. The central office of every leading managing agency firm has several departments, organized first on the lines of industry, and secondly in respect of the sections within an industry. Thus a firm like Andrew Yule & Co. has a jute department, a coal department, a tea department, and so on. And again these are further subdivided into a purchase department, for all the requirements of jute mills, a sales department, a financing department, and so on. In the case of certain firms, the purchasing department may cut right across all the different industries, buying the requirements, not only of the jute mill companies, but also of the tea companies, and so on. Whatever be the nature of the organization, the important point is that purchases for all the mill companies under one managing agency firm are made in common. Being in constant touch with the market and having a far better organization than any individual concern can have, the managing agency firm is able to supply an efficient buying organization and buy at the best prices. The requisition for purchase comes, of course, from each concern, but the time at which it is purchased is often the same for all, and the advantages of bulk purchase and the gains resulting from an intimate knowledge of the market accrue to all the concerns. As soon as a purchase is made, it is at once assigned to the particular concern for which the purchase is made so that changes in prices occurring later may not affect (adversely or favourably) the concern. When the purchases are made in London, a surcharge over the purchase rates is fixed for such supplies to cover the expenses of the buying. Where the managing agency firm has a London office, a definite percentage is paid.

In the same manner, several jute mills under one managing agency firm can and do have a much better selling organization than would be possible for any individual concern. When one man sells for eight or nine jute mills, the results are generally speaking better than can be achieved individually by eight or nine men of inferior quality and competence. The result is that the products of those jute companies take a much more prominent position in the market by virtue of the common sales organization than might be possible if each had to have an independent selling organization.

In respect of supervisory staff and administrative control, too, this integrated system of management has led to some very striking results, more particularly in the jute, tea, and coal-mining industries. A single tea garden cannot afford to maintain a good inspectorate staff to supervise quality and offer technical advice. It will be too expensive; whereas a group of gardens under one management can, and do, have a first-class inspectorate, the expenses of which are shared out in common by all. An interesting result of this feature is that when a new tea garden is to be opened up, a managing agent can easily find a good junior manager or assistant amongst his own staff as manager and employ him with confidence because of the general supervision by an efficient and trained inspecting staff. Nearly the same type of economy is noticeable in the coal companies. It has been pointed out that while the medium-sized coal companies cannot afford to employ a first-class engineer, it has been possible to have men of the grade of sub-engineers for each colliery, and to employ an expert engineer to supervise the work of the several smaller engineers in the mines. Thus a great economy has been possible, and the expenses of a supervisory staff are reduced and shared out, to the advantage of all.

Not less important is the economy in the cost of the administrative staff. The partners of at least the leading managing agency firms are men of great ability whose services could not be obtained by any one industrial concern operating alone. The high remuneration made possible by their managing several concerns affords the incentive to the partners of the managing agents to give their services and enables the industrial companies to have the advantage of the highest administrative talents at lower cost. How far actually industry benefits or has benefited by this system of management will be examined later. But it is necessary to point out that not only is this economy in administration a theoretical possibility, but in some cases at least an undoubted fact.

We have already reviewed the financial advantages accruing to industrial concerns from the managing agency system. It is only necessary here to stress two facts. In the first place, individual concerns have been better able to withstand depression or overcome the initial difficulties of every new activity because of the co-ordination in financing secured by managing agents. To that extent the economy of large-scale financial administration is secured. Secondly, smaller industrial companies are at no disadvantage compared to the larger ones both in the securing of permanent capital and in getting bank advances, for the credit of the managing agents enables the smaller concerns no less than the larger units to get equal financial facilities.

The managing agency system, then, ensures a co-ordination of the activities of all the units working under common management. In other words, administrative integration is a feature of the managing agency system at its best. Without any formal combination or amalgamation and without losing their independent legal and functional existence, these various units are enabled to realize some of the economies, if not of large-scale production, of large-scale organization. In other respects, too, the system ensures a certain economy which bears resemblance to the economies of vertical expansion. In so far as a jute mill, a coal company, a tea garden, and a boat company are all under common management, the products of one concern find a market, or at least a small outlet in the business of the others. Something has already been said of this in an earlier chapter, but it is necessary to underline its significance. Thus a boat company is almost assured of a certain quantity of transport which it can handle, because the goods of all the allied concerns will almost certainly be sent in the vessels of the boat company under the same management. Likewise a coal company is sure of finding an outlet for its product in the allied jute concern or a tea factory. Those concerns which need packing material may be expected to utilize the products of the jute company under the common managing agents. Thus partial self-sufficiency and a market common to all the products of the allied companies are sought to be achieved, and it is certainly an advantage to have a market, however small it may be, which is reliable, and can be controlled by the management.[1]

[1] The Group system of administration in the gold-mining industry of the Witwatersrand bears some striking resemblances to the managing agency system of industrial organization. In 1929 there were on the Witwatersrand thirty-three gold-producing companies which with a few exceptions were controlled by one or other of a few large corporations possessing strong financial resources, long and intimate experience of mining enterprises, and efficient technical and administrative staffs. One such corporation controls fourteen gold-producing companies, another controls seven, and so on. The individual companies are separate corporate entities, each having its own staff, managerial, technical, and secretarial; and their individual managerial authority and responsibility are jealously safeguarded.

The Group (or the controlling corporation) is able, while encouraging the best efforts of the separate managements, "to render to the individual companies a variety of valuable services which would not otherwise be available to them except at excessive, and in many instances prohibitive, cost. The Group maintains staffs of consulting engineers, consulting mechanical and electrical engineers, consulting metallurgists, and other technical experts whose energies are devoted to major technical problems of the mines under their supervision, to co-ordination of practice, and to the introduction of improvements in methods and appliances that the experiments and investigators constantly in progress frequently succeed in producing."

The Group organization also acts as head office and as secretaries of the individual companies, and in that capacity performs many valuable services. The Buying Department of the Group enables the smallest mining consumer of a particular commodity "to secure the advantage of the more favourable prices that apply to the collective group contracts for that commodity." For further interesting details regarding the Group system of organization the reader is referred to Mr. John Martin's article in the December issue of the *Economic Journal*, 1929, from which the above information has been extracted.

III

ATTEMPT TO SECURE UNIFORMITY IN DIVIDENDS

These conditions have brought about another result. Managing agents seek to secure as far as possible uniform results, and ensure to the shareholders of all the jute mills under the management the same rates of dividends within the limits which differences in location, technical conditions, etc., would permit. Sir Campbell Rhodes, the Head of the firm of Hoare, Miller & Co., at one of the writer's interviews with him, emphasized the natural tendency of a managing agency firm to treat all the jute mills under its control as one unit and show similar results. In the same manner the tea companies, the coal companies, the transport companies, etc., each group of units in an industry under the same managing agents may be expected to declare the same rate of profits over a period of time. At any rate, in the opinion of some of the partners of the managing agency firms, any wide divergences in the rates of dividends declared within an industrial group would have to be explained as due to certain exceptional factors.

To see how far in practice a uniform level of dividends has been declared in groups of units in an industry under the same managing agents, the dividends declared in the jute and tea companies have been analysed in the following tables. A study of the dividends declared in the shares of 31 jute mills managed by 5 different managing agents, one controlling 10, the others controlling 8, 5, 4, and 4 units respectively, has been made for 11 years from 1920 to 1930, and the results are shown in Statement 1. Statement 2 gives the average rate of dividend for 15 years from 1914 to 1928, of all the mills that have been working since 1914; and also the average rate of dividend for 5 years from 1928 to 1932. The figures do not seem to warrant any definite generalization regarding uniformity of profits. It is true that the mills under the management of Jardine & Skinner & Co. show over the period 1914–28, and again from 1928–32, a fairly uniform level of dividends. In the case of those under Andrew Yule & Co. and Bird & Co., the tendency is not sufficiently strong to justify

STATEMENT I

Giving profits per cent for each year

	1920	1921	1922	1923	1924	1925	1926	1927	1928	1929	1930
ANDREW YULE & CO., LTD.											
1. Albion ..	95	50	40	65	65	85	45	55	60	45	25
2. Belvedere	120	42	40	70	90	60	35	90	100	75	—
3. Budgebudge	130	45	42	60	55	55	38	70	90	60	28
4. Caledonia	140	40	70	72	100	85	30	95	120	85	45
5. Cheviot*	—	—	10	35	35	30	12	35	45	40	25
6. Delta ..	150	50	50	75	85	70	50	85	90	65	37
7. Lothian ..	100	35	40	55	70	45	22	70	80	55	28
8. National ..	100	45	30	45	45	47	22	38	42	35	19
9. New Central	190	85	55	60	100	90	40	85	105	75	—
10. Orient ..	—	—	18	20	25	20	15	30	35	35	18
BIRD & CO., LTD.											
1. Auckland	115	26	5	10	30	35	10	45	50	35	15
2. Clive ..	160	50	32	35	60	65	10	42	50	—	—
3. Dalhousie	160	65	35	45	60	65	25	75	80	67	—
4. Landsdowne	120	35	20	40	50	45	8	10	35	32	10
5. Lawrence	225	80	55	70	100	115	35	90	100	85	50
6. Northbrook	225	100	70	55	75	85	30	75	85	85	55
7. Standard ..	200	65	40	45	60	65	25	70	65	45	27
8. Union ..	265	50	25	45	90	115	40	115	120	95	50
MCLEOD & CO., LTD.											
1. Empire ..	200	70	40	50	70	80	30	55	85	80	—
2. Kelvin ..	300	100	70	85	110	120	60	85	125	110	—
3. Presidency*	—	—	—	10	15	8	17	20	17	—	—
4. Soorah ..	40	12	12	18	30	40	20	30	42	57	—
5. Chitananalsa†	—	—	—	—	—	—	—	—	—	—	—
BEGG, DUNLOP & CO.											
1. Alexandra	125	20	35	20	45	37	10	50	70	35	—
2. Alliance ..	175	70	50	72	80	105	15	35	80	70	—
3. Craig ..	—	—	—	—	—	—	—	—	—	2·5	—
4. Waverley ..	—	—	—	—	—	—	—	—	—	—	—
JARDINE & SKINNER & CO.											
1. Howrah ..	130	75	45	55	57	55	25	50	60	60	45
2. Kamarbethi	250	65	60	60	90	90	55	100	100	75	—
3. Kamkanrah	175	40	45	50	70	65	38	70	80	60	—
4. Reliance ..	130	75	65	75	90	95	65	100	115	120	90

* Started work only in 1919. † Started work only in 1926.

STATEMENT 2

Average rate of dividend declared for periods

	1914–28	1928–32
ANDREW YULE & CO., LTD.		
1.	65	32·5
2.	72	49
3.	74	42·5
4.	—	60
5.	—	27
6.	—	46
7.	—	38·5
8.	70	24
9.	—	49
10.	—	22
BIRD & CO., LTD.		
1.	45	22·5
2.	58	27
3.	66	47
4.	38	16
5.	98	58
6.	85	56·5
7.	76	35
8.	100	61
MCLEOD & CO., LTD.		
1.	74	46·5
2.	112	65
3.	—	8·5
4.	24	20
5.	—	—
BEGG, DUNLOP & CO., LTD.		
1.	40	21
2.	83	25
3.	—	—
4.	—	—
JARDINE & SKINNER & CO.		
1.	93	44
2.	93	48·5
3.	88	43
4.	72	83

STATEMENT 3

In the following statement the tea companies are classified according to their management. The average dividends declared for sixteen years from 1915 *to* 1930 *inclusive for each of the companies under the same managing agents have been worked out from the figures of dividends given in the "Investors' India Year Book." The total number of companies included in the table is* 55, *distributed as follows:* (a) *Duncan Bros. & Co.* 12, (b) *Williamson, Magor & Co.* 11, (c) *Andrew Yule & Co.* 9, (d) *Begg, Dunlop & Co.* 8, (e) *Octavius Steel & Co.* 8, (f) *Jardine & Skinner & Co.* 7.

	Average Dividend per cent for 16 Years from 1915–30 inclusive
DUNCAN BROS. & CO.	
1. Birpara Tea	29·5
2. Carru Tea	57
3. Ellenbarrie	20
4. Yungaram	14
5. Hantpara	47
6. Manabarrie	11
7. Nagsuree	80
8. North-Western Cachar	23·5
9. Patrokola	56
10. Phaskona	8
11. Runglis Rungliot	38
12. Teliapara	34
WILLIAMSON, MAGOR & CO.	
1. Bishnanth Tea	20·3
2. Borpukuri	16·5
3. Chamong Tea	9
4. Dimakuri	10
5. East Indian	8
6. Longview	1·5
7. Nagri Farm	26·5
8. Rajabarrie	3
9. Seajuli	27
10. Soom	8·5
11. Tukvar	23

	Average Dividend per cent for 16 Years from 1915–30 inclusive
ANDREW YULE & CO.	
1. Banarhat Tea	32
2. Choonabutti	57
3. Dilaram	12
4. Ergo	24·5
5. Hoolumgoorie	41
6. Jaybirpare	15
7. Mim	10
8. New Dooars	86
9. Singtom	18
BEGG, DUNLOP & CO.	
1. Amluckie Tea	8·5
2. Margarets Hope	10·6
3. Rancherra	24·5
4. Roopacherra	15
5. Runganotee	42
6. Sungna	20
7. Tirrihannah	10·5
8. Titabur	12
OCTAVIUS STEEL & CO.	
1. Alyne Pathemara	15
2. Chundeecherra	5
3. Eastern Cachar	10
4. Hattikhira	14
5. Kalacherra	4
6. Kaliti	25·6
7. Lohagar	25
8. Oodlabari	30
JARDINE & SKINNER & CO.	
1. Ballacherra Tea	23·5
2. Bardighi	33·5
3. Carron	5·6
4. Chandypore	11
5. Kallinugger and Khoreel	8
6. Kerseong and Darjeeling	1·7
7. Rydak Tea Syndicate	30

any general inference; but in the case of the remaining mills, the figures do not warrant any such conclusion.

Similarly for the tea industry, the dividends of 55 tea companies for 16 years from 1915 to 1930 have been taken from the *Investor's India Year Book*, and the average rate of profit over the period has been given in Statement 3. It will be seen from a scrutiny of the figures that it is not possible to say that any one of the managing agency firms referred to in the statement (Duncan Bros. & Co., Williamson, Magor & Co., Andrew Yule & Co., Begg, Dunlop, Octavius Steel, or Jardine & Skinner) has been able to declare the same rate of profits in the tea companies under its control. Indeed, it is not surprising that the units, whether of the tea industry, or of coal or even of jute industry do not show the same result even under the same management. Despite the administrative co-ordination secured under the managing agency system, differences in location, natural conditions, and even technical factors are so great between unit and unit that although managing agents might desire to bring about some uniformity in results, they would not succeed. This is particularly so in the tea and in the coal-mining industries, where location and the quality of the soil or of the mine are of great importance. Even in the jute industry where all the units are situated close to each other and the equipment and internal working are more uniform, there are bound to be differences owing to the differences in the size of the units and efficiency of the plant and differences in labour costs. For example, the jute mills in the Calcutta area are at a decided disadvantage compared with those situated at Titaghur, Kinkannara, Budgebudge, etc. The former are cramped for space and "have to pay higher wages for slightly inferior labour." All that can be stated is that managing agents aim as far as possible to achieve similar results and to bring about a uniform level of costs and profits whenever possible.

We thus see that the managing agency system has influenced the industrial structure of India in ways rather difficult to define, but of which the importance cannot be ignored. It has by no means eliminated competition in any industry; but what it has achieved is to eliminate competition as between the units under the same management and to achieve some economies pertaining to co-ordinated management and administration. Indian industry has so far given rise to few combinations of the monopolistic type. It has only witnessed some partial and unpremeditated efforts at rationalization brought about by the fact of common management. In the jute industry, there was perhaps no need for any special attempts at monopolistic combination, for the industry as a whole was in a strikingly prominent position in the world's market.

IV

THE CONFLICT OF INTERESTS BETWEEN MANAGING AGENTS AND SHAREHOLDERS

But these beneficial influences were not apparent in all cases, and indeed, owing to the methods adopted by some managing agents, more particularly in the Bombay Presidency, industry not only lost the gains of co-ordinated management, but found itself weakened by the system of common management. Before explaining the factors that have led to a weakness in organization, it is necessary to point out that the managing agency system of management, with all that it implies, carries with it great power for good and for evil. Even a good institution administered by incompetent or dishonest people is bound to result in injurious consequences. The managing agency system is by no means a perfect one. On the contrary, its leading characteristic is the possible disharmony and conflict of interests between the managing agents and the shareholders. In every large industrial concern all over the world there is a possibility of divided interests between the entrepreneurs and the shareholders. This conflict of interest does not necessarily mean that the shareholders are always right and that they are the victims of bad management. Where a high sense of duty prevails, the entrepreneurs, or the persons who actually control the industrial unit, are inspired by the laudable motive to see that the business is carried on successfully and that proper financial provision is made for growth and continuous development. Whilst the interest of the shareholder stops with his getting a dividend, those who administer the concern are not merely interested in their own dividends but anxious that a reserve is built up which would ensure ability to survive periods of depression and difficulty. Instances can be quoted when the shareholders have clamoured for more dividends, and but for the caution of the chief directors, ultimate success would have been sacrificed to immediate gains. We have stressed this aspect of the conflict of interests because it is often ignored, and the view is wrongly held that in all conflicts between the shareholders and the management the former must be right and the latter wrong.

Now the managing agency system presents an aspect of this divergence of interests in a different way. We may neglect cases where the shareholders in their ignorance or avidity seek to earn large immediate profit at the expense of the future growth of the concern; because the shareholders in India have not the power, even if they are so minded, to do anything to which the managing agents would not agree. In so far as the managing agents hold a large or even a considerable percentage of the shares of the company,[1] it may be supposed that their interests should coincide with those of the shareholders. But by their power of varying the amount of investment which they hold in each concern, they can always sell out if they think the concern would be losing in that year, or buy more if it be the contrary. When they buy the shares of the concern, they are at least strengthening the concern's business, even though their direct object is to make greater profit. But when they sell, clearly their interests are different from those of the ordinary shareholders, and what is worse, with their inside knowledge of the working of the concern during the year, knowledge which they alone possess, they are able to manipulate their holdings so as to make more profits when things are all right and incur the least loss when things go wrong. Although managing agents are not members of the Stock Exchanges in Calcutta and Bombay, they can easily get their transactions through with the assistance of their confidential

[1] See Appendix I, Chapter I.

brokers. In Bombay, and to a lesser extent in Calcutta, this has been going on, and although the better type of managing agents do not resort to these devices, the existence of this practice has undermined the confidence of the investors in the managing agency system and done injury even to the more scrupulous managing agents. Secondly, quite apart from the extent of the managing agents' holdings which may vary from time to time, a divergence of interests occurs because the managing agents regard the earnings from shares as subordinate to their earnings in other capacities and fields of activity. We here enter into a whole series of devices which have been resorted to by some of the managing agents, who have brought discredit to the system. We may first dispose of the least undesirable aspect of this divergence of interest. Whether the industrial company does well or not, a certain minimum commission is assured, and this in many cases includes both a sum of money for the office expenses of the managing agency firm and a further amount which has to be paid when the percentage remuneration on profits fails to yield to the managing agents a certain prescribed amount. Although the payment of a minimum commission may result in a certain amount of indifference to efficient management, no one can seriously question the fairness of an arrangement by which managing agents are guaranteed a certain minimum sum for all their arduous work. If there be some agents who are content with the minimum commission, they are either incompetent and deserve to be thrown out, or they must be holding so few shares in the concern that they do not identify themselves with the fortunes of the concern. Closely connected with this aspect is another point on which a word may be said here. Where the managing agents hold shares of widely different proportions in the concerns they manage, it may be that they neglect the interests of those in which their holdings are small, being content with just the minimum commission, and pay great attention to those in which their holdings are larger.

Although theoretically, and as has been found in practice too in Bengal, it is possible to ensure considerable economies by common purchase and sales organization and by a common administrative staff, the manner in which the system has been working in Bombay has not only failed to secure such advantages, but resulted in great waste. It is true that even in Bombay combined purchase of stores and raw materials has been adopted by some of the groups of mills under the same management;[1] but this is exceptional. Several managing agents receive a commission on their purchases and credit this commission to their own account. When this practice was objected to, it was not long before another device was adopted by which managing agents started a subsidiary company, which was appointed as agent for buying material and stores for all the concerns under their management, and the profits on such purchase went into the pockets of the agent.[2] Such commissions were very widespread and on nearly every contract of work done for the company a commission was received by the agents. Speculative purchases of raw cotton have not been unknown and when they turn out a loss, the losses are at once debited to the mill companies; whilst if there be a profit, it of course goes to the agents. The practice was not unknown in Calcutta too, where in some years the practice of speculative buying of raw jute came in for much criticism.[3]

Even in the sale of the mill products, commissions are charged and taken by the agents. Some of the managing agents are themselves guarantee brokers to their own mills and charge commission on sales of yarn and cloth. The extent to which this practice prevails can be gauged from the fact that twenty-nine mills have been discovered to be under an agreement with the mill agents by which the agents have the power to act as selling agents either

[1] Speech of the President of the Millowners' Association, Bombay, March 1930, *Indian Textile Journal*, p. 254.

[2] *Indian Tariff Board: Cotton Industry*, 1927, Vol. 2, p. 438.

[3] *Indian Textile Journal*, March 1912, p. 196. From an article in the *Capital*. Messrs. Leslie and Hindes, answering in the negative the question whether it was open to the managing agents of jute mills to take part in speculation now notorious under the name of "pink and white contracts," asked, "How can it be said that it is open to the managing agents to indulge in jute speculations which directly result in the raising of the price of jute to the jute mills?"

directly or indirectly by means of a separate selling organization controlled almost entirely by the managing agents.[1] The fact is that managing agents have found that the profits which they receive from their ownership of the shares in the mill companies are not so important as the profits which a large number of related side activities afford them. They have an interest in the stores business, cotton business, and coal business, and in a large number of allied activities. It is not on the profits of *Management* as such that they depend. A managing agency agreement is significant to them only in so far as it opens out to them a vast field of miscellaneous activities capable of yielding them larger profits.[2] Should, by chance, these activities land them in losses, the mill companies are there to which these losses can be passed on. Instead, therefore, of concentration of management being an advantage to the individual units, the manner in which the system is worked in some parts and by some agents results in weakness and the economies of co-ordination are entirely neutralized. While it would be wrong to say that the practices described above are universal in the cotton industry, there is little doubt that they are sufficiently widespread to cause the greatest distrust of the system. Broadly speaking, and subject to a good many exceptions both in Bombay and in Calcutta, while the best side of the managing agency system of organization is witnessed in Bengal, it has revealed itself in its unfavourable aspect in Bombay.

V

CO-ORDINATION OF FINANCE

The co-ordination of financial facilities which every combine or cartel in Germany or America attempts to secure cannot, of

[1] Memorandum submitted by the Bombay Shareholders' Association to the Indian Tariff Board on Cotton Industry in 1932.

[2] Arno Pearse, *Indian Cotton Mills*, p. 121: "A firm of mill managing agents told me that when they took over the business the old suppliers of cotton came offering them secret commission and added that their predecessors always had 2 per cent." See also *Indian Tariff Board: Cotton Industry*, Report, 1932, p. 87.

course, become a regular or systematic function of a managing agency firm. It is here that the chief difference between a cartel and the type of organization represented by the managing agency system comes in. The separate existence of each of the concerns under the managing agency system implies also a completely independent system of financing for each concern. In practice, however, there is a certain amount of inter-relation between the financial resources of the concerns under one and the same managing agency system. This inter-relation is secured in a number of ways. In the first place, the surplus funds of a concern are often taken over by the managing agents as deposits with them, and although the usual interest may be paid on them, they are utilized in their own agency businesses or loaned out to allied concerns. Indeed, in Bombay and Ahmedabad, and to a lesser extent in Calcutta, the practice prevails of receiving mill companies' deposits at bank rate on deposits, and of loaning the funds to allied concerns at the market rate for advances, and of pocketing the difference. Secondly, funds are borrowed in advance for the purpose of making extensions, and till the time they are actually needed, they are employed elsewhere in allied concerns or in the managing agents' own business. Thus it has been found that the balance sheets of many mill companies in Ahmedabad contain on the one side large borrowings, and at the same time on the other side large loans lent out at interest.[1] Thirdly, the surplus funds of one concern are invested permanently in the allied concerns by the same agency firm. Thus in 1922, the debentures of the Tata Mills were subscribed for to the extent of Rs. 60 lakhs by the three allied concerns managed by Messrs. Tata, Sons & Co., i.e. Nagpur Mills, Swadeshi Mills, and Ahmedabad Advance Mills.[2] In 1927 several mills under the agency of Messrs. Currimbhai, Ebrahim & Sons, Ltd., purchased shares of the Premier Mills under the same agents to the extent of nearly Rs. 14 lakhs.[3]

[1] *Indian Tariff Board: Cotton Industry*, 1927, Vol. 2, p. 514.

[2] Bombay Shareholders' Association Representation to the Tariff Board, June 1932.

[3] Ibid. See also *Indian Tariff Board: Cotton Industry*, Report, 1932, p. 85.

Instances of inter-company loans on short-term account can be found in the balance sheets of several mills both in Ahmedabad and Bombay, and the evidence of the Bombay Shareholders' Association has brought to light some important cases. They show that the practice is almost universal,[1] and the best managing agency firms, no less than the unsound and weak firms, have adopted the system.

Undoubtedly, at its best it is not one to which serious objection can be taken. It aims at the co-ordination of credit which every large-scale unified organization is entitled to do, and in other countries has done with success. Speaking of Germany, Mr. Whale points out how "even when no separate banking or financial organization is formed, the central offices of the big combines such as the *Vereinigte Stahlwerke* serve as intermediaries for the distribution of the balances between the affiliated undertakings and also for the investment of balances in the money market."[2] Surplus funds, if available have to be invested somewhere, and without sacrificing the interests of one concern, it is possible to afford financial facilities to others. But the system is full of dangerous possibilities, and in the hands of unscrupulous managing agents is bound to lead to serious abuses. Even where the managing agents are men of integrity and character, the system cannot be recommended as they would be influenced in their investment policies by considerations which, however unquestionable in their intentions, do, or are likely to do, injury to the shareholders of the company which has the surplus funds. Indeed, the theoretical possibilities, such as economy of credit, and better distribution of financial facilities, have not been realized, but on the contrary undesirable results have followed. In most cases assistance has been rendered to weak companies which had not much chance of successfully surviving the difficulties facing them, and resulted in sheer loss to the investing companies. From the social point of

[1] Bombay Shareholders' Association Representation to the Tariff Board, June 1932. See also *Indian Tariff Board: Cotton Industry*, Report, 1932, p. 85.

[2] P. B. Whale, *Joint-Stock Banking in Germany*, p. 307.

view it would be some justification if at least as a result of such financial aid the assisted companies were able to do well later. But in a large number of instances the only result has been a loss to the investing company with no social compensation at all. Some managing agents had even utilized the funds of the mill companies for speculating in shares and securities, but they must be regarded as exceptional.

Such have been the varied effects of the managing agency system on the structure of industry in India. That its influence has been of a mixed character is only to be expected because the system gives enormous power to the managing agents, which is bound to be abused by some persons. As will be suggested in the next chapter, the successful operation of the system can only be secured by control, partly external and legal, but mainly exerted by the industry itself. The divergence of interests between the shareholders and the managing agents is becoming more and more pronounced as managing agents become less and less the chief owners of the concerns under their management. But even in the case of an industry where the managing agents are the predominant owners of the businesses they control, there is from the social point of view a no less urgent need for developing some forms of external and internal control. In Ahmedabad, theoretically speaking, there should be no serious conflict of interests between the managing agents and the shareholders. Nearly 50 to 60 per cent of the shares of each concern are owned by the agents, and any diminution of dividends will hit the managing agents no less than the ordinary shareholders. One may, therefore, imagine that there can be no abuse in the Ahmedabad system. Even here conflict arises because, in the first place, so far as the agents are concerned, a small profit on shares will be enough for them, and they can make a total profit in a hundred and one ways. What matters to them is not so much the return on the shares they hold as the total remuneration. The system results, therefore, in a very poor return to the shareholders as such, which acts as a check to investment; or at any rate the inducement to investment in industrial concerns will never be very strong under the existing system. To this extent there is a divergence of interests even in concerns whose shares are predominantly held by the agents. Secondly, the abuses connected with the manner in which the system works have very serious and unfortunate results on the minds of the investing public. The good, no less than the bad, managing agents now suffer owing to this lack of confidence. The future industrial development of the country depends so much on the restoration of confidence among the investing public in the honesty and efficiency of the managing agency system that, equally in the interests of the country and of the managing agents themselves, the system should be rid of all its ugly features, so as to be able to perform for industry services even more valuable than it has done in the past.

VI

CO-OPERATION AMONG MANAGING AGENTS

An incidental result of the managing agency system in India has been the ability of industry to co-operate and combine for common ends. Judged by modern developments abroad, there is no reason to hold that the Indian entrepreneurs have been able to adopt economic co-operation to a greater extent than elsewhere, or that the managing agency system has sufficed to achieve the various forms of co-operative action so urgently required to ensure economic power. But the managing agency system has produced results which in the initial stage of a country's development could not have been secured if each concern had been in the hands of a separate Board of Management. Two or three instances will illustrate the point. A readiness to come to an agreement as, for instance, to work shorter hours, has been a characteristic feature of the jute industry of Bengal. The very first agreement to work shorter hours to which all the mills became parties was arrived at in 1886, and since then such co-operative action has become very common. Indeed, in the history of the jute industry since 1900, there have been only three years when the jute mills worked full time.[1] In all other years by common consent it was possible to work shorter hours because of the cohesiveness of the managing agency system. This result is all the more remarkable because most of the jute mill agents, as will be evident from the next chapter, were working on terms of remuneration which was based on production or on sale and not on profits. That the entrepreneurs were willing to subordinate their private interests to those of the industry as a whole is some testimony to the value of the managing agency system which has rendered co-operative action possible. Thus the concentration of business in the hands of a few managing agency firms has made it much easier for trade agreements to be made and observed than when there are a multitude of firms as in Lancashire for instance. Here again, without any legal or even formal combination, industry has been able to secure the advantages of concerted action.

This, however, is not to suggest that short-time working in the jute industry is an unmixed advantage. On the contrary it may be argued that the over-expansion in the jute industry would, but for the agreement to work short time, have received an inevitable check by the elimination of weaker firms. The agreement has had the effect of continuing a state of excessive development. It may be that the permanent interests of the jute industry might have been better served by free competition which, by eliminating the firms which have the higher costs of production, might have kept the remaining firms on a high level of efficiency. It is also true to state that while short-time working may be justified as a temporary measure in times of great depression, normal short-time working cannot be considered to be economical as industrial costs would be higher. But the point that is made here is that employers have been able to come together more easily to protect their own interests, because of the concentration of management which the managing agency system has brought about.

The tea industry is also marked by the same features of co-operative action, a result partly due to concentration of manage-

[1] Article in *Capital,* December 13, 1928, contributed by Sir Alexander Murray.

ment. The India Tea Association was formed as early as 1881, and here again co-operative action was rendered very easy because, although the number of tea companies was large, they were under a few managing agents. One of the achievements of the Association is the organization of a scientific department where research work in the field and laboratory has yielded very fruitful results. In this work, although Government shared a part of the expenses, the bulk of the expenditure was borne by a voluntary levy on all the gardens and tea companies of the managing agents. Another feature of the associated action of the managing agents is the voluntary restriction of tea production adopted on various occasions, the partial success of which was due to the ability of the agents to come together, and this was easy because of the concentration of tea gardens among a few leading managing agents. In the matter of propaganda for the larger consumption of tea, the Association was responsible for getting the Government of India to pass a Tea Cess Act in 1903, by which the funds collected by a levy on every pound of tea exported were to be utilized for the purpose of research and propaganda. In these and several other ways, co-operative action was facilitated by the managing agency system of organization.

In the Bombay cotton industry, although the Millowners' Association has been in existence since 1875 and has done valuable work of a general character, the extent of co-operative action has been until recent times quite limited. For one thing there has not been the same cohesiveness amongst the cotton millowners as among the jute mill agents, and the concentration of management (if we exclude exceptional firms which between them controlled 23 mills in 1930) is also less. However, on some occasions the Association has taken common action, particularly in regard to the general reduction in working hours. More recently, owing to the continued depression in the industry and the persistent labour unrest, the Association has been driven to take concerted action in drawing up a schedule of standard rates of wages, and the modification of rules applicable to labour. The growth of trade unionism in Bombay has been a factor in bringing home to the millowners the need for common action. The possibilities of co-operative action are even greater. Unlike the Japan Cotton Spinners' Association which controls the supply of raw material from India and elsewhere and arranges freights thereon, the Bombay Millowners' Association has done nothing in this direction, and has even permitted the loss of a big export trade in yarn to China and the Far East without taking any common action.

Further, what might have resulted in the best form of co-operation has been frustrated mainly by the unwillingness of some of the agents to join the proposed merger scheme, a result which reveals an unfavourable feature of the agency system. The object of the combine was to form a big organization with a view to securing a grouping of mills for specialization in particular kinds of cloth, joint buying and marketing, writing down of capital and co-operative efforts in all directions. A syndicate was actually formed to bear the expenses of engaging experts to value the assets of each mill company and to pay to any mill prepared to come into the merger a price for the assets, block being paid in ordinary shares, and stocks in cash. The idea was to run the organization without the managing agency system and to run it with a competent board of five or six directors and a chairman. The scheme matured so far that in September 1930 a meeting of mill agents, representing thirty-one mills, agreed to appoint a Manchester expert, and the expert actually went out and completed the task. But no further progress was made, and although several explanations have been forthcoming there is no doubt that the main reason for abandoning the scheme was that, on the one hand, with the increased protective duties the urge to rationalization no longer existed, and, on the other, some of the managing agents would not surrender their managing agency rights. The agency system with its "vested" rights has thus been a bar to progress.

Although for the moment the scheme has been abandoned, there is every chance of some meaure of organized co-operation in respect of buying and selling. The Millowners' Association has taken up seriously the better selling of their products, and the recent exhibitions, museums, special exhibition trains, and a number of propaganda activities bear witness to the possibility of extended co-operation. Experience in other countries shows that everywhere co-operation among the employers is increasing in face of the difficulties of finding new outlets for their products. It cannot, however, be stated that such results would not be secured without the managing agency system. But at its best the managing agency system does facilitate methods of co-operation owing to the concentration of businesses under common management.

But these possibilities have not always been achieved. Indeed, the fact that at a meeting of managing agents in Bombay, at which 31 mills were represented, it was proposed to run the new merger independent of the managing agency system is in itself a commentary of the small value which the agents themselves attach to the continuance of the system. Public opinion is strong that the system is costly and grossly inefficient, that its best aspects have not been visible in its working in Bombay and Ahmedabad, and that its continuance is inimical to industrial progress. How far these charges are really borne out by facts, and why the system has been even to-day working with reasonable success in Bengal, deserve to be fully examined in the light of the cost and efficiency of the managing agency system as it has been functioning in different parts of India.

CHAPTER IX

COST AND EFFICIENCY OF THE MANAGING AGENCY SYSTEM OF MANAGEMENT: ITS FUTURE

I

THE DOMINANCE OF THE MANAGING AGENT

Industrial development in India has been up to the present entirely bound up with the managing agency system of organization and control, and except in regard to joint-stock banking, no important industrial activity has been carried on independently of that system. It is therefore necessary to discuss in some detail the efficiency of this system of industrial management and to examine how far the system has been economical. At the outset it is necessary to distinguish the merits and defects of the system as such from those of the entrepreneurs represented in India by the managing agents. For while it is perfectly true that a reorganization and adaptation of the system to changed industrial conditions in India may promote efficiency, it should not be forgotten that, in so far as Indian industrial organization depends for its ultimate success upon the capacity and integrity of the entrepreneurs, it will have to rely for a long time to come upon the very same persons who are now directly or indirectly associated with the several managing agency firms. In one way or another they represent the quintessence of the industrial ability and experience available in the country, and whatever be the form of industrial control that is devised, they will undoubtedly remain the "captains" of industry. It is necessary to stress this aspect of the matter, for it is popularly supposed that if the managing agency system is abolished and industry controlled by Boards of Directors, with a managing director, secretary, or president as the chief executive officer, as in other countries, every difficulty will be resolved. That, surely, is not the case. In so far as inefficiency in India is due to the lack of ability, experience or character on the part of the men who are now managing agents, it can only be improved when a higher level of intelligence and integrity is secured.

Efficiency of industrial management depends in part upon the extent to which entrepreneurs enjoy the freedom to pursue a definite policy without being hampered by excessive interference. In this regard, managing agents in India have been at a great advantage, comparable with the freedom secured by some of the strong presidents of the American Boards of Directors. Something has already been said about the manner in which managing agents in India have been able to secure control; but it is necessary to consider this more fully. There are at least four ways in which they are able to ensure and maintain control of the industrial companies they manage. In the first place, they hold a certain minimum of the shares of the concern. It is difficult to estimate in each case the actual extent of their holdings, for the shares are held in various ways; e.g. (*a*) in the name of the managing agency firm, (*b*) in the name of the individuals who compose the partnership of the agency firm, (*c*) in the name of the relatives of the partners, and (*d*) in the name of the persons who are closely allied by business or personal relationship to the managing agents. The peculiarity of some of the family managing agency firms lies in the fact that the shares of the industrial company may be held in the names of the wives, children, sisters, and all the innumerable relatives that constitute the Indian joint family. By whatever methods the shares are held, a certain minimum is generally required to be held by the partners, who do so partly in their own interests and partly to maintain their agency rights.

In jute mills, however, a new feature is noticeable. The majority of the managing agents are so well assured of their tenure that they are content to hold only a small proportion of the shares.[1] They are aware that they have secured the confidence of the shareholders, and are therefore perfectly willing to take the chance of having the agency agreement renewed for another period of twenty-five or thirty years on the strength of other claims than that of their holdings. Increasingly they have become

[1] Refer to Chapter IV, Statement I.

more like an elected Board of Directors, but they have other ways of ensuring renewal of managing agency agreements.

Secondly, and perhaps this is the most important method, managing agents secure control by means of written agreements. These agreements may be classified under two headings, terminable agreements and practically non-terminable agreements. In Chapter I it was seen that some of the agreements gave rights of control to the managing agents and to their successors or inheritors in perpetuity. The Ahmedabad agency agreements illustrate the heritable character of the agency rights. Thus the Ajit Mills, Ahmedabad, started in 1931, have appointed agents who are to be the sole managing agents and are non-changeable, non-removable and permanent secretaries, treasurers and agents[1] (Clause 1 of the agreement). The New National Mills, Ltd., by Clause 2 of the agreement, provides that the appointment of the agents is not liable to be revoked or cancelled on any other ground except their voluntary resignation in writing.[2] These agreements are almost typical of the position in Ahmedabad. In Bombay the agreements are more elastic and provide for terminating the appointment, but in all such cases a three-fourths majority of shareholders is required, which, of course, is practically impossible to obtain. Permanent control is secured nearly as certainly as in Ahmedabad, and if there are constant changes in the management of some of the Bombay mill companies, it is due to the voluntary surrender of their position by the agents owing to their financial collapse or continued losses. The jute, coal, and tea industries have similar terms of agreement with their managing agents.[3]

The agreements not only confer the rights of management on the agents, but ensure compensation to the latter in case of winding up. A typical case in the Ahmedabad mill industry is that provided in the agreement entered into by the Ajit Mills, already referred to. "In case of winding up, agents are entitled to recover in priority over all other claims, ten times the average annual commission

[1] Replies to the Second Tariff Board's Questionnaire by the Bombay Shareholders' Association, 1932. [2] Ibid.

[3] Refer to Appendix III, Chapter I.

accrued during the preceding five years, and if the company shall not have existed so long, then a sum equivalent to ten times the commission accrued during the previous year"[1] (Clause 9 of the agency agreement). Again "no transfer of the company or amalgamation with another company is to take place unless the managing agents are appointed agents of the transferred company or of the amalgamated business." This provision directly militates against any grouping of mills or combination and creates a dangerous set of vested rights.

Although the Ahmedabad agreements contain from the point of view of the shareholders the most undesirable features, the agency agreements in Bombay and in Calcutta also ensure great freedom to the managing agents. In the majority of cases the managing agents are allowed to become buying and selling agents, and transact other business required to be done and to charge a commission on every such business. The evidence tendered by the Bombay Shareholders' Association before the Second Textile Tariff Board contains particulars of twenty-seven mills in Bombay under six different managing agents in which the agreements entered into by them provide that the managing agents be allowed "to act as muccadams or brokers of the company or selling agents," and that they shall be paid additional remuneration for such work.

The third method of securing control is through the managing agent's position as the chief creditor of the concern. The dependence of the industrial company on the finance supplied by managing agents automatically brings about a tightening of the grip of the latter on the industrial companies, and this is further strengthened by the fact that the agents are often the biggest debenture-holders, having a lien on the assets of the company.

Finally, their control is easily maintained by two further factors working in combination. While the managing agents' holdings, however small a percentage, are a good block of shares which, together with their friends' shares, can be used effectively,

[1] Replies to the Second Tariff Board's Questionnaire by the Bombay Shareholders' Association.

the remaining shareholders are distributed over long distances, and cannot come together and operate against the agents. Further, owing to the dependence of the industrial company on outside finance, any change, even if secured, will only mean a transfer of agency from one agency firm to another, and the knowledge that change implies only transfer from X to Y diminishes the inclination of the shareholders to throw out the existing agent, except in exceptional circumstances.

Owing to the operation of all the above influences, the powers enjoyed by the agents are enormous, and their freedom to pursue any policy they like remains unfettered—a state of affairs to which, except in the United States, it is difficult to find a parallel. The positive rights are reinforced by certain other advantages following from the unique position of the managing agents. The Boards of Directors of the industrial companies in India do not have the same importance as in other countries; they are nominees of the managing agents and controlled by the latter. Although there are even instances where the agency agreements definitely restrict the powers of the directors and "empower them to do only such acts and to exercise only such powers as are not exclusively vested in the agents," these restrictions are practically unnecessary. The extent to which directors' rights are allowed to be exercised and their abilities and talents utilized depends upon the discretion of the managing agents. Secondly, while in theory the auditors are appointed by the shareholders, in practice they are the nominees of the managing agents. It is obvious that within the wide latitude which auditors may permit themselves in their audit, managing agents have it in their power, if they are so inclined, to exhibit a picture hidden in some parts and magnified in others. Whatever may be the difficulties of the managing agents in India, want of power or lack of freedom is surely not one of them.

The real question is not so much what their powers are in theory, but how they have been exercised. Have their powers been utilized to bring about and maintain a high level of industrial efficiency? In attempting an answer to this question it is necessary to deal separately with the European managing agency system and the Indian managing agency system, as they reveal great differences in composition, achievements, and possibilities.

II

CHARACTER OF THE BRITISH MANAGING AGENCY FIRMS CONTRASTED WITH THE INDIAN. DIFFERENCES IN EFFICIENCY

One of the most striking differences between the European and the Indian managing agency firms lies in the methods adopted to secure efficiency of the managing agency firm as a going concern. The history of the British managing agency firm in India is a story of two types of ability intermingling in a continuous stream. The original founder or founders of the agency firm have their family represented on the firm from period to period, but there is always an outside element brought into the business which brings with it not only some capital and industrial experience but knowledge of the technical conditions of some industry or other. The family heir serves to maintain continuity in the ownership of the firm; but there are always two or more partners recruited from the firm's senior assistants. These latter continue as partners as long as their services are available, but on their retirement or death they are not succeeded by their sons, but their place is taken by other assistants from the industry. Such an arrangement retains the best features of the hereditary system and the selective system. It ensures both continuity and variety of experience. Thus in the firm of Andrew Yule & Co., now controlled by Messrs. Morgan, Grenfell & Co., the partners of the agency firm have an understanding that if one of them either wants to retire or transfer his share in the business, the rest of the partners will buy up his rights.[1] It is possible that the son or

[1] As the present head of Morgan, Grenfell & Co., who have purchased Andrew Yule & Co.'s rights, said to the writer, the late Sir D. Yule when he retired from active business took in a few partners, but these were not allotted any shares as such. They were given a definite share in the profits of the concern. After his death the partners had an agreement by which if any one died, the others would buy his shares out;

nephew or other near relation may be invited by the other partners to take his place; but if that happens it can only be because he possesses knowledge or experience considered by the remaining partners as invaluable to the firm. In this way the managing agency firm as a going concern constantly gets a fresh stream of industrial and technical experience, and while undoubtedly family influences do exist, weight is always given to considerations of efficiency and ability.

The Indian managing agency firms, on the other hand, with some notable exceptions, are not well organized for managerial or administrative purposes. From the commencement they had an initial handicap of a serious kind, and not all the years that have passed have secured any great improvement. Indian managing agency firms have been financial and not industrial in character. Even their best friends have always pointed to the want of technical knowledge on the part of the agents as a grave defect.[1] Indian firms in so far as they are family concerns allow the sons and heirs of the families to become managing agents irrespective of their ability to perform these tasks. The field of selection for managing agency functions is extremely limited. Even where the firms are partnerships on a more or less equal basis, e.g. where two or three persons control the firm, they become hereditary and the representatives of the families of these partners become the managing agents. It is, of course, not to be understood that the succession to a firm by the son or the heir of the family is necessarily a mistake; but when this occurs to the exclusion of other talents and experience, the results are unsatisfactory. Thus Indian agency firms have mostly exhibited one type of capacity, that is, mainly financial capacity, and are remarkably deficient in the element of expert technical knowledge. The result is that the fortunes of the firm in course of time fall into the hands of persons whose sole claim

and any new partner can only be taken with the consent of all the partners. The idea is that the firm must not lose its continuity and central purpose and direction.

[1] B. F. Madon's evidence before the *Indian Tariff Board: Cotton Industry*, 1927, Vol. 4, p. 34.

is the right of inheritance, or perhaps an assignment, when that is allowed in the agreement. Even the transference of agency rights is made mainly for financial reasons, and when an industrial company has to wind up, or has to seek another managing agency firm, it hands over the management to a capitalist firm richer in finance and not to one which may have a better industrial experience.

Again, Indian managing agency firms lack even the continuity usually to be found in such businesses. The powers of assigning the rights of agency firms vested with managing agents are exercised without any reference to the desire or the feeling of the shareholders or the interests of the industrial companies. This constitutes a serious disadvantage to the shareholders, who suddenly find that their properties are now administered by quite a new body of men who may be incompetent and undesirable. Several instances of transfer of management without the knowledge or consent of the shareholders have occurred in recent years, and the latest is the attempt to hand over the whole group of mills managed by Currimbhai, Ebrahim & Co. to the Government of the Nizam, which is the most important creditor of the mills by its having taken up a large amount of the debenture loan issued by the mill companies. In the hands of well-meaning and reputable managing agents, this power has been utilized to the great advantage of the industrial companies managed by them. When Tata & Co. went into partnership with the American syndicate for the financing and administering of all the Tata Power companies, they were able to secure not merely fresh capital for the firm's business, but valuable expert knowledge and technical experience, although the consent of the shareholders of the power companies had not been sought or obtained. But even when the results are so beneficial, as in this case, there is need for some restriction of the powers of the agents to bring about a transfer of their managerial rights.[1]

[1] The following from the *Annual Market Review*, a very sane and balanced annual review of current financial and marketing events in India, issued by Messrs. Premchad Roychand & Sons, is very relevant: "A one-half share in the Managing Agency of a powerful group of industrial concerns was sold to an American syndicate without the consent or even knowledge of the real holders of the property—the

In this connection the following clause, taken from the latest English Companies Act, is most relevant and appropriate, and similar legislation should be incorporated in the Indian Company law. Section 151 of the English Companies Act is as follows: "If in the case of any company provision is made by any agreement entered into between any person and the company for empowering a director or manager of the company to assign his office as such to another person, any assignment of office made in pursuance of the said provision shall, notwithstanding anything to the contrary contained in the said provision, be of no effect unless and until it is approved by a special resolution of the company." The incorporation of a similar provision in the Indian law is urgent and should not be delayed.

But this will not, by itself, be sufficient to ensure efficiency in the managing agency firm's organization. For that purpose the firm should adopt methods by which within itself it may possess men of varied experience and technical skill. The lapse of so many years has perhaps familiarized the Bombay and Ahmedabad mill

ordinary shareholders. The sale was made on the plea that it would secure the more efficient management of the enterprise. The answer is obvious. The handsome commission to the managing agents was paid for efficient service; if the agents were incapable of giving this efficient service, then they should have surrendered their responsibility with its large emoluments to the shareholders. Under present circumstances managing agents through the votes of Preference Shareholders can raise their rate of commission. They can promote new companies and buy their shares and debentures, in this way gravely prejudicing the interests of the ordinary shareholders in the stock of that company. There is a strong feeling that whilst the managing system might have been necessary in the early days of Indian industry—possibly without it the foundation of manufacturing industry would never have been laid—it has now outlived its purpose. Shareholders must be given the right to decide who shall manage their property; control of their investment should not be bartered in the market-place without their consent, and the drain on the industry of the agents' "commission" is an intolerable burden in these days of keen competition" (*Annual Market Review*, 1929, pp. 8–9). While it is not possible to agree with every statement contained in the above, no one will be disposed to question the desirability of getting the consent and approval of the shareholders when such important changes take place in the character of the management.

agents with the technical conditions of the cotton industry; but they are still generally deficient in technical experience. Attention should therefore be directed to the task of getting into the firm a continuous flow of varied talents, which can be maintained only by constantly recruiting men who have made good in various industrial concerns.

A second important difference between the European and Indian managing agency systems is that it is only the European managing agency system that reveals its distinctive features and harmonizes theory with practice. So long as a managing agency firm manages just one industrial company, the only effect is that it combines the financing function with that of management. But when a large number of units in different industries comes to be controlled by one managing agency firm, very interesting influences on the structure of industry are brought into play. If we exclude a few firms like Messrs. Tata, Sons & Co., practically all the Indian managing agents are concerned with one or two or a small number of units belonging to one and the same industry, and therefore have no such influence on the structure of industrial organization as the typical managing agency unit has. While even in these cases there are important differences between management by the ordinary Board of Directors and management by the Indian managing agency firms, they are from the larger point of view of minor importance. The continuance of the managing agency system in such circumstances does not produce those important economic consequences which one should regret to lose; its disappearance may therefore be regarded with equanimity. In a word, while its power for doing injury may be great, its capacity to do good is limited. So far as the Indian section of the managing agency system is concerned, its continuance can be explained and justified only because of the concentration of ability, experience, and capital in the hands of a few persons who have done great service to industrial development. If it became possible to persuade them to do for industry in an altered status what they have been doing as members of agency firms, the result would perhaps be wholly good. There are no benefits which would be lost by such a change, for those benefits are not the result of the system but of the ability and resources of the persons who run the system.

On the contrary, in the case of the European section of the system, both the nature of the organization and the men who run the agencies are equally important elements in industry. The administrative "integration" to which we referred in the last chapter is secured under the British managing agency system, and if, therefore, the system is given up, we shall lose some of the valuable advantages that are associated with it.

The failure to distinguish the essential and distinctive aspects of the managing agency system from its incidental results has led to its hasty condemnation and to a tendency to regard the defects of the Bombay managing agency system as affording justification for condemning the agency system as a whole. If an industrial company can dispense with the managing agency system of industrial finance, there is no reason why it may not be managed by a competent Board of Directors, with the help, if available, of the very persons who now comprise the managing agency firm. But where, as in the case of most of the British agency firms and a few Indian managing agency firms, several units in the same industry, and a considerable number of units in different industries are under the same management, there are great advantages of co-ordination and economy which would be lost if the agency system were abandoned. The danger of abuse exists in both cases; but the possibilities for good remain with the British agency system.

Thirdly, while it would be unsafe to speak decisively of the future of the Indian managing agency system, it is certain that the European managing agency system will long continue to function in India. This is because, apart from other reasons, it is an arrangement which eminently suits the British capitalists who are willing to invest money in India through the managing agents. The system further links up the British Indian firm with the corresponding British firm, and enables a large number of allied and miscellaneous activities to be carried on, resulting in increased profits.

III

OTHER FACTORS OF EFFICIENCY IN THE MANAGING AGENCY ORGANIZATION

With these considerations clearly in our mind, it is possible to consider certain other features bearing on the efficiency of managing agents as industrial administrators. We have to distinguish sharply between inefficiency or incompetence which affects the managing agents no less than the industrial company they manage, and the dis-economy resulting from divided interests between the company and the managing agents. In other words it is possible that although the managing agents may be able and efficient, the industrial company does not derive the benefits which properly should accrue to it from expert management. For instance, when managing agents have their own independent buying and selling organizations and carry on a miscellaneous range of activities, the profits arising from them may not be passed on to the share-holders, but may be retained by the managing agents. In this case the industrial company does not share in the economy and efficiency of management.

The internal organization of an Indian managing agency firm is not adapted to perform the various tasks of management and administration efficiently. There is little division of labour within the agency organization, and the control exercised by the agents in the details of the internal and external economies of a mill company is admittedly unsatisfactory. It is held that the Bombay mill agent is just a financing agent and not a real manager of the industrial company he manages, and although the statement is slightly exaggerated there is force in the argument that the agents leave too much to subordinates. This leads to slackness all round, and explains in part the growing difficulties of the Bombay cotton industry.

The organization of the mills in regard to the recruiting of labour is of the most loose description.[1] The "Sardar system of recruiting labour still prevails, and the labour turnover remains excessive with its well-known evil results. Although in some mills welfare work is carried on, it is not organized as a separate department and linked with the other departments. One of the important differences which the writer noticed between the factories in London, Birmingham, Manchester, Berlin, which he visited and those in Bombay with which he is familiar, was the way in which records[2] were kept in the former, and their absence in the latter. Some of the bigger mills in India have records of production, attendance, accidents,[3] etc., but these have not become a normal feature of industrial organization. Considerable difficulty was experienced by the Bombay Labour Department in its investigations relating to absenteeism owing to the absence of a system of record-keeping. On the other hand, even some of the smallest factories in England have an efficient system of factory control which enables them to ascertain at any hour on any day exactly how they stand in the matter of orders for goods, of production of the various kinds required, and of the time required to fulfil each of the orders received.[4] An efficient system of cost

[1] For a critical examination of the organization for recruiting labour, see the writer's *Industrial Welfare in India* and the *Report of the Royal Commission on Labour*, 1931.

[2] In the Austin Motor Works the writer found that safety questions were gone into in great detail. Every accident is thoroughly investigated and records kept. The card system maintained by J. Lyons & Co., London, is marvellous. Each worker has a card in which all information relating to him or her is recorded—previous service, kind of work assigned, attendance, leave, sickness, allowances, etc., are all recorded.

[3] The Tata Iron and Steel Works, Tatanagar, has an elaborate system of recording accidents. It also maintains a card for each worker and tries to get statistical data relating to output, absenteeism, labour turnover, etc.

[4] The writer is able to recall, for example, how on his visit to the Kalamazoo Print Works he was impressed by the card system of controlling the progress of each item of work. The cost of production of each item was ascertained by an efficient system of cost accounts. The time taken on each job by each worker was registered, efficiency measured, and waste of every kind discovered. By an efficient system of central

accounts is an indispensable part of the organization of every modern factory. It cannot be maintained that cost accounting has become a regular feature of the internal organization of Indian industrial companies. The lack of an efficient cost accounts system prevents a proper appreciation of the waste in the use of various materials like coal, stores, and other materials, in the employment of labour and in the use of other accessories of production.

WASTE IN INDUSTRY

The elimination of waste of all kinds in industry supplies the key to efficient production at the lowest cost. In this matter the responsibility rests with the management, for they have the greatest opportunity to effect improvements. In all countries a certain amount of waste is to be found, and only careful and detailed control will reveal the existence of such waste. Thus in the United States it was found that "there was constant interruption of work in many shoe-making firms through the workers having to wait for their work and materials and occasional shortage of racks for holding the shoes."[1]

In India, even in a modern and fairly efficient works such as the Tata Steel plant, several defects of control and management exist. The large amount of coal consumption is a chronic evil in India. With better supervision the percentage of ash in coking coal could be brought down in the Tata Steel Works.[2] Labour

control it was possible to know at any time at what particular stage of production a certain item was and when it would be completed. The factory has also evolved a system of giving units of cost to each item of production so that it may know which line of business is more profitable than another.

[1] *Waste in Industry, U.S.A.*, N.Y., 1931, "Over 50 per cent of the responsibility for wastes in industry can be placed at the door of the management and less than 25 per cent at the door of labour."

[2] *Indian Tariff Board Statutory Enquiry: Steel Industry*, 1927, Vol. 3, p. 8.

"In a mill using Esparto grass in Great Britain the consumption of coal was 1½ to 3 tons per ton of paper. In India it ranges from 5 to 7 tons, and

cost was still excessive in 1925, and too much hand labour was employed. Where mechanical loading and unloading was possible, hand labour was employed, resulting in excessive cost.[1] The maintenance of cost accounts could be improved in nearly all industrial concerns in India. It was found, for example, in the Steel Works that while the books showed a stock of 1,200 tons of plate, there was actually no stock in existence. No detailed records were kept, section by section, about the sales of each, e.g. of angles, channels, fish-plates, sheets, etc., and therefore it was not easy for the factory to know which sections were the most profitable and might be increased.[2] It is essential for every business to know what sort of market there is in the country, for the various classes of goods produced, and to know what sections are imported and on what scale. But most of the concerns do not equip themselves with adequate information and accurate data. Marketing research is not sufficiently practised in Indian industries.

In the cotton industry inefficient buying of raw cotton has often resulted in the purchase of cotton unsuitable to withstand the pressure when finer spinning is attempted. The use of inferior cotton and the lack of uniformity has led to too many breaks and to low production. Indian industry is full of waste and great economies will be possible in the use of materials and labour if organization is strengthened. For this purpose adequate information is necessary. The eye of the entrepreneur is sufficient to detect mistakes and waste in a small concern; but in the large cotton mills in Bombay and even in Ahmedabad a regular system of records is an essential preliminary to progress.

In the coal-mining industry the defect of organization is revealed in the very slow rate at which mechanical methods of raising coal have been employed. The introduction of electric power, the use of mechanical coal-cutters and labour-saving

this is far too high, even allowing for the lower calorific value of Indian coal," *Indian Tariff Board: Paper and Paper Pulp Industries*, 1925, p. 42.

[1] *Statutory Enquiry: Steel Industry*, 1927, Vol. 3,p. 333.

[2] Ibid., Vol. 3, p. 217.

appliances, and several other possible economies have not been effected. Part of the difficulty is due to the existence of too many small mines, which renders the introduction of machinery an uneconomic proposition. Amalgamation is a necessary preliminary to the elimination of waste. But even those mines which can introduce labour saving machinery and reduce costs have not done so as rapidly as they might have. There has been in certain months a regular shortage of "tubs" for holding coal, and the mine workers are unable to increase output on account of the deficiency in the supply of tubs.[1] There is much manual labour employed which should be replaced by machinery.

Indian entrepreneurs are slow in developing organizations for the purposes of propaganda and research. The recently formed Cement Concrete Association and the Sugar Mills Association are steps in the right direction. They afford evidence of the realization of the value of propaganda for popularizing the products of each industrial group. The Bombay Millowners' Association has only recently set itself to perform this task. A scheme is in contemplation by which the selling agents of the mills are to arrange for sending out travelling agents to study up-country markets[2] and report how best to meet the demands of consumers in those areas. The Association issues to its members a label which serves as a warranty of quality, but greater control is required to ensure standard. But so far no radical improvement in this matter has been attained. Managing agents have been content with spasmodic efforts to arrange an exhibition train to familiarize the people with the mill products, to take part in exhibitions organized by public bodies, and occasionally to pass on the information they secure from special correspondents to all the members. What is required is the combined employment of

[1] *Royal Commission on Labour*, Evidence, Vol. 4, Part 2, pp. 124–30.

[2] "Several mills have opened their own retail shops, the total number being twenty-seven. Several mills have also formed their own agencies in important up-country centres to deal more effectively with the demand for Bombay mill cloth" (*White Book on the Situation of the Cotton Textile Industry*, issued by the Bombay Government in 1930).

travelling sales agents, a permanent office and staff to whose upkeep several firms will contribute, or arrangements whereby the output of several firms may be disposed of both within the country and outside through the organization of a firm constituted for the purpose.

RESEARCH

The Balfour Committee on Industry and Trade pointed out, by way of contrast with Germany and the United States, that in England the recognition of the value of scientific research by industries concerned was "very imperfect."[1] Not only had the industries not undertaken sufficient research themselves, but their response to the propagandist efforts of the research associations in existence in England was poor and disheartening. It is hardly surprising that in India the conditions are worse. There are few research associations of any importance, and with the exception of the research carried on by the Tea Planters' Association and at some of the chemical works there has been very little industrial research by private enterprise worth speaking of. A certain amount of useful research has been carried on by Government in the Forest Research Institute at Dehra Dun, in the Bengal Tanning Institute, Calcutta, and the Madras Leather Trades Institute, Madras. Chemical research in certain branches of industry has been conducted in some of the pioneering factories in Madras. A number of investigations connected with the match industry have been made in Bengal and other subjects of investigation have included glue, sugar, lac, and glass. But the amount of work is not substantial considering the vastness of the field, and systematic work has been hampered by lack of well-equipped laboratories.[2] Had the recommendations of the Industrial Commission been carried into effect by the Government of India, we should have had long ago an efficient chemical service and an industrial

[1] *(Balfour) Committee on Industry and Trade*, Report, p. 286.

[2] For a detailed account of the work of Government in relation to research, education, and development of new industries, see *The State and Industry*, by A. G. Clow, Government of India, 1928.

engineering service, with a number of research institutes, but the Reforms Act of 1920, by provincializing the subject of industry, made the creation of an All-India Service impossible.[1] Thus Indian industry was deprived of the services which the State should render to it, and, left to its own resources, has been slow in organizing for research work.[2] Most of the Indian entrepreneurs have not even the necessary technical knowledge of industry and lack the true scientific spirit. They have been entirely dominated by empirical ideas of management, and such success as they have achieved is due to their financial resources and an early start. If industry is to become truly efficient, a good number of those who occupy responsible positions in industry should have a scientific habit of mind; that is to say, their minds should be receptive of the results of research and alert to its practical bearings. The old-fashioned type of men who have made some money in trade and commerce and gained some knowledge of industry by empirical methods of management are definitely an anachronism under modern conditions. Their continuance in Indian industry is responsible for the present parlous condition of many of our industries. Industry requires leaders with a scientific outlook, and if possible with scientific knowledge.

STATISTICAL INFORMATION AND GENERAL INTELLIGENCE

In the matter of equipping themselves with adequate information regarding internal and foreign markets, industries in India are backward. Speaking of the cotton industry, the Textile Tariff Board commented on the inadequacy of information in the hands of the Bombay Millowners' Association and recommended the constitution of a strong subcommittee, firstly to deal with all questions relating to the development of the export trade, and

[1] A. G. Clow, *The State and Industry*, 1928, Chapters III and IV.

[2] Indian industrialists have not shown any originality in designs and construction. The Japanese cotton industry has to its credit a number of useful inventions in machinery, and their automatic looms are now adopted in other countries. Indian cotton industry is deficient in this constructive faculty.

secondly to deal with all questions relating to the home market, finance, labour, registration of labels and numbers, and the supply of raw materials. Since then the Association has constituted several small committees for such purposes, but so far their work has not been much in evidence.

IV

THE NATURE AND QUALIFICATIONS OF THE DIRECTORS OF INDIAN INDUSTRIAL COMPANIES

One of the minor reasons for the existence and continuance of the (British) managing agency system was the difficulty of finding from among the European business men a sufficient number to constitute Boards of Directors for all the industrial companies floated in India. The scarcity of such men led to the system by which managing agents were the sole directors of businesses, and when the law required the management of a limited liability company to be in the hands of a Board of Directors, the managing agents found a few friends to serve on the Board and thus conformed to legal requirements. The same directors were nominated for all the companies under one managing agency firm and played a strictly subordinate role. Thus, in the case of 12 coal companies managed by Messrs. Andrew Yule & Co., 4 companies which had been founded before the Indian Companies Act of 1913 was passed still carry on without a Board of Directors. The remaining 8 companies have altogether only eight persons who serve on their Boards; two of them are on 6 Boards, one on 4, one on 3, one on 2, and the other three are on 1 Board each. In respect of 9 jute mills under the same managing agency firm, we find again that there are only eight persons on the Boards of all these companies. One person is on all the 8 Boards, one on 7, one on 6, one on 5, one on 2 and three are each on 1 Board. Of these eight persons, three are also directors of the coal companies under the same agency firm. Practically similar conditions exist in the case of the other companies under other managing agents. Thus in 1931, out of a total of 52 jute mills, about which information is given in the

Investor's India Year Book, two mills have no directors. The remaining 50 have on their Boards 92 persons.[1]

Pluralism.—In the Bombay cotton industry, it is held that there are cases where directors hold their position in far too many concerns, and this "pluralism" in directorship results in indifference and inability to perform the proper functions of a director. In the cotton mills in Bombay, it was found[2] that in 1927 one was director in 30 mill companies, one in 14, one in 13, three in 12, one in 10, one in 8, one in 6, one in 5.

Further, in the city of Bombay, one person is director of 65 industrial concerns, another of 42, a third of 34, a fourth of 12, a fifth of 14, a sixth of 29, a seventh of 26, and another of 29. One reason for this state of affairs is the managing agency system

[1] They are distributed as follows:

Jute

Director of—				
1 Firm	2 Firms but not more than 5	6 but not more than 10	11 but not more than 15	Over 16
58	27	6	0	1

(*Investor's India Year Book*, 1931–2.)

A characteristic feature of the list of directors is that every managing agency firm has three or four persons who are directors of all its companies.

Coal

Total number of persons who are directors of 72 coal companies is given as 80.

Director of—			
1 Company	2 to 5	6 to 10	11 to 15
36	31	8	5

Of these, four coal companies have no directors.

[2] *Rutnagur Cotton Mills*, pp. 254–80.

itself. The managing agents practically nominate the directors of all their companies, and they nominate one another. The Indian industrial companies have, therefore, Boards of Directors almost wholly manned by the representatives of the managing agents. Even the few men who are outside the managing agency firms are connected with the business of the managing agents in several ways, and therefore Indian industry does not contain on the Board of Management that variety of interests and experience needed for successful and efficient management. The few Indians that are nominated to the Boards of industrial companies under the British Managing Agents, become "stock" directors in all sorts of concerns.[1]

From the point of view of efficiency, two separate questions have to be discussed. Firstly, the system of multiple directors necessarily leads to a certain weakening of responsibility as no director, however able, will be in a position to look after the interests of more than a few concerns at a time. But this difficulty is not one peculiar to India. It is found all over the world. At the same time it is also to be noted that exceptional cases of persons having 100 directorships strike the imagination and lead to an exaggeration of the dangers resulting therefrom. In England, for example, an inquiry into the number of directorships which 30,000 individuals held revealed the following result.[2]

[1] *Indian Tariff Board: Paper and Paper Pulp Industries*, 1932, Vol. 1, p. 455.

[2] *Financial Democracy*, by Margaret Miller and Douglas Campbell, 1933, p. 107.

Companies	Number	Percentage
Under 5 ..	26,931	89·82
5–9	2,222	7·40
10–14	520	1·70
15–19	175	0·58
20–24	78	0·26
25–29	34	0·11
30–34	18	0·06
35–39	9	0·03
40 and over ..	13	0·04

These figures suffer from certain serious limitations. They cover only directors of the principal companies quoted in the Stock Exchange, and therefore exclude small companies in which these persons may be also directors. The list also excluded partnerships, and it is not known how many of the 30,000 persons are partners in various businesses. Still, despite the limitations, the table does warrant the conclusion that "pluralists" with sensational holdings of 50 directorships form a negligible group. Excessive pluralism is a relatively rare phenomenon.

Secondly, directorship implies different duties in different countries. What is not well understood in India is that, under the managing agency system, it is impossible to have a Board of Directors in the British sense of the term. Where so much depends upon the agents themselves, who are both entrepreneurs and directors of the industrial companies under their management, the duties of the remaining directors will be only very restricted. As will be pointed out presently, what the Indian system required was not a Board of Directors to be a mere ornament to the industrial organization, or the echo of the managing agents, but a Board of Control or Supervision with quite different functions from those of a British Board of Directors. In the existing structure of industrial organization in India, a Board of Directors is a superfluity, and those (other than managing agents) who are on it have no definite functions to perform; if they show excessive enthusiasm, they are simply dropped. In the words of an experienced industrial investor, "the majority of the Directors hardly take much interest in the concerns. If they are a bit active they go."[1] Sometimes provision is made in the managing agency agreement to curtail the powers of directors. Thus, in some of the agreements between the cotton-mill companies in Ahmedabad and the managing agents, it is prescribed "that the directors are to do such acts and to exercise only such powers as are not exclusively vested in the agents," and since enormous

[1] *Indian Tariff Board: Cotton Industry*, 1927, Vol. 4, Evidence of J. A. Wadia.

power is vested in the agents, directors are virtually mere figure-heads.

V

BOARD OF DIRECTORS, AN ANOMALY IN THE INDIAN SYSTEM

Criticism, therefore, of the "multiple" directorships in India is entirely beside the mark. Even if by law it were provided that no person shall be a director in more than three or four companies, the root of the difficulty in India would remain. Under the managing agency system there is no place for a Board of Directors who can effectively function; but there is every need for a Board of Supervision and Control. One of the unfortunate results of reproducing English legislation in the entirely different industrial conditions of India is the lack of control over the managing agency system of industrial management. The Government did not realize that the managing agency system was quite different from the English method of industrial management, and that the company law should recognize that vital distinction. The argument that in so far as managing agents were "directors" they were controlled by the provisions applying to the Directors under the Indian Companies Act, entirely misses the special position occupied by the managing agents. On a British Board of Directors, although the Managing Director may occupy a predominant position, he has to carry with him the remaining directors in every important policy and action; but under the Indian managing agency system, the directors cannot have any independence. What is even more important to recognize is that it is not desirable to fetter the managing agents by the addition of directors who are legally and theoretically supposed to have the same duties and functions and the same status as the managing agents, but who actually have very little power. In a word, the managing agency system and the system of control by a Board of Directors are mutually exclusive and opposite. The failure to recognize this fact has led to the perpetuation of a number of undesirable consequences which could have been remedied by proper legislation.

NEED FOR A BOARD OF SUPERVISION

What is therefore required is to interpose between the managing agents who are the real "directors of industry," and the shareholders, some body or committee of men who must be entrusted with quite specific powers, but whose functions will be very different. Germany and Holland afford examples of great value to India. In Holland, business concerns do not possess Boards of Directors in the British sense of the term. A small body known as the "commissarissen" is appointed whose duty it is to supervise and report to the shareholders upon the activities of the "Directeuren."[1] In Germany, the Aufsichtsrat performs functions similar to those of the Dutch commissarissen. These functions are important, and include the securing of all relevant information to be placed with the shareholders, the approval of the company's balance-sheet, the right to be consulted on every important new policy and so on. Indian company law must likewise recognize the existence of the managing agency system and provide for the constitution of a Board of Supervision which, while leaving administration in the hands of the managing agents, may exercise general supervision and act as adviser and guide to them, and be responsible to the shareholders for the supply of accurate information. It should also be provided that the balance sheets of the companies managed by managing agents should, before being presented at the shareholders' meeting, be approved by this Board.

The adoption of this proposal would have another result of an even more desirable kind. The persons whose functions start by protecting the interests of the shareholders and watching the activities of the managing agents will soon grow into a body of men who have an understanding and insight into the problems of industrial administration. One of the less desirable consequences of the managing agency system of administration is its failure to train a band of new men for the task of directing industry. By reducing the "directors" to mere figureheads and by weakening their responsibilities, the system killed all incentive to learn and

[1] *Financial Democracy* by M. Miller and D. Campbell, 1933, p. 47.

understand, and industry was not able to revitalize itself by drawing from the experience and talents of persons outside the ranks of the managing agents. In the circumstances the question whether the existing directors of industrial companies (under the managing agency system) are men with industrial experience and technical qualifications ceases to have as much importance as is usually supposed. Able men, if they are available, constitute themselves into managing agency firms, and if they are directors of companies for which they are not managing agents they do not take much interest. In practice, therefore, the only persons who count are the managing agents, and so far as technical and administrative efficiency is concerned it is their efficiency that is important. If, therefore, in Bombay out of 175 persons who were directors of its cotton mills in 1927, there were only 11 men with technical qualifications, and the other 149 belonged to the merchant class, and 15 were lawyers, it only means that the managing agency firms in Bombay seriously lack one of the essential qualifications for successful management and administration, a point to which reference has already been made. Of these 175 directors, 95 are agency directors, including under that term partners and others connected with one agency firm or another in Bombay, and 80 are outsiders not connected with any managing agency firm, who are practically nominated by the managing agents. These outside directors, even if they are able and experienced men, lack the power and the incentive to be of any real use to industry.

On the other hand, the experience that the Board of Supervisors would gain as a result of its performing certain definitely assigned, though limited, functions will bring about a wider dispersion of industrial knowledge and experience. A nucleus of men possessing intimate acquaintance with the general problems of industrial management would thus be formed, who would be able to supply the necessary basis for the constitution of a Board of Directors for companies that may be formed outside the managing agency system. For, as will be pointed out later, in the future industrial organization of the country there will be ample room for both the managing agency system and the system of management by Boards of Directors on the English model to work side by side. A wider diffusion of industrial knowledge brought about by the establishment of a Committee of Shareholders, or a Board of Supervision would enable certain industrial companies not needing the special type of financial and managerial services which managing agents alone can render to find enough men of competence to undertake this task. Looked at from any point of view, the constitution of an intermediary body between the managing agents and the shareholders with responsibility for performing certain definite duties would fill a very important gap in the industrial organization of the country, and the Indian Company Law must be amended with a view to providing for the compulsory constitution of a body like this in all cases where the managing agency system prevails.

VI

REMUNERATION OF MANAGING AGENTS: COST TO INDUSTRY

It is now necessary to examine how far the payments made to the managing agents for their services have been fair and reasonable, and whether Indian industry has had to pay heavily for its entrepreneurs. The remuneration to managing agents takes several forms. In the first place, whatever may be the system of remunerating the agents, a certain fixed monthly or annual sum of money is given to them for their head office expenses in all industries.[1] In so far as this is paid to cover the out-of-pocket expenses incurred by the managing agency firm in the running of the mill companies under their charge, the payment is clearly justifiable. Managing agents provide valuable secretarial and clerical services on behalf of the industrial companies under their control, which would have to spend more if each were to have a self-contained office of its own. Criticism is, however, made that they charge (*a*)

[1] The expenses on head office account are for the following (among other) purposes. Work in connection with the board and annual meetings; the maintenance of share register and transfer of shares; work involved in buying and selling, insurance, advertising, and correspondence. See also *Indian Tariff Board: Cotton Industry*, Report, 1932, p. 88.

an excessive amount towards head office expenses account, and (*b*) that under cover of office expenses, they seek to gain extra remuneration. As regards the former, taking the managing agents as a whole, their charges towards office expenses are reasonable. From the statement of accounts submitted to the Second Textile Tariff Board by the Bombay Millowners' Association, it is seen that the office allowances during the years 1927–30 averaged about Rs. 7,000 per mill company per annum,[1] a sum which cannot be considered excessive. But it is not all mill companies that are charged for office expenses. Confining ourselves to those that actually pay towards office maintenance, we find that 31 mills paid altogether Rs. 5,16,800 in 1928, making an average of Rs. 16,670 per mill.[2] Even this figure is not high or unfair. But the real point is not so much the size of the allowances, as the question whether (*a*) the mill company gets full value for its expenditure on the head office of the managing agents, and (*b*) what exactly do head office expenses imply. An allowance of Rs. 24,000 per annum may be a very economical item of expenditure in the case of one mill company, whereas Rs. 2,400 may be just a waste of expenditure in the case of another, if the managing agent of the first renders valuable services and the managing agent of the second does nothing of the kind.

In the jute industry office allowances are charged by some managing agents, and in these cases Rs. 200 to Rs. 500 per mill is usual, although in one or two cases Rs. 1,000 to Rs. 1,200 is received.[3] In all the industries managed by the Bengal managing agents, whether they be paper mill companies, tea gardens, coal companies or cement companies, managing agents receive an allowance on account of their head office expenses. A statement

[1] *Indian Textile Journal*. Summary of the Memorandum submitted by the Bombay Millowners' Association to the Indian Tariff Board (Cotton Industry), 1931.

[2] Evidence submitted by the Bombay Shareholders' Association.

[3] *Indian Tariff Board: Cotton Industry*, 1927, Vol. 3, p. 323. Also *Indian Textile Journal*, March 1904, where full details are given for a number of jute mills. There has not been any considerable change in the system of remuneration since then.

is appended at the end of this chapter giving for each industry a few typical cases of the amount of head office expenses paid.[1] But some managing agents who are paid on the basis of profits definitely seek to get a minimum return through charging more than is strictly necessary for office expenses, and in those instances the charges for office expenses present an altogether different aspect, which will be examined presently.

Another feature common to all the systems of remunerating the managing agents is the payment of a certain minimum sum as "commission," that is payable under all circumstances, whether the industrial concerns make profit or not. The principle underlying this guarantee of a certain minimum remuneration is obviously fair. It is that adverse general economic conditions should not debar the managing agents from getting some remuneration for their services of management which in India, of course, include financing as well. The evidence submitted by the Bombay Shareholders' Association before the Second Textile Tariff Board inquiry shows that 36 out of 58 mill companies about which the association was able to get information have been paying a minimum remuneration, varying with the size of the unit from Rs. 1,200 to Rs. 72,000 per annum, and in one case it amounted to Rs. 120,000. The average minimum per mill worked out at Rs. 33,000. In the jute industry, as would be evident from the extract quoted from the articles of association of some jute mill companies in an earlier chapter, a minimum commission varying from Rs. 24,000 to Rs. 50,000 (depending upon the size of each mill company) is very commonly guaranteed to the managing agents. In the paper industry, too, there is a similar arrangement.[2] The cases where no minimum commission is charged are those where the managing agents are paid a commission on output or gross sales, and are certain to get a sure return. Where the remuneration is on the basis of profit, the minimum commission

[1] Information extracted for each industry from the Evidence of Applicants for Protection tendered to the Tariff Board.

[2] *Tariff Board: Paper and Paper Pulp Industries*, Evidence, Vol. 1, 1932, p. 580.

is usually guaranteed; if it is not, the managing agents charge a much greater allowance towards their head office expenses, which include remuneration for their managerial work. As has been pointed out by Sir T. Catto in his evidence before the Tariff Board inquiry relating to the paper industry, "if we were paid by commission on profits, our office allowances would need to be considerably larger. At present, the agent knows that he can rely on something out of his commission on output. In the case of commission on profits which may or may not materialize, the usual practice is for the office expenses to be put up at a higher rate."[1] We thus get a somewhat complicated and composite system of payment to the managing agents which is made up of at least two separate elements: (*a*) payment for secretarial and clerical duties performed by the managing agents on behalf of the companies concerned, (*b*) guaranteeing to them a certain minimum remuneration which takes the form of an additional charge towards head office expenses or of a definite minimum commission.

It would simplify matters enormously if some uniform practice were adopted by managing agents. Obviously the best course would be to treat head office allowances as an item of cost to be reimbursed by the industrial company and not to treat them as a source of remuneration. Where the remuneration to the agents takes the form of a percentage on profits, a minimum guarantee is fair and equitable, but this must be secured by an explicit agreement and not indirectly by increasing the charge on account of office allowances.

SYSTEMS OF REMUNERATION

Over and above payments for office expenses and a minimum commission the management receive: (*a*) commission on production, or (*b*) commission on sale, or (*c*) commission on profit. When the cotton industry was first established in Bombay, and when mule spinning was in vogue, the managing agents received a commission based on the output of yarn (3 pies per lb. of yarn).

[1] *Tariff Board: Paper and Paper Pulp Industries*, Evidence, Vol. I, 1932, p. 580.

The system was not injurious when productive output was low, but with the introduction of ring spindles, production increased and the defects of a system which sacrificed quality to quantity and which enabled agents to make enormous profits, even if the mills were producing at a loss, became apparent. It was in 1886 that the system which had already been adopted in Nagpur by the late Sir J. N. Tata was introduced in Bombay by Messrs. Greaves Cotton Co., Ltd., i.e. the system of commission on profits, usually 10 per cent. Thereafter the change-over was rapid, and at present a commission on profit has become almost universal in the Bombay section of the cotton industry. Of the 71 mills which were members of the Bombay Millowners' Association in 1928, only one mill paid commission on production; one mill was managed by a managing director whose remuneration was fixed by the Board of Directors; 8 mills paid commission on sale, and 61 mills paid on profit.[1] Ahmedabad started like Bombay with the system of commission on output but has now switched over to commission on sales. The rate of commission is usually 3½ per cent of gross proceeds of sale. In the other industrial centres of the cotton industry, the most common method is that of a commission on output, but there is a fair number which pay commission on sales. It is usually provided in the agreement that when the companies incur losses, a portion of the commission must be relinquished by the managing agents.

In the jute industry, the majority of the mills still pay on gross sales.[2] There are some mills which pay a commission on profit in addition to a minimum commission and a generous allowance for office expenses. Since the managing agents in Bengal have a variety of enterprises under their control, they have chosen either the one or the other with suitable variations to secure themselves against inadequate remuneration. An inquiry made as long ago as

[1] Letter from the Secretary of the Bombay Millowners' Association to the Bombay Shareholders' Association. (Memorandum of evidence submitted by the latter.)

[2] *Indian Tariff Board: Cotton Industry*, 1927, Vol. 3, p. 323. Also *Paper and Paper Pulp Industries*, Evidence, 1925, Vol. 1, p. 580.

1904 revealed that of 23 jute concerns whose methods of paying their management were investigated, 15 paid on gross sales and 7 on profits, one being a private company.[1] This position has not altered since then, as the evidence given before the Tariff Board enquiries shows.[2] In the tea industry, the usual terms are a minimum amount when a garden is laid out and subsequently a commission of $2\frac{1}{2}$ per cent on sale proceeds and a further $2\frac{1}{2}$ per cent on profits;[3] 10 per cent on profits is the usual return to managing agents in the coal industry.[4] With the important exception of the Indian Paper Mills Co., the paper industry pays to its managing agents a commission based on profits, usually about 10 per cent.[5] In the cement industry the commission on profits is almost universally prevalent in all the units.[6] Both the systems of the commission on profit and commission on gross sale proceeds exist in the sugar industry.[7] The Tata Iron & Steel Co. was paying its managing agents only 5 per cent on its profits, but when the agreement came to be revised in 1916 a very interesting method of remuneration was devised by which managing agents were to share in a slowly rising degree in the prosperity of the company. It was agreed that "provided that Messrs. Tata, Sons & Co. agree not to compete with the company by promoting or by taking up agency of a company manufacturing pig-iron, steel, and other products (description of the several kinds of products turned out in the works is here given) the agency will be continued for another thirty years from 1916. Upon the expiration of the extended term, the agency of the firm do continue until the agents shall resign or shall be removed from their office by the company

1 *Indian Textile Journal*, 1904, quoting extract from *Capital*, Calcutta.

2 *Indian Tariff Board: Paper and Paper Pulp Industries*, 1925, Vol. 1, p. 580.

3 *Indian Tariff Board: Cotton Industry*, 1927, Vol. 3, p. 323.

4 *Indian Tariff Board: Paper and Paper Pulp Industries*, 1925, Vol. 1, p. 201.

5 Ibid., 1925, pp. 128–30, 240–60. Also 1932, Vol. 1, pp. 393, 455, 480 *et seq.*

6 *Indian Tariff Board: Cement Industry*, 1925, Vol. 1, pp. 33, 86, 242 *et seq.*

7 *Indian Tariff Board: Sugar Industry*, 1932, Vol. 1, pp. 86, 98.

after twelve calendar months' notice in writing. The remuneration shall be as follows: 5 per cent on net profits subject to a minimum of Rs. 50,000. When the dividend declared exceeds 8 per cent and does not exceed 10 per cent, agents' commission will be 7 per cent, when it exceeds 10 per cent and does not exceed 12 per cent the commission will be 8 per cent; when it exceeds 12 per cent the commission will be 9 per cent."[1] It was also provided that for purposes of calculation, net profits shall be taken after making full allowances and deductions from revenue for interest on loans and debentures, and after deducting 3 per cent for depreciation.

Now this agreement is in many ways exceptional and sound. In most of the agreements where a commission on profits is provided for, the profits are calculated after making full allowances and deductions from revenue for interest on loans and deposits, and working expenses chargeable against profits, but "*without any deductions for or in respect of interest on debentures or of any amount carried to insurance, reserve, depreciation or sinking fund, or to any other special fund or in respect of any expenditure on capital account.*"[2] The system of calculating profits payable to the managing agents does not, with rare exceptions like those under the agency of Tata, Sons & Co., provide for deductions for depreciation. However undesirable from the point of view of the shareholders this arrangement may be by which the managing agent gets a percentage on profit before depreciation, it need not in itself adversely affect the financial position of the industrial company, and, contrary to the popular view, it may be stated that managing agents have under this scheme no direct inducement to starve the depreciation fund as full allowances for depreciation may be made without reducing their own remuneration. If, however, the system of paying on the basis of gross profit has an

[1] *Indian Textile Journal*, August 1913, p. 343.

[2] Extract from the evidence given by the Indian Cement Co. before the Tariff Board, Evidence tendered by Applicants, p. 85. Also *Tariff Board: Cotton Industry*, Report, 1927, p. 147. *Tariff Board: Paper and Pulp Industries*, 1932, Vol. 1, p. 393.

undesirable effect on depreciation account, it is because of its indirect rather than direct effects. Where managing agents succeed in providing themselves with some remuneration by this means, they have to meet the clamorous demand of the shareholders who feel with some justification that when the agents were able to make some profit, they, too, should have some dividend. In their anxiety to meet this demand, no provision is made for depreciation, and profits are declared out of sums which should have been credited to depreciation account. The psychological effects of this system on the shareholders and through them on the managing agents are distinctly injurious to the ultimate interests of industry. The cotton industry in Ahmedabad and Bombay has for long years been generally ill provided with reserves for depreciation. As long ago as 1903, Mr. B. J. Padshah of Tata, Sons & Co., in his memorandum on the financial position of the Bombay cotton industry, pointed out that even first-class mills, numbering at the time, according to him, 16, had provided much smaller sums than those usually provided for in British mills of equal rank for depreciation, that it was only one-half of the amount calculated on the basis of original cost of fixed plant, sanctioned by first-class British mills and 15 per cent less than that allowed by mills of the second class of efficiency in England.[1] Mr. J. H. Fisher, of J. H. Fisher & Co., commenting upon the system of allocating funds for depreciation in the Bombay cotton industry, stated that " in this country (England) it would not be considered sound policy to allow less than 2½ per cent on the 'original' cost of fixed plant," and that the practice in India of making allowance of less than 4 per cent., based on the depreciated value each year, was not desirable.[2] The Tariff Board in 1927, after drawing pointed attention to the lack of uniformity in Bombay and Ahmedabad in respect of the system of allotting funds for depreciation, and to the urgent need of providing adequate reserves for depreciation, recommended that "depreciation, including any amount which may be in arrears, should invariably be regarded as a first charge

[1] *Indian Textile Journal*, March 1903.
[2] Ibid., April 1903.

on profits."[1] Even after this we find that in 1928, although nine mills declared a dividend, only five provided for depreciation in that year.[2] Lack of a proper depreciation reserve is characteristic of other industries besides the cotton industry. The paper industry affords instances of exactly the same feature. The Titaghur paper mills and the Upper India Couper Mills declared high dividends in boom years and provided so little for depreciation that they were later in difficulties.[3]

It is not the managing agency system of remuneration based on gross profits that is responsible for this chronic insufficiency of depreciation reserve. Theoretically, as their remuneration would not be diminished by any allowances towards depreciation account, the contrary must be the result. But the psychological reactions of this system of remuneration and the belief that depreciation is not an item of cost, but on the contrary, only one of the several ways in which profits may be distributed, have produced results injurious to industrial progress. Hence it is desirable that in all cases where the remuneration is based on profit it should be based on net profits, i.e. after all charges on loans and debentures are met, and after full allowance for depreciation is made.

Of the three systems in vogue in Indian industries, there is no doubt that the system of commission on profits is, as pointed out by the Textile Tariff Board, undoubtedly the best. But there are certain features in each which deserve notice. When prices are falling and industry continues in a depressed state, the commission on profits will result in such inadequate remuneration to the managing agent that, unless he is guaranteed a minimum commission, he cannot afford to continue his managerial and financial functions. On the other hand, when prices are going up and industry is booming, a managing agent would, under this system, be realizing high profits, higher than under either of the other two systems. One reason why in Ahmedabad there was a rapid

[1] *Indian Tariff Board: Cotton Industry*, Report, p. 148.

[2] *Indian Textile Journal*, July 1929.

[3] *Indian Tariff Board: Paper and Paper Pulp Industries*, 1925, Vol. 1, p. 374.

switch-off from the old system of commission on output, to that on gross sales, or on profit, was that in a boom period remuneration based on output does not yield as good returns to the managing agents as that based on profits or on sale. Payment on output is an uneconomical method of remuneration. It not only tends to draw attention away from quality to quantity, but removes the incentive to the efficient working, management, and marketing of product. The theoretical objections against it are so overwhelming that but for its being worked in a reasonable manner by managing agents it would have broken down long ago. Although similar objections may be advanced against the system of payment on gross sales, its peculiarity is that in years of depression it enables the managing agents to realize some reasonable remuneration, and in years of boom it gives better opportunities for the shareholders to share in the prosperity of the boom than under the system of payment on profit. From the point of view of the managing agent, then, commission on sales, if it does not secure to him as high a profit in boom years as under the other systems, does not also reduce his return so adversely in lean years as that on profit does. Provided, therefore, managing agents do not bring about an alteration in the method of remuneration just when industry is on a rising tide, commission on sales will not really work out adversely to the industrial companies over a long period. It is only fair that in times of adversity managing agents should share adequately in the difficulties of the industrial companies (and this cannot happen if the system of remuneration on production prevails) and that in times of prosperity the shareholders should share to a greater degree in the increased profits of the concern (and this can be better secured under the commission on sale system than on the commission on profit system). The choice, therefore, lies between the system of remuneration based on profits and that on sales. Over a fairly long period it may be a matter of indifference which is adopted were it not for one decisive factor which points to the superiority of the profit system. Where the managing agent is paid on gross sales his interest becomes divorced from that of the shareholder by making him reluctant to agree to work short-time in the interests of the industry as a whole and even gives him a profit on unprofitable business.

VII

ARE PAYMENTS TO MANAGING AGENTS EXCESSIVE?

But whatever be the system of remuneration in vogue, the real questions are: "Have the payments to the managing agents been excessive, unfair and inequitable?" Have they absorbed such a large portion of the profits of industry that investment has been checked owing to the low return to the shareholders?" These are difficult questions, but some answer must be attempted in view of their great theoretical and practical importance. There is, however, no standard by which remuneration to entrepreneurs who, as in India, perform varied functions, may be measured and judged. But two propositions of general acceptance may be laid down. In the first place, so long as industry is more or less privately organized and privately owned, the division of profits between the managing agents and a few of their friends has not the same importance as when the shares have been taken up by the investing public. Even in Ahmedabad, where, although the bulk of the shares are owned by the managing agents and their friends, the public are gradually seeking to come in and share in the development of the industry, the question of equitable arrangement has become one of great practical importance. Further from the social point of view, unless the investors are left with a reasonable rate of dividend, fresh capital will not flow into industry and industrial development will be arrested. Secondly, the burden of payment must gradually be scaled down as experience is gained and as an industry becomes well established. Pioneer industrial enterprises will naturally have to pay the managing agents more amply than industries like cotton and jute which have been established for a long time, and which do not involve any great risk or call for qualities difficult to be found. What this means is that in the case of all new industrial enterprises or even in the case of an old industry in a new centre, a higher reward to the managing agents will be justified, but after the first ten or fifteen years, the agreement should be revised and the payment reduced to what would be regarded as fair remuneration to a Board of Directors with a managing director. In the early years of an industrial company, the financial service of the managing agents is important and will have to be rewarded.

In the light of the above considerations, the managing agency system of administration tends to become increasingly costly and burdensome with time unless, of course, at successive revisions of agreement the rate of remuneration is reduced. There can be no justification for providing, as has been done in some of the agreements in the newly started Ahmedabad cotton mills, a return to managing agents of "4 per cent commission on the total sale proceeds of yarn, cloth, and other manufactures and any other materials whatever sold by the company together with 5 per cent on total amounts of bills for ginning, pressing, dyeing, bleaching, baling and bundling and other work done by the company,"[1] This is far in excess of the usual 2½ per cent on gross sale proceeds and is an unfair arrangement. Neglecting these exceptionally costly methods prevalent in Ahmedabad, and confining ourselves to the Bombay section of the cotton industry, it may be stated that, provided the mills are managed honestly and efficiently, 10 per cent on profits cannot be considered to be too liberal or unfair. It is true that in times of difficulty even the minimum yearly commission bears too hard on the industrial companies, as will be evident from the following table. But considering the financial

	Number of Mills Repre-sented	Profit or Loss without Charging Depreciation Rupees	Profit or Loss after Allowing for Depreciation Rupees	Agents' Office Allowance Rupees	Net Commission Drawn Rupees	Total Allowances and Commission Drawn Rupees
1927	75	15,700,435	−736,309	547,569	2,539,908	3,087,477
1928	73	−12,646,416	−29,877,920	516,541	1,315,684	1,832,225
1929	76	−7,184,940	−23,066,994	470,211	1,555,962	2,026,173
1930	71	−9,422,570	−23,698,662	470,158	875,286	1,345,444

[1] Bombay Shareholders' Association replies to the Tariff Board Questionnaire, where relevant articles of agreement are quoted in Appendix B.

functions of the managing agents in that critical period, the minimum commission should not be grudged. Further, managing agents have been quite ready to forego a large portion of their minimum commission in times of stress and difficulty.[1]

What really makes the system of payment burdensome is not the size of remuneration but the incompetence and indifference of managing agents. The statement made years ago by a writer in *Capital* in respect of the jute industry is of wider application and remains as true now as when it was made. Reviewing the methods of remuneration prevalent in the jute mills in his time he concluded thus, "A comparison of the commission paid with the profits of jute mills will show that the race is not always to the swift nor the battle to the strong. For it would seem that some of the agents who are highly paid have shown much better results than those who are only moderately remunerated. But there is no doubt that a commission based on the output of the mills or on gross sales may press hardly in bad times. The main question is one of good management."[2] Provided the managing agents do not seek to add to their commission by various miscellaneous activities, the direct payment for their services would not weaken the finan-

[1] The Managing Agents of C.P. Portland Cement Co., Ltd., have foregone their commission since 1922 (*Tariff Board: Cement Industry*, 1925, Evidence by Applicants, p. 33.)

In 1928, in the Bombay cotton industry managing agents of seventy-three cotton mills gave up by way of commission Rs. 191,004. In addition they also surrendered Rs. 739,825 in the same year, being interest on the loans and debentures due to them (Arno Pearse, *The Cotton Industry of India*, 1930, p. 67).

Amount of commission given up by the Ahmedabad Mill Agents:

	Rupees
1922	52,638
1923	158,621
1924	459,709
1925	117,522
1926	327,740
1927	212,834 (Ibid., p. 68).

See also Memorandum submitted by the Bombay Millowners' Association to the Second Cotton Tariff Board, 1932.

[2] Quoted in the *Indian Textile Journal*, March 1904.

cial position of an industrial company.[1] This is not to say that in the case of industries like cotton, jute, and tea, the payment to the managing agents cannot be reduced without impairing efficiency. On the contrary, some of the managing agents themselves have recognized that they take away a rather large slice of profits, leaving too little for the investors. Thus, speaking in 1916 at a meeting of the shareholders of the Tata Iron & Steel Co., the late Sir Dorab Tata said "from a table of profits and agency commissions of several mill companies in 1915, I find that the commission averages from 20 to 25 per cent of the profits and that in one case the agents were paid Rs. 22,000, and the profit was Rs. 89,000, out of which Rs. 40,000 was carried to a depreciation fund. The agents were thus paid as much as 45 per cent of the net profits."[2] Although some reduction in remuneration is clearly desirable, and in the case of older industries perfectly justifiable, the real lines of solution lie first in removing some of the abuses connected with the system and secondly in ensuring better service from the managing agents. This raises the whole future of the managing agency system, and something must now be said about it.

VIII

FUTURE OF THE MANAGING AGENCY SYSTEM. METHODS OF IMPROVEMENT. ALTERNATIVES

It is dangerous to prophesy; but perhaps it may be safely predicted that the future of the managing agency system lies mostly in the hands of the managing agents themselves. That the managing agency system will continue to exist for a long time most certainly in Bengal, no one acquainted with its past history and present position will dispute. Equally will it go on functioning in Bombay and other parts of India, though its range of influence may be

[1] As evidence of this point may be quoted the prosperous Bombay Dyeing & Spinning Co. managed by Messrs. Nowrosje Wadia & Sons, who do not pocket any commission on purchases of any kind, but who are also paid 10 per cent on profits.

[2] *Indian Textile Journal*, August 1916.

confined to some industries only. But whether it will live in an anaemic state until it languishes at last, or whether it will continue in vigour and usefulness as it has done in the past, depends entirely upon the development of certain forms of control, both from within and without. The managing agency system can still justify itself in two important ways. Where it has the opportunity of performing the useful function of co-ordinated and centralized control in administration great economy can be achieved under the system. Again, where much pioneering work is involved in the establishment of new industries, and where financing requires not merely large resources but considerable waiting, the managing agency system can be of the greatest value to the country. In industries established long ago and not involving difficult problems of finance or high technical ability, there is no special need for their services and a Board of Directors can manage as well. Further, in industries of national importance like public utilities, it is dangerous to adopt a system which confers such enormous power on the managing agents. In the future industrial organization of the country it must be fully recognized that both the managing agency system and the Board of Directors system should exist and perform useful functions, and that the field is sufficiently large and varied to be cultivated by different types of ability.

ASSOCIATION OF MANAGING AGENTS

If this is recognized, certain important results follow. Managing agents must develop certain internal rules of conduct and control with a view not merely to eradicate the undesirable elements that have crept into the system, but to develop and strengthen those features that justify its continuance. For this purpose the most essential thing is to form an association of managing agents, membership of which would imply a recognition of responsibilities and conformity to prescribed standards of conduct. Even in Bombay where the agency system is temporarily discredited, its disrepute is due to the lack of a standard of conduct by which the action of the less scrupulous agents may be judged and condemned. Had there been an organization to lay down the conditions and circumstances in which commission for extraneous work done by managing agents may be appropriated by them, or the limitations under which they may be allowed to carry on subsidiary enterprises, and to regulate the manner in which managing agency rights may be transferred, many of the evils now prevalent in the Bombay Presidency might have been avoided. A self-regulating organization is the best insurance for the safety and permanence of the managing agency system.

But in the creation of this organization, both the European and the Indian sections must unite. How much industrial development in India is due to the enterprise of the British and Indian managing agents has been made clear in the foregoing pages. Further progress depends, however, upon co-operation between these two sections, and each will gain by association with the other. The Indian managing agents will find their experience enriched by a knowledge of the methods of co-ordination and control successfully adopted by British managing agents. In turn the latter will find that in new fields of activity their chances of success improve by closer contact with Indian business men and by co-operation with them. Such co-operation will, by inspiring confidence in the investing public, enable a larger amount of capital to be drawn into industry. It is because of the isolation of the managing agents from one another that they have been unwilling or unable to take up new and risky enterprises, and were criticized by the Industrial Commission with perfect justification as exhibiting "undue reluctance to embark on new ventures." From the social point of view no less than from their private point of view, co-operation in the economic sphere is bound to result in great advantage. The method of "Konsortium" to which we referred in an earlier chapter as a valuable means of achieving success among the bankers applies in no less degree in the industrial field to the European and Indian managing agents. That, for the moment, differences between the European and Indian managing agents exist on a number of issues is true; but in the great majority of cases there is enough common ground for co-operation. Nor can isolation solve the difficulties that exist. The sooner the two sections come together and work with understanding and develop rules of conduct which will raise the general tone of industrial management, the easier will be the solution of a number of unsolved difficulties.

Whatever view is held about the immediate practicability of the proposal outlined above, there can be no disagreement as to its importance both in regard to its influence on the agency system as a whole and on the course of industrial development in India. Recent developments indicate that there is no ground for pessimism and that sooner or later some forms of co-operative action are bound to be developed. In January 1933, at the instance of the Bengal Chamber of Commerce, the Associated Chambers of Commerce of India accepted a resolution to call into being an Indian Employers' Federation, consisting of the more important industrial concerns of India, both Indian and European.[1] What we have suggested would be the logical outcome of the evolution of the managing agency systems, Indian and European. In any case, the establishment of an Association of Managing Agents, Indian and European, for the purpose of regulating the conduct and activities of the managing agents and for affording opportunities for closer contact and intimacy between the two is an end which deserves to be sought and achieved.

IMPROVEMENT OF THEIR INTERNAL ORGANIZATION

Next, managing agency firms should seek to improve their internal organization. This is particularly urgent in the case of the Indian managing agency firms. In some cases managing agency firms comprise persons whose title to manage a concern consists less in their industrial and technical abilities than in their possession of some capital. Unless they are able to get and utilize the services of persons with industrial experience and technical knowledge, it is almost inevitable that their management should be inefficient. It would be dangerous to hand over the management

[1] *Indian Finance*, January 7, 1933.

to the unfettered control of a weak or incompetent managing agent. The continuance of the managing agency system in Bombay and Ahmedabad implies an obligation on the managing agents to recognize their social and public responsibilities. The tendency for the agency to be passed from father to son or to some other relative, and to be regarded in the light of a family possession does not conduce to efficiency "since it does not follow that business capacity is inherited with the succession to the agency."[1] In the circumstances the wisest course will be for managing agents to regard their firm purely as a business concern, and to draw in continuously a fresh stream of outside ability which will infuse life and vigour into the business.

REFORM OF THE COMPANY LAW

Although these reforms from within are urgent and should be carried out, it will be foolish to ignore the existence of certain evils under the managing agency system, which must be put an end to and which the country cannot afford to leave to the uncertain action of the managing agencies to remedy. The Indian Companies Act should be amended, and there should be a frank recognition of the enormous power of managing agents in the industrial structure of the country. Nothing has done more to enable abuses to creep into the system than the failure of the Indian Companies Act to distinguish between the British system and the Indian system of company management. The complacency with which the Honourable Mr. Clark disposed of the criticism of the Indian Companies Bill by stating that the managing agent "was either a director, in which case the rules applying to the directors will apply to him or not a director in which case his relationship was governed by contract,"[2] has led to more unfortunate results than he ever foresaw. As has been pointed out, there should be recognized in the Companies Act a new body which would have certain definite functions and which could serve as an intermediary between

[1] *Indian Tariff Board: Cotton Industry*, Report, 1927, p. 88.
[2] *Indian Textile Journal*, August 1912, pp. 371–2.

the managing agent and the shareholders. The appointment of auditors should be made with the approval of this body. One of the incidental consequences of the managing agency system has been the sterilization of the activities of auditors, who depend both for their appointment and continuance on the goodwill of the managing agents. In some cases audit is carried out by an auditor who is related to the managing agent of the mills the accounts of which are under audit.[1] It is not to be supposed that the auditors become corrupt or dishonest, but human nature being what it is, they are willing to connive or wink at practices which in a more independent position they would be sure to expose. The appointment of auditors for auditing the accounts of industrial companies under the management of agency firms must have the approval of the proposed Board of Supervisors.

There are those who think that the managing agency system has outlived its usefulness and that it must go. No one who has followed the evolution and work of the managing agents, described in the foregoing pages, will agree with such a view. That there are defects, even of a serious kind, may be admitted, but they are capable of solution. On the other hand, in some ways it will be a great advantage for the country to have the continued services of agency firms with ripe experience and great financial resources. Managing agents perform a wide variety of functions which cannot all be undertaken by ordinary Boards of Directors.

At the same time in the future industrial organization it may be expected that there will be increasing opportunities for Boards of Directors to function. As each new industry gets started and as experience is gained by the Board of Supervisors, the earlier risks of pioneering and organizing would disappear, and the field would become clear for ordinary management typified by a Board of Directors. The managing agency firms will be the spearhead of industry and the vanguard of the industrial army of leaders; the Board of Directors will follow in their footsteps. Each will gain from contact with the other and the country will be the richer on account of this variety in its industrial leadership.

[1] *Indian Tariff Board: Cotton Industry*, Report, 1927, p. 149.

STATEMENT

Office allowances charged by Managing Agents in respect of the concerns they manage

Cotton Industry[1]	Rupees
Apollo Mills	24,000
Bradbury	12,000
David	12,000
Gokak	24,000
Kohinoor	6,000
Madras United Spinning and Weaving Mills ..	30,000
Phoenix	18,000
Sassoon Spinning & Weaving Co.	18,000
Tata Mills	14,400
Vishnu Cotton Mill	18,000
Simplex Mills Co.	24,000
Kastoorchand Mills	12,000
Cement Industry	Head Office Expenses Rupees
C.P.'s Portland Cement Co., Ltd.	51,000
Indian Cement Co., Ltd.	45,000
Gwalior Cement Co., Ltd.	20,000
Dwarka Cement Co., Ltd.	71,000
Katni Cement and Industrial Co., Ltd. ..	97,200

In the case of the cement and sugar companies, the Head Office expenses include all expenditures incurred by the managing agents on behalf of the concerns they manage. They are not therefore strictly comparable with the mere allowances charged by managing agents of cotton, paper, and other companies.

Sugar Industry, 1928–9	Rupees
Cawnpore Sugar Works, Ltd.	1,05,850
Champaran Sugar Co.	46,664
Ryam Sugar Co.	31,635
Purtabpore Sugar Co.	15,014
	Head Office Allowance
Punjab Sugar Corporation	12,800
Paper Industry	
Titaghur Paper Mills	24,000
Indian Paper Co.	12,000
Deccan Paper Mills	9,600
Match Industry	
Bhagiratti Match Factory	1,200
New Sunderhan Match Factory	6,000

[1] Information extracted from the Replies to the Tariff Board Questionnaire sent by the Bombay Shareholders' Association.

CHAPTER X

WAGES, STANDARD OF LIVING AND EFFICIENCY OF THE INDUSTRIAL WORKER

I

WAGES, standard of living, and industrial efficiency are intimately related to one another, both as cause and effect. The problem of wages may be regarded from two points of view; as a means of livelihood for the worker and his dependants, and as an item of productive costs. The employer is primarily interested in the wages cost per unit of output and the worker in the amount of necessaries and luxuries which his nominal wages can buy. Although the two objectives may seem to be widely different, they are brought nearer to each other by the reactions of wages on the standard of living and through it on industrial efficiency. It is true that this effect may not be always immediate or direct. Indeed, in so far as low wages also imply low labour cost—and this is often possible in certain trades employing low grade manual labour—the employer may remain unconcerned about the workers' efficiency. Equally is it conceivable that an increase of wages may have little effect in improving the standard of living of the workers and their efficiency. But over a long period of time, and from the national point of view the securing of a reasonable standard of earnings for the worker is an essential requisite of industrial efficiency.

The Indian industrial worker is in receipt of wages which are insufficient to satisfy even the primary needs of civilized existence. This is hardly surprising as his efficiency, judged by any standard, is low, and his desire to improve his standard of living is not intense, or at least does not stimulate him to make great efforts at improving it. Poverty cuts at the root of ambition, initiative and desire, and leads to bad conditions of living; bad conditions lead to inefficiency and inefficiency leads to poverty.

Thus the usual vicious circle is formed, so difficult to break unless attacked at as many points as possible. No easy or immediate solution is possible, and long, patient, and continuous work in the task of improving the conditions of life and employment of the worker can alone bring about progress.

EFFICIENCY

Comparisons are usually made of the number of workers required in India and in other countries for doing a certain quantity of work with a view to measuring efficiency. It is almost impossible to claim any scientific accuracy for such comparisons as apart from their limited scope "it is impossible to say that such quantitative measurements have taken account of all the other factors involved, such as differences in machinery, organization, etc."[1] The economic life of each nation is adjusted to a certain rate of movement at which equilibrium is achieved, and unless the "tempo" is speeded up all round it may not be possible to secure results of any permanent value in any single sphere. This point is of considerable importance, and explains why it will be difficult to raise the efficiency of the industrial worker unless at the same time a change in the general attitude of a people to the tempo of industrial activities is also secured. There is no doubt that part of the reason for the "arrested" economic development of India to which Dr. Anstey has referred in her *Economic Development of India*, is to be found in the slower movement of economic activities to which all classes of people, no less than the worker, are accustomed.

In spite of the limitations from which all comparisons of relative efficiencies of workers in different countries suffer, it will not be altogether valueless to consider some estimates of the efficiency of the workers in different industries in India compared with that of the workers in other countries. The evidence tendered by the employers of industry in India before the Royal Commission on Labour, supplies us with data which may be utilized for this purpose.

[1] *Report of the Royal Commission on Labour*, 1931, p. 208.

The Cotton Industry.—According to the Cotton Yarn Association, Ltd., while in the spinning section of a Japanese mill, 18 operatives manage to look after 1,000 spindles on an average (count 20's), in India for the same number of spindles 30 to 31 operatives are required.[1] According to the *Bombay Labour Gazette*, the usual number of operatives required for 1,000 spindles in India is even higher, i.e. 33.[2] However imperfect this comparison may be, it conveys some idea of the difference. Whereas a competent tenter in Japan attends to two sides, and in England to three, in China and India only one side of the ring frame is attended to by a worker. The number of spindles on each side of the frame is about 200. In some of the mills in Ahmedabad,[3] tenters look after two sides of a ring frame, but this is not usual. Moreover, the output per spindle in India for ten hours (20's yarn) is only 5·7502, whereas in England it is 6·6602, and in Japan 8·02.[4]

In respect of weaving, 48 operatives look after 100 looms in Japan, while in India 98 operatives are required for the same number of looms,[5] (including all processes leading up to weaving). According to Mr. Arno Pearse, the average number of looms tended by one operative in Japan is 5·5 as against 4 in England and 2 in Bombay and Ahmedabad, and 1 in other centres in India. In a very few mills the number of looms per operative is 3, and in two mills in Madras a weaver minds 6 automatic looms. In Japan the weavers are mostly girls, and hence the efficiency of the Indian weavers is even less than the figures indicate. From the point of view of labour costs in weaving, the following figures given by Mr. Sasakura of Japan are of interest:[6]

[1] Quoted with approval by the Bombay Millowners' Association. Evidence, *Royal Commission on Labour*, Vol. 1, Part 1, p. 401.

[2] *Bombay Labour Gazette*, September 1926.

[3] *Report on an Enquiry into wages and hours of labour in the Cotton Mill Industry*, 1926, p. 39.

[4] Arno Pearse, *The Cotton Industry of India*, 1930.

[5] According to *Bombay Labour Gazette*, September 1926, the number is 87.

[6] *Royal Commission on Labour*, Evidence, Vol. 1, Part 1, p. 498.

	Total Number of Operatives	Total Wage Bill per Day	Wages per 100 Looms per Day
		Rupees	Rupees
Japanese Mill, 840 looms	175½ (weavers 140, all girls)	334·21	39·78
Bombay Standard, 840 looms ..	465	920·37	109·56
Manchester Mill (Bombay), 800 looms	318	680·78	85·09

Even assuming that productive output per loom is the same, the labour costs in weaving are in one case 112 per cent, and in another 176 per cent higher than in Japan.

With the introduction of the "Efficiency" scheme in certain mills in Bombay in 1927 and 1928 it was to be expected that the standard of efficiency in spinning and weaving would improve; but unfortunately the introduction of the efficiency system in the group of mills controlled by Messrs. E. D. Sassoon & Co., Ltd., was attended with such serious unrest and interruption to work that progress has been checked. Success depends upon the attitude of labour to rationalization schemes, and so far labour in Bombay has been hostile towards labour-saving and improved appliances and machinery. In part it also depends upon the ability of the millowners to rationalize their plants on the Japanese model, and to standardize all processes with a view to raising the level of output in all directions. Both the Sassoon group and James Finlay & Co. before actually introducing the new scheme, carefully planned out things in advance with the object of (*a*) fixing standards of production and quality for each machine in the mill, (*b*) arranging systematic checking so that these standards might be maintained, and (*c*) fixing a standard of cotton for each mixing, and arranging the quality of mixing to suit the quality of the fabrics to be manufactured. Old and out-of-date machinery was scrapped and replaced by machinery of the most efficient type. The layout of the machinery was also improved. "Weavers were required to work three looms instead of two, and every facility was given them. Larger pirns were provided for the shuttles to cut down the labour involved in shuttling. Improved methods of handling the cloth and giving out work were adopted."[1] But the workers went on strike, influenced by all sorts of considerations, based partly on ignorance, but mainly on prejudice and fear of having to work harder or face unemployment.

Jute industry.—As in the cotton industry, so in jute there has been very little increase in the workers' efficiency during the last thirty or forty years. Owing to the pressure of foreign competition and the glare of publicity which the cotton industry has had to face, some attempts have been made as pointed out above to raise the efficiency of the cotton-mill worker; but the jute industry has not had the same incentive, or the necessity to effect improvement. The industry has been able to make profits owing to its monopolistic position, and has adopted other means of strengthening its condition than by increasing the efficiency of the industrial worker. The difference in efficiency between the cotton-mill worker in India and elsewhere exists also in the jute mills and "one foreign worker, either in Dundee or the Continent has to do work that requires the services of two operatives in India."[2] It is not, according to the Jute Mills Association, that the work is unduly hard or that climatic conditions render the work more difficult to be done, but simply because "this has been the custom so far as the Calcutta jute mills are concerned."[3] This explanation makes it all the more regrettable that the jute mill employers have not turned their attention to raising the level of efficiency of the workers. The fact is that although the Indian jute mill worker compared with the foreign worker is inefficient in relation to output, the labour cost to the jute mill employer is slightly less, and cost efficiency as contrasted with work efficiency is higher. The wages of the jute operatives range from about one shilling to three shillings a day, and these are definitely much lower than

[1] Quoted from the Report of the Chief Inspector of Factories, Bombay, on page 247 of the *Report of the Bombay Strike Enquiry Committee.*

[2] *Royal Commission on Labour,* Vol. 5, Part 1, p. 304, Evidence of the Jute Mills Association.

[3] Ibid.

the difference in efficiency would justify. The lack of an incentive to reduce labour costs has been the chief reason for the continued inefficiency of the industrial worker in the jute industry. Had there been a strong and well-organized trade union organization among the jute mill workers, wages would have increased and employers would have extracted better work from the operatives, and both classes might have benefited. The jute mill industry is an outstanding example of an industry where trade unionism of the proper type might have achieved results of permanent value to the workers.

Coal-Mining Industry.—Considering the character of the supply of mining labour in India, it is not surprising that efficiency is low. Labour for the coal mines is recruited from certain aboriginal hill tribes who have not taken to mining as a permanent occupation, but only as a temporary means of adding to their agricultural income. Some of the collieries have given the workers some cultivable land with a view to making them stay permanently. But as the supply of such land is limited, it has not been possible to settle more than a small percentage of mining labour permanently near the coalfields. Labour is thus extremely migratory, and with a low standard of living has no great inducement to earn high wages. The result is that the Indian miner cuts and loads only three tubs of coal of 13 cwt. each per day with the help of an assistant, although he could certainly do more. It is to be noted that conditions in Indian mines, i.e. thickness of seams and depth from surface are in favour of the miner when compared with most other countries. As has been pointed out, "In the Jharia coalfield, the output from which is more than half the total for British India, the coal is in seams ranging from 40 to 100 feet in thickness. Much of the coal is mined at a depth of only 150 to 350 feet. Where the method of "getting" is by the aid of the coal-cutting machine there is no cramping of space for the working of the machine."[1] In the light of the above the output of the Indian miner compared to that of miners in other countries must be considered

[1] *Report on Labour Conditions in India by Purcell and Hallsworth*, 1928, p. 25.

to be very low. The following statement shows the tons of coal produced per annum per person employed.[1]

India (1928)	131 tons
Japan (1926)	132 tons
Great Britain (1928)	250 tons
America (1926)	780 tons
Germany (1925)	234 tons
Transvaal (1926)	426 tons

Although there had been some slight increase of output since 1923 when the *per capita* output was only 103 tons, the increased productivity was partly due to an increase in the number of coal-cutting machines used in collieries. The number of coal-cutting machines increased from 93 in 1923 to 146 in 1928,[2] and this increase has raised output per worker. It is, of course, difficult to say whether independently of the increase in the number of machines and consequently of output, there has been an increase in the efficiency of the worker. But the fact that the miner is willing to make use of these tools is itself an indication of increasing efficiency. On the other hand, it has been stated that there has been a distinct advance in efficiency among the skilled labour such as engine-men, pump-men, mechanics and electricians, and among the subordinate supervising staff.[3]

Iron and Steel and Engineering Industry.—The iron and steel industries have given much greater attention to the training of labour, and although the time during which the schemes have been in force has not been very long, the result is not unsatisfactory. The work involves a good deal of heavy, and at times exceptionally arduous, labour and "the Indian workman compared individually to the European workman is not so strong physically, nor has he the stamina to continue work of this nature for so long a period."[4] The experience of the Tata Steel works is that it employs in rela-

[1] Evidence of the Chief Inspector of Mines in India, *Royal Commission on Labour*, Vol. 4, Part 1, p. 234.

[2] Ibid., Vol. 4, Part 1, p. 234.

[3] Ibid., p. 247; also Vol. 5, Part 1, p. 186.

[4] Ibid., Vol. 5, Part 1, p. 200.

tion to output a far greater number of employees than a similar plant would in Western countries.[1] On the other hand, the tinplate industry records distinct progress in the efficiency of the skilled workers. Within six years the Tin Plate Co. of India, Ltd., succeeded in training men for all positions in their "Hot Mills," i.e. heaters, roughers and rollers, and have Indian foremen or instructors. They have also been able to train Indians as shearers, pricklers, annealers, etc., but are still dependent on foreign labour for work requiring finer skill, e.g. judgment of the temperature of the furnaces. Despite the progress that has been achieved, the Indian tinplate worker is still inefficient compared with the European or American worker. The Welsh Plate and Sheet Manufacturers' Association, in their representation to the Tariff Board (1926) stated that the total number of employees for a mill equipment similar to the Indian Tin Plate Company operating three shifts, and producing 36,000 tons annually, would be between 710 and 720, whereas actually there were employed in India 2,734. This gives a rate of 1 to 3·6, but owing to the progress achieved since then, the proportion is now said to work out as 1 to 2·8.[2] A committee which investigated the working of the Indian Railway workshops stated that while in England on the L.M.S. Railway, 4·4 persons were required for doing certain kinds of work in a locomotive workshop, in India 20·25 persons were required.

It is not necessary to examine the conditions in other industries; but the general position may be summarized thus—unskilled labour is still generally very inefficient, mainly owing to constant migration from agriculture to industry and back, irregular attendance and a lack of familiarity with machines and labour-saving appliances. The testimony of employers in every industry is unanimous that the efficiency of the skilled workers, and of some of the supervising staff, has increased in recent years. But there is a general concensus of opinion that continuous and sustained effort is often lacking in all grades of labour. Lack of initiative, inability

[1] *Royal Commission on Labour*, Vol. 4, Evidence, Part 1, p. 161.
[2] Ibid., p. 179.

to face a new situation, and a tendency to follow routine methods seem to be the defects of even the supervising staff. Above all, labour of all kinds requires continued personal supervision. An absentee management or one so overburdened with office work that frequent visits to the works are not easy, would lead inevitably to slack and easy-going work. Even the supervising staff, which may be expected to know their responsibility, suffer from the same defect, and unless efficiently supervised and "overlooked" are apt to get slack, and the general slackness communicates itself rapidly to all grades of labour, resulting in the establishment of a low standard of work.

It should be observed in all comparisons that are made that the conditions of work are not the same. It is admitted on all hands that far better help and facilities are given to the workers in foreign countries by way of tools and standardized materials than are given to Indian workers. There is greater co-operation between the various parts of an industrial plant in the West than in India, and although it is difficult to say in such cases which is the cause and which the effect, the failure of the management to standardize conditions of production impairs efficiency. Whatever may be the cause, and however imperfect the comparisons may be there is no doubt that the Indian industrial worker "produces less per unit than the worker in any other country claiming to rank as a leading industrial nation."[1]

II

WAGES

Such inefficiency has revealed itself as cause and effect in the Indian worker's earnings, which are very low indeed. The evidence collected by the Royal Commission on Labour has supplied us with the figures of rates of wages in all important industries. Unfortunately, "the very wide variations which exist both in the methods of payment and the manner in which the rates are fixed not only between centre and centre, but also as between unit and

[1] *Report of the Royal Commission on Labour*, p. 208.

unit in a particular centre"[1] render any general statements applying to all localities extremely hazardous. In the cotton mills in Ahmedabad there is not only a complete lack of uniformity "in the methods adopted in calculating the different additions and deductions before arriving at the final earnings," but also wide variations "in the methods adopted for different classes of workers in a particular mill."[2] In the jute industry again, although the mills are located within a small area and could easily adopt uniform methods of remuneration owing to the uniformity both in the conditions of production and in the classes of goods produced, there has been so far no attempt at securing any standardized methods of remunerating the workers. The Indian Jute Mills Association tried to explain away the variations in the rates and systems of payment in terms of differences in cost of living in different manufacturing areas. But as has been pointed out by the Government of Bengal, "perhaps in no industry in the world, situated in such a circumscribed area, is the wage position more inchoate. The mills, grouped under different managing agents, work under wage systems which have developed many local idiosyncrasies during long or short years of their existence. Even in mills under the same managing agents there are differences which, to persons not acquainted with the position, seem incredible. For example, in two mills situated in the same area and separated from each other by little more than a boundary wall, under the same managing agents, there is practically not a single entry of wages which is the same. In three mills under the same managing agents, situated within a stone's throw of each other, the rates in one mill have for many years been higher than those in the other two mills. In other groups of mills, situated close to each other and under different managing agents the wage rates are kept, or supposed to be kept, strictly secret. The total earnings are not necessarily kept secret, but each prides itself on having been able to declare piece-rates or bonus rates which are better than

[1] *Report of an Enquiry into wages and hours of labour in the Cotton Mill Industry* (Bombay Labour Office), 1926, p. 29.

[2] Ibid.

the rates of the neighbouring mills."[1] The degree of differentiation existing in wage rates for identical processes in the jute industry is indeed amazing, and the figures of earnings of the workers in the jute industry given by the Jute Mills Association have to be accepted as only approximate and general.

Similar variations exist in most of the industries in India in regard to wage rates and within an industry are to be found different methods of payment in different localities. For example, spinners are paid in Bombay by time, while in other centres they are paid by piece rates. The absence of standardization was commented upon by the first Textile Tariff Board, and the Royal Commission on Labour has more recently recommended the adoption of some uniform practice in the cotton, jute, and other industries. Owing to these difficulties the most useful method of bringing out the differences between one centre and another in an industry and between one industry and another is to present the figures of average daily or monthly earnings of different classes of workers in each industry. It is true that equal monthly earnings do not necessarily imply equal wage rates. The former may be affected by (*a*) efficiency, (*b*) regularity of work or otherwise, (*c*) hours of work, (*d*) days of rest, etc. Where differences in efficiency between one centre and another are appreciable and where irregularity and absenteeism are excessive in one centre as compared to another, we may take note of them. But as a rough indication of the rates of wages paid these figures will not be without value, and from the point of view of the welfare of the workers, their earnings are after all the most decisive, subject to differences in cost of living and in wisdom in spending the income.

Wages in the Cotton Industry.—Reliable figures of the earnings of the workers in the cotton mills in Bombay, Ahmedabad, and Sholapur are available as a result of a detailed inquiry by the Bombay Labour Office in 1926. The average *daily* earnings of all operatives in the cotton mills in these three centres are as follows:

[1] Quoted in the *Report of the Royal Commission on Labour*, pp. 215–16.

Average Daily Earnings

	Men	Women	Children	All Adults
Bombay ..	Rs. 1–8–0	Rs. 0–11–1	—	Rs. 1–5–3
Ahmedabad ..	1–6–8	0–12–6	Rs. 0–5–6	1–4–8
Sholapur ..	1–0–5	0–6–8	0–4–0	0–14–8
Average Monthly Earnings of Full-Time Workers				
Bombay ..	Rs. 44–3–6	Rs. 20–4–6	—	Rs. 40–4–6
Ahmedabad ..	38–4–0	21–1–6	Rs. 9–4–6	34–14–0
Sholapur ..	26–10–2	11–6–7	6–13–10	24–16–1

These figures are those of the earnings of all operatives; but a better idea may be formed of the relative wages in these centres by a reference to the earnings of important classes of operatives. The following are the average daily earnings of weavers, spinners, winders and reelers in the cotton industry in Bombay, etc.

Class of Labour	Bombay		Ahmedabad		Sholapur	
	Men	Women	Men	Women	Men	Women
Weavers—						
2 looms ..	Rs. 1–13–4	—	1–13–5	—	1–9–9	—
3 looms ..	Rs. 2–8–6	—	2–6–6	—	—	—
Ring Spinning:						
(*a*) Siders ..	Rs. 1–0–3	0–15–2	0–15–2	0–15–1	0–11–5	0–11–0
(*b*) Farmallas (Followers)	Rs. 0–15–5	0–14–3	—	—	0–9–2	0–8–8
(*c*) Doffers .	Rs. 0–12–1	0–11–5	0–10–7	0–10–5	0–8–1	0–7–10
Winders—						
Time ..	Rs. 0–14–10	0–13–1	0–13–3	0–11–2	0–7–10	—
Piece ..	Rs. 1–1–4	0–12–10	0–15–2	0–12–7	—	0–6–4
Reelers—						
Time ..	—	0–7–11	0–13–2	0–9–7	0–9–0	0–8–10
Piece ..	—	0–10–11	0–15–0	0–14–5	—	0–6–9

The above table brings out the fact that wages in Bombay city are higher than in Ahmedabad and Sholapur. The differences between Bombay and Ahmedabad are actually greater than the above figures would suggest; for the mills in Ahmedabad produce yarns of higher counts, and weave cloths of finer quality than those in Bombay. Whereas only 33·4 per cent of the total output of yarn produced in Bombay in 1926 was over 20 counts, in Ahmedabad it was 59·17 per cent. The character of production has a vital bearing on rates of wages and hence it should be concluded that in relation to the quality of production, wages in Bombay are much higher than in Ahmedabad. Secondly, a larger percentage of weavers in Ahmedabad are working three looms than in Bombay, and hence, although the earnings would necessarily be greater, the actual rates of wages are less in Ahmedabad. While only 73 persons among the weavers included in the study minded more than two looms in Bombay, the number was 205 in Ahmedabad, the percentage respectively being 0·6 and 4·5.

That Bombay pays the highest wages not only absolutely, but in relation to efficiency will be clear from the fact that according to the Tariff Board (1927) of the manufacturing charges per spindle per day, wages in Bombay amounted to 5.04 pies, while the figure was 3.86 for the up-country mills; again, of the manufacturing charges per loom per day, wages in Bombay were 317.64 pies, whereas up-country mills had only 255.50 pies as wages cost. The differences between wages in Bombay and in other centres are well brought out by the average earnings of workers taken from the standard muster of a representative mill in 1926 in each centre and supplied to the Tariff Board.[1] Standard muster is the muster roll kept by each mill indicating the number of operatives in each department, and also showing the monthly rates for workers on fixed wages and the remuneration per unit for piece workers. The average wages shown against piece workers are those earned during the month on the basis of the piece rate given in the standard muster.

It is unfortunate that the Tariff Board has not given also the number of spindles or looms or other machines attended to by one worker in each centre. But since the mills that have been

[1] *Report*, p. 113.

selected are representative ones, it may be assumed that efficiency is more or less the same, and that a weaver usually attends to 2 looms, and that the usual number of spindles per operative is about 180 to 200. These figures would thus indicate the high rates of wages paid in Bombay and to a less extent in Ahmedabad, compared with other centres. Some centres in the Madras Presi-

Monthly Earnings of Workers in a Representative Mill in each Centre

	Bombay	Ahmedabad	Cawnpore
1. Blow-room Tenters (Time)	Rs. 29-0-0	23-10-0	16-14-6
2. Card-room Tenters (Time)	Rs. 27-4-0	24-7-6	23-12-0
3. Frame Tenters (Piece) ..	Rs. 37-12-0	29-6-0	27-3-0
4. Ring Frame Sideboys (Time)	Rs. 29-12-0	26-7-6	15-10-0
5. Winders (Piece)	Rs. 21-4-0	23-1-0	27-13-0
6. Weavers (Piece)	Rs. 47-12-0	47-15-9	32-7-0
7. Folders (Time)	Rs. 29-0-0	25-11-3	14-6-0

	Delhi	Nagpur	Madras
1. Blow-room Tenters (Time)	Rs. 19-0-0	24-0-0	25-14-6
2. Card-room Tenters (Time)	Rs. 14-0-0	24-0-0	23-3-3
3. Frame Tenters (Piece) ..	Rs. 25-0-0	30-12-0	25-2-0
4. Ring Frame Sideboys (Time)	Rs. 20-0-0	24-0-0	14-10-8 (*a*) 17-15-0 (*b*)
5. Winders (Piece)	Rs. 25-0-0	18-8-0	21-8-0
6. Weavers (Piece)	Rs. 35-0-0	41-0-0	34-7-0
7. Folders (Time)	Rs. 20-0-0	24-0-0	26-3-5

(*a*) For minding 180 spindles.
(*b*) For minding 240 spindles.

dency, such as Coimbatore and Madura, pay wages substantially lower than those given above for a mill in Madras city.

From the point of view of the worker in Bombay, it may be the high wages he secures do not afford him the same degree of comfort as his confrère in other centres gets with lower wages. To the differences in cost of living we shall return later; but it is relevant to point out that an improvement in the economic position of the Bombay worker can only be secured by methods other than a direct increase in money wages for the same amount of work.

Wages in Jute Mills.—The jute mill worker is in some ways worse off than the cotton mill worker; for not only are his money wages low, but they are made lower still by organized short time work in the industry. Most of the mills work only for four days a week, and a few for five days, but nearly all conform to the restricted hours of work agreed upon by the Jute Mills Association. The wages of jute-mill operatives range from 10 annas to Rs. 2.0.0 a day, but their total earnings are poor. Warp spinners received in 1926 about Rs. 13.4.0 a month, and weft spinners Rs. 16, and both were paid by time. Warp winders and weft winders are on piece rates and receive higher wages, their average earnings per month in 1926 amounting to Rs. 21.6.0 and Rs. 26.8.0 respectively.[1] The following statement of average weekly earnings of jute-mill workers by the Jute Mills Association, Calcutta, will give an idea of the wages in that industry. The figures relate to 1929.[2]

Department	Multiple Shift	
	Four-Day Week	Five-Day Week
Sacking Weaving ..	Rs. 8–2–9	9–3–0
Hessian Weaving ..	Rs. 5–15–0	7–4–9
Sacking Winding ..	Rs. 4–9–6	5–1–3
Hessian Winding ..	Rs. 4–8–7	5–6–0
Sacking Spinning ..	Rs. 2–9–6	3–4–9
Hessian Spinning ..	Rs. 3–0–3	3–14–0
Batching	Rs. 2–12–9	3–9–9

The above statement of wages may be compared with the following, where the average monthly earnings of the operatives

[1] *Report of the Chief Inspector of Factories*, 1928, p. 38.
[2] *Report of the Royal Commission on Labour*, p. 199.

have been obtained from actual payments in representative jute mills in 1926.[1]

Sacking Weavers	..	Rs. 29-5-0	(Piece Work)
Hessian Weavers	..	Rs. 28-3-0	(Piece Work)
Warp Winders	..	Rs. 21-6-0	(Piece Work)
Weft Winders	..	Rs. 26-8-0	(Piece Work)
Warp Spinners	..	Rs. 13-4-0	(Time Work)
Weft Spinners	..	Rs. 16-0-0	(Time Work)
Batching (cutters)	..	Rs. 16-4-0	(Time Work)

Wages in Coal Mines.—The report of the Chief Inspector of Mines (1930) contains particulars of the daily earnings of different classes of mining workers, and the figures have been obtained in a form prescribed by the regulations framed under the Indian Mines Act. The average daily earnings have been obtained by dividing the total amount paid in wages for work done in a month by the aggregate daily attendance in that month.

The following figures represent average daily earnings of men workers during the month of December 1929.

	Underground			
	Miners	Loaders	Skilled Labour	Unskilled Labour
1. Jharia Coalfield	Rs. 0-13-6	0-11-0	0-12-9	0-9-9
2. Raniganj Coalfield ..	Rs. 0-13-0	0-10-3	0-12-13	0-9-0
3. Giridih Coalfield ..	Rs. 0-12-9	0-12-0	0-14-3	0-8-0

	Open Working				Surface	
	Miners	Loaders	Skilled Labour	Unskilled Labour	Skilled Labour	Unskilled Labour
1. ..	Rs. 0-13-9	0-11-6	0-10-3	0-10-0	0-13-3	0-6-9
2. ..	Rs. 0-9-0	0-7-0	0-11-6	0-8-0	0-11-6	0-6-0
3. ..	Rs. 0-11-9	0-6-3	0-9-0	0-8-0	0 14-9	0-5-0

[1] *Report of the Chief Inspector of Factories*, 1928, pp. 37-8.

Women are employed mostly as coal carriers, and get about 7 to 9 annas a day, but unskilled women workers get less. Wages in the tin and salt mines are much higher, the average daily earnings of miners being Rs. 1.9.0 and Rs. 1.6.3 respectively.

These figures must be accepted with some reserve, as has been pointed out by the Royal Commission on Labour. In the first place the returns submitted by the mine owners are not subjected to any official check, and secondly the attendance of the miner is extremely irregular. According to the Government of Bihar and Orissa, who made an estimate from the family budgets they collected, the average monthly earnings of a coal cutter are in the neighbourhood of Rs. 10 to 15. This is likely to be the more correct figure, as other evidence confirms it. The miner is paid 7 annas per tub of coal, and the daily output is about two or three tubs, which represents the work of the cutter and the loader. The number of days that a miner works is about 18 to 20 days in a month, and it is unlikely that he will be able to earn more than Rs. 15.

Wages in the Iron and Steel and Engineering Industries.—These industries necessarily show a wide variation of rates and earnings owing to the variety of work and the great differences in skill. In Jamshedpur a fitter receives R. 1 a day, a carpenter Rs. 1.4.0, a driller Rs. 1.8.0, a mason Rs. 1.4.0, and a boiler attender Rs. 3 a day.[1] The Royal Commission on Labour state, "taking five typical occupations, masons, carpenters, blacksmiths, fitters, and turners—the earnings are highest in Bombay City and Ahmedabad. Masons there earn from Rs. 50 to 70 a month, carpenters and blacksmiths from Rs. 60 to Rs. 75, and fitters and turners between Rs. 65 and Rs. 80. In Sholapur the rates are appreciably lower. They are lowest in Madras, Bengal, Bihar and Orissa, and the United Provinces where the average monthly earnings of masons are in the neighbourhood of Rs. 30, of carpenters about Rs. 35, and of blacksmiths, fitters and turners about Rs. 40. Midway between these two extremes come the Central Provinces, Burma, the Punjab and Delhi in the order named."[2]

[1] *Royal Commission on Labour*, Vol. 4, Part 1, p. 177.
[2] Ibid., p. 199.

Wages in Tea Gardens.—The wages of the Assam tea gardens are for the most part based on piece rates. The older system known as the *hazira* and *ticca* system under which the worker gets a certain wage (*hazira*) for performing a standard task and overtime rates (*ticca*) for additional work has now been replaced to a large extent by the "unit" system. Under this system, payment is made for each unit of work, and the basic principle is to give the worker great latitude in the matter of attendance, and to leave it to him to earn as much or as little as he likes. These piece-work earnings are therefore liable to considerable variations owing to the latitude allowed to the worker, of which he takes full advantage, owing to his other subsidiary occupations. Statistics of average monthly earnings are published in the annual reports on immigrant labour published by the Government of Assam, but they represent not *actual* earnings, but monthly earnings of an average worker if he did not absent himself on a single working day—a condition which is hardly ever fulfilled. On this calculation, the figures in the report for 1929–30 give the average monthly earnings in the Assam Valley as Rs. 13.8.7 for men, Rs. 11.1.7 for women, and Rs. 7.8.6 for children. The earnings include overtime, diet, rations, and subsistence allowance and bonus.

In considering the above, it has to be noted that while absenteeism, which is high in the tea gardens, would reduce the earnings to figures considerably less than those given here, the workers are in receipt of certain other concessions, the value of which in some cases is very important. Every garden worker receives free housing, medical facilities, and firewood, and some receive land for cultivation either free or at a very low rent. Other concessions include free grazing for the cattle of the workers, free fuel, supply of rice at concession rates, and advances without interest. The first two "are not regarded as concessions" and the fourth is "frequently regarded with suspicion." Apart from concessions, there are two other factors which strengthen the economic condition of the worker. Most of the workers find employment in family groups, and all the members of a worker's family are wage earners.

Secondly there is some standardization in the matter of wages, which enables every worker to get as much as any one can receive in any other garden. It is true that this "standardization" of wages has now been adopted in their own interests by the employers; and the Royal Commission have recommended a definite wage-fixing machinery to be adopted in co-operation with the workers. But even the existing system does ensure at least a uniform minimum all over the Assam gardens, however low that minimum may be. The introduction of minimum wage-fixing machinery would have the important effect not only of strengthening the existing arrangement, but also probably of raising wage levels. Although the economic condition of the tea garden worker is still very poor, there has been a distinct improvement owing to the increase in his cash earnings and the fall in the cost of living during the past decade.

The Unskilled Industrial Worker.—The lowest-paid industrial workers are those regularly employed on manual work in factories and other industrial establishments on wages ranging in many centres from Rs. 10 to Rs. 15 a month. In the Bombay Presidency and Burma they earn from about Rs. 20 to Rs. 25. But on the whole, their economic condition is deplorable, although their earnings are higher than those of the agricultural workers.

	Percentage of Cases Earning Monthly Wage of—						
	Less than Rs. 13	Rs. 13 but less than Rs. 17½	Rs. 17½ but less than Rs. 22½	Rs. 22½ but less than Rs. 27½	Rs. 27½ but less than Rs. 32½	Rs. 32½	Total Number of Cases, 1925–9
United Provinces	26	27	15	9	7	16	304
Madras	22	25	19	15	4	15	110
Central Provinces	18	38	17	8	4	15	209
Bihar and Orissa	21	24	21	12	8	14	717
Bengal	13	18	18	15	10	26	873
Punjab	10	16	36	10	7	21	324
Bombay	3	10	19	23	13	32	1,273
Burma	1	3	10	16	27	43	186

The table on page 372 given by the Royal Commission on Labour prepared from the statistics available with the Workmen's Compensation Commissioners in all provinces of India gives a general picture of wage levels in different provinces, particularly for the semi-skilled operatives in organized industry. The figures relate to the five years, 1925–9 inclusive. Despite their limitations owing to the fact that the workers whose cases have been combined to furnish the statistics cannot be considered as constituting a representative class, they are not without value as a picture of general wage levels.

It will be seen from the above that Burma and Bombay have the highest wage levels, while wages are lowest in the Central Provinces, Madras and the United Provinces. Bengal and Bihar and Orissa and the Punjab are intermediate.

III

REAL WAGES AND THE ECONOMIC CONDITION OF THE WORKER

So far we have been dealing with money wages; but it is real wages, i.e., what the wages can buy, that really determine the welfare of the worker. The position of the worker before the war and in the years after the war up to 1920 has been analysed in the *Economic Development of India* by V. Anstey. But the uncertainty in the worker's economic improvement in the post-war period, to which, writing in 1928, she has referred, may now be stated to exist no longer. That compared to 1920 there has been a distinct improvement in the condition of the worker may not be denied, although, owing to the continued depression in industry, the opportunities for employment have not kept pace with needs. But those that are actually employed do have higher wages. The broad facts of the matter may be stated in a few words. A sharp rise in prices took place towards and after the end of the war. Increases in wages were granted in the leading industries, but up to the end of 1921 wages lagged behind prices. From 1922 there has been an increase in wages and the peak of prices reached in 1920 gradually fell so that by 1923 the workers were generally better off than before the war. Since then prices have fallen substantially. The Calcutta and the Bombay Index Numbers of wholesale prices fell to 172 and 181 respectively in 1923 from 201 and 206 respectively in 1920, and have been steadily falling since then as the statement of index numbers of wholesale prices at the end will show. During all this period, although a slight fall in wages has taken place, the fall has not been commensurate with that of prices. The evidence of the representatives of every industry bears testimony to increases in wages in recent years in some cases so that altogether the wages of those actually in employment are higher than ever before the war.

But this is not to say that the wages now secured by the industrial worker are sufficient to ensure a reasonable standard of living. "Standard of living" is so indefinite and varying in conception that in a vast country like India any attempt to compare and measure the standards in different provinces cannot be successful. Much less will it be possible to draw any comparisons of value between one country and another. Even a standard like "minimum of subsistence" has different meanings in different provinces owing to the varying needs of those localities. In Madras the writer was associated with an inquiry into the minimum needs of subsistence of a Madras working-class family in 1917 which resulted in a figure of Rs. 17.8.0 as the sum required to maintain the family of four persons (man, wife, and two children) above the poverty line. In 1932, applying the same standard, the writer found that at the then prevailing levels of prices for each of the commodities that constituted the family budget, the figure was as low as Rs. 14.12.0. But as has been pointed out in the *Economic Development of India*, this will not be regarded as at all applicable to a city like Bombay.

The only way of bringing out the prevailing standards of living is to outline the results of inquiries conducted by Government and other bodies into the family budgets of working-class families in different industrial centres in India. But the material available is extremely defective. In a number of cases sufficient care had not been exercised in the selection of cases and greater attention to sampling would have produced better results. However, the investigations into family budgets in Sholapur and Ahmedabad and Bombay by the Bombay Labour Office in 1925 and 1926 and 1931, and the Memorandum submitted to the Royal Commission on Labour dealing with the standard of living of workers in Madras Presidency, United Provinces, Central Provinces, Bihar, and Orissa are at least sufficient to throw some light on the general economic conditions of the workers in these provinces. We have also a special report on an Enquiry into the Standard of Living of Jute Mill Workers in Bengal, and all these are sufficient to make one realize the workers' chief difficulties, although they may be inadequate for any quantitative analysis to be made.

It is not possible or necessary to give full details of the various quantities of things bought and consumed by the families whose budgets have been investigated. But it may be useful to set out in each case, (*a*) the percentage of income spent on food, (*b*) clothing, and (*c*) fuel and lighting, (*d*) on house rent, and (*e*) on interest on debt.

These statistics are, of course, not comparable. In the first place, they are of varying degrees of accuracy. Secondly, some budgets contain detailed information relating to all items of expenditure, including liquor, interest on debt and repayment of debt. Others are frankly guesses on the part of the investigators. Thirdly, although the budgets collected specially for the Royal Commission on Labour were designed to be those of workers whose incomes were below Rs. 50 a month, so that "evidence of the same character" might be available, owing to the divergence in the methods of selection, the results are not strictly comparable. For example, in some inquiries the sampling method was adopted, whilst in others there was no system in the selection of particular families. Finally, in the case of the workers in Ahmedabad and Sholapur the inquiry relates mainly to cotton-mill workers who are better paid than most industrial workers. The statistics therefore refer in those cases to groups of workers who are by comparison favourably situated. But in spite of all such limitations, the figures do suggest a striking feature which cannot be missed. The large proportion spent on the primary necessaries of life is evidence of the insufficiency of the wages, and of the very low margins between subsistence and starvation available to the workers. The four main items of expenditure absorb over 75 per cent of the total

	Food	Clothing	Fuel and Light	House Rent	Interest on Debt
	Per cent	Per cent	Per cent	Per cent	Per cent
Sholapur	49·25	11·86	9·60	6·27	6·65
Ahmedabad	57·90	9·45	7·40	11·86	(not available)
Madras City	60·71	3·84	7·54	8·29	87·35 of the families under inquiry in debt
Coimbatore	60·04	6·54	6·84	4·20	83 in debt
Cawnpore	48·12	7·44	6·02	8·76	71 in debt
Lucknow	52·04	8·16	7·38	6·73	70 in debt
Gorakpur	44·93	7·33	4·51	3·06	34 in debt
Nagpur	64·15	9·03	4·29	2·73	62 in debt
Calcutta (jute mill workers)	64·9	7·40	7·13	4·74	76 in debt
Bombay (*Labour Gazette*)	59·56	—	8·2	8·8	—

Railway Workers in—	Food	Clothing	Fuel and Light	House Rent
		Per cent	Per cent	Per cent
United Provinces	55·11	7·75	5·65	3·93
Bihar and Orissa	59·1	6·8	4·4	1·8
Bengal	53·1	5·8	4·4	4·3

NOTE.—The above figures are taken from Vol. 11, Evidence, *Royal Commission on Labour*, 1931.

income; but if we include other necessaries such as expenditure on washing, household utensils, bedding and hairdressing, the percentage will come to about 85. These facts emphasize the poverty of the industrial worker and incidentally his inefficiency.

The worker is not free to spend all his income.—But what makes his position worse is that in most cases the worker is not free to spend all his wages on himself and his family. The Indian worker spends much more on his dependent relatives than is usually the case elsewhere. But the heaviest inroad upon his income arises out of his dependence on the moneylender, and the budgets of the workers' families, collected in every province and locality, reveal the existence of a large amount of debt incurred by the workers on account of marriage, sickness, and death, and insufficient incomes to meet the primary necessaries of life. Indebtedness is almost universal, and is the major cause of the low standard of living of the workers. From the table of expenditure given above it will be seen that in most industrial centres the proportion of families or individuals who are in debt is not less than two-thirds of the whole. The amount of debt is variously estimated, but in the opinion of the Royal Commission on Labour it is not less than three months' wages in the majority of cases, and is often far in excess of this amount. As the Commission have pointed out, "many, indeed, are born in debt, and it evokes both admiration and regret to find how commonly a son assumes responsibility for his father's debt, an obligation which rests on religious and social but seldom on legal sanctions."[1] The debt thus taken up is seldom capable of being extinguished, and the burden is aggravated out of all proportion by the high rate of interest which has to be paid. A common rate is "one anna in the rupee" per month, and this is 75 per cent per annum; but lower and higher rates also exist. The inquiry made into the standard of living of the South Indian Railway workers states "More than 80 per cent of the loans are obtained from moneylenders whose usual rate of interest ranges from one anna in the rupee or 75 per cent to 2 annas in the rupee or 150 per cent."[2] The report of the Special Officer on the standard of living of jute-mill workers states that the maximum interest charged is 325 per cent, or 1 anna per rupee *per week*. This is generally for small sums. The minimum is 18 per cent

[1] *Report of the Royal Commission on Labour*, p. 224.
[2] Ibid., Vol. II, pp. 302–10.

but the average rate of interest is 78 per cent.[1] The Bombay, Sholapur, and Ahmedabad budgets reveal an interest burden of 24 to 75 per cent. The inquiries made for the Royal Commission into the standard of living in the United Provinces give 75 per cent as the commonest rate in Cawnpore, the next commonest rate being 37 per cent.

In view of the serious diminution of the worker's income on account of the excessive burden of their debt, it would be dangerous to assume that real wages are in any sense a measure of their standard of living or that the one is equivalent to the other. We have also to reckon with another factor in India. It has been urged by many employers that the Indian worker has a fixed standard of living which is on a very low level, that when he has earned enough to maintain that level he ceases to make any further effort, and that therefore increased rates of wages do not have the same reactions with him as with the workers in foreign countries. The supply of labour may diminish as a result of higher rates of wages, and it cannot be denied that this has been actually found to be the case in the coal-mining industry, and to a smaller degree in the tea gardens. But this conception of a fixed standard of expenditure applying to industrial workers all over India is not tenable in the light of such progress as has been achieved. If this were true, it would be impossible to raise the standard of living of the workers except by coercion; but as has been pointed out already within the last decade, there has been a general improvement in the standard of living of all classes of workers. Indeed, when one examines this conception closely, it is found that the theory is born out of a combination of two kinds of experience, one general and the other special. The general experience of all employers is what Dr. Anstey calls "an uneconomic" outlook on life, a feature that is found not only among the workers but among all classes of people in India. That ambition and intense desire to raise standards are not particularly vigorous with many workers may at once be admitted. But the differences between the workers in India and elsewhere

[1] Standard of living of jute mill workers, *Report on Inquiry*, 1930, p. 24.

are differences, not of uniform intensity but of varying degree. Some workers in India are only just a little less ambitious than their confrères elsewhere; while there may be found in other countries workers who are even less ambitious than some of the workers in India. The reason for the persistence of this conception of a fixed standard is that in the coal-mining industry, and in tea gardens, workers are a special class of people who are usually lacking in enterprise and ambition. The coalminer's ambition is to return to his village as quickly as possible, and if a fortnight's continuous work rather than three week's work would give him sufficient to go back with some savings, he would go back sooner and give less time to mining. The tea garden worker in so far as he has his own rice lands to cultivate, is perfectly justified in working less on the garden, and if higher rates enable him to absent himself from the garden for a longer period it is not to be supposed that he is either lacking in ambition to improve his standard of living or spending his time wastefully. Some workers in the tea gardens are unusually lacking in foresight and ambition, but they cannot afford justification for any sweeping statement of the fixity of standards in India. The truth is that the "uneconomic" outlook of most of the people of India, combined with an extraordinary degree of willingness to put up with sufferings, makes it more difficult to supply quick incentives to work by increase of wages. More time will be required for wages to exert their full influence in India than elsewhere.

Employers need not, therefore, be deterred from raising wages by any fear that workers will not respond to the incentives thus offered. On the contrary, among the semi-skilled and skilled workers, wages do have a very important and even quick effect. In the Buckingham and Carnatic Mills, Madras, the workers have both raised their standard of living and become more efficient on account of the increased wages supplemented by training. These mills have the pick of the labour supply, and the writer knows how much the workers in the other textile mills in Madras City desire to qualify themselves for entering those two mills. Similar features can be reproduced elsewhere.

IV

INDUSTRIAL WELFARE

WELFARE WORK

But even assuming that increase in wages does not have an immediate effect on standard of living and on efficiency, there are several ways open to the employer to bring about the desired improvement. For reasons entirely different from those applying to the coal-mining industry in India, the cotton mill industry of Bombay city must set itself to the task of raising the efficiency of workers by means other than an increase in money wages. From the point of view of the workers the wages are so largely absorbed by high rents and other high costs of living that they are regarded as insufficient. But any further increase in wages is practically out of the question unless efficiency increases and labour costs can be reduced. The only way of ensuring that wages are not dissipated in wasteful expenditure or not lost to creditors, and so on is to let any additions that employers can afford be spent on what is known as "welfare work." Apart from its humanitarian aspect, its economic aspect, in the special circumstances of India, is even more important. If wages and the standard of living are not identical in different parts of India owing to various reasons, and if increased wages would not necessarily improve the standard and raise efficiency, the opportunity for welfare work becomes correspondingly greater and more extensive. For the money spent by the employers in improving the conditions of their workpeople is bound to react indirectly to their own benefit, and is certain to benefit the workers directly. Public money spent in promoting the well-being of the workers may fail in its purpose "because the workers may for one reason or other fail to avail themselves of the opportunities."[1] But when an employer spends money and energy in improving the conditions of the workers, the results are certain because the workers are tied definitely to the factory for a certain number of hours every day and thus "in bettering these conditions, there is a splendid opportunity for reacting beneficially

[1] A. C. Pigou, *Essays in Applied Economics*, 1927, p. 16.

on their character and their lives."[1] The employer occupies a unique position by virtue of his power to exercise a kind, paternal supervision over the workpeople, and can influence them to pursue their education and use the various other things provided by him. Thus while the worker has the choice of his own methods of spending his income, the employer may seek to meet part of the needs of the worker by taking responsibility for expenditure on education, recreation, and other amenities of life, on travel, on insurance, and on a large number of other items on which the Indian worker at present practically spends nothing.

Again, it is possible for the employer to bring about an increase in the earnings of the workers without adding to labour cost. Absenteeism in Indian industries is still very high, and this, combined with irregular attendance even on days when they actually work, reduces earnings seriously. Any steps which the employers take to increase the regularity of employment will do everyone good. In some industries, casual employment and the retention of too many workers in reserve as substitute workers, diminish the earnings of those in employment. The substitution of regular for irregular workers, whatever may be its temporary disadvantages, is likely in the end to be beneficial to both the workers and the employers. It must be the function of a Welfare Department if one is organized, to examine the case of each worker, to see if he receives fair and adequate earnings and to assist him in the earning of the wages that his efficiency warrants.

The scope of Welfare Work in India would necessarily differ from that in other countries. One of the most interesting differences which the writer noticed while he was on a visit to the British and Continental factories was that in contrast to Indian methods of welfare work, much greater attention was given to improving the internal conditions in the factory to suit the needs of the worker. Again the organization of canteens and medical and surgical and dental dispensaries has been done with a thoroughness which is lacking in India. In a factory like the Austin Motor Works, or the great German Siemens works near Berlin, which

[1] A. C. Pigou, *Essays in Applied Economics*, 1927, p. 16.

the writer visited, the management have rightly devoted much attention to improving the methods of quick and cheap transport for the workers so that the workers coming from a distance of three to ten miles may reach the factories quickly and at very low cost. In this they have been able to secure the co-operation of transport companies, and the thousands of workers employed are thus able to get back to their homes as quickly as possible.

In the housing of the workers, the employers in Great Britain and Germany assist in the provision of houses by public authorities rather than build houses directly and let them out. Even here, of course, there exist differences. At Bournville and Port Sunlight some of the workers are housed on the land and often in buildings constructed by the employers. But as a general statement it may be said that the task of providing suitable houses is regarded as belonging to the local authorities, and that employers can only co-operate in that task. In India, partly owing to the poverty of the local authorities and their apathy, and partly also owing to the feeling that much of the evils of overcrowding and slum conditions is directly traceable to the growth of factories, public opinion demands more from the employers. The housing of the workers thus became part of the welfare activities of every important factory in India.

Again the problems connected with the employment of women in India differ much from those in Western countries. At most of the factories which the writer visited in England and the Continent, he found that as soon as a girl desired to marry, she was expected to vacate her job. The reasons for this were variously explained, but the general opinion seemed to prevail that a married woman must be supported by the husband, and that in the face of the large amount of unemployment no married woman should be allowed to stand in the way of an unmarried girl. On the other hand, in India welfare work is associated largely with the granting of maternity benefits and the establishment of crèches in the factory with a view to ensuring that the children of the large number of women at work may be properly taken care of. There are several other features which distinguish welfare activities in India and Europe, such as the greater attention given in Europe to all kinds of sport activities and games, and the development of recreation facilities for men and women. The scope of these activities must necessarily differ as between countries.

It is unnecessary to discuss the principles of Welfare Work, or describe the directions in which further development in India should take place. A reference may be made to Chapters XI and XII of the writer's *Industrial Welfare in India*. The Royal Commission have fully gone into the methods of improving the conditions of life and work of the worker, and their report, together with a considerable number of publications on Indian labour affords enough material on the subject. On the question of housing and health, we have again had some useful inquiries in recent years.[1] But the Royal Commission have done the most valuable piece of work in making detailed recommendations to improve the housing and health conditions of the worker.

Trade Union Organization.—Finally a part of the responsibility for improvement lies on the workers themselves. The history of the trade union movement in India, the aims and achievements of unions in the short period of their existence, their shortcomings and defects have been described and examined in Chapters XIII and XIV of the writer's work already referred to. But it may be useful here shortly to explain the weakness of the organization and suggest lines of improvement. In the first place, the movement has been too long in the hands of outsiders. It is necessary to get rid of the outside elements who now control policy and to retain them only as counsellors and advisers. The unions have often been made pawns in the political game played by some of the outside politicians who control the movement. The development of leadership from within the ranks of labour is the unions' first task. The

[1] A. R. Burnett Hurst's *Labour and Housing in Bombay* contains a very detailed account of the housing conditions in the city of Bombay and presents a picture of the sordid conditions in which the workers are housed. Raj Bahadur Gupta's *Labour and Housing in India* is also a useful piece of work.

need for educating the workers to occupy responsible places on the managing committees of unions is most urgent, and in the starting and organizing of a training institute for the purpose, unions may legitimately look forward to some external assistance, such as universities and other educational institutions, in the arrangement of some courses of instruction for the workers. An equally urgent step is the extension of the sphere of trade union activities in several directions. Too long have most of the unions concentrated in practice on a limited range of tasks. Their attitude has been so far negative and critical and not constructive or educational. What is required is to create interest among the workers and induce them to take a steady and intelligent interest in the work of the unions. Co-operative credit and co-operative stores, the organization and maintenance of reading-rooms, libraries, the conduct of special adult educational courses, the provision of legal assistance and other benefits, these are the kinds of useful activities which may be taken up by unions. Thirdly, unions should have a full-time official staff like those of Great Britain, and an able and intelligent secretariat staff should be constituted to perform the varied functions of a modern trade union. Unions cannot any longer afford to rely on the voluntary service of outsiders, nor will it be possible for workers who have done a day's work in a factory or railway to find the time or energy required to manage a union. With the existing resources, it may be difficult to provide a whole-time staff at once, but when the first step is taken, the creation of whole-time staff may itself be the means of increasing substantially the union's resources on account of the increase in membership which will be its direct outcome.

Trade unions must aim at limiting their objects to ends definitely realizable within a measurable distance of time. Already in Bombay the movement has come to grief by adopting revolutionary and communistic principles of action. The Bombay Girni Kamgar union has done far more to hinder the growth of the trade-union movement than the most reactionary employer.

Above all, trade unions must recognize the simple economic truth that wages depend upon efficiency and that therefore the workers should co-operate with the management in raising productive efficiency. The General Strike in Bombay in 1929 was directly the outcome of the unwillingness of labour to accept the "efficiency" scheme sought to be introduced by some mills in the city. Their refusal to mind more looms, their ca'canny methods and their reactionary outlook are fatal to the progress of the workers, and their leadership has been greatly defective.

CONCLUSION

The efficiency of the Indian worker is undoubtedly low, and it is so closely bound up not only with the existing wages and standard of living, but with habits, ideas and tradition, deep-rooted and long-surviving, that it is impossible to hope for any sudden or rapid improvement. Climate and physique have had a great deal to do with inefficiency. In recent years there has come about a great change in the attitude of the people and Government towards problems of health, housing, and sanitation. The willingness of the people to permit large expenditure in these directions is the most hopeful feature of the situation, although there has not been the same willingness to tax themselves for it. A desire to industrialize the country as rapidly as possible has led to greater attention to problems of efficiency; but unfortunately there has been a tendency to exaggeration. On the one hand, defects have been magnified and exaggerated, and on the other the difficulties of increasing the efficiency of the worker have been grossly understated. The Royal Commission on Labour have done most valuable service in bringing to light the serious difficulties which the problem presents, and their recommendations have been framed with a view to break the vicious circle of low efficiency, low wages, and low standard of living at as many points as possible. Time and thought and a will to achieve are necessary for success in this direction. But if the recommendations of the Commission are carried out, there is no reason to fear that the inefficiency of the Indian worker will remain a permanent handicap. The future of industrial development in India will depend upon the extent to which the employers, workers, and the State co-operate in improving the conditions of life and work of the industrial workers, and upon the rapidity or otherwise of the change in the attitude of the country towards modern industrial life.

STATEMENT I

Index Numbers of Wholesale Prices in India

	Calcutta (*Indian Trade Journal*)	Bombay (*Labour Gazette*, Bombay)	Bombay Cost of Living Index (*Labour Gazette*, Bombay)
1914	100	100	100
1915	112	—	107
1916	128	—	110
1917	145	—	119
1918	178	**239**	154
1919	196	223	175
1920	**201**	216	**183**
1921	178	198	173
1922	176	187	164
1923	172	181	154
1924	173	182	157
1925	159	163	155
1926	148	149	155
1927	148	147	154
1928	145	146	147
1929	141	145	149
1930	116	126	137
1931	96	109	110
1932	91	109	102

SELECT BIBLIOGRAPHY

OFFICIAL PUBLICATIONS AND REPORTS

Indian Tariff Board. Cotton Textile Industry Enquiry, 1927, Vols. 1 to 4. Sugar Industry Report, 1931. Vol. 1, Written Evidence; Vol. 2, Oral Evidence, 1932.

Report of the Indian Tariff Board *re* the grant of protection to cement industry, 3 vols., 1924–5. Coal Industry, 2 vols., 1926. Match Industry, 5 vols., 1928–9. Paper and Paper Pulp Industries, 4 vols., 1924–5; and 1931, Vol. 1, 1932. Steel Industry (1924), Evidence, Vols. 1 to 3, 1924. Supplementary Protection to Steel Industry, 2 vols., 1925. Statutory Enquiry relating to the Steel Industry, 1926–7, 8 vols.

Royal Commission on Indian Currency and Finance, 1926; Report, Vol. 1, Cmd. 2687; Appendices, Vols. 2 and 3; Minutes of Evidence taken in India, Vol. 4; in London, Vol. 5.

Report of the External Capital Committee, 1925.

Report of the Royal Commission on Labour, 1931, Cmd. 3883. Evidence, Vols. 1 to 11 in eighteen parts.

The Indian Central Banking Enquiry Committee, 1931. Vol. 1, Part 1, Majority Report; Vol. 1, Part 2, Minority Report; Vol. 2, Written Evidence; Vol. 3, Oral Evidence; Vol. 4, Discussion with Foreign Experts.

Provincial Banking Enquiry Committees, Reports and Evidence, Bombay, Central Provinces, Bihar and Orissa, Punjab, Madras, United Provinces, Bengal, Assam, Burma.

Indian Fiscal Commission, 1922, Report, and Evidence, Vols. 1 to 3.

Indian Industrial Commission, 1916–18. Report, Appendices to the Report, and Evidence. Vols. 1 to 5.

Indian Economic Enquiry Committee, 1925, Report. Evidence, Vols. 1 and 2.

Statistical Abstract for British India (Annual).

Report of the Controller of the Currency (Annual).

Statistical Tables relating to Banks in India (Annual).

Report of the Registrar of Joint-Stock Companies (Annual).

Large Industrial Establishments in India (Biennial).

Annual Review of the Trade of India.

Preliminary Report on the Water Power Resources of India (Hydro-Electric Survey of India, 1919).

Triennial Report of the Department of Hydro-Electric Survey of India, 1922.

India Munitions Board Handbook, Calcutta, 1919.

Report of the Chief Inspector of Mines (Annual).

All-India Income-Tax Reports and Returns for the Year 1922–3, *et. seq.*

Report of the India Sugar Committee, 1920, Simla.

Royal Commission on Agriculture, 1928. Report and Appendix to Report.

Report of the Coalfields Committee, 1920.

Report of the Indian Coal Committee, 1925.

Indian Coal Statistics, Government of India, 1931.

Report of the Bombay Stock Exchange Enquiry Committee, 1924.

Report of the Bombay Strike Enquiry Committee, 1928–9.

Court of Enquiry into Cotton Mill Strikes, Government of Bombay, 1931.

Note on the Working of the Indian Trade Unions Act of 1926 for the year 1930.

Report of an Enquiry into the Standard of Living of Jute Mill Workers in Bengal, 1930.

Report on an Enquiry into Family Budgets of Cotton Mill Workers in Sholapur, 1928; in Ahmedabad; in Bombay.

Report on an Enquiry into Wages and Hours of Labour in the Cotton Mills Industry in 1921, 1923, and 1926, Bombay.

Bulletin No. 3. Index numbers showing the changes in the cost of living of industrial workers in Nagpur, Sholapur, and Jubbulpore, 1929, with amendment to Bulletin No. 3.

Prices and Wages in India (Annual).

Indian Railway Rates Advisory Committee Reports and Proceedings.

Committee on Industry and Trade (Balfour Committee).

Survey of Industrial Relations, 1926.

Survey of Overseas Markets, 1927.

Factors in Industrial and Commercial Efficiency, 1927.

Further Factors in Industrial and Commercial Efficiency, 1928.

Survey of Textile Industries, 1928.

Survey of Metal Industries, 1928.

Final Report of the Committee, 1929.

Report of the Committee on Finance and Industry (Macmillan Committee). Cmd. 3897, 1931. Evidence, Vols. 1 and 2.

Report of the Royal Commission on the Coal Industry (Samuel Commission), 1926.

Proceedings of the Sugar Conference, 1933 (Simla).

Moral and Material Progress of India (Annual).

Legislative Assembly Debates.

JOURNALS, PERIODICALS, AND OCCASIONAL REPORTS

The Economic Journal.
Quarterly Journal of Economics.
Journal of the Royal Statistical Society.
The Economist.
The Statist.
Labour Gazette (Government of Bombay).
Round Table.
Indian Journal of Economics.
Indian Finance.
Capital (Weekly).
Indian Industries Trade and Transport Supplement (Annual).
Investor's India Year Book.
Report of the Millowners' Association, Bombay (Annual).
Report of the Millowners' Association, Ahmedabad (Annual).
Indian Textile Journal, 1894, *et seq.*
Indian Year Book.

ANSTEY (VERA), The Economic Development of India, 1929.
BASTER (A. S. J.), The Imperial Banks, 1929.
BOWLEY (A. L.), The National Income, 1924.
BROOKINGS INSTITUTE, The Tariff in relation to Iron and Steel, 1929.
BURNETT-HURST (A. R.), Labour and Housing in Bombay, 1925.
CLOW (A. G.), The State and Industry, 1928.
COTTON (C. W. E.), Handbook of Commercial Information for India, Calcutta, 1924.
DEY (H. L.), The Indian Tariff Problem (George Allen & Unwin Ltd.), 1933.
DUBEY (D. L.), Indian Public Debt, 1930.
DUNCAN (J. C.), Principles of Industrial Management, N.Y. 1931.
FONG (H. D.), Cotton Industry and Trade in China, 1932.
FOXWELL (H. S.), Papers on Current Finance, 1919.

GERSTENBERG (C. W.), Financial Organization and Management, N.Y., 1924.
GUPTA (RAJ BAHADUR), Labour and Housing in India, 1930.
HARDY (G. S.), Report on the Import Tariff on Cotton Piecegoods and on External Competition in Cotton Piecegoods Trade, Calcutta, 1930.
HARRIS (F. R.), Life of J. N. Tata, 1925.
JAIN (L. C.), Indigenous Banking in India, 1929.
JAIN (L. C.), Monetary Problems of India, 1933.
JONES (E. D.), Administration of Industrial Enterprises, N.Y., 1917.
KEYNES (J. M.), A Treatise on Money, Vols. 1 and 2, 1930.
KIMBALL (D. S.), Principles of Industrial Organization, N.Y., 1913.
KIMBALL (D. S.), Industrial Economics, N.Y., 1929.
LAVINGTON (F.), The English Capital Market, 1921.
LEAGUE OF NATIONS, Memorandum on Commercial Banks, 1913–29 (1931).
LOKANATHAN (P. S.), Industrial Welfare in India, 1929.
LOVETT (PAT), The Mirror of Investment, 1927.
MARQUAND (H. A.), The Dynamics of Industrial Combination, 1931.
MARSHALL (ALFRED), Industry and Trade, 1919.
MEAD (E. S.), Corporation Finance, N.Y., 1933 (Sixth Edition).
MILLER (M.), and CAMPBELL (D.), Financial Democracy, 1933.
NOEL-PATON (F.), Notes on Sugar in India, 1911.
OHLIN (B.), Inter-regional and International Trade, 1933.
PARKINSON (H.), Scientific Investment, 1932.
PEARSE (ARNO), The Cotton Industry of India, 1930.
PEARSE (ARNO), The Cotton Industry of Japan and China, 1929.
PIGOU (A. C.), Essays in Applied Economics, 1923.
PILLAI (P. P.), Economic Conditions in India, 1925.
Recent Economic Changes, N.Y., Report of a Committee appointed by the President of the U.S.A. Vols. 1 and 2, 1929.
REED (M.), The Indian Peasant Uprooted, 1931.
RIPLEY (W. Z.), Railroads: Finance and Organization, 1915.
ROBINSON (E. A. G.), The Structure of Competitive Industry, 1931.
RUTNAGUR (S. M.), The Bombay Industries: the Cotton Mills, 1927.
SHIRRAS (FINDLAY), Indian Finance and Banking, 1919.
SINHA (H.), Early European Banking in India, 1927.
SMITH (RUSSEL), Principles of Industrial Management, N.Y., 1915.
SONI (H. R.), Indian Industry and its Problems: Vol. 1, Factors in Industrial Development, 1932.
SRINIVASAN (K. C.), Indian Railway Rates, 1928.
TAUSSIG (F. W.), Some Aspects of the Tariff Question, 1915.

URWICK (L.), The Meaning of Rationalization, 1929.

UTLEY (F.), Lancashire and the Far East (George Allen & Unwin Ltd.), 1931.

VON BECKERATH, Industrial Organization: An Economic Interpretation, University of Bonn, N.Y., 1933.

WACHA (D. E.), Life of J. N. Tata, 1918.

WALLACE (D. R.), The Romance of Jute, 1928, second edition.

Waste in Industry, By the Committee on Elimination of Waste in Industry of the Federated American Engineering Societies, N.Y., 1921.

WEBER (A.), Theory of the Location of Industries, Edited by C. J. Friedrich, English edition, 1929.

WHALE (P. B.), Joint-Stock Banking in Germany, 1930.

WILLIS (H. PARKER) and BECKHART (B. H.), Foreign Banking Systems, 1929.

WITHERS (HARTLEY), The Quicksands of the City, 1930.

INDEX